Better Homes and Gardens®

Garden Flowers
you can grow

© 1980 by Meredith Corporation, Des Moines, Iowa. All Rights Reserved.
Printed in the United States of America. First Edition. First Printing.
Library of Congress Catalog Card Number: 79-90781
ISBN: 0-696-00595-6

**BETTER HOMES AND
GARDENS® BOOKS**

Editor in Chief: James A. Autry
Editorial Director: Neil Kuehnl
Executive Art Director:
    William J. Yates

Editor: Gerald M. Knox
Art Director: Ernest Shelton
Associate Art Directors:
    Neoma Alt West, Randall Yontz
Copy and Production Editors:
    David Kirchner, Lamont Olson,
    David A. Walsh
Assistant Art Director:
    Harijs Priekulis
Senior Graphic Designer:
    Faith Berven
Graphic Designers: Linda Ford,
    Sheryl Veenschoten, Tom Wegner

Garden and Outdoor Living Editor:
    Beverly Garrett
Senior Garden Editors:
    Steven Coulter, Marjorie P. Groves
Associate Garden Editor:
    Douglas A. Jimerson

Garden Flowers You Can Grow

Editors: Steven Coulter, Marjorie P. Groves
Graphic Designer: Randall Yontz
Copy and Production Editor:
    David A. Walsh

CONTENTS

Perennials and Biennials _____ **6**
Using Perennials _____ 8
Perennial Know-How _____ 10
Perennial Favorites: Iris _____ 16
Perennial Favorites: Peonies _____ 18
Perennial Favorites: Daylilies _____ 20
Perennial Favorites: Hardy Lilies ___ 22
Perennial Favorites: Chrysanthemums _ 24
ABCs of Perennials _____ 26
Biennials _____ 66

Annuals in the Garden _____ **68**
Old-fashioned Mixed Flower Beds ___ 70
Flashy Flowers Massed Together ____ 74
Beautiful Borders _____ 78
How to Plan a Border _____ 80
The Versatility of Annuals _____ 82
Planters for Close-Up Color _____ 84
Annuals for Special Uses _____ 88
Annuals in Pots _____ 90
Strawberry Jars _____ 92
Hanging Baskets _____ 94
Problem Areas _____ 96
Climbing Annuals _____ 100
Annuals for Special Situations _____ 102
Annual Basics _____ 104
ABCs of Annuals _____ 114

The Wonder of Roses _____ **144**
The History of the Rose _____ 146
Roses' Role in the Garden _____ 150

Basics of Rose Care _____ 174
Old Garden Roses _____ 186
Shrub-Like Roses _____ 190
Hybrid Tea Roses _____ 194
Grandifloras _____ 202
Floribundas _____ 204
Tree Roses _____ 210
Climbing Roses _____ 212
Miniature Roses _____ 216

Flowering Bulbs: Hardy Bulbs 222
How to Use Bulbs _____ 224
Hardy Bulbs: Tulips _____ 226
Hardy Bulbs: Daffodils _____ 228
Hardy Bulbs: Other Favorites _____ 230
Bulb Know-How _____ 234
Tender Bulbs: Gladiolus _____ 238
Tender Bulbs: Dahlia _____ 240
Tender Bulbs: Tuberous Begonia ___ 242
Tender Bulbs: Calla Lily
   and Exotics _____ 246
Summer Bulb Storage _____ 250

Specialties _____ **252**
Wildflowers _____ 254
Enjoy Garden Flowers Indoors _____ 262
How to Handle Cut Flowers _____ 264
How to Dry Flowers _____ 272
Zones of Plant Hardiness _____ 278

Index _____ **280**

INTRODUCTION

For centuries, gardeners have cultivated flowers for the beauty they offer. Shakespeare wrote, "Flowers are like the pleasures of the world." Years later, Longfellow exclaimed, "How like they are to human things." Today we, too, appreciate their color and fragrance, and the life they bring to a garden. Flowers, whether growing outdoors or cut and brought inside, are an always-welcome sight.

Wherever you live, you can enjoy your own homegrown blooms from early spring until winter. Start with tulips, daffodils, and other early-season bulbs. Continue with peonies, iris, daylilies, phlox, chrysanthemums, and other reliable perennials that bloom year after year. Count on petunias, marigolds, zinnias, and other annuals for colorful flowers from early summer until the end of the season. Let tender bulbs such as gladiolus, dahlias, cannas, begonias, and callas brighten your summer flower beds. And don't forget the universally beloved rose. Combinations of these favorites can give you brilliant color, such as in this late-spring garden (left), throughout the gardening season. A sweep of flowers from one end of this garden to the other and large areas of identical plants make meandering masses of color more effective than the color you would get with smaller groupings. Little paths through the garden provide access for planting, watering, trimming, and other general maintenance jobs.

To help you with your garden plans, we compiled this treasury of the flower-growing advice we've published in the past few years. You'll find concise information on how to choose and use your favorite annuals, perennials, bulbs, and roses, plus what you need to know about soil preparation, planting, and care. Look, too, for information on how to handle cut flowers so they'll last longer in arrangements, how to dry blooms, how to create fragrant potpourris from petals and spices, and more. In short, here's everything you need to know to grow and enjoy garden flowers for years to come.

Perennials and Biennials

What are they and
what can they
do for you?

No one knows quite how long ago the love for gardening was first felt by human beings; but we do know that in America, the early settlers from England brought with them seeds and roots of well-loved plants to grow in colonial gardens.

In the years since, gardens have never ceased to fascinate Americans as the frontier pushed ever westward, at last to the Pacific Ocean and a climate far different from that of New England, where frigid winters were a real threat.

In a country as vast as ours, what may be a perennial plant in one area may not be so in another. But nowhere in America is there a lack of perennial plants that can serve as the backbone of a flower border. In zones 9 and 10, these may well differ widely from the hardy perennials counted upon to appear year after year in Northern zones.

The first thing a beginning gardener should do is to study a zonal map (see pages 278 and 279), then look for plants suited to your climate. Or, if you're an experienced gardener confronted by a need to move— something that often

happens in this ever-mobile world in which we live— it's time to seek new plants that will take the place of older friends and rediscover the fun and excitement of learning to garden well under a new group of climatic conditions, seasons for planting and bloom, different types of soil, and annual expected amount of rainfall. These are just a few of the factors you should take into account as you do perennial planting plans. Wherever you live, it pays to understand your climate.

Biennials are usually described as plants that bloom the year following their sowing, then die. But as you will learn on the pages to follow, many of the biennials often

self-sow so cheerfully that they behave like perennials in many climates. Several of them—foxglove, hollyhocks, Canterbury-bells—are graceful verticals whose height can lend distinction to the back-of-the-border area in your garden.

Taken together, the plant group we know as perennials and biennials can give you great joy with little work and combine beautifully with annuals—amiable plants also deserving of your admiration.

Thus far, the main role of perennials here discussed has been as valuable members of flowering borders. But there are many plants within the group that play other roles as well —ground covers in sun or shade; color in rock gardens; bouquets to take into the house; heralds of spring from hardy bulbs and native wildflowers; and exotic tufts produced by ornamental grasses. Each of these uses of perennials will be discussed in later sections of this book.

One of the major factors determining success or failure with perennials—other than zonal hardiness which has already been discussed —is quality of soil and advance preparation of a bed. Have a soil test made before you begin setting out plants. Usually your state's agricultural college or its extension services will do this for you. Only then can you learn the pH factor of the soil and if it is necessary to sweeten a too-acid soil or add acid to an overly alkaline soil.

Preparation in advance of planting can't be over-rated. For small areas this can be done with a spade by digging down 12 to 24 inches, thoroughly cultivating soil as you go, then adding whatever's necessary: coarse sand and small gravel, peat moss, well-rotted manure, bone

meal, and balanced fertilizer are possibilities. Someone has said: "Always dig a $5 hole for a $1 plant." The basic meaning is clear: the better your preparation of a bed for a plant, the greater will be your rewards in its health, longevity, and productivity.

Plan to keep a garden diary, noting when and where you set out plants and recording dates of bloom over a number of seasons. And make a genuine effort to learn the botanical —as well as the common—names of your plants. So many plants of a variety of species are called by the same common name in various parts of the country that the only real way to know for certain what's growing in your garden is to learn its botanical name.

Finally, remember the old adage concerning perennials: the first year it sleeps; the second year it creeps; the third year it leaps. With this trite but true saying in mind, you'll find it easier to be patient with a perennial plant that takes off a bit slowly at first.

Using Perennials

Versatility is one of the qualities of hardy perennials that makes them so highly valued by flower gardeners everywhere. If you want bloom from earliest spring right up to killing frost, there are plants in the perennial family to do the job.

The photographs on these pages suggest some of the many ways in which perennials may be put to work: as edgings along garden paths; in mixed borders, perhaps combined in pleasing ways with annuals; in shady spots where you'd still like color; and in rock gardens as handsome partners to blooming shrubs and low-growing evergreens. Or, for a fragrant garden, look to perennials—some of them herbs—to perfume the air around you from narcissus-time until frost.

Massed plantings of sweet williams, calendulas, pinks, yellow and white violas, and azaleas form brilliant strips at either side of a garden path.

Rose-pink hardy phlox B. Symons-Jeune is in view at lower right foreground, along with baby's-breath Bristol Fairy. Next to phlox is Cambridge Scarlet bee-balm with achillea Coronation Gold and gloriosa daisy. Back of these are semi-double Heliopsis scabra. To their left is lythrum Morden's Pink.

Mixing annuals and perennials lends an old-fashioned air to this border. Grouped are calendulas, sweet williams, pink Iceland poppies, and pansies (left).

Yellow-edged, large-leaf Siebold hosta (above) finds flattering companions in rudbeckia Goldsturm, white phlox, all in a shady spot between shrub plantings.

Looking as if Nature were the artist, this interesting rock garden is the result of careful design that turned a troublesome slope into a lovely sight. Pink mounds in foreground are creeping phlox. Rock cress bears the tiny white bloom (lower left). To its left is Hino-Crimson azalea, Miriam azalea (pink), and Delaware Valley White azalea. Tulips and daffodils outline the upper ledge. Primroses and basket-of-gold alyssum are the other colorful perennials that are in such pleasant contrast with the cool gray of stone and the green of several low-growing evergreens nearby.

For a drift of cool white bloom in June, choose cerastium, also called snow-in-summer. It's a spreader, so cut back each year to desired size. Plant in sun—it's drought tolerant. Zone 2.

Perennial Know-How

Hardy perennials that flower for brief or lengthy periods are desirable garden plants no matter where you grow them. But in a mixed border, they're absolutely indispensable.

If you're just starting your perennial border, you'll almost certainly rely on some annuals to fill bare spots during part of the season. But if you plan well, you'll eventually have a handsome mixed border of all perennials.

To achieve this, draw up a plan (see following pages). Make lists of those varieties best suited to the conditions of soil and light you can offer, and then buy or grow from seed the perennials you need to fill the border space available. Keep heights and colors in mind as you plant.

CHOOSE PERENNIALS BY HEIGHT

Front-of-the-Border (Dwarf to 15 inches)	Mid-Border (15 to 30 inches)	Back-of-the-Border (Over 30 inches)
Anemone (Anemone canadensis)	Allium (bulb)	Anchusa (variety Dropmore)
Aster (dwarf Michaelmas varieties)	Astilbe	Aster, hardy (Michaelmas daisies)
Baby's-breath (Gypsophila repens)	Baby's-breath (gypsophila)	Baptisia (false indigo)
Bellflower (Campanula carpatica)	Balloon flower (platycodon)	Coneflower (rudbeckia)
Bugloss (anchusa)	Bee-balm (monarda)	Delphinium (species varieties)
Candytuft (iberis)	Bleeding-heart (dicentra)	Daylily (hemerocallis)
Chrysanthemum (cushion varieties)	Butterfly weed (Asclepias tuberosa)	Foxglove (some varieties such as Excelsior hybrids)*
Cinquefoil (potentilla)	Chrysanthemum (many varieties)	Globe thistle (echinops)
Cranesbill geranium	Columbine (aquilegia)	Goldenrod (solidago)
Crocus (bulb)	Coreopsis	Helenium
Dwarf iris varieties	Coralbells (heuchera)	Heliopsis
English daisy (bellis)*	Delphinium	Heliotrope (centranthus)
Feverfew	Gaillardia	Hollyhock (Alcea rosea)*
Flax (linum)	Gas plant (dictamnus)	Hibiscus
Grape hyacinth (bulb)	Iris	Iris (spuria and Japanese)
Hyacinth (bulb)	Foxglove (digitalis)*	Liatris (gayfeather)
Lavender	Lilies (many varieties)	Lilies (many hybrid varieties)
Narcissi (miniature varieties; bulbs)	Lobelia	Lupine
Painted daisy (pyrethrum)	Loosestrife (lythrum)	Mullein (verbascum)
Pinks (dianthus)	Peony	Phlox
Phlox (Phlox subulata)	Poppy (papaver)	Sunflower (helianthus)
Plumbago (dwarf)	Phlox	Thermopsis (Carolina lupine)
Primrose (primula)	Rudbeckia	Yarrow (achillea, variety Coronation Gold)
Salvia, perennial blue sage	Shasta daisy	Yucca
Silver Mound (artemisia)	Spiderwort (tradescantia)	
Stokesia (Stoke's aster)	Tulips	*Biennial
Tulip (botanical varieties; bulb)	Virginia bluebells (mertensia)	
Veronica (some varieties)		
Viola		

You're already doing something to increase your perennial know-how: reading a book. But also study seed and plant catalogs and garden columns in your local newspaper. Some are extremely well-done, with accurate information on zonal hardiness and culture for many varieties. And, if you're lucky enough to live near a large nursery of perennial plants, by all means pay a visit (check first to learn the days and hours when the public is invited to tour).

It's also a good idea to write your own garden book—in the form of a diary. Note in it the varieties planted (whether seed or plants), and the time of planting. Follow up with notes on time of bloom, temperature lows and highs, flower color, health problems, and a record of the rainfall.

Be sure to keep an accurate chart of where you've set plants, and mark with a name-stake all that emerge late, whose foliage disappears from view after blooming. This could prevent losing a plant by digging into a spot that appears—deceptively—to be bare.

APPROXIMATE BLOOM DATES

Spring *February through early May*	Summer *Mid-May through August*	Fall *Late August to Frost*
Alkanet (anchusa) *Anemone canadensis* Artemisia Silver Mound Basket-of-gold alyssum Crocus (bulb) Bleeding-heart Dwarf iris Grape hyacinth (muscari; bulb) Hyacinth (bulb) Iberis (candytuft) *Phlox subulata* *Scilla siberica* (bulb) Tulip (botanical varieties; bulb) Viola Virginia bluebells (mertensia)	Astilbe Baby's-breath (gypsophila) Balloon flower (platycodon) Bellflower (campanula) Bee-balm (monarda) Butterfly weed (*Asclepias tuberosa*) Columbine (aquilegia) Coreopsis Coralbells (heuchera) Daylily (hemerocallis) Delphinium Gaillardia Gayfeather (liatris) Gas plant (dictamnus) Globe thistle (echinops) Heliopsis Helenium Iris Lilies (bulb) Lobelia Loosestrife (lythrum) Peony Poppy (papaver) Phlox Rudbekia Salvia (perennial blue sage) Shasta daisy Spiderwort (tradescantia) Thermopsis (Carolina lupine) Veronica Yarrow	Aster, hardy (Michaelmas daisy) Christmas rose Chrysanthemum Candytuft (iberis variety Autumn Snow) Daylilies (hemerocallis) late-season varieties Dianthus (Allwoodi "alpinus") Sedum Tradescantia (Blue Stone) **Note:** Many of the "summer" perennials will continue to bloom until frost if dead bloom is regularly removed and the plant is not allowed to go to seed earlier in the season. A few of the early varieties, such as viola, may well have a second season of bloom if the fall is cool and the moisture supply is sufficient.

Perennial Know-How

Once you've decided on the kinds of perennials you'll grow in your border, it's time to make a placement chart. Though some will be short, some mid-height, and others tall, all will look best if they're planted according to height—preferably in groups of at least three per variety.

If possible, install a backdrop for the show in the form of a hedge, fence, or garden wall. This will also protect against strong winds, and will help keep plants from toppling in a sudden storm. And, it's good protection from wintry blasts even when the garden's not in bloom.

SUNNY PERENNIAL BORDER

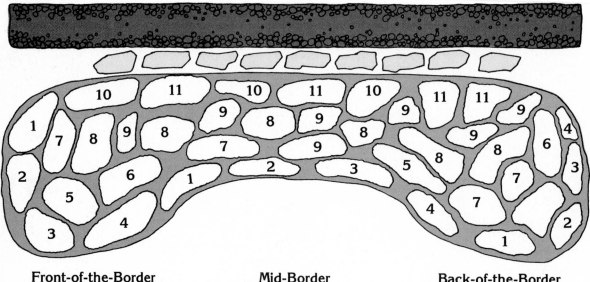

Front-of-the-Border
1. crocus
2. species tulips
3. iberis snowflake
4. basket-of-gold alyssum

Mid-Border
5. hyacinth
6. tulip (Plant early and late varieties to lengthen the season.)
7. narcissus
8. daylilies (hemerocallis) (In this spot, choose varieties under 30 inches.)
9. iris (Include bearded, spuria, Siberian, and Japanese varieties.)

Back-of-the-Border
10. delphinium (Choose tall, large-flowering kinds such as Pacific Coast hybrids, Blackmore, Langdon, and Bishop.)
11. lilies (Choose Pacific hybrid varieties.)

Note: Depending on your color scheme, such annuals as zinnias and marigolds, or geraniums and coleus could be set into areas where bulb foliage has yellowed and ripened off, leaving unattractive bare spots for much of the summer season. Note, also, that daylilies have been purposefully positioned so that their foliage will emerge slowly, ready to cover some of the spots made bare by ripened-off bulb foliage. Stepping-stones placed between the border and background hedge help make cultivation easier.

Unless your border's narrower than 3 feet, it's important to allow for reaching plants from either back or front—for planting, weeding, fertilizing and so on. Stepping-stones of natural flagstone, or a brick path are two practical solutions. If you pour pea gravel between stones and along the path, you'll avoid awkward weeding. Lay plastic under stones to inhibit weeds.

Note that the sunny border is planned for 25 feet in length, and the shady border for 10. If you'd like yours either longer or shorter, simply repeat or decrease plant groupings to fit the desired length of bed.

In both garden plans, the lists of plants are only suggestions. For each one, there are a number of others that would work equally well. See the charts on these two pages, and the later section, "ABCs of Perennials," for helpful alternate selections.

PART-SHADE PERENNIAL BORDER

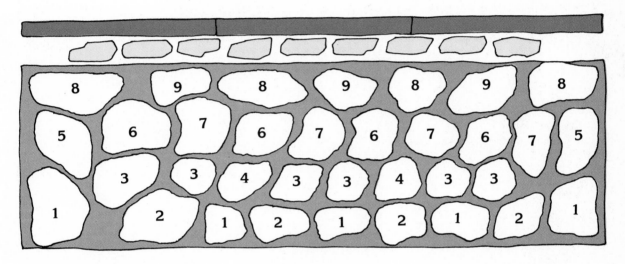

Front-of-the-Border
1. hardy cyclamen (or small-leaf hosta, such as *Hosta lancifolia*)
2. primrose (primula)
3. astilbe
4. bleeding-heart (*Dicentra spectabilis*)

Mid-Border
5. hosta (large leaf varieties such as *Hosta fortunei* or *Hosta sieboldiana*)
6. Siberian iris (available in a range of blues, whites, and purples)
7. globeflower (trollius)

Back-of-the-Border
8. false indigo (*Baptisia australis*)
9. loosestrife (lythrum variety Morden's Gleam)

Note: "Part-shade" here means that the location receives morning and perhaps late afternoon sun, but not midday sun. If shade is not too dense, daylilies are an excellent choice for back-of-the-border plantings; they will not bloom as heavily as in full sun, but will give an adequate performance. The Goldsturm rudbeckia is also a good mid-border alternate choice, as it, too, blooms satisfactorily if shade's not too dense. Stepping-stones placed between the border and the background fence make for easier cultivation.

Perennial Know-How

Some nurseries and garden stores sell perennials already growing in containers. In both fall and spring, perennials are also available as dormant, bare-root plants. You can plant dormant roots with very little risk of loss. In northern zones, fall-planted roots start growing at the normal time in the spring.

SOIL PREPARATION

Whether you're planting perennials in a bed, border, or other area, always prepare the soil thoroughly before you plant. The best soil lies near the surface. So if you must remove sod, strip off the top layer, trying not to take off more than an inch of soil.

Locate all perennial plants at least 3 feet from any tree or shrub so they won't have to compete with massive roots. Use a spading fork to remove grass and weak roots, as illustrated above. Spade the soil well, turning it over to a depth of 8 to 10 inches. Then rake the soil to level it, removing all stones and breaking up clods. Use the fork to work in a 2- to 4-inch layer of peat moss or well-rotted cow manure. (*Exception:* Omit manure in preparing bulb beds.) Organic matter improves the soil structure and provides better growing conditions for all plants.

It's wise when preparing a large bed to take the steps outlined above in the fall. Then leave the area unplanted until spring so winter rains and snows have time to mix in all additives and the soil can naturally settle into place.

If your soil has an overly high clay content—heavy, sticky, and hard to work—you should fork in coarse sand and fine gravel as well as peat until you have a lighter mix. Vermiculite or perlite can also be used to good advantage to lighten this type of garden soil.

If you move into a fairly new home and discover that the builder has put a very thin layer of topsoil

over clay, your best bet is to tackle the problem at once, before you attempt any planting. Decide on the place or places where you want perennial beds and remove at least 3 feet of poor soil in those areas. Have loads of black dirt brought in to replace soil removed.

If this sounds like a drastic step, remember that it will certainly be easier to do now than later. And it could make all the difference between a good and a poor future garden.

PLANTING

It's difficult to generalize about planting perennials because each is quite individual. However, here are some steps to help ensure success. First, set the plants at the proper depth—at the same level they grew the previous season. You can see marks of the former depth on the dormant roots you buy. Next, provide adequate space for roots so they're not crowded. Dig a hole several inches larger in diameter than the width of the roots and spread roots out so they can quickly get established. It often helps to build up a low cone of earth at the bottom of the hole so you can easily space roots out over the cone. Then, gradually sprinkle in soil.

Remember that your main goal in transplanting—whether new

plants or those you obtain through division of your older plants—is to avoid shocking plants. Don't let roots dry out or break off. They're the plant's lifeline to food, moisture, and good health.

Choose a day to plant that is cool, cloudy, or even a bit rainy. If it's warm or sunny, keep plant roots shaded and covered with layers of water-soaked newspaper until you're ready to plant. Lift plants gently and set at the same level at which they formerly grew.

Gradually fill in earth about the roots and firm the soil to eliminate all air pockets. Water thoroughly immediately after transplanting and continue to water every day until soaking rains make certain the new plants are settled in.

If you plant in the fall, mark the location of new plants. Some are quite late to emerge in spring, and you can easily forget their location if it's unstaked. Cover them with a light mulch for the winter, then remove it in the spring as plants first appear. But keep some mulch handy in case a late frost should make it advisable to re-cover the young, tender shoots.

Don't use raked leaves as mulch. Winter snows and rains turn them into a soggy mass that doesn't perform the most important function of mulch: not to keep plants warmer, but to prevent the soil from heaving when rapid

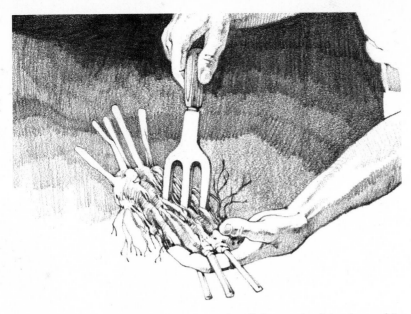

temperature changes cause freezing and thawing.

Much better materials to use for winter mulch are straw, hay, or pruned branches of evergreens. If you haven't enough evergreens for the entire job, use what you have as a top layer. The greens will improve the appearance of the mulch and help hold it in place.

DIVIDING

You can divide some perennial roots by gently tearing off sections. In the case of tuberous or woody roots, it's best to use a hand fork or a sharp knife. Don't try to make too many divisions out of one plant, and be sure each division has adequate roots to sustain it while it's recovering from the shock of division. In the case of peonies, be sure to have at least three "eyes" on each division, or you'll wait a long time before you have bloom from them. Five-eye divisions will often bloom the first season after you divide.

When dividing any plants, it's a good idea to wash soil away from the roots so you can see what you're doing. Direct the hose stream away from the base of the stems to avoid bud injury. Keep as many roots attached to each division as possible, but trim away any damaged roots. If any part of the division looks dead or diseased,

trim all the way back to clean, white tissue. Replant as soon as possible after dividing any perennials.

Shown above is the correct use of a hand fork to divide roots of such perennials as hemerocallis.

WINTER PROTECTION

In addition to the general mulch previously described, there are other ways to cut down on losses of plants to winter freezes. Several of them are described and illustrated below. None takes much time or costly equipment, but each may save you the loss of a valued plant.

Put a protective covering over small tufts of fall growth. An inverted flowerpot over a madonna lily keeps mulch from packing around the new shoot.

If you live in an area where winter temperatures frequently fall below freezing and often remain at low levels for prolonged periods of time, you will have to protect all beds of perennial plants with a general layer of mulch, as has been described. The best time to mulch for complete plant protection is as soon as possible after the first killing frost. (This is usually preceded in cold climates by one or more "light" frosts which nip the tops but do not kill plant foliage back to the ground.)

Before you put on mulch, clear the beds of all dead foliage and weeds, cutting stems of plants back to within 2 inches of the soil; then add fertilizer, such as bone meal or a general garden fertilizer.

For perennial beds exposed to wind, here's an easy way to keep mulch in place. Lay on sections of poultry wire weighted down at intervals with bricks or stones.

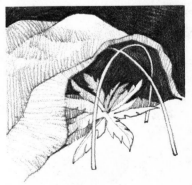

Make a frame of crossed wire loops to protect fall growth of Oriental poppies. Cover with burlap and pile soil on edges to hold in place.

PERENNIAL FAVORITES

Iris

T he irresistible iris is undisputed queen of many perennial borders from spring on into early summer. The beginner is apt to think only of the tall bearded varieties such as Red Storm, shown above. But there are a large group of others in the tribe: early blooming dwarfs; Siberians; and spuria, which blooms after the bearded iris have closed for the season. Also late to bloom are Japanese iris with their unbelievably huge and upturned faces that measure up to 10 inches in diameter.

Plant spuria iris—this one's Dawn Candle—in rich, moist soil in full sun.

Japanese iris Driven Snow (white), Good Omen (purple), Stippled Ripples (variegated).

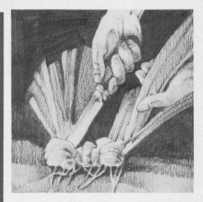

1 Clumps of bearded iris need to be dug up, divided, and replanted about every 3 years. Use a sharp knife to separate the rhizomes, and make sure each division has a strong section of roots.

2 After separating, clean, and trim off decayed or corky ends of rhizomes. Check for borers; cut them out. Trim the foliage to a fan shape.

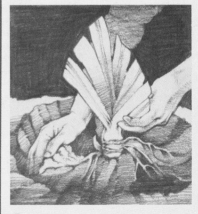

3 Be sure to prepare the soil well before planting new divisions. Spade in plant food and compost. Place rhizome on a ridge of soil.

PERENNIAL FAVORITES
Peonies

Think peony, if you want a plant that's generous in rewarding you for minimal care. Once they're established for a year or two, you can count on armloads of bloom in spring. Fertilize after blooming.

Tree peonies like Kagura Jishi, shown above, don't die back each fall as do herbaceous types. The trees bloom earlier, also.

June Brilliant (herbaceous) truly glows.

Mercy, also herbaceous, is a single type.

1 While undisturbed peonies will often bloom faithfully for a century, it's good garden practice to lift and divide herbaceous peonies about once every 10 years. And this task can be done only in the fall.

First, dig a shallow trench just outside the edge of the clump. When plant is completely encircled, pry under root mass with a spade, as you lift from the top, using stems as a "handle" to pull with.

Use a hose to wash away all soil so you can see clearly where "eyes" are located on roots. This helps you to decide on how many sturdy divisions you should make. Making too many means a longer wait for bloom.

2 Use a sturdy, well-sharpened knife to make the divisions. No division should have fewer than 3 eyes; divisions having from 5 to 8 eyes are better, since newly set-out plants can be expected to perform well the following spring. It takes at least two years for 3-eye divisions to bloom significantly.

This is a fact worth remembering when buying new peony plants from a nurseryman. The difference in prices usually reflects the number of eyes your plant will have. Newer introductions will also cost more than the older favorites. Pick both early and late bloomers for a longer period of peony color in the spring.

3 To plant a new division, begin by digging a deep hole (2 feet) in a sunny location and replacing subsoil with fresh topsoil, unless subsoil in your area is exceptionally rich. To encourage sturdy growth, add humus and bone meal to soil you replace in hole. Do **not** use peat moss or cow manure, however.

Set divisions 3 feet apart. Be sure that eyes are 1 to 2 inches below soil surface—no more, no less. Measure to be sure. Spread roots over firm mound formed at bottom of hole. Fill with more topsoil and water in well. Fertilize after each season's bloom. In cold climate areas, mulch with 2 to 4 inches of straw or leaves.

19

PERENNIAL FAVORITES
Daylilies

T he Greeks had a word for this summer star: Hemerocallis, meaning "beautiful for a day," and that describes well the plant's bloom schedule. Each stem will have from 5 to 10 buds; as one fades, another soon opens.

Modern hybridizers have developed varieties which bloom early, mid-season, and late— allowing you flowers from May on into the month of September.

Colors range from yellow through peach, orange, pink, mauve, and red. The delicate melon-color Ruth Lehman (36 in.), above, belongs to the mid-season bloom group.

There are numerous tall varieties—28 to 36 inches—that make perfect back-of-border plants. Others bloom at heights as low as 15 inches—suitable for mid- and front-of-border spots.

Winnetka (22 to 24 in.), mid-season.

Soft Whisper (28 to 30 in.), mid-season.

Showy trio: Shooting Star (38 in.), Golden West (center right), Crimson Pirate (30 in.).

Newly purchased plants or divisions of your established clumps should be planted 1 foot apart. Dig holes to a depth of 10 to 12 inches, then center a mound of earth in each hole. Set in all plants at depth at which they formerly grew, spreading roots over mound. Fill in with soil; water well.

Hemerocallis may be set into the garden in either spring or fall, and are subject to virtually no disease. They flower most in sun, although they perform adequately in shady locations as well.

Daylilies are actually very undemanding about the soil in which they grow, but will benefit from fertilizing, either in fall or early spring. Mulch the planting bed to hinder weed growth.

Recommended long-time favorites in the mid-season class—and therefore less costly—include Evelyn Claar (33 in., pink); Kindly Light (30 in., citrus yellow); Hesperus (42 in., chrome yellow); Mabel Fuller (38 in., cardinal red); The Doctor (36 in., deep red); and Stars Over Dallas (34 in., pale yellow).

21

PERENNIAL FAVORITES
Hardy Lilies

Over recent decades, hybridizers of hardy lilies have worked magic to give us bulbs that will perform handsomely and, if planted where drainage is good and the site mostly sunny, offer few problems of maintenance or disease control. Select lilies by flowering time to have some in bloom all summer. Imperial Gold, above, is one of the June-July bloomers.

Old-fashioned favorites, tiger lilies bloom in July-August.

July-August bloomer Imperial Crimson.

Joan Evans (orange) and Destiny (yellow) flower in June-July.

PERENNIAL FAVORITES

Chrysanthemums

Gardeners everywhere are indebted to the Chinese and Japanese who have grown and hybridized the chrysanthemum for thousands of years. The spectacular mum shown above is Potomac, an unusual single, two-foot plant with a 5- to 7-inch bloom. Choose varieties grown locally for gardens of the North where deep frost comes early. Or, try growing in pots sunken in the garden, to be brought indoors to bloom in a sunny window prior to killing frost. The best practice for cold regions is to select cold-hardy and early blooming varieties to avoid having hard frost kill off budded chrysanthemums before they unfurl. Look to early blooming cushion-type mums for September flowering, well ahead of expected freeze dates in most areas.

Tantalizer, spider, bears 12-in. flowers; Yellow Arcadia, pompon, with 2-in. bloom.

1 If a mature plant needs dividing, wait until it's 3 inches tall in spring. Dig up and pull apart, selecting sturdy shoots to set in fertile soil in sun.

2 When transplanting, shoots should be spaced 1 foot apart. Cut or pinch ¾ inch off top of each newly planted division. When a plant is six inches tall, prune again. In the North, last pruning is July 15. This keeps plants shorter and denser.

3 For bushy, heavily budded plants, every 10 days use a light feeding of balanced plant fertilizer, either liquid or dry, and well watered in. Use mulch of grass clippings, shredded bark, or compost applied 2 inches thick to keep roots cool and conserve ground moisture.

Powder Puff, yellow anemone, flowers to 5 in.; Deanna Lee, pompon, 3½-in. bloom.

25

ABCs
of
Perennials

When you plant perennials, you plant for long-lasting beauty. And you hope for minimal care on your part. To achieve these two desirable—and reasonable—goals, make plans before you plant. With perennials, if you've planned and planted well, you can expect to sit back and admire the results of your efforts for years to come.

But planning and planting techniques are all-important, and it is to this section that you should look for vital facts on season of bloom, zonal hardiness (see also pages 278 and 279), height of plant at maturity, preferences as to sun or shade, soil type, color or colors available, and special cultural information. So, whether you're a new or an experienced garden hand, check this section before you decide whether and where to add a new member to your garden.

Oriental poppies are available in a wide range of colors.

A

ACHILLEA
see yarrow

ACONITUM
see monkshood

ADONIS
(Adonis vernalis); also called spring adonis

ZONE: 3   **HEIGHT:** 12 inches
FLOWER COLOR: yellow
BLOOM TIME: March-April
LIGHT: sun or light shade
PROPAGATION: seed or root division

Blooming early, along with snow-drops, adonis has solitary, terminal flowers on leafy stems. Foliage is narrow and very finely cut.

Culture is easy in any average soil, though the plant prefers moist woodsy earth. Use adonis at the front of a mixed perennial border that includes spring-flowering bulbs, or plant in a rock garden.

Grow new plants from seed in summer or divide and replant established clumps in late spring, summer, or fall.

AGERATUM
(Eupatorium coelestinum); also called hardy ageratum

ZONE: 3   **HEIGHT:** 2 feet
FLOWER COLOR: blue
BLOOM TIME: August-September
LIGHT: part-shade
PROPAGATION: root division

Also called mist flower, this hardy perennial is a valuable addition to mixed borders in need of late summer color—especially in the blue range. It takes its common name from annual ageratum, which is not a relative, although they do bear some similarities, especially in color of bloom.

No special culture is needed for this easy-to-grow plant, but it is at its best in light shade.

Reproduces readily in the form of spreading clumps. Spring is the best time to lift, divide, and replant.

ALYSSUM
(Aurinia saxatilis); also called basket-of-gold

ZONE: 3   **HEIGHT:** 12 to 15 inches
FLOWER COLOR: yellow
BLOOM TIME: early spring
LIGHT: sun or part-sun
PROPAGATION: seed, stem cuttings, or root division

Ordinary garden soil suits this hardy perennial, which flowers most prolifically in full sun.

A. saxatilis 'citrina' is the most

floriferous variety; *A. saxatilis 'compacta'* has similar growth habits but is somewhat shorter.

Note that this is *not* the plant referred to as "sweet alyssum," which is an annual of wide usage, a dwarf in habit, and available in white, blues, pinks, and purples.

ALKANET
see anchusa

ANCHUSA
(Anchusa azurea); also called alkanet

ZONE: 3   **HEIGHT:** 1 to 4 feet
FLOWER COLOR: blue
BLOOM TIME: June onward
LIGHT: sun or part-sun
PROPAGATION: root division in spring or fall

Depending upon the variety you pick, this perennial forget-me-not grows up to 4 feet tall (*Anchusa azurea*, Dropmore variety), or only 12 inches (Little John).

Bright blue flowers on plants of pyramidal form with somewhat rough or hairy foliage are characteristic of all varieties.

If spent bloom is regularly cut (not allowed to go to seed), this plant will often continue to bloom into September. Clumps multiply at a slow rate. If more rapid increase is wanted, allow plants to go to seed.

ANTHEMIS
(Anthemis tinctoria); also called golden marguerite

ZONE: 3   **HEIGHT:** 30 to 36 inches
FLOWER COLOR: yellow
BLOOM TIME: June to frost
LIGHT: sun or part-shade
PROPAGATION: root division

Any garden soil seems to suit this long-flowering perennial. Two-inch-wide blooms of a deep yellow appear on plants which may grow as tall as 3 feet under ideal conditions. Generous with its bloom, it's good as a mid-border plant, allowing you to cut long-lasting bouquets during all summer months. Divide established clumps to start new plants.

AQUILEGIA
see columbine

ARMERIA
see thrift

ARTEMISIA
(Artemisia sp.); also called wormwood

ZONE: 3   **HEIGHT:** 6 inches
FLOWER COLOR: silver-gray foliage
BLOOM TIME: spring through summer
LIGHT: sun, part-shade
PROPAGATION: cuttings or root division

Silver Mound, *Artemisia schmidtiana,* is the most widely known of cultivated artemisias. Its cool, ferny foliage contrasts well with the green leaves and the colorful bloom of other plants in a mixed perennial border. Use it as a transition plant between bloom colors that could clash if set next to each other. It's a good rock garden plant as well, with mounds spreading out to as much as a foot in width.

If mid-season heat makes it look ragged, cut back sharply. It will soon put up fresh growth.

Another favorite, *A. stellerana,* grows 2 feet tall, and is called dusty miller or old woman, having the same trait of white-looking foliage as does Silver Mound. It, too, is useful in borders, though at mid- rather than front-of-the-border locations. Thrives in almost any type of garden soil.

A. abrotanum, called old man or southernwood, reaches 2 to 3 feet tall with fragrant, gray foliage and small yellow flowers in August.

Silver King artemisia (*A. ludoviciana*) has silvery gray leaves and can reach a height of 3½ feet.

Propagate the shrubby artemisias such as Silver Mound by rooting stem cuttings in a cold frame in autumn. For herbaceous artemisias on which stems die back in the fall, such as Silver King, increase by root division in late fall or early spring.

As with many common names, a certain amount of confusion exists here, also. Some seed catalogs list a perennial cineraria as "dusty miller" in both dwarf and taller varieties. These have the silver-white foliage that is typical of the artemisias discussed above, and they may be put to similar uses.

ASCLEPIAS
see butterfly weed

ASTER
(Aster sp.); also called michaelmas daisy

ZONE: 4   **HEIGHT:** to 48 inches
FLOWER COLOR: pinks, blues, purples
BLOOM TIME: most kinds bloom late summer-fall
LIGHT: sun or part-shade
PROPAGATION: root division in spring or fall

Hardy asters demand no more than adequate sun and water to supply you with important late bloom—mostly in August and September. Among the best-loved of the many varieties available are:

Harrington's Pink, Sailor Boy (violet flowers with yellow eyes), and Boningale White (double, with yellow eyes).

There are other hardy asters that do not bloom at such tall heights, and a few that bloom all summer. Best of this last named group is *Aster frikarti,* which does bloom from June to frost, with flowers of lavender-blue, and stems from 24 to 30 inches tall.

Among the dwarfs of the tribe—plants that grow 8 to 15 inches tall—are Jenny—15 inches, cyclamen-red bloom—and Romany—6 to 8 inches tall, with violet flowers from early September until frost.

Tall-growing varieties should be lifted, divided, and replanted about every three years. As with chrysanthemums, throw out woody center portions of plants, divide healthy parts, and re-set about a foot apart. Clumps spread quite rapidly, but new plants do not come true from seed.

If you pinch tops back sharply in June, tallest varieties can be kept somewhat shorter. Left unpinched, tallest varieties will probably have to be staked in August.

ASTILBE
(Astilbe arendsi);
also called false spirea

ZONE: 4   **HEIGHT:** 15 to 30 inches
FLOWER COLOR: pink, red, white, salmon
BLOOM TIME: June-July
LIGHT: sun-shade
PROPAGATION: root division in spring or fall

This handsome plant supplies the answer to a question that plagues many gardeners who want color in shade. Although it will perform in sun, it much prefers shade, and puts up big, feathery plumes of bloom above neatly formed dark green fern-like leaves.

Astilbes prefer a damp location, but will perform adequately in almost any soil. They're hardy enough to use as ground cover in shady spots, and will bring welcome color to mid-border locations in mixed perennial gardens.

If summers are long and hot in the zone where you live, be sure to mulch around base of astilbes to retain needed ground moisture.

B

BABY'S-BREATH
(Gypsophila paniculata)

ZONE: 3   **HEIGHT:** 4 feet
FLOWER COLOR: white, pink
BLOOM TIME: June-July
LIGHT: full sun
PROPAGATION: root cuttings in midsummer

Perennial baby's-breath needs well-drained alkaline soil, full sun, and lots of space if it is to be at its best. Because plants grow almost as wide as they are tall, set new plants about 6 feet apart in the location where you'll want them permanently. They send down a tap root that makes it virtually impossible to move big plants with success.

Because they are so tall, with rather weak stems, they'll need to be well staked so wind and rain won't send them sprawling over their neighbors in the perennial border.

But they are worth the trouble—as a source for cut and dried flowers, as well as for their feathery charm in the border itself.

Well-loved varieties include Bristol Fairy (white) and Pink Fairy. Both are doubles.

There is a creeping variety of the plant, *Gypsophila repens* (either white or pink) that grows only a few inches tall and is best suited to rockeries.

BALLOON FLOWER
(Platycodon grandiflorus)

ZONE: 3   **HEIGHT:** 20 inches
FLOWER COLOR: blue, pink, white
BLOOM TIME: July-August
LIGHT: sun
PROPAGATION: sow seed in spring or summer, or buy root starts

Most popular in its blue form, this hardy perennial takes a year or two to become well established, then goes on to bloom for years. It gets its common name from the fact that buds are round and puffy before they open, resembling tiny balloons. The fleshy, tuber-like roots should be planted so crowns are just below the soil level, with at least 1 foot

ZONE: 3   HEIGHT: 4 to 5 feet
FLOWER COLOR: deep blue
BLOOM TIME: June
LIGHT: sun or part-shade
PROPAGATION: seed or root division

Native to North America, baptisia is a very hardy perennial, able to withstand drought. Although it will grow in full sun, it prefers some shade. Flowers resemble those of the pea family but are of an intense, dark blue. If pods are left on the plant, wild birds will eat seeds during the winter months.

This plant is ideal for sloping banks, but is not without problems in a perennial border, since it grows rankly, once established, and may need staking while in bloom. *Baptisia australis* (blue) is best suited to perennial gardens. *B. tinctoria,* which has yellow flowers, often is grown in wild gardens. *B. alba* is one of several white species.

BASKET-OF-GOLD
see alyssum

BEE-BALM
(Monarda didyma); also known as bergamot

ZONE: 4   HEIGHT: 2 to 3 feet
FLOWER COLOR: pink, red, purple, white
BLOOM TIME: July-August
LIGHT: sun or part-shade
PROPAGATION: root division

Bee-balm is indeed attractive to bees as well as to hummingbirds.

Valuable as a mid-border plant, it is extremely hardy and withstands drought. Even when not in bloom, it's easily recognized from its square stem. Not at all fussy as to soil, bee-balm will perform well even in fairly sandy or heavy soil, though it does best in a lighter loam. Clumps increase rather rapidly, and more plants may be had by lifting, dividing, and replanting divisions in early spring.

between plants. Don't try to move them once they're planted.

It is not difficult to grow this plant from seed. Start seed in late summer when nights begin to be cool. Transplant to a cold frame for the winter, then move into garden after all frost danger has passed.

BAPTISIA
(Baptisia australis); also known as blue or false indigo

Variety Cambridge Scarlet puts out brilliant bloom from late June on into September, and is attractive when planted close to yellow daylilies.

BELLFLOWER
see campanula

BELLIS
(Bellis perennis); also known as English daisy

ZONE: 3   HEIGHT: 6 to 8 inches
FLOWER COLOR: pink, white, red
BLOOM TIME: spring
LIGHT: part-shade
PROPAGATION: seed or root division

These dainty plants make attractive companions to spring-flowering bulbs, but resent long, hot, dry summers, under which conditions they behave as biennials rather than perennials. If pansies do well for you, so will English daisies.

To grow from seed, sow in late summer or early autumn in a protected location or cold frame, then transplant into flower border or bed as early as the ground can be worked. Space the plants 5 inches apart, and if growing conditions are suitable, they will self-sow generously.

BLEEDING-HEART
(Dicentra spectabilis)

ZONE: 4   **HEIGHT:** 24 inches
FLOWER COLOR: pink
BLOOM TIME: early spring
LIGHT: part-shade
PROPAGATION: cuttings or root division

This old-fashioned favorite has lacy foliage, and sends up racemes loaded with gracefully drooping pink, heart-shaped flowers. Plant about 24 inches apart, as the clump will gradually increase in size.

When set close to flowering bulbs and either annual or perennial (anchusa) forget-me-nots, bleeding-heart has endearing charm in the spring garden.

As summer progresses, foliage is prone to die back. For this reason, it's wise to mark location with a stake to avoid disturbing the root if you plan to overplant bulb areas with annuals for summer color.

In recent years, some shorter varieties of bleeding-heart have been introduced and described in plant catalogs as "blooming all summer." These, however, are not as reliably hardy as *Dicentra spectabilis* described above, nor do they tolerate heat well.

BLUE FALSE INDIGO
see baptisia

BLUE MARGUERITE
see felicia

BRUNNERA
(Brunnera macrophylla); also known as Siberian forget-me-not and Siberian bugloss

ZONE: 4   **HEIGHT:** 18 inches ·
FLOWER COLOR: blue
BLOOM TIME: May
LIGHT: part-shade
PROPAGATION: seed or root cuttings

Sometimes listed as *Anchusa myosotidiflora,* brunnera should be thought of as a half-hardy perennial. The bloom closely resembles that of the perennial forget-me-not, *A. azurea,* but it appears earlier, and

therefore has value as a complement to the spring flowering bulbs. May be grown from seed sown in late summer, then transplanted into the border as early as the soil can be worked.

In fact, it's wise to allow some bloom to go to seed, saving it in case the mother plant fails to emerge after a fall and winter of adverse weather conditions. Seed also may be sown indoors in early spring (March-April), but young plants are unlikely to bloom that same spring.

BUGLOSS
see brunnera

BUTTERCUPS
(Ranunculus sp.)

ZONE: 4   **HEIGHT:** 18 inches
FLOWER COLOR: yellow
BLOOM TIME: May
LIGHT: sun or part-shade
PROPAGATION: seed or root division

An enormous family, the buttercups include many wildflowers. One that's particularly worth growing in the mixed perennial garden is *Ranunculus acris.* It has double shiny yellow flowers on stems from 12 to 18 inches tall, with attractive, deeply cut leaves.

Acris is a creeper and sends out a large number of runners each spring. But these are not difficult to control if you simply pull them off before they take root. Their yellow flowers are a pleasant contrast to the blues and purples of bearded iris, with which their season of bloom coincides.

R. amplexicaulis, 10 to 12 inches high, is a good candidate for the rock garden.

BUTTERFLY WEED
(*Asclepias tuberosa*)

ZONE: 4 **HEIGHT:** 2 to 3 feet
FLOWER COLOR: orange
BLOOM TIME: summer
LIGHT: sun
PROPAGATION: seed or division
Butterflies are attracted to the umbels of brilliant orange bloom on this hardy perennial. Flowering from July to September, it fills a gap in the mixed perennial border season of bloom and is most welcome.

Not fussy about soil, this plant must have good drainage and sun if it is to perform at its best.

It makes its greatest effect when set out in groups of three or more. Try to plant where you'll want permanent growth, as large plants are very difficult to move.

Seemingly unaffected by any plant disease, butterfly weed is handsome in bouquets of cut flowers and is long-lasting. But as it's slow to come up in spring, clumps should be marked to avoid damage when cultivating or planting at that season of the year.

C

CAMPANULA
(*Campanula* sp.); also known as bellflower

ZONE: 3 **HEIGHT:** 8 to 36 inches
FLOWER COLOR: blue, white
BLOOM TIME: June
LIGHT: sun, light shade
PROPAGATION: root division
in early spring
There are so many attractive members of this family—some hardy all the way from zone 3 southward, others not hardy farther north than zone 5—that it is difficult to choose any one or two as "best."

Campanula carpatica makes an excellent edging plant, sends up blue bloom all summer, and is hardy zone 3 southward. Its relative, *C. carpatica alba,* has the same growth habits but bears white flowers.

C. glomerata has both blue and white varieties that grow 18 to 20 inches tall, bloom throughout June and July, and are ideal mixed border plants. They multiply generously in zone 4 southward.

C. persicifolia, or peach-bells, has white or blue nodding flowers up to 1½ inches long on 3-foot stems. Some varieties that are July flowering include doubles. Set plants of this variety 10 to 12 inches apart. Zone 3.

C. lactiflora varieties are generally not hardy north of zone 5. They are part-shade tolerant, and colors are mostly in the blue range.

All campanula should have winter protection; plants should be lifted,

divided, and replanted every two or three years to ensure hardiness. Do this after the bloom period ends.

All require moderately rich, well-drained soil. Since none is easily grown from seed, it is advisable to start with young plants, set out in spring.

C. medium, a member of this family commonly called Canterbury-bells, is a biennial rather than a perennial and is covered on page 66.

CANDYTUFT
(*Iberis sempervirens*)

ZONE: 3 **HEIGHT:** 4 to 8 inches
FLOWER COLOR: white
BLOOM TIME: May
LIGHT: sun
PROPAGATION: seed, stem cuttings, or division

Perennial candytuft has foliage that stays evergreen in mild climates; it dies down where winters are severe. Cut the tips back an inch or two right after the blooming season.

Use candytuft as an edging, as a companion to May-flowering tulips, or in rock gardens. Plants require a rich, well-drained garden soil. If your soil is poor, improve it by adding generous amounts of compost; if there is too much clay, incorporate coarse sand and fine pebbles with compost.

One variety, Autumn Snow, blooms again in September, after having bloomed in May, then stays in bloom until frost. It's 7 inches tall.

Variety Pygmy grows only 4 inches tall, and is easily propagated by division. Or, use cuttings taken in the spring, rooted in vermiculite, and then planted. Makes a good underplanting to May tulips.

CANTERBURY-BELLS
see campanula

CARDINAL FLOWER
see lobelia

CATANANCHE
see cupid's-dart

CATCHFLY
see lychnis

CENTAUREA
(Centaurea montana) also known as mountain bluet, cornflower, or perennial bachelor's button

ZONE: 4   HEIGHT: 2 feet
FLOWER COLOR: blue, yellow
BLOOM TIME: June-July
LIGHT: sun, part-sun
PROPAGATION: root division or seed

Most members of the centaurea family are annuals, including *Centaurea cyanus*, also called bachelor's button.

C. montana is one of the perennials with silvery leaves and blue bloom measuring up to 3 inches across. The variety *C. montana citrina* has similar growth habits, but blooms are lemon-yellow in color.

None is fussy about soil, though good drainage is important. Use them in a mixed border for mid-season color and for cut flowers.

To propagate from seed, sow in late summer, when nights are cool, then transplant to a cold frame for the winter. Set into border after all frost danger has passed. They will bloom that summer.

CENTRANTHUS
see Jupiter's-beard

CERASTIUM
(Cerastium tomentosum); also known as snow-in-summer

ZONE: 2   HEIGHT: 6 inches
FLOWER COLOR: white
BLOOM TIME: summer
LIGHT: sun
PROPAGATION: seed, cuttings, or division

Cerastium can be a pest if planted in a mixed border, as it has the tenacity and the will to reproduce fairly rampantly. But if you have a dry, sunny spot, choose it for a cool, silvery-looking ground cover.

Although it puts forth white flowers in early summer, cerastium is grown more for the foliage than for bloom. It survives in soil that is almost pure sand. Space 10 inches apart as plants spread to 8 inches

each. It's easy to grow from seed sown in late spring in areas where you want growth. It won't bloom the first season, but it will put on a good foliage display and become well established by the second year.

CERATOSTIGMA
see leadwort

CHINESE-LANTERN
(Physalis alkekengi)

ZONE: 3   HEIGHT: 2 feet
FLOWER COLOR: bright red "lanterns"
BLOOM TIME: July-August
LIGHT: sun, part-sun
PROPAGATION: seed or root division

Easy to grow from seed, Chinese-lantern plants should be given a bed of their own. They're such pervasive growers that they tend to "take over" and so are undesirable members of a mixed perennial border.

The plant is grown almost entirely for its red, hollow, inflated husks which enclose the fruit.

Cut stems when husks are red and keep in a cool, dry place. They make delightful additions to the dried arrangements of autumn.

CHRISTMAS ROSE

see helleborus

CHRYSANTHEMUM

(Chrysanthemum morifolium); also known as hardy chrysanthemum; also see painted daisy, shasta daisy, and feverfew.

ZONE: 3-5   **HEIGHT:** 28 inches
FLOWER COLOR: white, yellow, bronze, purple, red
BLOOM TIME: autumn
LIGHT: full sun
PROPAGATION: root division in spring or cuttings

Garden-grown chrysanthemums belong on everyone's "best-loved" group of perennials, not only for their beauty, but also because they bloom so late in the season, when almost every other garden plant has closed its color show for the year.

Time of bloom for most hardy chrysanthemums is determined by day length. As days grow shorter, this particular plant is stimulated to come into bloom. This is why you can buy mums from the florist's greenhouse the year 'round. He can simulate nature's time clock with the use of artificial light and heavy polyethylene to cover plants early, and thus fool them into bloom.

Choose chrysanthemum varieties to match your season. That is, pick those that will bloom before the expected date of first killing frost. Most can take a light frost—where night temperatures dip only slightly below 32° F., then rise rapidly. And you can protect plants on nights when light frost is expected by covering overnight with old sheets or newspapers weighted down so the wind can't carry them off. But don't use plastic bags. Cold easily penetrates them and they will not prevent frost damage.

Major types of chrysanthemums developed over the years by plant hybridizers include:

Cushion chrysanthemums: 12 to 18 inches tall; compact growth with lots of bloom. Good for cutting and for use in the mixed border or in separate beds. Among this group are quite a few early bloomers good for areas where frost arrives early. Almost every color you can think of in the chrysanthemum range is represented by some member of this group.

Decorative chrysanthemums: These plants are taller and less compact in growth habits than are cushion mums. Most will need staking to prevent toppling by strong autumn winds. All are excellent for cut flowers. Bloom dates tend to be in late September. All the usual colors are included in this variety.

Pompon chrysanthemums: Habit of growth is closer to cushion than to decorative mums, but more spreading. The group is excellent for cut flowers, but not as attractive in the mixed border. Grow in a cutting garden, if possible. Bloom dates range from mid- to late-September.

Spider chrysanthemums: Tightly rolled petals give this type a unique appearance. Many varieties are not hardy and must be greenhouse-grown. There are a few, however—including Geisha Girl (lilac), which blooms late-September on 24-inch stems, and Sun Spider in mid-September—that are reliably hardy as far north as zone 5 if given winter protection.

Spoon chrysanthemums: So-called by reason of their petals —tight tubes which open out at tips to a spoon shape. Heights vary from 18 to 24 inches. Give winter protection in colder climates.

For photos of some chrysanthemum varieties and illustrated instructions on how to plant and divide mums, see pages 24 and 25.

CINQUEFOIL

see potentilla

COLUMBINE

(Aquilegia sp.)

ZONE: 3   **HEIGHT:** 24 to 30 inches
FLOWER COLOR: yellow, red, pink, blue, white
BLOOM TIME: June
LIGHT: sun, part-sun
PROPAGATION: seed or root starts

The native American wildflower *Aquilegia canadensis* and its hybridized relatives form an admirable group of hardy perennials that deserve a place in the mixed border. The native plant has red sepals and yellow spurs on flowers that dance to the slightest breeze on 12- to 24-inch stalks. It needs full sun and prefers rather dry, sandy soil, though it's tolerant of other kinds.

Its hybrid relatives include varieties with yellow, white, blue, rose, and crimson bloom. McKana Hybrids, a recent strain, comes in

bright colors and grows 30 inches tall. Hardy zone 4 southward. Seed comes in a mixture of colors.

A. caerulea, or Rocky Mountain columbine, is one of the loveliest of columbines, having long spurs and blooming on 1- to 2-foot stems.

Foliage of all columbines is fan-shaped in varying shades of green, depending on the variety.

To insure perennial quality, cut all spent bloom before it starts to make seed. When flowering period has ended, cut foliage back to about 4 inches. New growth will arise and the plant will be stronger.

Established plants are difficult to move or divide. To increase your supply, start new ones from seed sown in late summer, winter in a cold frame, and transplant to the garden when frost danger passes. Or, purchase new plants in spring.

CONEFLOWER
see rudbeckia

CORALBELLS
(Heuchera sanguinea); also called alumroot

ZONE: 3 **HEIGHT:** 18 inches
FLOWER COLOR: white, pink, red, chartreuse
BLOOM TIME: June-September
LIGHT: sun, part-sun
PROPAGATION: seed or root division

Attractive mounds of leaves make this an attractive plant in or out of bloom. But it blooms over such a long season that it's a valuable member of a mixed perennial border and equally good in separate beds. Leaf mound stays low (8 inches), but tall bloom spikes reach upward, loaded with tiny bell-shaped flowers. The coral or pinkish-red

color is most common, and the one from which the plant takes its species name—sanguinea. But there are other attractive kinds such as White Cloud with creamy-white bells, and Chartreuse, with flowers of a soft chartreuse hue.

Heuchera plants perform best in a rich, moist, well-drained soil, but they grow satisfactorily in almost any kind of garden soil.

Smaller, new plants form around the base of the mother plant and make it easy for you to increase your supply. Dig up and divide about every three years, separating new plants from old. Replant 12 inches apart.

COREOPSIS
(Coreopsis sp.); also known as perennial tickseed

ZONE: 4 **HEIGHT:** 16 to 30 inches
FLOWER COLOR: yellow
BLOOM TIME: August to frost
LIGHT: full sun
PROPAGATION: seed or root division

With daisy-like flowers on plants that are mostly in the 20- to 30-inch range, coreopsis make choice additions to the mixed perennial border because they stay in bloom for such a long period of time. And they're not fussy about soil type.

There are both single and double varieties to choose from. Baby Sun, a dwarf, covers 16- to 18-inch plants with golden bloom all summer.

To grow from seed, plant in late summer in a cold frame or in a protected place. Transplant into the perennial border after all frost danger has passed. You may grow seed indoors in early spring, transplanting to the garden when frost danger has passed, with a good chance of getting some bloom during the first season.

Or, you can send for roots in spring from a mail-order nursery.

CORNFLOWER
see centaurea

CRANESBILL GERANIUM
see geranium

CUPID'S-DART
(Catananche caerulea)

ZONE: 4   **HEIGHT:** 15 to 18 inches
FLOWER COLOR: blue, white
BLOOM TIME: July-September
LIGHT: sun, part-sun
PROPAGATION: seed or root division

The common name of this hardy garden perennial comes from the Greek use of the plant in making love potions. Today the plant is grown for its bloom, which makes good bouquet material and is easily dried for winter arrangements.

Flowers are reminiscent of blue cornflowers borne on stems that rise above rosettes of green leaves.

Sow seeds indoors in early spring and transplant seedlings in the garden after the weather is frost-free. Or, sow directly in the garden after the soil warms. If you have an established clump of cupid's-dart, you can divide plants in the spring.

D

DAYLILIES
(Hemerocallis sp.)

ZONE: 2   **HEIGHT:** 20 to 48 inches
FLOWER COLOR: yellow, orange, pink, red
BLOOM TIME: summer-autumn
LIGHT: sun, part-sun, part-shade
PROPAGATION: root division

"Beautiful for a day" is the translation of the Greek word for this beautiful and trouble-free plant, but it's a misleading way to describe the bloom habits of the daylily. Since each flower stalk is loaded with buds, as one opens, blooms for a day, then dies, others are growing larger, ready to open on succeeding days.

Daylilies have received intensive hybridizing for a good many years, and collectors who pride themselves on having each new introduction in their garden will need ample bankrolls. When a new variety is first offered, it's obviously in short supply and may command up to $75 or more for a division.

But for the average gardener, there are so many old favorites on the market that cost need never be important. Actually, if the plant has been on the market a number of years, it has proven itself, though its price has grown small. As little as $1.50 can buy you a strong division of a sturdy favorite that will rapidly increase in your own garden in a few years' time.

In selecting daylilies, consider color, height, and season of bloom. This last-named feature is important if you want a long blooming season. The early daylilies will start to bloom in June; mid-season varieties, in July-August; and late daylilies that begin blooming in August carry on well into September, though this group is much smaller than the mid-season.

Plant catalogs will indicate whether the bloom stays "open evenings"—important if you'd like some to decorate the table. Look, too, for indications of "repeat bloom." Some that bloom early put on a second late show.

Although daylilies are undemanding as to soil type, it's wise to fertilize them in fall or very early spring. Set each new plant a foot away from its neighbor. Plants can be moved at any time of the year without endangering their life, though the foliage may wilt a bit if you choose a hot summer day. The best time to lift and divide is early spring, when new shoots emerge.

For color illustrations of some varieties and additional cultural advice, see pages 20 and 21.

Both for appearance's sake and for the good of the plant (to prevent it from forming seed and wasting energy that otherwise would go to increasing plant size), it's good practice to pick off spent bloom regularly.

DELPHINIUM
(Delphinium sp.)

ZONE: 3   **HEIGHT:** to 8 feet
FLOWER COLOR: white, blue, yellow, pink, lavender
BLOOM TIME: June, repeat in autumn
LIGHT: sun
PROPAGATION: seed or root division

Spring is the time to plant delphiniums. It's best to start with sturdy nursery plants for the impressive hybrid varieties such as the famous Round Table series of Pacific Coast Hybrids, or the English Blackmore and Langdon Hybrids. If you choose to start from seed, sow indoors or in a cold frame in early spring.

When you order your plants or sow seeds, it's time to start preparing the outdoor bed that will receive them. Delphiniums are known as "heavy feeders," which means you must supply them with extremely rich soil. Cover the bed with at least 2 inches of well-rotted cow manure or compost, or a mixture of the two. Space this in to a depth of 6 to 8 inches. Next, spread 5-10-5 fertilizer in proportions recommended on package. Add an additional 2 inches of compost or manure, spade this in thoroughly, and soak the bed or wait for a heavy rain. When soil has dried enough to be workable, you're ready to set out new plants.

Space plants 2 feet apart, setting crown at soil level—not below. Water well after planting and, if natural rainfall does not do the job for you, continue watering on a regular basis until plant is well established. After bloom stalks form, keep soil around the roots well watered but avoid soaking the bloom unnecessarily.

Even when you set out all plants of the same hybrid strain, they'll bloom at different times—a virtue if you like to prolong the season.

Set stakes in place and be ready to fasten bloom stems to them well ahead of the time buds begin to open. Few sights are sadder than a fallen delphinium stem, in full bloom, all for lack of staking.

When bloom ends on each plant, cut bloom stalk off just below lowest bloom. New leaves will come up at the plant's base and, when this occurs, cut off remainder of stalk.

Many plants will produce a fall crop of bloom, though on much shorter stems than the first bloom.

To keep plants strong, it will be necessary to continue adding manure and compost to soil every year, in late fall or early spring.

DIANTHUS
(Dianthus sp.); also known as pinks

ZONE: 3-7   HEIGHT: 3 to 24 inches
FLOWER COLOR: pink, white, red
BLOOM TIME: summer
LIGHT: sun, part-sun
PROPAGATION: seed, cuttings, or division

The family of pinks is a large one, including both annual and perennial varieties. Carnations and sweet william are both members of the pink family, as are the gilly flowers which are mentioned by Shakespeare.

Some of the best are *Dianthus alpinus,* only 3 to 4 inches tall and a perfect candidate for rock gardens; and *D. allwoodi,* with very sweetly scented flowers, some double, in a mixture of colors. If you cut off spent bloom regularly, these plants will stay in nearly continuous bloom from June until September. This one is hardy from zone 3 southward. Stems reach 15 inches.

Sweet william, *D. barbatus,* hardy from zone 4 south, bears bloom in umbels of bright color at the top of 1½-foot stems. It's usually grown as a biennial, though it does seed itself in if growing conditions suit it and thus behaves as a perennial. When setting out new plants, space them 10 inches apart.

All pinks like sunny garden spots with good drainage and a soil that is neutral or tends slightly toward the alkaline side. If your soil is acidic, use lime to make it more alkaline.

Pinks are easy to grow from seed sown in the garden as soon as soil warms. You may also make cuttings of varieties or colors you especially like, rooting them in a non-organic material such as vermiculite and setting them into the garden when root growth is adequate. Another way to renew plants is to divide established clumps in the spring.

DICENTRA
see bleeding heart

DICTAMNUS
see gas plant

DORONICUM
(Doronicum cordatum); also known as leopard's-bane

ZONE: 4   HEIGHT: 24 inches
FLOWER COLOR: yellow
BLOOM TIME: spring
LIGHT: sun, part-shade
PROPAGATION: root division

Earliest to bloom of all the tribe of daisy-like plants, *Doronicum cordatum* is eye-catching when grown close to Virginia bluebells, *Mertensia virginica*. Like that plant, foliage of doronicum also tends to disappear during the summer, so locations should be marked.

The hardiest variety of the several doronicums available on the market is Madam Mason. It's undemanding as to soil type and will sometimes put on a second show of bloom if you cut off first bloom promptly as it fades. This variety usually holds its foliage all summer.

To ensure plant hardiness, clumps should be divided and reset at least every other year. Fertilize in late fall or very early spring.

DRAGONHEAD
see physostegia

DUSTY MILLER
see artemisia

E

ECHINOPS
see globe thistle

ENGLISH DAISY
see bellis

EUPATORIUM
see ageratum

EUPHORBIA
see spurge

F

FALSE DRAGONHEAD
see physostegia

FELICIA
(Felicia amelloides); also known as blue marguerite and blue daisy

ZONE: 5   **HEIGHT:** 1 to 3 feet
FLOWER COLOR: blue
BLOOM TIME: early summer to October
LIGHT: sun, part-shade
PROPAGATION: seed and cuttings

A tender perennial, felicia is best grown in climates where winters are mild, or else resown each spring as an annual. Its flowers resemble the common daisy and are as large as an inch across. The plant is a generous bloomer, supplying a source of cut flowers as well as color in the mixed perennial border.

When main bloom period ends in late summer, it is often possible to get a second, though sparser, flowering if you cut the entire plant back severely, inducing a burst of new growth.

Felicia can be grown from seed sown in early spring. It also self-sows if some bloom is not clipped off the plant, but let go to seed. Or, you can take cuttings of established plants.

FEVERFEW
(Chrysanthemum parthenium)

ZONE: 3   **HEIGHT:** to 30 inches
FLOWER COLOR: cream
BLOOM TIME: summer
LIGHT: sun, part-sun
PROPAGATION: root division

Some catalogs may list this perennial as matricaria. It's an old-fashioned flower, attractive when planted between brilliant clumps of flowering plants for contrast, and good also for bouquets, as it's long-lasting. Flower heads measure only about ¾ of an inch across, but many are borne on each stem. Foliage and bloom have a pleasantly aromatic scent.

If spent bloom is cut off promptly, feverfew usually blooms from June through September.

Clumps increase in size and ought to be lifted, divided, and replanted about every third year.

FILIPENDULA
see meadowsweet

FLAX
(Linum sp.)

ZONE: 4   **HEIGHT:** 12 to 18 inches
FLOWER COLOR: blue, yellow
BLOOM TIME: summer
LIGHT: full sun
PROPAGATION: seed, cuttings, or root division

Although most cultivated types of flax are of medium height, there is a dwarf form, *Linum perenne alpinum,* suited to the rock garden and bearing blue flowers in spring.

Other more commonly grown and longer blooming kinds include *L. flavum* which blooms profusely all summer, with feathery foliage and showy yellow flowers on 15-inch stems. A cultivated variety, Heavenly Blue, produces brightest blue flowers on 12- to 18-inch stems and has recurring periods of bloom all summer, especially if spent flowers are promptly cut and plants are not allowed to go to seed.

Blue flax makes a lovely companion to white phlox, white campanula, and cream-colored feverfew.

Increase your supply of plants by dividing in early spring. Set divisions 8 to 10 inches apart. Or, take cuttings and root them. Plants started from seeds sown in spring seldom bloom until the second year.

FLEABANE
(Erigeron sp.)

ZONE: 3   **HEIGHT:** 10 to 36 inches
FLOWER COLOR: pink, lavender, white, blue, orange
BLOOM TIME: summer
LIGHT: sun, part-shade
PROPAGATION: root division

The fleabanes are undemanding as far as soil is concerned, and adapt easily to varying light conditions.

Members of the family that are good subjects for mixed flower borders include *Erigeron coulteri* or mountain daisy, hardy zone 6 southward and bearing white or

lavender bloom in summer; *E. aurantiacus,* which produces orange blooms and grows just 10 inches high; and *E. speciosus,* showy or Oregon fleabane (zone 4), with rose, lilac, or white blooms resembling those of hardy asters. This species and its cultivars will bloom mid- to late-summer. Hybridized varieties to consider include Azure Fairy. Its lavender flowers are semi-double and are borne on 30-inch stems. It is in constant bloom for most of June and July. Forrester's Darling has bright pink semi-double flowers with the same growth habits as *E. speciosus* (zone 3).

G

GAILLARDIA
(Gaillardia aristata); also known as blanket flower

ZONE: 3   **HEIGHT:** 12 to 30 inches
FLOWER COLOR: gold, orange, red
BLOOM TIME: summer
LIGHT: full sun
PROPAGATION: root division

Good border plants, most varieties fit into mid-border locations. Gaillardia also is rewarding as a cut flower.

A rich though light and well-drained soil gets the best results from this showy plant. But it will

39

tolerate quite sandy soil and seaside conditions. There is also an annual gaillardia.

Hybrid perennials that make fine border plants include Burgundy, with wine-red bloom that can be as large as 3 inches across and reach 30 inches in height; Monarch strain, which comes in a range of colors; and Yellow Queen, its name accurately describing its color.

Goblin, a dwarf variety, is only 8 to 12 inches tall, with dark red flowers bordered in yellow. It blooms from July onward.

Should your plant fail to send up new foliage the spring after planting, do not discard the root. Dig it up, and divide and replant the divisions from 10 to 12 inches apart. The crown of the plant may be dead; if so, discard that section only.

GAS PLANT
(Dictamnus sp.)

ZONE: 3   **HEIGHT:** 1½ to 2½ feet
FLOWER COLOR: white, pink
BLOOM TIME: summer
LIGHT: sun
PROPAGATION: buy started plants or sow from seed

The odd name of this favorite garden perennial comes from the fact that, on a hot night when no breezes are stirring, you can often produce a small burst of flame if you hold a lighted match over the blooms.

Once established, dictamnus is very long lived, but don't try to move an established plant; you will probably lose the plant if you do.

Since dictamnus is not easy to raise from seed, you will probably have the best luck if you start with a purchased young plant. Plants grow slowly, but do eventually grow into big clumps, so allow for this by spacing 3 feet apart in locations where you want permanent growth. If you do start from seed, sow in the spring or fall and let seedlings grow for a full garden season before attempting to move them.

Provide a sunny and well-drained location for dictamnus. They bloom during June and July, but the foliage remains attractive after the flowering season has passed. Late blooming bearded iris and spuria iris are enhanced by being planted close to clumps of dictamnus.

Dictamnus albus grows about 30 inches tall with spikes of white flowers in June and July. *D. albus rubra* puts up pink bloom but resembles the white variety in every other way. Both are about 30 inches tall at maturity and are also good to use as cut flowers.

GAYFEATHER
see liatris

GENTIAN
(Gentiana sp.)

ZONE: 4   **HEIGHT:** 4 to 18 inches
FLOWER COLOR: blue, violet, rarely white or yellow
BLOOM TIME: July-September
LIGHT: light shade
PROPAGATION: cuttings or root division

The original gentians were mountain flowers brought to

English gardens long ago, then hybridized to a considerable extent to produce a few varieties that grow as tall as 18 inches. The mountain species were mostly dwarf, and descendants are still in use, largely as rock garden specimens.

Considered rather difficult to establish, gentians have been known to take as long as a year to germinate. It is, therefore, much better to purchase young plants than to try to grow them from seed.

It is probably unwise to attempt to grow this beautiful plant if you live in areas with long, hot, and dry summers.

Gentiana lutea is the yellow variety of the gentian group, rarely offered in plant catalogs. *G. andrewsi,* also called the closed or bottle gentian, is one of the most widely grown members of the family. Flowers are a deep purplish-blue. They bloom in July and August if planted in moist soil, and will tolerate light shade. *G. saponaria* is also fairly widely cultivated. It has blue flowers borne on solitary stems 8 to 18 inches in height in autumn.

The fringed gentian, a wildflower celebrated in verse, is an endangered species. Under no circumstances should it be picked or dug if encountered in the wild. It's offered by a few plantsmen who deal in wildflowers.

GERANIUM

(Geranium sp.); also known
as cranesbill geranium

ZONE: 4 **HEIGHT:** dwarf to 10 in.
FLOWER COLOR: pink, red, purple
BLOOM TIME: early spring
LIGHT: sun
PROPAGATION: root division

Several members of this true
geranium family (what we most
often refer to as geraniums are really
pelargoniums) make ideal rockery
plants or edgings at the front of
a mixed border. So long as there
is good drainage, they will grow
in any soil.

Of the dwarf forms, *Geranium
cinereum 'splendens'* has deep
pink blooms, but grows only 3
inches tall and is not hardy north
of zone 6. *G. dalmaticum* has pale
pink bloom veined with crimson. It
spreads rapidly, but is not difficult
to keep in control by pulling
unwanted young plants as they
appear at the edges of the main
plant. In fall, leaves turn red,
making spots of welcome color
when most perennials are no
longer in bloom.

G. himalayense produces
purplish flowers on 10-inch stems,
and continues to bloom from May to
August. *G. sanguineum,* a
European native, is generous with its
red-purple flowers, also from May to
August. Cut tops back after the first
heavy bloom period and roots will
send up new shoots. If you want
more of this plant, simply allow it
to go to seed.

Propagate any of these geraniums
by division in either late fall or in
early spring.

GERBERA

(Gerbera jamesoni); also known
as transvaal daisy

ZONE: 8 **HEIGHT:** 18 inches
FLOWER COLOR: cream, pink,
yellow, rose, orange-red, violet
BLOOM TIME: summer
LIGHT: sun, part-shade
PROPAGATION: seed, root
division, or cuttings

Not for harsh climates, these
showy plants can be grown well
in zones 8 through 10. Bloom may
be as large as 4 inches across,
on stems tall enough to make
them valuable as cut flowers.

Gray-green foliage grows in the
form of a basal rosette from which
flower stems emerge.

Purchase roots unless you're
ready to wait a year for bloom from
seed. Or, you can root cuttings taken
from side shoots. Set roots so crown
is at soil level or just above, and
plant in late fall.

Clumps should be lifted, divided,
and replanted every three to four
years. Plant 8 to 10 inches apart.

In the north, gerbera makes
a good, cool greenhouse plant,
supplying bloom in spring from
roots planted in pots late in the
preceding summer.

GEUM

(Geum sp.); also known as avens

ZONE: 5 **HEIGHT:** 1½ to 2 feet
FLOWER COLOR: yellow, orange,
scarlet
BLOOM TIME: summer
LIGHT: full sun
PROPAGATION: seed or root
division

Not for hot climates, this plant
requires a rich, well-drained soil full
of organic matter such as leaf mold
or compost that will retain moisture
during summer months. Clumps
increase in size, but rather slowly;
the plants should reach maturity
within three years.

Hardy to zone 5 if provided with winter protection is Heldreichi geum, with bold foliage up to 12 inches and bold double orange flowers on 18-inch stems.

Lady Stratheden, developed from a Chilean cultivar, has yellow, double bloom on 2-foot stems, and is not hardy north of zone 6.

Mrs. Bradshaw (zone 6) has bright red flowers on 2-foot stems.

These plants put on their main show of bloom in June and July, but some bloom may occur up to October.

They can be grown from seed sown in late summer, wintered over in a cold frame, and set into the garden after all danger of frost has passed.

GLOBEFLOWER
(Trollius europaeus)

ZONE: 3 **HEIGHT:** 30 inches
FLOWER COLOR: yellow, orange
BLOOM TIME: May-June
LIGHT: part-shade
PROPAGATION: seed or root division

Large flowers of ball shape on tall, sturdy stems make this a most desirable plant if you can supply the moist, partly shady location it needs.

Spade in plenty of humus before planting, and mulch to retain moisture during hot months.

Byrnes Giant has deep yellow flowers of large size, and Prichard's Giant is similar, but a deeper shade of golden-yellow. Golden Nugget *(Trollius ledebouri)* blooms from June to August.

Foliage is attractive even when the plant is not in bloom, and cut flowers are long-lasting. Plants often send up sporadic bloom well after the major season is past.

Set plants 8 to 10 inches apart and let them serve as complements to late-blooming iris and June-blooming lily varieties. They are most attractive when set out in groups of three or more. Plant in spring when soil has warmed. Trollius are not difficult to grow from seed sown outdoors in spring, but will provide no bloom until the following year.

GLOBE THISTLE
(Echinops exaltatus)

ZONE: 4 **HEIGHT:** 4 feet
FLOWER COLOR: blue; (foliage is silvery)
BLOOM TIME: July
LIGHT: sun, part-sun
PROPAGATION: seed or root division

Not to be confused with the farmer's pest, the Canadian thistle, the globe thistle is a highly

recommended hardy perennial for back-of-the-border placement.

Any ordinary garden soil will be suitable, and they grow well in either full sun or light shade. The flower heads are globe-shaped.

Use globe thistles of the variety Taplow Blue as the perfect accompaniment to yellow daylilies that bloom at the same time. Bloom is also one to dry for fall arrangements. Cut stems to desired length and hang, head down, in a cool, dry place out of sunlight so the blue color won't fade.

Set young plants into the border in spring, when ground has warmed.

GOLDENROD
see solidago

GYPSOPHILA
see baby's-breath

H

HELENIUM
(Helenium autumnale); also known as false sunflower or sneeze-weed

ZONE: 3 **HEIGHT:** 3 to 4 feet
FLOWER COLOR: yellow, mixed gold, red
BLOOM TIME: late-summer
LIGHT: sun
PROPAGATION: seed, root division, or cuttings

A valuable member of any mixed border of perennial plants, helenium gives its major burst of color at a time when little else is in bloom—August into September. It's tolerant of soil—almost any type will do—and takes heat well.

The brilliant variety starts to bloom about the middle of August and goes on for the next six weeks. The flowers are a mixture of reds and oranges—the colors of turning leaves. Bruno sports deep mahogany-red flowers. Butterpat is solid-colored—a rich, clear yellow.

Heleniums are good plants to supply cut flowers when most phlox are gone and chrysanthemums haven't yet begun their show. They grow vigorously and benefit from being lifted, divided, and replanted in early spring every other year.

HELIANTHUS
(Helianthus decapetalus multiflorus); also known as perennial sunflower

ZONE: 4   **HEIGHT:** 3 feet
FLOWER COLOR: pale to deep yellow
BLOOM TIME: July to frost
LIGHT: sun
PROPAGATION: seed or root division

Well suited to any sunny, dry spot in your garden, the helianthus bloom resembles small sunflowers (it's a relative of the annual sunflower). Although it survives

drought, it produces lots more bloom when watered regularly.

The multiflorus variety sold by nurseries will give you big sprays of nearly double flowers from July on.

This plant probably is best grown in a bed to itself because it grows rampantly and could become a pest in a mixed border.

Set out plants in spring. Or sow seed in spring, but don't expect bloom until the next year.

HELIOPSIS
(Heliopsis helianthoides); also known as oxeye

ZONE: 3   **HEIGHT:** to 5 feet
FLOWER COLOR: yellow, orange
BLOOM TIME: summer
LIGHT: sun, part-sun
PROPAGATION: division or cuttings

Another of the late-summer flowering perennials, heliopsis is entirely hardy and is especially welcome because it fills a garden gap, flowering after most perennials have finished the season, but before chrysanthemums come into bloom.

Its culture is the same as that of helianthus, but it is less-often grown

because of the availability of a wider selection of good plants among the genus helianthus. One variety of heliopsis, however, does deserve more attention than it receives: pitcherana. This is a dwarf, bushier than the taller varieties and reaching only 2 to 3 feet in height. It is well-suited to the perennial border and also valuable as a source of cut flowers. It tolerates drought and does well even in dry places.

Similar to pitcherana is scabra, sporting deep yellow flowers with dark centers. Blooms measure up to 3 inches across, appear from July until frost, and are good both as cut flowers and in dried arrangements. The mature plant is 3 feet tall.

To keep your plants in peak shape, divide every three years. If you want more plants but don't want to divide clumps, take cuttings during the summer.

HEMEROCALLIS
see daylily

HELLEBORUS
also known as Christmas rose *(Helleborus niger)* or Lenten rose *(H. orientalis)*

ZONE: 4   **HEIGHT:** 12 inches
FLOWER COLOR: white, pink, purple, green
BLOOM TIME: late fall to spring
LIGHT: shade
PROPAGATION: sow seeds in early fall, or divide

Ideally, helleborus should be grown in the shade of trees, since it requires moist, woodsy soil that's

43

rich in humus. Add leaf mold and well-rotted cow manure if your soil is not up to the needs of this plant.

The season of bloom depends very much on the weather. Long, mild falls with ample rainfall might permit bloom of Christmas rose in late autumn.

Where killing frost comes early, the plant must be protected. A discarded storm window turned into a cold frame-like structure, with bricks to support it, works well. Mulch with marsh hay or straw.

In such cases, bloom will probably not come until spring. It should also be kept in mind that the plant matures quite slowly and will not be able to produce bloom until the second or third season. Once this plant is established, do not move unless it's essential. If you must move plants, or want to divide them, wait until August or September. Lift plants carefully, taking care not to break the brittle roots.

HOSTA
(*Hosta* sp.); also known as plantain lily or funkia

ZONE: 3   HEIGHT: dwarf to 30 in.
FLOWER COLOR: white, blue, violet, lilac
BLOOM TIME: July-August
LIGHT: shade, part-shade
PROPAGATION: division or seed

As an extremely decorative and easy-to-grow plant for shaded areas, it's difficult to think of any that can rival the hostas. Grown primarily for their foliage, the many species and varieties bloom at various times from early to late summer.

Some have sweet-scented bloom in the form of pendant bell-shaped flowers on tall stems that emerge from the rosette mat of foliage. Probably the most outstanding hosta for fragrant bloom is *Hosta plantaginea 'grandiflora'*, which shows very fragrant flowers on 30-inch stems in late August and September. This one is somewhat less hardy than the rest and should be planted in spring rather than fall. Give it winter protection the first year. Thereafter, it will satisfactorily adapt to colder weather.

Other hostas to grow for their handsome foliage include: *H. decorata 'marginata'*, oval green leaves enhanced by a white margin, with lavender bloom in August on 20-inch stems; *H. fortunei 'viridis-marginata'*, oval leaves of chartreuse hue in spring, gradually becoming a solid light green in summer; *H. lancifolia* with much narrower leaves than most hostas—a shiny dark green in color and producing lavender flowers on 2-foot stems in late August or early September; *H. sieboldi,* also known as the seersucker hosta, which grows 2 to 3 feet high and has huge leaves marked with overall puckered patterns; and *H. undulata,* with wavy green and white variegated foliage.

Although hostas like rich, moist soil, they survive hot dry spells and perform adequately in quite poor garden soils.

Clumps of hosta increase in size each year and are easy to divide. In a few years' time, you can easily double your supply of any particular variety. This is a real virtue if you become a hosta addict and begin

to buy some of the new, high-priced introductions. Trading more expensive plants with other hosta fanciers makes the hobby less expensive to pursue.

Varieties listed here, however, have been long on the market and are not in the "high priced" group. Use them as a ground cover under shade trees, as edgings for shaded driveways, and in separate beds of several varieties so planted as to make pleasing contrasts of size, leaf shape, and hue.

HYPERICUM
(*Hypericum patulum*); also known as St. John's wort

ZONE: 5   HEIGHT: 2 to 3 feet
FLOWER COLOR: yellow
BLOOM TIME: May-August
LIGHT: sun, part-sun
PROPAGATION: division or cuttings

The large genus of hypericum includes a great many varieties of shrubs and sub-shrubs (woody stems), but only a few are of interest as garden perennials. All of them tolerate a sandy soil.

One variety well suited to use in the mixed perennial border is Hidcote, which freely produces its yellow flowers that may be as large as 2 inches across. Foliage tends to be evergreen, though even if it dies back, new growth will come up from the roots in spring and produce bloom by midsummer. Given good winter protection, it has been known to survive in zone 4, though there it must be winter-protected, and will probably die back anyway. Other reliable varieties are Sun Goddess and Sungold—both reaching heights of 3 to 4 feet.

Divide early in the spring, or take cuttings anytime.

I

IBERIS
see candytuft

ICELAND POPPY
(*Papaver nudicaule*)

ZONE: 2-5 **HEIGHT:** 12 inches
FLOWER COLOR: white, pink, red, yellow, orange
BLOOM TIME: May
LIGHT: sun, part-sun
PROPAGATION: seed

This poppy, as its common name indicates, had its origin in the arctic areas and is most rewarding in areas

where summers are fairly cool. It also may be grown as a winter annual in the South.

If you live where summers are apt to be long, hot, and dry, forget the Iceland poppy and turn to its relative, the Oriental poppy, for gorgeous early-summer bloom.

Dainty flowers 3 inches across and sweetly fragrant are in bloom at the same time as many of the hardy bulbs, and are pretty in the spring mixed-perennial garden.

In the North, sow seed in early spring and expect some flowers the first season, with full bloom from the plants the second year.

Further south, sow seed in early autumn for early spring bloom. In warm areas, treat the plant as an annual.

INDIGO
see Baptisia

IRIS
(*Iris* sp.)

ZONE: 3 south   **HEIGHT:** dwarf to 38 inches
FLOWER COLOR: white, yellow, orange, red, pink, rose, lavender, purple, blue
BLOOM TIME: spring and summer
LIGHT: sun, part-sun
PROPAGATION: division

The iris tribe is so vast that it is extremely difficult to generalize about, except to say that its members are among the most beautiful perennials you can possibly find for your garden and that there are some kinds that will grow well for you almost anywhere.

There are bulbous, tuberous, and rhizomatous kinds. But for the purpose of this discussion, iris will be presented by the following classes: bulbous, tall bearded, dwarf bearded, Dutch, Japanese, Siberian, and spuria, with recommended varieties listed and described.

For color photographs and further cultural information on iris, see pages 16 and 17.

The Bulbous Iris
Beardless dwarfs remain reasonably perennial in zone 4 with winter protection, but more

dependably so in zones 5 to 8. Plant beardless iris in the fall. *Iris danfordiae,* with vivid yellow flowers not much bigger than a hybrid crocus, may appear as early as late February, according to the season, but certainly by early March. This, of course, makes them subject to possible frost damage in colder zones, though it does not normally kill the bulb.

I. reticulata Joyce has large flowers for its class, with pale blue falls blotched with orange and blue uprights; Violet Beauty is deep purple with an orange blotch, and Spring Time is pale blue with white markings on the dark blue falls. Reticulata iris want an alkaline soil; if yours is on the acidic side, dust with lime after the blooming period ends each year.

Both danfordiae and reticulata iris grow only 4 to 6 inches tall. Use them at the front of a mixed border or in a rock garden. Let foliage ripen and turn yellow naturally.

Dutch iris, also bulbous, may be grown successfully in the garden in zones 5 and 6, but success is doubtful if temperatures sink below zero. If you decide to try your luck with Dutch iris, purchase only a few bulbs to begin with and see how you fare. Plant 3 inches deep and 4 inches apart. The variety *I. xiphium* Franz Hals sports violet standards and violet-bronze falls; Sunshine is solidly bright yellow; pale blue Wedgwood has yellow blotches on the falls; and White Perfection makes a good neighbor to any of the colored varieties.

Tall Bearded Iris

This iris group abounds in such a multitude of spectacular beauties that it's hard to choose among them, except on the basis of colors you want. Almost all in this category are reliably hardy in zones 3 and 4 if winter protection is provided. Plant all bearded iris in the fall.

These iris must have good drainage or rhizomes will rot. Depth of planting is very important: rhizome should be barely below soil surface. If planted too deep, there will be no bloom. It's best practice to prepare the bed for iris some weeks before planting. Spade a fertilizer with a low nitrogen count into the soil at about an ounce to the square foot. Also dig in compost or well-rotted manure, though this shouldn't touch the rhizomes as it may cause infection. Topdress each plant in spring with superphosphate—about ¼ cup to each plant.

Bearded iris should be lifted, divided, and replanted about every five years. Follow directions on fertilizing the soil as for initial planting, keep weeds away from the base of plants, and retain soil moisture with mulch.

The one serious cultural problem tall bearded iris present is the likelihood that they'll be infested by iris borers. If you are loath to resort to insecticides, you can get rid of this pest by lifting any plant whose leaves display a telltale wet-looking streak, and searching for, cutting out, and destroying the borer before replanting the rhizome. The only other method of control is to use a contact insecticide each spring when new growth is about 3 inches

tall, repeating twice more at weekly intervals. This method will not kill any borers already present, but will prevent new infection.

Dwarf Bearded Varieties

Mostly 10 to 12 inches tall, the dwarf iris tend to flower early—in May in all but the most northerly zones. Many are sweet-scented. Use them in the rock garden or at the front of mixed perennial borders.

Gleaming Gold is 12 inches tall and a very brilliant yellow; Bright White matches its name to perfection, and is only 10 inches tall; Pepita, also ten-inch, is a lovely gentian blue with a deeper blotch on the falls.

Dwarf bearded iris may be planted in either spring or fall.

Japanese Iris

I. kaempferi belong in general to the beardless group, but are a quite distinct category within that group. The Japanese have developed the Higo strain that has startlingly large bloom—as wide as 8 inches across—growing on stems tall enough to qualify as important back-of-the-border plants. Some varieties are as tall as 4 to 5 feet. Most bloom in June.

Japanese iris prefer moist soil but cannot tolerate standing water. Nor can they take acidic soil. Use lime to neutralize yours if it's naturally on the acidic side.

Plants multiply fairly quickly, so you can increase your supply by lifting, dividing, and replanting about every three years.

Among the Higo strain, these are a few of the outstanding varieties: Ise, with a 6- to 8-inch bloom of very pale blue, veined with purple and yellow at the base of petals; Nara, with 8- to 9-inch double flowers of deep violet color that bloom in July, a little later than most, on sturdy, 40-inch stems; and Over the Waves, with very ruffled petals of pure white edged in pale purple, borne on 4- to 5-foot stems.

Siberian Iris

Easiest to grow of all iris and seldom attacked by any pests are the Siberian iris, *(I. sibirica)*. Prepare the bed for these plants by digging down about 12 inches and enriching soil with humus, compost, or peat moss along with a fertilizer low in nitrogen.

In established clumps, roots go deep, making plants drought-resistant. Clumps continue to grow in size, but do not require digging and separating to remain vigorous. Of course, you may separate plants if you want to repeat identical clumps throughout the length of a mixed border—something that is quite effective.

Older varieties such as Perry's Blue, Caesar's Brother (purple), and Snow Queen are still very much worth growing. Plants remain in bloom for two to three weeks in June, and supply bouquets to take indoors. All grow to about 3 feet in height with dark green foliage that remains attractive when bloom ends. All prefer sun but will bloom in part-shade.

In making original plantings of Siberian iris, plant several single divisions from 3 to 4 inches apart to form a clump.

Among the newer introductions in the Siberian iris group—most of which are slightly taller than the older kinds already mentioned—Blue Brilliant is an especially attractive variety, growing to 39 inches. *I. s.* Cambridge has big turquoise-color bloom on stems 36 inches tall. And *I. s.* Lights of Paris, with yellow centers, reaches a height of 35 inches.

Spuria Iris

Hardiest of any of the herbaceous irises, the spurias are also the last of the iris tribe to bloom, following on the heels of the late tall bearded kinds. They belong to the beardless group and grow as tall as 36 to 50 inches, with sturdy green spear-like leaves that remain attractive long after the bloom is gone.

Spurias need good drainage, soil that's rich in compost, and deeper planting than do the bearded kinds.

Cover strong roots with 2 inches of soil and place them in full sun, if possible. You will not need to dig up and divide this iris—just let clumps increase naturally. Plant in fall for the root development that must take place before you can get bloom. Don't expect spectacular amounts of bloom for the first year or two; but from then on you'll be able to cut big, long-lasting bouquets.

Recommended varieties include solid yellow Sunny Days, pale blue Morning Tide, and ruffled white Wake Robin.

J

JACOB'S-LADDER
(Polemonium caeruleum); also known as Greek valerian

ZONE: 4   **HEIGHT:** 1½ feet
FLOWER COLOR: blue
BLOOM TIME: spring
LIGHT: shade, part-shade
PROPAGATION: self-sown seed, division

Clusters of sky-blue flowers and attractive ferny foliage make Jacob's-ladder an excellent companion to narcissus, as they bloom at about the same time. Totally undemanding about soil type, they need some shade and moisture. There is a white variety of this plant, *Polemonium caeruleum album,* though it is less attractive in most garden placements than the blue one.

There is also the relative *P. reptans,* sometimes called by the common name of bluebell, which grows 2 feet tall and also bears clusters of drooping blue flowers. The culture is the same as for *P. caeruleum,* and it blooms at approximately the same time.

Polemoniums self-sow readily. Pull out unwanted plants or transplant to a new location where you want to establish a stand.

JUPITER'S-BEARD
(Centranthus ruber); also known as red valerian

ZONE: 4   **HEIGHT:** 3 feet
FLOWER COLOR: rose, white
BLOOM TIME: summer
LIGHT: sun, part-sun
PROPAGATION: seed or root division

No plant could bloom more reliably than the red valerian; it produces clusters of flowers in midsummer with little effort on your part.

On all counts, Ruber variety is a very satisfactory perennial that grows 3 feet tall and bears its sweet-scented rose flowers on 30-inch stems.

You can increase your supply of this plant by lifting, dividing, and transplanting divisions in early spring. But the plant is also a generous self-sower, so you may need do nothing but wait for it to increase by its own seed. If you don't want plants to spread, pull seedlings.

Albus is the white form of this same plant, and has the same form and habits, except that it does not produce much seed.

Set out new plants in spring, spacing 18 inches apart. Average garden soil is satisfactory.

K

KNIPHOFIA
see poker plant

L

LAMB'S-EARS
see stachys

LAVENDER
(Lavandula angustifolia)

ZONE: 5   **HEIGHT:** 15 to 30 inches
FLOWER COLOR: blue, lavender
BLOOM TIME: mid- to late-summer
LIGHT: sun
PROPAGATION: seed, divisions, stem cuttings

Lavender is one of the most fragrant plants in border or herb gardens. There are three commonly grown varieties. English or true lavender, the showiest, produces the most fragrant flowers and is often used in potpourris and sachets. Spike lavender produces larger, more fragrant leaves. And French lavender, slightly less popular, is grown primarily as a bath fragrance.

Start seeds of all varieties indoors ten to twelve weeks before the last expected frost. Germination and survival rates are low, so be sure to sow extra seeds, or plant stem cuttings or divisions from established plants. Plant seedlings outdoors in a sunny location after all danger of frost is passed.

Harvest fresh leaves as needed and flower heads before they open. Hang cut stems upside down in a shady, well ventilated area until dry. In cold climate areas, mulch with 2 to 3 inches of leaves or straw for winter protection.

LEADWORT

(*Ceratostigma plumbaginoides*); also known as plumbago

ZONE: 6 **HEIGHT:** 1 foot
FLOWER COLOR: blue
BLOOM TIME: August-September
LIGHT: sun, part-shade
PROPAGATION: division or cuttings

Bright blue phlox-like bloom and shiny green leaves recommend this plant as a ground cover or as an edging at the front of mixed borders. Leadwort is also effective in rock gardens.

Foliage turns an attractive bronze color in fall. Plants require well-drained soil, and need winter protection if grown as far north as zone 6.

Set plants 1 to 2 feet apart; they'll spread fairly rapidly by means of underground roots, and are easy to propagate by division.

LENTEN ROSE
see helleborus

LIATRIS
(*Liatris* sp.); also known as gayfeather

ZONE: 3 **HEIGHT:** 4 feet
FLOWER COLOR: rose, purple, white
BLOOM TIME: summer-autumn
LIGHT: sun, light shade
PROPAGATION: seed or root division

Not widely used, this native of North America deserves more attention for use in the mixed perennial border. It's also good for cutting and drying.

Liatris pycnostachya has purple flowers on 4-foot stems in July and August. *L. scariosa* White Spire has white flowers on 40-inch stems, blooming in August and continuing well into September. *L. spicata montana* Kobold is a dwarf and grows only from 18 to 24 inches tall. Its red-purple bloom begins in July and continues to September.

An undemanding and hardy perennial, gayfeather likes light soils that are on the sandy side.

LILIES, HARDY
(*Lilium* sp.)

ZONE: 3 **HEIGHT:** 2 to 8 feet
FLOWER COLOR: white, orange, red, salmon, yellow, maroon, pink, crimson
BLOOM TIME: June-September, depending on variety
LIGHT: sun to part-sun
PROPAGATION: bulbs

All lilies demand well-drained soil and like to have their "heads in the sun, feet in the shade." This makes hardy lilies perfect candidates for mixed perennial borders, although they are just as handsome planted in groups by themselves, with hedges as background. Plant lilies in the fall.

Except for the martagons and the Madonna lilies, lily bulbs should be planted from 4 to 8 inches deep, measuring from the base of the lily bulb. The Madonna lily should be covered with not more than an inch of soil and should put up top growth before frost if they are to bloom the following season. Plant martagon lilies about 2 inches deep.

It's important to remember that lilies are never truly dormant, and so should be planted promptly when you buy or receive a shipment.

When planting, add a handful of bone meal to the bottom of each hole you dig. After covering the bulb with soil, spread the planting bed with a 2- to 3-inch layer of straw for winter protection and early weed control in the spring.

If you use lilies in flower arrangements, don't cut longer stems than you need. Severe cutting can cause loss of the plant. Lilies need stems and leaves to build up bulb strength for next season's bloom.

It's not harmful to cut off individual lilies to float in decorative bowls and dishes. Also, cut off spent flowers, leaving stems and leaves intact.

A good lily collection should include early, mid-season and late-blooming varieties for a continuous display of color. Some of the most popular, disease-resistant varieties of hardy lilies include:

Early flowering—Bittersweet, Nova, Regal, Improved Strain, and Sonata.
Mid-season flowering—Imperial Crimson Strain, Pink Perfection Strain, Golden Splendor Strain, and Harlequin Hybrids.
Late-season flowering—Tiger Lily, Imperial Silver Strain, Imperial Gold Strain, and Redband Hybrids.

LINUM
see flax

LOBELIA
(Lobelia cardinalis); also called cardinal flower

ZONE: 2   **HEIGHT:** 24 to 30 in.
FLOWER COLOR: bright red
BLOOM TIME: late summer to early fall
LIGHT: shade
PROPAGATION: root division or stem cuttings in midsummer

Lobelia cardinalis is one of the handsomest of plants to grow in shade. Its tall, spike form makes it good for back-of-the-border.

It grows best planted in groups, and plants should be set 6 inches apart. Each plant will send up from four to six bloom spikes.

Another perennial lobelia also worth growing in shade is a variety called *L. spicata.* It has stems of about the same height as the cardinal flower, but its bloom is blue.

Less hardy than its relative, it is hardy in zone 4 with good winter protection. This one, too, is easily propagated by root division, either in early spring or in fall. It blooms from June to September.

LOOSESTRIFE
(Lythrum sp.)

ZONE: 3   **HEIGHT:** to 4 feet
FLOWER COLOR: pink, purple, red
BLOOM TIME: June to September
LIGHT: part-shade to full sun
PROPAGATION: root division in early spring, or cuttings

A long-time favorite in the tribe of lythrums is the vivid purple Dropmore, which blooms freely all summer long, with 20- to 36-inch spikes of bloom that recommend it for mid- or back-border placement.

Thick mulch pays dividends since the lythrums do best in moist soil, though they also require good drainage.

Morden's Gleam, as close to red as you will find among lythrums, grows as tall as 4 feet.

49

Morden's Pink flourishes in sunny locations. Each plant eventually grows into a clump as large as 3 feet wide, and 3 to 4 feet tall.

To insure the perennial nature of any lythrum variety, plants should be lifted, divided, and replanted every three years. Space plants 3 feet apart when making original plantings or when replanting divisions of old plants.

Although new plants may be set into the garden in either spring or fall, early spring is the time to divide older, established plants. After dividing, make sure newly set plants receive ample water the first year to encourage rapid growth of the new feeder root system.

LUNGWORT
(Pulmonaria sp.)

ZONE: 3 **HEIGHT:** 10 to 15 in.
FLOWER COLOR: blue, pink, rose
BLOOM TIME: April-May
LIGHT: shade or part-shade
PROPAGATION: division in early spring

Another common name of this valuable perennial is blue cowslip—more attractive than lungwort. But the latter name is more widely used, as folklore reveals that this plant was once believed efficacious in the treatment of diseases of the lungs.

There are several species in cultivation. Foliage of all plants in the lungwort family is splashed with silvery white blotches, and the plant is especially effective if planted near hardy spring bulbs in bloom during April and May.

Pulmonaria saccharata Pink Dawn does well in almost any soil, even if it is continuously moist. Flowers are an attractive shade of rosy pink.

Plants are from 12 to 15 inches tall and spread fairly rapidly. With frequent division, it's possible to start with a few plants and, in a few years' time, have enough to cover a large area. Set plants 10 inches apart.

The variety known as Mrs. Moon is very similar to Pink Dawn but is slightly shorter—from 10 to 12 inches tall. Its flowers start out pink, but gradually turn to blue as they open and mature.

Unlike Virginia bluebells which it resembles, the foliage of lungwort remains visible and attractive throughout the garden season (the foliage of Virginia bluebells ripens and disappears within a few weeks after blooming).

LUPINE
(Lupinus sp.)

ZONES: 4-7 **HEIGHT:** 3 to 5 feet
FLOWER COLOR: blue, pink, red, yellow, purple, also bi-colors in a wide variety of combinations
BLOOM TIME: spring into summer in temperate climates
LIGHT: full sun
PROPAGATION: seed or purchased plants

Wild varieties of lupine are found in temperate zones of many countries. But only the Russell Hybrids, developed by an English nurseryman, are well suited to growing in the mixed perennial

border, and then only if you live where summers are mild. These plants cannot take intense heat and hot winds.

Although it's possible to buy seed of the Russell Hybrids, the average gardener will prefer to buy plants, since it takes two years from planting before the plant flowers well.

Lupine bloom, borne on tall spikes, is sweetpea-like in form, and makes a striking impression planted in fairly large groups. When you purchase young plants that have been field-grown, you will probably not be offered an exact color choice, other than blue and white, and carmine or coppery shades. But as almost all of these colors are harmonious when planted next to each other, this will not be a great disadvantage to most gardeners.

If the climate is right—on the cool and moist side—the soil may be heavy or sandy and you will still get healthy growth with many long-lasting stalks of flowers.

LYCHNIS

(*Lychnis* sp.); also called catchfly or Maltese-cross

ZONE: 3 **HEIGHT:** 12 to 36 in.
FLOWER COLOR: range of reds
BLOOM TIME: May through July
LIGHT: full sun
PROPAGATION: seed or division

Related to the pinks, lychnis is a valued summer perennial for the mixed border. Big heads of brightly colored bloom are attention-getters at front- or mid-border locations, depending upon the variety you choose to grow.

Foot-high *Lychnis Haageana* hybrids put out blooms that can measure as wide as 2 inches across. Available in mixed colors only, these include a range of salmons, oranges, and reds that are all compatible. Place at the front of the border.

The variety *L. chalcedonica*, known as scarlet Maltese-cross, is from 2½ to 3 feet tall, with big bloom heads on sturdy stalks, and is effective at back-of-the-border locations. Its main period of bloom is in June and July. A very hardy variety, it thrives in ordinary soil and multiplies rapidly. Lift, divide, and replant every three years, and allow 18 inches of space between newly set plants.

If you plan to grow lychnis from seed, you may sow it in spring and will probably have bloom by August of the same season. Autumn-sown seed will bloom the following spring, in May or June.

LYTHRUM
see loosestrife

M-N

MEADOW RUE
see thalictrum

MEADOWSWEET

(*Filipendula vulgaris*); also called dropwort

ZONE: 4 **HEIGHT:** 18 inches
FLOWER COLOR: pink buds; white mature flowers
BLOOM TIME: July to August
LIGHT: sun or part-shade
PROPAGATION: seed or division

Meadowsweet is great for wild gardens, but adapts well to cultivated sites as well.

Seed can be obtained from plantsmen who specialize in wildflowers. Or, you may be able to locate a friend who will give you a clump to start in your own garden. It multiplies rapidly and can be lifted, divided, and replanted every few years until you have the supply you want.

One of meadowsweet's values is that it can help fill in a period when many hardy perennials have ended their season. Too, it's very undemanding as to soil, though it does require moisture if it is to bloom well.

Clusters of double flowers are carried on straight stems arising from rosettes of fern-like foliage.

As often happens with common plant names, there is another plant also called meadowsweet to which filipendula is unrelated. It is of the rose family, *Spiraea latifolia*, and is of shrub-like habit, with plumes of

fragrant pink flowers in summer. You may find it in the woods from Newfoundland as far south as Virginia. But don't dig it up, as it is an endangered species.

MERTENSIA
see Virginia bluebells

MONARDA
see bee-balm

MONKSHOOD

(*Aconitum* sp.)

ZONE: 3 **HEIGHT:** 3 to 5 feet
FLOWER COLOR: blue, purple-blue, yellow, white
BLOOM TIME: July, August, September
LIGHT: sun or light-shade
PROPAGATION: seed or root division

Because they bloom in late summer and fill a void before the chrysanthemums come into flower, monkshood finds a welcome in many perennial borders.

The plant needs a constant supply of moisture, but rejects any location where water stands. Be sure to choose a well-drained planting site.

Barker's variety, which grows to 4 feet in height, is perfect at the back of the border and its blue-purple bloom contrasts in striking fashion with many of the yellow daylilies that are in bloom during the same late-summer period.

Aconitum carmichaeli (formerly known as *A. wilsoni*) grows to 5 feet tall and puts up big spikes of rich blue flowers. It's also an excellent daylily companion.

Golden Yellow Monkshood, to 3 feet, combines well with clumps of white or purple phlox.

Seed should be sown in late summer, with seedling plants set into a cold frame for the winter and moved to the garden when frost danger has passed. These plants usually bloom the second season.

Roots of all varieties are poisonous and care should be taken not to plant them where children or animals can get to them.

MULLEIN
see verbascum

O

OBEDIENCE
see physostegia

OENOTHERA
(*Oenothera* sp.); also called sundrops and evening primrose

ZONE: 3 or 4, depending on variety
HEIGHT: 12 to 18 inches
FLOWER COLOR: golden yellow
BLOOM TIME: June through August
LIGHT: full sun
PROPAGATION: seed or root division

The hardiest of the species and the most often cultivated in perennial borders is the variety Highlight (zone 3). Very free-flowering, it displays flat trusses of cup-shaped bloom and is most effective when it is grown in good-sized groups.

Oenothera fruticosa's flowers are a somewhat paler yellow, and it forms an 18-inch plant (zone 4).

O. missourensis, just 12 inches tall, has blooms that measure up to 4 inches in diameter, and is hardy from zone 4 southward.

All varieties need well-drained soil, on the sandy side, but enriched before planting with well-rotted manure. Set out new plants 8 inches apart in spring or fall.

P-Q

PAINTED DAISY
(*Chrysanthemum coccineum*); also known as pyrethrum

ZONE: 4   **HEIGHT:** 14 to 24 in.
FLOWER COLOR: white, pink, and red
BLOOM TIME: June-July
LIGHT: sun
PROPAGATION: root division or seed

This member of the chrysanthemum family blooms in

June, about the same time as the bearded iris.

Its fern-like foliage and colorful bloom make it a useful mixed perennial border plant, grown in a mid-border placement. Allow about a foot between plants. Each clump will spread, and in two to three years you can lift, divide, and replant to increase your supply. The best time to divide is late-summer.

To start new plants, sow seed in spring, or set out root starts purchased from the nursery. Both single and double forms are available in nursery starts.

Painted daisies need a rich soil and ample moisture. If your soil is poor, prepare the bed by spading in compost, leaf mold, or well-rotted cow manure. Water the location thoroughly and let stand for several days before setting in new plants.

PAPAVER
see poppy

PENSTEMON
(*Penstemon* sp.)

ZONE: 3 to 5, depending on variety
HEIGHT: 12 to 20 inches
FLOWER COLOR: blue, purple, red, rose
BLOOM TIME: June-July
LIGHT: sun or light-shade
PROPAGATION: seed or root division

The spiky growth habit of this attractive perennial makes it a useful plant to give variety to a border containing many rounded-form plants—such as daisies, bee-balm, helenium, and gaillardia.

Flowers are reminiscent in shape of foxglove, with many blooms on each stem, and are good as cutting flowers as well as in the border.

One recommended variety, Firebird, has ruby-color blooms on 18- to 24-inch stems. It's easy to grow, free from pests, and free-flowering. Zone 5.

Penstemon newberryi is somewhat shorter—12-inch stems—with rose-purple bloom in June. Prune it back after the first flowering and you'll almost certainly have a second crop of flowers at summer's end. Zone 5.

An extra-hardy (zone 3) variety, Rose Elf grows 18 to 20 inches tall, with flowers of a clear rose color blooming freely from June until the arrival of frost.

If drainage is good and plants have ample water during the summer months, the penstemons are an easily grown perennial, with a long period of bloom. Plant in the spring or in the fall, spacing 10 inches apart.

PEONY
(*Paeonia* sp.)

ZONE: 3 **HEIGHT:** 18 to 30 inches
FLOWER COLOR: white, range of reds, pinks; yellows occurring in tree peony group
BLOOM TIME: May-June
LIGHT: sun or part-sun
PROPAGATION: root division in fall for herbaceous types

Double herbaceous peonies are a major event of early summer in almost every part of our country. Huge blooms and attractive green foliage that remains good-looking when bloom has disappeared are their endearing qualities. So are their resistance to virtually all pests, their

long-life qualities, and their ability to withstand periods of drought in hot summers. Their range of colors and forms (see pages 18 and 19 for illustrations of several varieties) puts peonies in the almost-indispensable group of perennials for most flower gardeners.

Well-planted (see pages 18 and 19), your peonies will require almost no attention from you other than working some fertilizer into the soil around each plant when its season of bloom is over. You may leave plants undisturbed for a great many years—up to twenty. Or, if you wish more of the same kind, you can divide and replant about once every six to ten years.

In addition to the double peony which is best known, there are attractive singles, Japanese, and semi-double varieties. And there is also the less-widely-known tree peony, so called because, unlike the herbaceous types just listed, its woody branches do not die down to the ground in winter. At maturity, tree peonies grow up to 6 feet tall and may bear as many as 80 blooms—a truly striking sight in a spring garden.

Among the herbaceous peonies, there are early-, mid-, and late-season blooming varieties. Choose some of each to prolong the time you can enjoy these flowers in the garden and in magnificent bouquets. Many are quite fragrant.

Fall is the best time to set out new peony plants. See that they are watered well and regularly until frost hardens the soil. Then put on a protective layer of mulch, using straw, hay, or clippings from your evergreens. It will not be necessary to continue this winter protection after the first year.

In its first spring, a peony plant may sometimes show signs of wilt that is fungus-produced. In such cases, fungicide sprays will control the problem. Cut off and burn any affected stalks. This measure will not be necessary in following years, once the plant has become established and produces sturdier shoots in spring.

If you are anxious to produce the largest possible bloom, you'll want to "disbud" bloom stalks by cutting off side shoots. It will be necessary to supply some support for these heavy-headed beauties, so stake all outside stems to prevent them from toppling over in heavy wind or rain.

Don't allow seed heads to form. When flowers shatter, clip away the entire flower head. And, after the first killing frost, cut off dead foliage and remove all weeds that encircle the plants.

Tree peonies

Never make the mistake of cutting down woody stems of a tree peony as you would the leafy stems of the herbaceous varieties. If you do, you may find yourself with no tree peony the following spring, but instead, an herbaceous peony (tree peonies are grafted to the more hardy herbaceous peony root stock). After a few years, the herbaceous peony roots wither away and the tree peony's roots become firmly established.

After the initial planting of a tree peony in fall, be sure to keep it well-watered until frost. Then cover with an upside-down bushel basket weighted to stay in place through winter months. This protective measure need not be taken in following years.

In spring, after the second year, work a pound of bone meal into the topsoil surrounding each plant, taking care not to dig so deeply as to damage shallow roots.

Tree peonies bloom slightly ahead of herbaceous peonies each year, and remain handsome shrubs for the rest of the season until frost causes leaves to fall. As with herbaceous peonies, clip off the entire heads when blooms shatter. Do not allow to go to seed.

Recommended varieties

The immense popularity of peonies makes them the subject of continuing crossbreeding by a number of growers. And when a new variety is produced and put on the market, it is certain to carry a high price tag for a few years, until quantities available are large enough to meet demand.

But unless you become a peony fancier, there is no need to spend much per plant to have a wide variety of beautiful and time-tested varieties for your garden. For less than five dollars, you may expect field-grown plants that have from three to five "eyes," ready to bloom the spring after planting. (Your plant will increase in size more rapidly if you do not cut stems of the first year's bloom; cut sparingly from crops for the next year or two.)

Single and Japanese varieties are mostly mid-season bloomers, except for hybrids which are all early.

In the white-cream list, Bu-Te, Krinkled White, and Pico are all popular; pink Barrington Belle and Sea Shell rank high; and red Hari-Ai-Nin and White Cap top the lists. Among hybrids of these categories, choose Sprite (white), Flame (pink), and Burma Ruby, or Scarlett O'Hara (red) for early season bloom.

Semi-doubles that head many favorite lists are: Miss America (white), Liebschen (pink), and the

Mighty Mo and Hoosierland (reds). Hybrids in this class, blooming a bit earlier (mid-season) than those just listed, include these sure-to-please varieties: Coral Charm and Paula Fay (pinks); and Carina and Red Glory (reds).

Doubles, probably the most popular of all herbaceous peonies, include these top-sellers: Moon River, Bowl of Cream, Festiva Maxima (white-blush-creams); Dolorodell, Mrs. F. D. Roosevelt, Dinner Plate, First Lady (early) and Pink Jazz (pinks); and Jay Cee and Cherry Hill (reds). Of these, Cherry Hill is early, and Jay Cee is a mid-season bloomer.

Tree Peonies will cost more to buy than herbaceous kinds because they involve the labor of grafting scions onto herbaceous roots.

Among the American hybrid varieties that sell most widely are these choice plants: Black Pirate (dark red), Coronal (ivory blushed with rose), Golden Hind (clear yellow bloom, maroon flares), High Noon (lemon yellow), Princess (mauve), Redon (pink), Renown (copper red), and Vesuvian (dark red, fully double). All of these tree peonies are reliably hardy in zone 4, and with protection, in zone 3.

Japanese tree peony hybrids that top popularity lists include: Fuson No Tsukasa and Godaishy (whites); Yachiyo Tsubaki and Hanakisoi (pinks); Higurashi and Taiyo (reds); and Kamata Fugi and Rimpo (purples). Of the yellow tree peony hybrids, Alice Harding is probably the universally favorite variety.

PHLOX
(*Phlox* sp.)

ZONE: 4   **HEIGHT:** to 4 feet
FLOWER COLOR: white, pinks, reds, lavenders, purples
BLOOM TIME: July until frost
LIGHT: sun, part-sun
PROPAGATION: root division

For fragrance, magnificent trusses of colorful bloom that are very long-lasting, and ease of culture, the perennial hardy phlox is deservedly popular.

A major factor in growing phlox successfully is advance preparation of the bed. Soil should be deeply spaded and enriched with bone meal or other organic plant food. Plants should be set at least 1 foot apart and kept well-drained. Spacing is especially important if you are to avoid the one pest phlox are subject to: mold on foliage. While it will not kill the plant, mold is certainly unsightly. But if air circulates freely, the danger of mold is minimal.

Keep plants thinned out so that each supports no more than four or five stalks. Divide roots about every three years, and clip off bloom heads before they go to seed. Plants from such seed will not be true (most will be unlovely shades of lavender), and if any of these appear, pull and destroy them. The best time to divide and replant is early spring.

The most important work in hybrid phlox development has been done by the late Captain Symons-Jeune. Many varieties

created by him have brilliant "eyes" that contrast nicely with the main color of the florets: pink centers on white florets, red centers on pink florets, etc.

In mixed perennial borders, set phlox at back-of-border positions and use them as accompaniments to daylilies, tall hardy asters, or rudbeckia. Phlox, somewhat like lilies, prefer to have their "feet" in the shade, but their "heads" in the sun, so a mulch is helpful. When watering, always use a soaker hose or other method of keeping water on the soil, rather than spraying from above. This helps control mold.

Recommended whites include: Iceberg (white with red eye), White Admiral, and Mount Fujiyama. Outstanding lavender-through-purple phlox are: Lilac Time, Russian Violet, and Royalty. In the pink-through-red group, these are favorites: B. Symons-Jeune (rose pink with crimson eye), Fairy's Petticoat (pale pink with deep pink eye), Dodo Hanbury Forbes (clear pink), Prince Charming (flame red), Windsor (rose red), Starfire (brilliant red), and Othello (clear red).

A rarity in the phlox tribe is the dwarf Pinafore Pink, which seldom reaches a height of more than 6 inches. Use it at the front of the border for a novel effect.

PHYSALIS
see Chinese-lantern

PHYSOSTEGIA
(*Physostegia* sp.); also called false dragonhead or obedience plant

ZONE: 3 **HEIGHT:** to 2½ feet
FLOWER COLOR: white, pink
BLOOM TIME: July to September
LIGHT: sun
PROPAGATION: root division

The wildflower *Physostegia virginiana* has been hybridized by plantsmen and is a good addition to perennial borders. Flowers are carried on tall spikes or branching racemes and will remind you in their form of foxglove (digitalis).

Most attractive grown in groups, individual plants should be spaced 12 inches apart. Roots will spread quite rapidly and may be divided every two years. New plants may be set out in either spring or fall.

P. virginiana Vivid is about 20 inches tall, and has flowers of a fine, deep pink. Grow it at mid-border position alongside Shasta daisies or other flowers of round form for a pleasing contrast.

Summer Snow, as its name suggests, puts out pure white bloom on 2½-foot stems. It may be used at mid- or back-border positions in mixed perennial borders, or is handsome grown in large clumps by itself.

PINCUSHION FLOWER
see scabiosa

PINKS
see dianthus

PLANTAIN LILY
see hosta

PLATYCODON
see balloon flower

PLUMBAGO
see leadwort

POLEMONIUM
see Jacob's-ladder

POKER PLANT
(*Kniphofia* sp.); also called torch lily

ZONE: 5   **HEIGHT:** 3 to 5 feet
FLOWER COLOR: white, pastels, vivid yellows, reds
BLOOM TIME: spring through summer
LIGHT: sun or part-sun
PROPAGATION: root division

For this South African native, hybridizers have developed a number of good varieties which are reasonably hardy, but which will require winter mulching in the northern zones.

Flower stalks rise up from grass-like mounds of foliage with many drooping blooms on the terminal end, forming a poker-like cluster from which the plant takes its common name.

When the period of flowering ends, cut away flower spikes, and cut old leaves to an inch or so above the ground in the fall. New foliage will come up in the spring.

Set new plants which have fleshy roots into a sunny, well-drained location in the spring, and allow 18 inches of space between them.

POPPY
(*Papaver orientale*)

ZONE: 2   **HEIGHT:** 2 to 4 feet
FLOWER COLOR: red, white, pink, orange, lavender
BLOOM TIME: early summer
LIGHT: full sun
PROPAGATION: root division

Today's Oriental poppies—hybrids developed from varieties that grow wild in Mediterranean countries—are eye-dazzling in both size and color range. Flower heads often measure 6 to 8 inches across with soft, gleaming petals reminiscent of the finest silk cloth.

Whatever the flower color, it is often enhanced by the sharp contrast of near-black splotches at the base of petals.

Easy to please where soil is concerned, they perform most handsomely in rich loam. New plants must be set out in August or September when plants are dormant. Try to place where you'll want permanent growth, for poppies deeply resent moves. Place the crown 2 or 3 inches below the surrounding soil level and space plants 15 to 18 inches apart. Keep well-watered till frost hardens the ground. In the first season, supply a mulch for winter protection or mound soil over the plant's crown. This step will be unnecessary in following years.

Just don't expect bountiful bloom the first spring after planting Oriental poppies. It takes them a while to get "settled in." But in years thereafter, you should be amply rewarded for your patience by these "show-offs" of the perennial world.

Choose a sunny and well-drained location for poppies. If possible, place them behind plants (such as daylilies) whose foliage will hide poppy foliage as it ripens, then gradually withers away following the bloom season.

Recommended varieties

Barr's White is universally chosen as an outstanding poppy, and is most striking planted alongside a strong red such as Glowing Embers or Surprise. Good pinks are Helen Elizabeth and Lighthouse. Rosy varieties you'll like include Curlilocks, Salome, and the well-named Watermelon.

In the coral-to-orange range, try Tangerine, Pandora (8-inch bloom!), or Bonfire. Lavender Glory (lavender is a less-common color among Oriental poppies) is dramatic with three large basal splotches of black.

The Iceland poppy is a close relative of the Oriental species. For information on this plant, see Iceland poppy.

PYRETHRUM
see painted daisy

POTENTILLA

(*Potentilla* sp.); also known as cinquefoil

ZONE: 4-5 **HEIGHT:** 3 to 18 inches
FLOWER COLOR: yellow, cerise, orange
BLOOM TIME: June to frost
LIGHT: sun or part-sun
PROPAGATION: root division

In its short varieties, potentilla is very useful as an edging for a mixed border, or to grow in a rock garden. Cinquefoil, its other name, derives from the fact that leaves are "five-fingered." The plant form resembles that of creeping wild strawberries. Natives in the northern zones of the United States, they are hardy and will grow readily in any type of soil. Blooms resemble wild roses, but on a smaller scale.

Potentilla aurea puts on most of its color show with a profusion of small yellow flowers in May and June. It's only 3 inches tall, Zone 4.

P. nepalensis Miss Willmott grows to 1 foot in height, with cerise bloom all summer. Zone 4.

Lady Rolleston, 18 inches tall, bears 1½- to 2-inch bloom of orange-gold hue from June to September. It's hardy from zone 5 south. *P. verna* is a low-growing creeper with mat-like foliage.

PRIMROSE

(*Primula* sp.)

ZONE: 3, 4, or 5, depending on variety
HEIGHT: to 12 inches
FLOWER COLOR: white, pink, blue, red, gold, mixed
BLOOM TIME: early spring
LIGHT: shade or part-shade
PROPAGATION: seed or root division

The primrose family, a very large one, includes a few that are relatively easy to grow if you can provide them with the right location and climatic conditions. All demand soils rich in peat, whether natural or a supplement, and ample moisture. When you set out new plants, allow 4 to 6 inches of space between each.

The polyanthus strain is apt to be the one you'll prefer because of its relatively large bloom borne on 9-inch stems. Bloom colors of the polyanthus variety are brilliant pinks, reds, yellows, scarlets, and purples, as well as white. They are usually offered in mixtures, as exact colors are difficult to guarantee (zone 3).

Primula vulgaris, the true English primrose, has creamy-yellow flowers with a deeper yellow eye on 4- to 5-inch stems. It's well-suited to the rock garden or as an edging for a shady mixed border (zone 5).

P. denticulata produces bloom in the lavender-to-purple range and has stems as tall as 12 inches. It's hardy from zone 4 south.

P. Japonica Millar's Crimson has candelabra-like bloom arranged in whorls around the stalk. Individual blooms are 1 inch in width, with stems as tall as 2 feet (zone 5).

Premier variety has exceptional bloom—up to 3 inches across in a wide range of colors (zone 5).

All members of the primrose group are subject to red spider. To control this pest, flush plants thoroughly with water as soon as hot weather begins, and continue to do so periodically throughout the summer. Once a plant is infected, it's hard to cure.

R

RUDBEKIA

(*Rudbekia* sp.); also known as coneflower

ZONE: 3 **HEIGHT:** to 30 inches
FLOWER COLOR: yellow-gold
BLOOM TIME: July until frost
LIGHT: sun or part-sun
PROPAGATION: root division

Close relatives of the black- or brown-eyed susan (a biennial), there are two cultivated varieties of the coneflower that can and should be grown in almost any mixed perennial border. They are Gold Drop and Goldsturm, both of which grow easily and compactly, and produce large golden-yellow bloom during a period when few other perennials are flowering. Gold Drop is double; Goldsturm, single.

Both withstand heat and drought well, and neither is subject to damage by insect or disease. They flower most freely in full sun, but will tolerate a surprising amount of shade and still put out a good supply of bloom.

Fall's the time to set out new plants, or to lift and divide.

S

SALVIA

(*Salvia* sp.); also known as sage

ZONE: 4   HEIGHT: to 3 feet
FLOWER COLOR: blue, blue-violet, red
BLOOM TIME: summer to autumn
LIGHT: sun
PROPAGATION: division
Perennial plants with blue flowers that bloom mid- or late-summer are not easy to find, but blue sage is one

that meets these specifications. Flowers are borne on spikes or racemes, and spent stems should be regularly cut away to keep the plant blooming steadily.

Any average garden soil will suit these plants, and they spread quite rapidly. Set out new plants in early spring, spacing them 10 inches apart, then divide and replant every three years.

The variety East Friesland produces 18-inch flower spikes in June and continues to bloom all summer. Flowers are an intense hue of violet-tinged blue, and are good to cut for indoor use.

The Pitcher's sage displays gentian blue flowers borne on a shrubby plant that grows as tall as 3 feet. This variety, grown in zone 4, will require a protected location and winter mulch.

The cooking herb, *S. officinalis*, can be grown from seed or root starts purchased from a nursery. But scarlet sage, *Salvia splendens*, takes on shrubby characteristics and so isn't used as often in the perennial border.

SANTOLINA

(*Santolina chamaecyparissus*); also called lavender cotton

ZONE: 6   HEIGHT: to 2 feet
FLOWER COLOR: yellow
BLOOM SEASON: June-July
LIGHT: sun
PROPAGATION: division
Several varieties of this small shrub-like plant are grown mainly for their attractive aromatic foliage (reminiscent of lavender), as edgings for mixed borders, as low hedges, or in rock gardens. Several varieties have feathery foliage of a silvery hue that makes a pleasing contrast with the bright flower colors in a mixed border.

Santolinas aren't winter-hardy north of zone 6, but some northern gardeners grow plants in pots and keep them in a cold frame for the winter. They also lend themselves to growing as bonsai and can be wintered over as a houseplant in a sunny window.

Santolinas bloom in June and July, with yellow button-like flowers. Plants should be pruned after the

flowering period ends.

You may plant either in spring or fall, spacing plants 6 inches apart in sandy soil and full sun.

Recommended varieties include Nana, that will reach a height of 8 inches but should be kept pruned to 6 when used as a miniature hedge of silvery gray; Neapolitana, also silver-leaved with graceful pendulous branches; and *Santolina virens*, with dark evergreen foliage, which will tolerate poor soil and hot summer sun.

SCABIOSA

(*Scabiosa* sp.); also known as pincushion flower

ZONE: 5   HEIGHT: to 30 inches
FLOWER COLOR: white, blue, lavender
BLOOM TIME: summer
LIGHT: sun
PROPAGATION: seed or root division
Named for its protruding white stamens above a cushion-like bloom—giving the appearance of pins stuck into a pincushion—this plant is effective in mixed borders and makes an excellent cut flower.

Both giant and dwarf strains are obtainable—the dwarfs reaching a height of 18 inches; the giants, 2½ feet.

Seed may be sown in fall and carried through the winter in a cold frame, ready to set into the open garden as soon as frost danger has passed. These seedlings will bloom in early summer.

Spring-planted seed may bloom by late summer of the first year after planting. Seeds of both the dwarf and giant types are sold in mixed, rather than individual, colors.

SEDUM
(*Sedum* sp.); also called stonecrop

ZONE: 3 **HEIGHT:** dwarf to 2 feet
FLOWER COLOR: orange, yellow, red, pink, cream, white, rust-brown
BLOOM TIME: spring or late summer
LIGHT: sun
PROPAGATION: root division

The sedums, fleshy-leaved plants equipped for storing up water and so able to withstand periods of drought, serve many useful garden purposes: in rockeries, as edgings for borders, and—for a few—as good border plants themselves.

Most bloom in summer, but there also are a few spring-blooming sedums. Some have colorful foliage even when not in bloom.

Spring is the best time to set out new plants, and they should be spaced 12 to 15 inches apart, as most varieties increase rapidly.

Sedum kamtschaticum is one of the most dramatic varieties, sending up many bright orange clusters of bloom from July on. When autumn arrives, the rich, dark green foliage becomes red and gold. Its height of 3 to 4 inches makes it suitable as an edging for a border, or to plant in rock gardens.

S. kamtschaticum variegatum has all the same growth patterns as the previous variety, but its foliage carries a band of white. Plant alternating clumps of these two for an attractive pattern.

The floriferous form of *S. kamtschaticum* comes originally from Siberia, and is especially hardy. Never growing to more than 6 inches, the plant is covered with golden-yellow bloom during July and August. Use it as a border edging or in a rock garden.

S. telephium Indian Chief, a plant that is from 10 to 14 inches tall, has gray-green foliage, with each stem topped in early autumn by an umbel of copper-colored bloom. Each plant produces 10 or more bloom stems, making this variety a good choice for perennial borders.

S. Maximum atropurpureum is often called the mahogany plant because of its foliage color. Creamy rose blooms appear in August. Use it in flower arrangements as well as in the mixed perennial border. It's from 18 to 24 inches in height.

S. sieboldi has plump, silvery gray foliage, and in early September, bright pink bloom on 6- to 9-inch stems. Variegatum, the variegated form of *S. sieboldi* just described, has foliage that is sprinkled with cream-colored spots.

S. spectabile Meteor grows to 18 inches tall. Foliage is gray-green, with flowers appearing in umbels of red in summer. It's effective in mixed borders and in bouquets.

The Star Dust form of spectabile has blue-green leaves and puts up big flower heads of ivory bloom in late summer. It's 18 inches tall.

S. spathulifolium Capa Blanca, an English import, is a low-growing, slow-spreading sedum with blue-green foliage in rosettes. Bright yellow bloom appears in May or early June.

S. Spurium Dragon's Blood is one of the dwarfs—an inch or two tall—that remains in bloom from July to September. The foliage takes on the tints of deciduous trees in autumn.

SHASTA DAISY
(*Chrysanthemum maximum* or *C. x superbum*)

ZONE: 4 **HEIGHT:** 2 to 3 feet
FLOWER COLOR: white with yellow centers
BLOOM TIME: early summer
LIGHT: sun, part-sun
PROPAGATION: seed or root division

59

Among the many varieties of shasta daisy, you'll find both singles and doubles that will be outstanding in a mixed perennial border. They are not, however, reliably winter-hardy and will need winter protection in zone 4.

Set new plants a foot apart in rich soil, mulching around the base to retain moisture. If you start from seed, sow in spring.

Every other spring, you should lift, divide, and replant divisions to keep plants healthy. Under good growing conditions, bloom can be 3 to 4 inches across, excellent for cutting as well as for border display. Variety Alaska is a good single; Marconi, a recommended double shasta.

SNOW-IN-SUMMER

see cerastium

SOLIDAGO

(*Solidago* sp.); also called hybrid goldenrod

ZONE: 3 **HEIGHT:** to 3 feet
FLOWER COLOR: rich gold
BLOOM TIME: August-September
LIGHT: sun or part-sun
PROPAGATION: root divisions

If you're one who thinks of this stately plant as a weed, think again. It has been falsely accused of causing hay fever, but it is ragweed pollen—its timetable coinciding closely with goldenrod—that is the villain. If you've visited the majestic herbaceous borders maintained by many of the colleges of Oxford, you've seen it dramatically used and much admired.

Consider planting it at the back of a mixed border in clumps that alternate with hardy asters in purple hues. They make a stunning combination when both are in bloom.

The Golden Mosa variety is a strong branching plant with tapered bloom trusses of deep yellow-gold. It's about 3 feet tall.

SPEEDWELL

see veronica

SPURGE

(*Euphorbia* sp.)

ZONE: 4 **HEIGHT:** 12 to 15 inches
FLOWER COLOR: yellow
BLOOM TIME: April-May
LIGHT: sun or part-sun
PROPAGATION: root division

The euphorbias are most often used in rock gardens, but they are also good accent plants for mixed borders. They thrive in hot, dry sunny spots that would kill off many perennials.

Euphorbia epithymoides, sometimes called milkwort (all plants of this genus have a sticky,

milky fluid in their veins), is bushy in form, grows 12 to 15 inches tall, and puts out yellow bracts of bloom in May. As summer progresses, these change to a rosy-bronze, but foliage remains deep green throughout the season. Although it spreads readily, you can keep it where you wish if you pull up any unwanted plants in the spring. This is also a good time for separating and replanting clumps if you want to increase your stock of this and other euphorbias.

Milkwort is a formal-looking plant that works well in the border or rock garden.

E. myrsinites, cushion spurge, is a prostrate plant that has stiff blue-green foliage growing in spiral whorls about the stems. Heads of yellow bloom appear in April and May. Use it in rock gardens and as a ground cover in hot, dry, and sunny locations.

STACHYS

(*Stachys* sp.); also known as lambs-ears or betony

ZONE: 4 **HEIGHT:** 8 to 12 inches
FLOWER COLOR: red
BLOOM TIME: summer
LIGHT: sun or part-sun
PROPAGATION: root division

Often seen in old-fashioned gardens, stachys has been increasing in popularity in recent years because of its ease of care, willingness to grow in poor soil, and effective contrast of color and texture in the mixed perennial flower border.

Its common name is an accurate description of its soft, furry foliage; the bloom is insignificant.

The inviting, woolly-white leaves of *Stachys byzantina* reach a height of about 8 inches. A taller variety of the plant matures at 10 to 12 inches and has leaves that are 6 to 8 inches long. Red flowers rise 10 to 12 inches above foliage when the plant is in bloom.

STOKESIA

(*Stokesia laevis*); also known as Stoke's aster

ZONE: 5   **HEIGHT:** 12 to 15 inches
FLOWER COLOR: light blue or white
BLOOM TIME: July into September
LIGHT: sun
PROPAGATION: root division

A valuable midsummer-into-autumn bloomer in the perennial garden, stokesia is quite undemanding except for sun and good drainage. It may be planted either in early spring or autumn, but leave 6 inches of space between each plant.

Blue Danube is the most commonly grown stokesia. Its light blue flowers, which can be up to 5 inches in diameter, may remind you more of bachelor's-buttons than of asters. Place this one toward the front of a mixed border.

Silver Moon stokesia is a hybrid of Blue Danube with the same growth habits. Big white flowers are tinged with blue-to-lavender at the center of the bloom.

SUNDROPS
see oenothera

SWEET WILLIAM
see dianthus

T-U

THALICTRUM

(*Thalictrum* sp.); also known as meadow rue

ZONE: 3   **HEIGHT:** 3 to 4 feet
FLOWER COLOR: yellow, white, lavender
BLOOM TIME: June-July
LIGHT: shade, part-shade
PROPAGATION: seed or root division

The graceful foliage of thalictrum is similar to that of columbines, and there are several varieties to choose from if you're willing to grow these plants from seed. Only *Thalictrum minus* is widely offered as a plant by growers. It blooms in July with fragrant heads of green-tinged yellow bloom. All meadow rues are good in perennial borders that are partly shaded.

T. polygamum, tall meadow rue, is 5 to 7 feet tall, bears white bloom in panicles, and blooms from July onward. It requires winter protection if grown north of zone 4.

T. rochebrunianum, lavender mist meadow rue, is only 3 feet tall, has lavender bloom with yellow stamens, and blooms from May to September.

T. speciosissimum (glaucum), dusty meadow rue, has frothy yellow

bloom heads in summer. Hardy from zone 5 southward, it grows 3 to 4 feet tall.

To obtain seed of the various meadow rues described here, secure catalogs from plantsmen who are specialists in wildflowers. Some of these wildflower specialists also sell field-grown plants.

If you do grow from seed, the best time to sow is late summer; transfer seedlings to a cold frame for the winter, and set into the open garden in early spring. All varieties should bloom that season.

Seed sown in early spring probably will not bloom until the next garden season.

THERMOPSIS

(*Thermopsis caroliniana*); also known as Carolina lupine

ZONE: 3   **HEIGHT:** 3 to 4 feet
FLOWER COLOR: yellow
BLOOM TIME: June-July
LIGHT: sun
PROPAGATION: root division or seed

Although there are a good many plants in the genus, only the one described here, Carolina lupine, is widely offered for sale by plantsmen.

The plant has graceful form, attractive dark green leaves, and sends up spikes of sweet pea-like bloom in midsummer.

For climates where summers are often hot and dry, this is a plant to count on—unlike the true lupines which cannot tolerate spells of hot, dry weather.

Set out new plants or divisions in either early spring or autumn. Or, sow seed in early fall. Space plants 18 inches apart.

THRIFT

(*Armeria maritima*); also called sea thrift and sea pink

ZONE: 3   **HEIGHT:** dwarf
FLOWER COLOR: rose, white
BLOOM TIME: May to July
LIGHT: full sun
PROPAGATION: root division

This appealing family of small hardy perennials is most often used in rock gardens. Although certainly effective in such placements, it also lends itself well to use as an edging plant for a mixed perennial border. It's attractive all season.

Its major requirements are full sun and a well-drained site, but it is not at all fussy about soil type.

New plants may be set out in the spring or autumn, about 8 or 10 inches apart. Each will soon form a tidy mound of foliage from which flower stems arise.

The white form of *Armeria maritima* sends up many 5-inch bloom stems in the form of tufts of very narrow leaves that rise above its low mat of dark green foliage.

Another one is 6 inches tall and bears many vivid rosy heads of bloom in May and June. Foliage is evergreen.

Royal Rose, a hybrid developed from the variety just described, puts up 15-inch flower stems bearing pink globe-shaped blooms.

TRANSVAAL DAISY

see *gerbera*

TROLLIUS

see *globeflower*

V-W-X

VERBASCUM

(*Verbascum* sp.); also called mullein

ZONE: 5   **HEIGHT:** 30 inches to 6 feet
FLOWER COLOR: yellow, white, pink, salmon, violet
BLOOM TIME: June to October
LIGHT: full sun
PROPAGATION: root division

For those hot, dry spots unfriendly to many perennials, try verbascum. Furry gray foliage makes this an interesting contrast plant in a mixed border. And tall forms make good back-border subjects. Just give it plenty of sun and a well-drained location to get good performance.

Verbascum phoeniceum comes in mixed colors—white, pink, salmon, and violet—blooming from June until October. It grows from 3 to 6 feet tall, depending on how well the planting location suits its needs, and is hardy from zone 6 southward.

Pink Domino, 4 feet tall, has pink flowers with maroon eyes.

VERONICA

(*Veronica* sp.); also known as speedwell

ZONE: 3 **HEIGHT:** 6 to 36 inches
FLOWER COLOR: shades of blue, white, pink
BLOOM TIME: June to September
LIGHT: sun
PROPAGATION: root division

This large genus includes both shrub and perennial plants, but shrub forms are hardy only in the warmest zones of our country.

Among the perennial plants, there is a good range of sizes, suiting some for use in rock gardens or as low edgings for borders, and others for placement at mid- or back-of-the-border.

All varieties should have bloom stems cut off as soon as flowers fade to encourage a longer season of

bloom. Once planted, veronica should not be moved. But if a move is unavoidable, do it in early autumn and keep the plant well-watered until the ground freezes.

Veronica alpina alba puts on a show of white bloom that continues all summer if spent bloom stalks are faithfully removed and not allowed to go to seed. It's just 6 inches tall, and so is ideal for use in rock gardens, or as an edging for a mixed perennial border.

Spikes of bloom of the Barcarolle variety are rose-pink in color, and the plant, 10 inches tall. Flowers

keep coming from June until late August if spent bloom is cut.

Crater Lake Blue is a free-flowering variety that's at its best in early summer. Colorful spikes of deep sky blue bloom grow on sturdy 18-inch stems.

Blue Giantess bears deep blue flowers on spikes that can reach 3½ feet in height, while the Rosea variety, just 1½ feet tall, has bloom spikes of a rosy pink. Icicle is a pure white, has 18-inch flower spikes, and is a good cut flower.

VIOLA

(*Viola* sp.)

ZONE: 3 to 5, depending on variety
HEIGHT: 4 to 6 inches
FLOWER COLOR: blue, purple, pink, white
BLOOM TIME: early spring
LIGHT: part-shade
PROPAGATION: root division

Violas are relatives of pansies, but are a good deal easier to keep perennial. There are two major groups within the genus: sweet (*Viola odorata*) and tufted (*V. cornuta*). Both want good garden loam which has been enriched with leaf mold, well-rotted manure, or peat. Soil must be moist, though it should have good drainage.

However, even if you can meet these conditions in spring, violas aren't for you if your area is accustomed to long, hot, dry summers. In that case, you may have to grow them from seed and replant when you lose plants to adverse weather conditions.

To grow violas from seed, sow in late summer, transplant seedlings to a cold frame for the winter, and, for bloom that season, set out into garden location as early as the ground can be worked. Space plants 10 to 12 inches apart.

Seed sown in early spring will probably bloom that fall. Many viola varieties will produce a smaller fall crop every year if weather conditions are right: enough rain and no early spell of frost.

In the *Viola odorata* group, Rosina produces generous amounts of fragrant pink bloom on 8-inch stems. Zone 3.

Red Giant, with fragrant long-stemmed, red-violet flowers, develops into a good-sized clump quite rapidly, with leaves larger than most violas. Zone 4.

Royal Robe has violet-blue bloom on 6-inch stems. This variety can take somewhat more sun than can most other violas. Zone 4.

White Czar, like Royal Robe, is also tolerant of part-sun locations and has big flowers on 6-inch stems. Zone 4.

In the cornuta group, the variety Catherine Sharp is a very desirable plant. It produces generous amounts of bloom over long periods, and plants rapidly increase in size. By the second year, a clump may measure a whopping 24 inches across. Zone 3.

Floraire is one of the earliest to bloom, its lavender-blue flowers touched with darker splotches of color. If summers are cool, it may continue to bloom for the entire season. Zone 3.

Purple Glory has deep velvety-purple bloom with a yellow eye. Bloom stems are from 5 to 8 inches long, and plants are hardy from zone 3 southward.

Jersey Gem Alba is a white variety of similar growth habits to Purple Glory. Zone 3.

VIRGINIA BLUEBELLS
(Mertensia virginica)

ZONE: 3   **HEIGHT:** 18 to 24 inches
FLOWER COLOR: blue
BLOOM TIME: early spring
LIGHT: shade, part-shade
PROPAGATION: root division

Lovely companions to the spring-flowering bulbs, clumps of Virginia bluebells are easy to grow, make no special demands about soil type, and prefer light shade.

Although they're especially handsome when naturalized on a grassy slope, you must be prepared to leave the area unmowed until foliage yellows and dies back.

Mertensia virginica has tubular shaped flowers of sky-blue color on 18- to 24-inch stems that sway in spring breezes. Flowers turn pink as they open fully and mature.

Y

YARROW
(Achillea sp.)

ZONE: 3   **HEIGHT:** 6 inches to 3 feet
FLOWER COLOR: white, red, yellow
BLOOM TIME: June to September
LIGHT: sun or part-sun
PROPAGATION: root division

Most varieties of achillea are on the tall side—2 to 3 feet—though there are also varieties that are mat-like, with flowers borne on 4-

to 6-inch stems. Some are excellent to cut, dry, and use in fall bouquets, with Coronation Gold one that's especially suited to this use. Fern-like foliage is typical of the achillea varieties.

These plants perform well in dry locations and are not fussy about soil, but do best in good loam.

Achillea ageratifolia, a low-growing variety, is well-suited to use in rock gardens or as an edging for borders. Single, daisy-like bloom on 4- to 6-inch stems begins in June and goes on until September. This variety needs alkaline soil; if yours is acidic, have a sample analyzed and add the correct amount of lime to sweeten it.

Coronation Gold, already cited as good for drying, grows to 3 feet and is in bloom from June to August.

A. millefolium Fire King, as its name suggests, has rosy-red flower heads on 24-inch stems. Foliage is a silver-gray in color.

A. ptarmica Angel's Breath looks like a larger-size variety of baby's-breath, its white rosettes of bloom in clusters at the tips of 18-inch stems. The plant is bushy in habit.

A. filipendulina Moonshine produces canary-yellow bloom on umbels on 18- to 24-inch stems. It's in bloom from June to September, and foliage is silver-gray color.

YUCCA
(Yucca sp.)

ZONE: 4   **HEIGHT:** 3 to 6 feet
FLOWER COLOR: creamy white
BLOOM TIME: summer
LIGHT: sun
PROPAGATION: root division

Striking all season long because of its sword-like ball of pointed foliage, yuccas put on their show of bloom in spectacular fashion, sending up bloom spikes that can be as tall as 6 feet, with half their length covered by creamy-white, bell-shaped flowers.

For a hot, dry, sunny location, the yucca is one of the best suited plants. It demands good drainage, but little else in the way of care.

Yucca filamentosa has evergreen foliage, and puts up flower spikes that are at least 3 feet in height.

Y. filamentosa Bright Edge, a newer variegated form, carries a band of gold edging on its deep green spiky leaves. Use this one for accent in a doorway planting where there's sun and well-drained soil.

Y. flaccida Ivory Tower is the most spectacular of the varieties listed here, with bloom spikes which may be as tall as 5 or 6 feet and are laden with creamy-white flowers that grow upright, rather than pendant.

Gas plant, in both white and pink varieties, blooms all summer long.

Biennials

The renowned, late horticulturist, Liberty Hyde Bailey, defined biennials as "plants that bloom a year after seeds are sown, then make seeds and die." But there are confusing factors about such well-known biennials as foxglove, honesty, and hollyhock: they self-sow or multiply by off-shoots, often seeming to be perennial.

The best way to grow biennials from seed, except in warmer zones, is to plant seed outdoors in early August, transplanting to a cold frame before frost. Set plants into garden in May.

Double hollyhocks, like their single cousins, need full sun.

ALPINE FORGET-ME-NOT

Myosotis alpestris, grown as a low (1-foot) carpet of sky-blue under the brilliant spring-flowering bulbs, creates an unforgettable sight.

This plant prefers moist soil and a half-shaded location. It has little tolerance for the hot weather of summer, and goes to seed when that season arrives.

Left undisturbed for a time, it sends up seedling plants which you can transfer to a cold frame or protected area for plants to set into your border next spring. Transplant to border as soon as the ground can be worked.

If you live where springs tend to be long and cool, you can wait for the ground to thaw, plant seed outdoors, and have bloom within 6 weeks.

CANTERBURY-BELLS

Campanula medium, blooming in early summer, could be the star of the mixed flower border.

On 2-foot stems, single cups may measure as much as 3 inches in depth, framed by "saucers" 3 to 4 inches across.

This plant is available in both single and double forms, and in shades of blue, rose, and white. Use it to best advantage in a middle-of-the-border location.

Sow seed of this biennial in August; transplant to a cold frame for the winter, and set out in spring when all danger of frost has passed.

ENGLISH DAISY

Bellis perennis, opposite bottom, is aster-like in appearance, endearing for prolific bloom in the spring on 4- to 6-inch plants.

Perfect for front-of-border placement, it requires moist soil and grows best in part-shade. Flower colors vary from pink to deep rose.

FOXGLOVE

Digitalis purpurea, opposite above, is one of the graceful verticals that are so effective in combination with plants of more bushy growth habit. Most varieties are from 4 to 6 feet tall, although one variety, Foxy, forms a bushy plant of only 3 feet in height at maturity. Seed for foxglove is commonly sold in a mixture that includes white, cream, yellow, rose, red, and lavender. The Giant Rusty variety, however, produces all rusty-red flowers with bearded lips. Six feet tall, it needs staking. All foxglove varieties bloom in June or early July, in sun or part-shade.

HOLLYHOCK

Alcea rosea so readily seeds itself that many take it for a true perennial, and it is sometimes so listed in seed catalogs. In a clump against a garden wall or fence, hollyhocks make a fine sight. They need full sun to make strong stems, and even then, tall types (6 to 8 feet) will often require staking.

Or, use hollyhocks as a back-of-the-border plant. From July onward, you will enjoy single or double blooms in pink, white, red, yellow, and lavender shades.

HONESTY

Lunaria annua, also known as the money plant, is grown largely for its charm as a dried flower, lending the shining silver glow of its 2-inch round seed pods to winter bouquets.

Plants grow from 1½ to 3 feet tall. This biennial is so apt to reseed itself that, in most climates, the main chore may be to pull the unwanted seedlings each spring.

PANSY

Viola tricolor, for all its charming pansy "faces," may not be worth the effort it takes to grow from seed if your area is apt to have springs that are short and often abruptly ended by a spell of hot, dry weather.

Then, buy young plants and set out as early in spring as you dare; plant near spring flowering bulbs in a moist, part-shade location.

SWEET WILLIAM

Dianthus barbatus is another self-sower of great vigor and, in most years, will behave like a perennial. Blooming in May and June on 12- to 20-inch stems (or 5 to 6 inches for the newer dwarfs), they're popular both for their color and fragrance in borders. Roundabout (mixed reds, roses, and pinks) and Wee Willie (red) are both 4-inch dwarfs. Plant in a sunny, well-drained garden location.

Graceful, tall foxglove, above, and low-growing English daisy, below, are rewarding biennials. Alternate clumps of English daisies and pansies for an effective early spring border.

67

Annuals In the Garden

What are they and what can they do for you?

Annuals grow seed-to-flower in a surprisingly short time, producing bold color summer-long. You can grow annuals from seeds on a sunny windowsill in early spring to plant out later, or buy seedling plants in flats at a local outlet.

These quick-growing blooms stand well alone, or as fillers in your newest perennial plots. Plant the sturdy seedlings in good soil, water them well, then stand back and watch while they mature and flower in the boldest colors.

It is difficult to dream up a color, shape, or size that's not available in annual flowers. If you love zinnias and want a small flower in a rosy hue, consider the dwarf Rose Buttons. Or, for the very brightest red, look for the All-America winner, Red Sun. It almost seems to glow from within. In zinnias, you may choose from giants to dwarfs in shaggy, quill, or button forms. For mixed colors, look for the very large State Fair and the medium-sized Cut and Come again. Zenith and Fruit Bowl have shaggy blossoms in super sizes.

If you're hooked on marigolds, get acquainted with Primrose Lady, Showboat, and Yellow Galore. These are recent award winners of fine substance—excellent as container plants or in separate beds. Marigolds also run the gamut from very big to very small; from carnation pompons

to nugget edgers; and then to the single French marigold best known as Naughty Marietta, a golden yellow splashed with maroon at the base of the petals. Further, there is a whole family of petites, such as Red Pygmy in a mahogany hue. "Spectacular," "everblooming," and "easy-to-grow" are frequent words of praise for marigolds. They give a continuing source of golden color right up until frost.

A third popular annual is the petunia. It doesn't offer tall, medium, and short sizes, but it is available in a host of grandiflora, ruffled, single, and double flower forms. And in each of these, there's a wide choice of colors. Candy Apple is a vivid red; Glacier, an icy white; and Ballerina, soft salmon. All are grandifloras and

are superb as bedding plants or in hanging baskets. If you pick off flower heads as they fade, the plants will bloom from early summer until frost. And as an added bonus, most have a spicy fragrance. In full-flower, the giant doubles have a strong color impact. The bicolors come in sparkling combinations. Some prefer the multiflora (many-flowered) singles in Summer Sun yellow, Comanche red, or Coral satin. All are vigorous, free-blooming plants of great value in expanding a garden's floral impact.

Hybridizers bring to annuals a steady stream of accomplishment. They've taken the celosia to new heights with Red Fox and Fireglow. They've given us the orange Sunset cosmos, the Bravo dianthus, the Carefree and Showgirl geraniums, Majorette and Silver Puffs hollyhocks, the Golden Gleam nasturtium, and the Blaze verbena.

If you buy annuals in flats from a nursery specialist, arrange in the fall to have unusual plants grown to your order. Ask for gazanias, blue salvia, white or yellow marguerites, salpiglossis, and sweet scabiosa. If you're looking for something different, search out the little-known garden treasures generally listed in major seed catalogs.

The best medium for growing annual seeds is milled sphagnum moss available at most seed stores.

Packed in a plastic bag, the moss should be practically sterile. Wet down the moss overnight, drain away the excess water, and then put the moss in pots or flats sufficient to hold your seed crop. To plant, scatter seed thinly over the top and slip the moist concoction into a plastic bag, holding the plastic film away from the seeded surface with three or four short stakes. Tie the bag closed with a rubber band and place in a warm, light place, free from drafts. The moisture will rise each day, condense on the plastic at night, and return to the container. After two months, transplant seedlings to separate pots.

Annuals for Show

Old-Fashioned Mixed Flower Beds

Make a big splash with just a little cash by growing masses of old-fashioned flowers from seed or from seedlings purchased in flats. Choose marigolds, petunias, zinnias, and snapdragons for brilliant, fresh color, great masses of bloom, and heady fragrance. With a little work, you can parlay a few dollars' worth of seeds or a batch of seedlings into a wealth of beauty. Costs vary from place to place and season to season, but no matter how you figure it, annuals are your best bargain.

Plant the taller zinnias, marigolds, and a few cosmos toward the rear as a backdrop, with snapdragons and petunias midway, and pansies and ageratum up front. Mingle the clumps so they look less regimented than a row-on-row fruit market display.

If you buy a package mix, expect to get tall and short plants in a crazy-quilt pattern. To establish some focus, you can add a few shrub roses or dwarf dahlias to the center of the bed.

Enjoy bright, tumbling color through a long summer season with dahlias, sweet williams, violas, pansies, marigolds, and petunias.

Plant a red-gold mix of dahlias, dianthus, asters, and marigolds.

Old-Fashioned Mixed Flower Beds

Old-fashioned? Yes. Charming? Precisely. There is excitement in the random happenstance of mixed beds. You can create this same beauty in any planting pocket that gets at least six hours of sun a day. We've become so accustomed to the prolific bloom of annuals that we expect success well before it is our rightful due. And these near-instant plants can be a real solace while your perennials are getting established.

To keep the flowers coming after the first big burst of color, learn the art of deadheading. Each week, cut off all faded blooms before they can go to seed. Not only does this keep the beds looking neat, it encourages the plants to continue making blooms as they try to set seed before the frosts come. Plants will flower longer if they don't have to spend their energies producing seed.

Combine California poppies with dwarf phlox and forget-me-nots.

Pink and white petunias, pansies, ageratum, and Iceland poppies form a kaleidoscope of flower color on top of a retaining wall.

Bold color comes from zinnias planted with purple-blue statice, yellow dahlias, and two-toned red gaillardias.

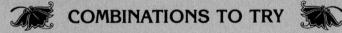

COMBINATIONS TO TRY

Blue Blazer ageratum with white alyssum
Red amaranthus with pink snapdragons
Orange calendula with orange cosmos
White candytuft with purple lobelia
Castor bean plant with orange tithonia
Cornflowers with white field daisies
Rose-purple cleome with white gypsophila
Blue larkspur with Iceland poppies
Dianthus in pink, red, and white
Forget-me-nots with California poppies
Gaillardia with yellow coreopsis
Godetia with rose-colored nicotiana
Hollyhocks in a mix of colors
Petunias in deep blue with red verbena
Iceland poppies in a sea of blue lobelia
Celosia in a mix of red and gold
Gazanias with blue verbena

Nemesia and bachelor's-buttons
Red Sun zinnias with red celosia
Coleus with Rocket snapdragons
Dwarf yellow marigolds with pansies
Giant marigolds with tall, pink zinnias
Phlox drummondi with *Nigella damascena*
Four-o'clocks with white cosmos
Nasturtiums with yellow petunias
Hartwegi lupines with blue flowering flax
White cleome with giant gold marigolds

Annuals range from tender to hardy depending upon the severity of the climate. Check with your local suppliers for varieties that do well in your region. If your season is short, start your tender annuals indoors.

Flashy Flowers Massed Together

There's a wonderful sense of extravagance in the mass planting of one kind of flower or in the subtle blending of near-colors of the same plant. If you prefer the bold statement, then mass planting is definitely for you. It places focus on a robust strain, gives authority to the design, and makes for easy care.

Carry the strong impact theory further by choosing plants that are round and squat for the widest burst of color. Low mounds, close by each, hog the sunlight and leave little room for weed growth. Tall plants make a big show for a short time, but low mounds tend to survive better against heavy rains and wind. Either way, mass plantings assure bright color and beauty without all the bother.

Petunias remain the showplace favorite. The flowers love bright sun and the plants spread wide enough to support 20 to 30 blooms at one time. The choices are many—double, two-toned, and upright or cascading varieties in a whole rainbow of colors. Many are so sweetly fragrant that they're too sticky to touch. Still, it's worthwhile to pick off dead blooms to maintain the pristine quality of the beds and to keep the showy flowers coming.

Calendulas are easy, almost obliging annuals of medium height. They bloom mid- to late-summer in unbelievable shades of orange and gold. You can sow them in a sunny bed or container and have masses of strong color in a short time. They're great, too, as cutting flowers. Take what you want from the bushy plants; you'll never miss them in your garden. Buy new seed each year, and cut away faded flowers to prevent self-seeding. The volunteers revert to lesser strains and are not as vigorous as the parent stock. Sow calendula seeds in early spring.

White and salmon-colored petunias combine with blue ageratum.

Orange Gem calendulas glow with dazzling color in late summer.

Flashy Flowers Massed Together

Tall-growing salvia is useful as a colorful property divider.

Dwarf dahlias mass well as border plants.

 GOOD VARIETIES TO MASS

For sunny areas where heat-resistance is essential, try Joseph's Coat amaranth, four-o'clocks, sunflowers, gloriosa daisies, and the drought-resistant zinnias, Classic and Mexican. On a long sweeping curve, set out Jetfire celosia; and as an airy backdrop, use cleome (spiderflower). Statice does well in the garden and dries well for winter bouquets. Remember annual vines for a quick wall cover. Use *Cobaea scandens,* a purple climber, and morning-glories in Heavenly Blue, Pearly Gates, and Scarlett O'Hara. For a feathery stand, use cosmos in the orange-reds—Diablo and Sunset. Zinnias may be at the end of the alphabet, but they rank first as bedders. Their range in height, size, and color is remarkable. Because of its low branching habit, Magic Charms dianthus makes showy color spring into fall, in pink, crimson, coral, or white. Rocket and Regal snapdragons make long-lasting companions for medium-to-dwarf marigolds. Use double petunias in Red or Blue Bouquet, or the tawny white Champagne. In yellows, consider Sunburst or Summer Sun. For garden fragrance, try Nicki-Pink or White—the heavy-flowering nicotiana. In shade, use impatiens.

The large-flowered pansy varieties are easily combined to make an attractive low bed.

Beautiful Borders

Add annuals for brighter border bloom.

In days past, a fine floral border was designed around perennials alone. But today, less-classical gardeners use annuals and shrub roses for even brighter displays.

The basic aim of a border is a continuing show from plants that bloom in an overlapping sequence. Beds are generally 4 to 6 feet wide, with taller plants at the rear, and medium and low varieties up forward. Start the bed or beds with good, rich garden loam, or add leaf mold, manure, or compost as amendments and additives. Remember, this is a long-term project, so do it well.

Plant iris, peonies, daylilies, phlox, and chrysanthemums in large groups or drifts. Then select a few secondary varieties—shastas and sweet rockets with iris, and lythrum or veronica as fillers for peonies, poppies, and phlox.

You can also use annuals to fill the temporary gaps in your border plan. As shown here, add geraniums, petunias, and lobelia to fill in the forward spaces; follow with some medium and giant marigolds in a range of warm colors; and in the rear, include a dozen or so very elegant dahlias.

A floral border tends to peak several times through the summer. For example, first comes iris, trollius, and poppies; later, daylilies, peonies, phlox, and achillea; and toward the end of the summer, hardy asters, mums, liatris, and solidago. For each of these peaks, there are annuals that can intensify the display. Pansies, lobelia, and tiny marigolds are valuable early; petunias, snapdragons and zinnias carry through most of the summer; and cosmos, coreopsis, and calendula can intensify the golden colors well into fall.

Perennials seem to follow a natural sequence of color with the seasons. Blues and lavenders dominate in the spring, accented by touches of yellow here and there. In early summer, the emphasis shifts toward pinks and then reds laced with brighter golden hues. As fall approaches, the colors tend to intensify. Orange rudbeckia, deep purple asters, and bronze and maroon chrysanthemums signal the year's final color fling.

How to Plan a Border

A well-planned garden offers breathtaking beauty every season of the year. Crocus, scilla, then daffodils and tulips inaugurate the frost-free season; primroses, violets, and trollius follow soon after. By late May and early June, peonies, iris, and poppies are the prime attraction. All these are perennial plants, but there are many fine annuals that can be added to enhance a border display.

Sweet alyssum and lobelias make fine front edgings, while petunias and salvia enliven the middle ground. You can use a screen of spiky snapdragons or larkspur to hide the ripening leaves of spring-flowering bulbs. And while geraniums, marigolds, and zinnias dance among the early perennials, they can become so vigorous by midsummer as to claim prime attention in the border.

But always your goal should be toward plant harmony in relative size, color, and texture. The annuals and perennials should be compatible—happily married in one glorious union.

There should be a flow of shape as well as color in a floral border. As the season progresses, low mounds are replaced by bigger, taller plants, rising in time to new dominance in the overall pattern. Delphinium, liatris, and solidago reach upward in narrow spires, while cosmos and cleome spread wide, still keeping pace. The aim is to have at least two or three kinds of plants in fine flower at any given moment.

Keeping a border trim is a continuing obligation. Cut back stems and stalks as they dry or wither, and pull out early blooming annuals as they falter to make room for more robust varieties. Continue watering into fall if you want to extend the prime flowering season. Then, as autumn comes, you can cut back and take away all debris, or retain some dry flowers as standing bouquets to decorate the garden until they're weighed down by heavy winter snows.

A few plants may self-seed and reappear in the spring, but you can pull them up with the weeds or give extra-good seedlings to friends.

FOR AN ALL-ANNUAL BORDER

To plant a border 5x15 feet, select a sunny site, preferably with good garden loam. If you have poor soil that is heavy with clay, mix in sharp sand. Or, add clay if your soil drains too quickly. Manure, humus, compost, and/or leaf mold can be added to improve the nutritional properties of the soil.

As a border backdrop, use larkspur in blue, pink, or white, together with rose or white cleome. Then choose Peter Pan zinnias in their vivid mixed colors, mostly pinks to reds, to complement Gold Galore marigolds for the middle area. On the forward third of the bed, use alternate drifts of petunias in bright red, and ageratum in white or blue. Then, to finish off the design, run a row of wax begonias or sweet alyssum across the front edge of the border.

LATE-SUMMER ANNUALS

These johnny-come-lately blooms are important to the waning floral border. The newer dwarf dahlias listed in seed catalogs will flower in their first season of growth. Blooms are waxy bright in golden yellows, pink, orange, and red. Treat them as you would zinnias.

Rely, too, on annual asters, now available in vivid new tall, medium, and dwarf varieties. Plant out seedlings when danger of frost has passed. Also, try an English introduction, brachycome or Swan River daisy, which produces a thick carpet of purple flowers. It's easy to grow, superb for bedding, and nice for cutting. A gypsy mix of orange and gold calendulas can help carry the season to a glorious end. And the new striped, or pygmy four-o'clocks bloom right up to frost.

Today's hollyhocks deserve an equally high place in the fall garden in all their Madcap, Majorette, and Silver Puffs designs.

Consider, too, oxypetalum or southern star. Its wide arching sprays of silver-blue starry blooms give forth from June till the end of October. Sow directly outdoors in April, then save them for use indoors as a winter pot plant. Polygonum, known also as Magic Carpet, is a vigorous, creeping form with deep-crimson leaves and dainty rose-pink flowers. It's useful as a covering for slopes, or as a spiky border edging.

ANNUALS FOR MIXED PLANTINGS

When planning to add annuals to an existing perennial border, consider these varieties. In the dwarf to 1-foot size: baby-blue-eyes or nemophila, with cup-shaped blooms; annual candytuft with white flower spires; blue browallia for sun or shade; coleus for exciting color and shape in its foliage; and echium, a light purple favorite of butterflies. Use impatiens for compact plants, free-flowering lobelia in dark-blue as striking edging plants, and all the dwarf marigolds in golden yellow. Also remember nasturtium—now available in dwarf, semi-trailing, and climbing strains—and pansies in solid colors. Use pinks, petunias, vinca, sweet alyssum, verbena, wax begonia, and dwarf zinnias.

Annuals of intermediate height include arctotis, balsam, calliopsis or coreopsis, and clarkia, as well as geranium, gaillardia, and nemesia. Further, consider mignonette, nigella, other marigolds, sweet william, and stocks. And any list should include cockscomb, centurea, and zinnia.

For tall back-of-the-border plants, the choices are wide. There's an annual poinsettia (euphorbia), baby's-breath or gypsophila, tall bachelor's-button (Centaurea cyanus), and bells-of-Ireland. Others include cosmos, celosia, gloriosa daisies, heliotrope, kochia, larkspur, marigold, summer aster, nicotiana, snapdragon, salpiglossis, snow-on-the-mountain, and zinnia. All these and more are available, so study the plants before choosing.

As the season mellows, calendulas and snapdragons add to the perennial show, and marigolds replace fading poppies.

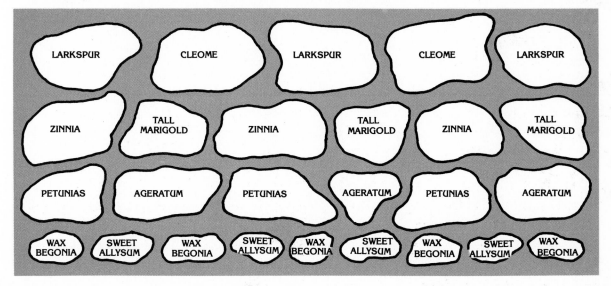

LARKSPUR
CLEOME
LARKSPUR
CLEOME
LARKSPUR

ZINNIA
TALL MARIGOLD
ZINNIA
TALL MARIGOLD
ZINNIA
TALL MARIGOLD

PETUNIAS
AGERATUM
PETUNIAS
AGERATUM
PETUNIAS
AGERATUM

WAX BEGONIA
SWEET ALLYSUM
WAX BEGONIA
SWEET ALLYSUM
WAX BEGONIA
SWEET ALLYSUM
WAX BEGONIA
SWEET ALLYSUM
WAX BEGONIA

Topper snapdragons offer tall flowery spires in vivid colors.

The Versatility of Annuals

The choice of annuals is so vast and versatile, you should be able to find exactly the right variety to brighten any nook or cranny in your garden. Garden annuals are typically a good deal more brilliant than most perennials. They grow in petite, squat, thick, tall, thin, and feathery forms, with near-endless color variety. However, when planting out small spaces, it's best to concentrate on one or, at most, two kinds of plants.

Beside a flight of steps, plant Empress candytuft seeds, and expect flowers in about two months. Try an edging of hybrid dianthus, Snowflake, or Queen of Hearts for fragrance all summer long. And put some zing in life with a mix of Bright Lights cosmos and Sunny Boy calendula.

Gazanias have daisy shapes, but come in wild, exciting colors. Pot them up in the fall to enjoy indoors. For evening pleasure, grow four-o'clocks in the striped Jingles and Petticoat strains. Then use zinnias in dwarf to giant varieties, and low-growing Peter Pan in a wonderful mix of luscious colors. Fruit Bowl is taller, with 5- and 6-inch blooms. You can start a prairie garden by adding sunflowers, larkspur, gilia, liatris, and goldenrod to a sunny rise of ground, or give soft color to a tree-shaded corner with *Vinca rosea*.

For a back fence line, plant sweet peas. Revive a few oldies, but test such new hybrids as Galaxy and Jet Set, too. All are sweet-scented. Morning-glories Early Call and Heavenly Blue are other favorites. Try the butterfly and wedding bell shapes of snapdragons, along with the Rocket strains. Asters come in new and surprising variations, from Carpet Ball to Super Princess. These and calendulas are good for cutting, too.

If you're weary of lawn mowing, rake up the thatch and try planting a packet of mixed flowers.

A walk edged with yellow marigolds.

Enliven a shady corner with fuchsia and impatiens in many pinks.

Planters for Close-Up Color

Annuals take kindly to pot culture, and because of their brilliant colors, make ideal floral accents in raised beds, hanging baskets, or big containers. What's more, container planting is particularly useful where garden plots are small since it encourages multiple use of terrace space for both plants and people. In addition, you can rearrange containers to change the emphasis, alter the mood, or bring out plants as they come into peak bloom.

With the great development of new colors and strains, there is an extra excitement with annuals. New hybrids extend the color range of the big three—petunias, zinnias, and marigolds—and give us new shapes and sizes. With this accomplished, hybridizers turned their fine talents to snapdragons, dianthus, impatiens, and even cosmos.

Each of these departures is evaluated by the All-America Selections judges, and the best are tagged on seed packets as AAS winners. Each breakthrough can be an adventure for the enterprising gardener, and some winners are so worthy, they remain favorites for years afterward. Container gardening is a good way to study the plants and make your own award judgments. Then, with little effort, you can place your favorites out front where they show to best advantage.

It's easy to garden in pots wherever you live. You can cultivate lush plants on a desert patio, or cacti in a container of gritty sand beside a marshy place. If space is limited, hang baskets from the ceiling or set small pots of tiny plants on a porch railing. And, use window boxes on a ledge or sill for suspended pockets of coleus, geraniums, and trailing ivy.

When choosing material for your low planter arrangements, don't overlook the foliage plants amaranthus, dusty miller, coleus, caladium, and flowering kale. The dusty miller and the kale can be a foil for brilliant zinnias or marigolds. By contrast, the coleus and caladium have enough exceptional coloring to stand alone.

Another great advantage of planter boxes and containers is that they let you tailor the soil to the needs of special plants. More often in the garden, you must grow only what your soil can support.

While we're extolling the virtues of container gardening, we should also be aware of its handicaps. Soil in raised planters or containers tends to dry out faster, and therefore needs more watering. But frequent watering washes away soil nutrients faster and that means more care and replacement. And, because container plants are viewed close-up, there may be a greater inclination to primp and trim. But altogether, these are minor obligations, and relatively painless. Just don't choose containers that are so large and heavy you can't move them about. If you must think big, build yourself a small dolly to roll your plants around. Or use three short lengths of pipe for the same purpose.

Spanish brocade marigolds vie with green-eyed gloriosa daisies.

Low retaining walls of brick, wood, or stone can 'contain' a garden plot to good purpose by directing traffic to other sections of the garden or doubling as casual seats or benches. They permit you to introduce rich garden loam into a limited area, and also make watering chores much easier. Low walls and raised beds strengthen the garden design, and also make weeding and cultivating easier, with less stooping. If you're short of brick or stone, lay up chunks of broken sidewalk concrete as a dry wall, cascading petunias along the top and adding succulents to the outer crevices. If your soil is sandy and drains too quickly, first line the planter with several inches of clay.

Choose your flower colors with the thoughtfulness of an artist. For a rounded sphere of dappling color, mix tiny blue lobelia with dwarf marigolds and white sweet alyssum in a moss-filled basket. Add a few of the seedlings to the sides of the basket as you mound the moss across the top, putting the biggest and stoutest plants in the center. Water at least every other day, except when the rains do it for you, but withhold water when the moss feels soggy. For other surprising combinations, try flowering kale interrupted by little button zinnias in many colors, scarlet carefree geraniums in a bed of English ivy, or Jewel Box celosia in a velvet mix of colors.

Raised beds, close by a terrace, can offer another kind of beauty and one we often overlook—fragrance. There is an ongoing debate about the merits of marigold and nasturtium, but most will concede the nicotiana and scented geraniums are a real delight. Some find petunias too sweet to live with, dianthus just right, and carnations a bit spicy. Annuals you may choose from include the sweet pea, sweet-sultan, and sweet alyssum, mignonette, four-o'clocks, stocks, verbena, candytuft, and heliotrope. Tansy and chrysanthemums, like marigold, have pungent odors. Add some herbs like basil, thyme, dill, fennel, and mint to the flowers for an unforgettable scent combination.

All-America zinnias Rosy Future and Torch are astoundingly big and brilliant. They make a great color show in a patio corner.

Planters for Close-Up Color

Movable gardening is a practical concept when you have handsome wood planters and patio boxes to work with. The well-designed boxes below can be spread across a window wall, picked up and moved in line as a barrier on the edge of a terrace, or placed on a wide flight of steps. If you start with a good basic design of square or rectangular shapes, you can interlock the boxes in a zigzag fashion, or group them around a central point. You can rearrange them at will.

Timing is another trick to be learned early. In the boxes below, icy-white Glacier petunias were bought as starter plants, set out first, and then nasturtium seed was sown around them. In mild climates, you can plant pansy seed around spring-flowering bulbs in the fall. But in harsher climes, wait until spring and add pansy plants as the tulips or daffodils send up leaf blades to show their location.

Calendulas can be sown in a bed of primroses, to come into flower as the primroses lose their punch. And blue petunia seedlings can be planted in a bed strewn with annual forget-me-not seeds. Both should come to maturity at about the same time and keep good company. If you're looking for an easy-care garden, combine low-growing coreopsis with white Carpet of Snow sweet alyssum. And after planting your favorite petunias, start a casual

planting of Iceland poppies and statice between.

If you want to set a style for your garden, you should decide whether you prefer pastel flower shades or a far bolder mix of brilliant and sometimes clashing colors. Fortunately, most annuals are available in gentle and vivid hues so you can have the kind you want.

However, if none of the colors pleases you, try concentrating on neutrals with gray and white. This will take some doing, as an all-white plot needs the drama of various flower forms—the feathery spider flower, the ubiquitous daisy, the white zinnia, and even the white marigold.

Style comes, too, from careful design as well as controlled color. If you want the casual look, show it in random planting and a loosely-woven design. Or if you prefer to be earth-shaking, gather all

This trio of flower-filled boxes can be viewed from either indoors or out. The petunias and nasturtiums flourish in the bright sun.

In a trough made from railroad ties, three kinds of marigolds mingle with petunias and ageratum. Curly parsley adds a crisp note.

the wild colors you can muster, and juxtapose them one against the other in big bold beds.

Although it looks quite permanent, the long planter box shown above is indeed movable, and provides a fine display of color at the edge of a concrete patio. Eight-foot railroad ties are stacked two-high, joined together with 2-foot end pieces, and held in place with heavy spikes. The framed unit has no base and sits directly on the concrete deck. The wood container is filled with good soil, heavy with humus and well-laced with sand for good drainage. In it, a concentrated planting of robust annuals produces a wide display of maximum brilliance.

If you have a sheltered garden where the winds are gentle, try growing taller annuals in containers. There is dancing beauty in a wiry stand of pink cosmos, giant asters, or the very bright Flaming Fountain amaranthus. And although compact plantings of stout marigolds give intense globes of color, a loosely-branched display of marguerite, celosia, or cleome also can be a delightful surprise. If you stay with cosmos or cornflowers because they do best, you can still work wonders by putting individual colors and heights in separate pots.

Houseplants that have been moved outdoors for the summer can be embellished with extra bits of annual color, too. Seedling plants of lobelia or sweet alyssum can be added to full-grown geraniums to cascade over the rims. Or a scattering of sedum seeds might be dropped in scuffed soil around the base of a jade tree. If the sedum crowds the jade, dig it out and pot alone.

87

Annuals for Special Uses

Bright Spots on City Windows

Window boxes are a great way to improve your city view *and* share your flowers with neighbors. Below is one with extras: tubs of geraniums plus strung-up vegetables and indoor plants. It's rigged with six shelf brackets screwed to a balcony wall (with the landlord's OK), but the same setup would work with a conventional window, too.

If your balcony gets little sun, use shade-loving plants—wax begonias or impatiens—to keep the area colorful. It's perfect, too, for starting new plants from stem cuttings that the wind might knock off, or for snippets from shaggy houseplants. Use a ball of twine and a couple window-top appendages to build a morning-glory cage by running strings at 3-inch intervals around the rim of the window box and up to a U-shaped rod above. Soak the seeds overnight and plant in groups of three around each string upright. Then plant a flat of giant pansies in the remaining space; you can pick them for indoor use.

Build a saddlebag planter by joining two boxes to fit over your porch or balcony railing. A third box is mounted on the saddle bridge to sit, nail-free, on top of the rail. The three-part unit is secured by wiring the saddle boxes to a couple of railing uprights. Plant the top box with petunias, add morning glories at either end to trail along the rail, then start vining nasturtium or black-eyed susan vine in the remaining space for further screening.

With window boxes and railing units, arrange your plants first for indoor view, and then for outsiders looking in. For added privacy, include a few tall plants, or use scarlet runner beans or climbing tomatoes to cover the entire window opening. Add a few herbs along the inside edge for gourmet clipping.

Containers are also good set on stair treads and planted with cascading varieties to drape through the balustrade. They're handsome, too, stood on rough-hewn pedestals, 6x6 posts, or fruit market crates as an entry display. Any of these spots can make a setting for browallia, impatiens, wax begonias, or coleus. Monitor your displays, watching for signs of too much midday heat, wind damage, or too much shade. Then rearrange the plants to their individual likings until they seem content.

Most window boxes are built with 1x10 boards. Redwood boxes are most durable, and resist rot. But before adding soil, drill ½-inch holes in the box bottom and spread a layer of screening and 2 inches of perlite or vermiculite to assure good drainage. Then you can either fill with good garden loam or set in a row of potted geraniums and ivy, filling the spaces between with vermiculite to keep the unit light in weight. Remember that a 4-foot window box filled with wet soil can be very heavy. If the box hangs over a sidewalk, you must be doubly sure that the weather or the box's own weight cannot dislodge it to fall to the ground or on passersby.

If you have to go to the roof to find a place to garden, choose a protected corner beside a chimney wall and out of the wind. Spread out some old planking around the edges of your new domain to hold your container plants while distributing their weight across a wider span of roof beams. If your roof is tarred and graveled, you can use a square of artificial turf to protect the surface and give the illusion of a lawn. Then, gather together a group of barrel halves, soy tubs, or surplus window boxes, raising them an inch off the turf or planks for better circulation.

In containers near the chimney and parapets, plant climbing annuals, cup-and-saucer vine, thunbergia, or passion flower vine. String them up to the chimney top or across a portable lattice made from an expansion gate or old ladders. Then add a tray or two of potted pansies, weeping lobelia, sweet william, and shirley poppies. And bring your dracena and variegated geraniums up into a shaded corner for the summer. Garden with commercially prepared soil-less compost instead of earth. It's lighter than normal soil, but contains all needed nutrients.

The rest is up to you—from benches to lounge chairs to canopies to night lights. A roof garden can give you a new view of your life in the city.

Grow bright flowers anywhere within reach of a watering can.

The glorious crimson of far-reaching geraniums makes viewing this window box a two-way pleasure.

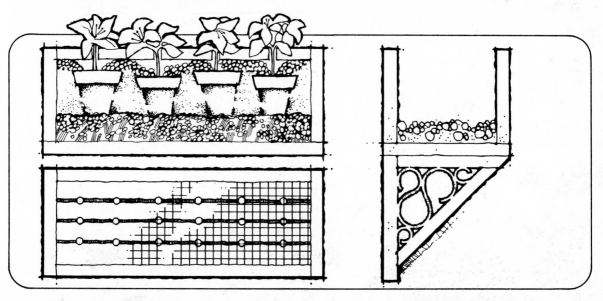

Annuals in Pots

Choose plants with vivid colors to decorate a small porch or balcony, and change them with the season. Use primrose in spring, and mums in the fall.

Maneuverability is your biggest asset in container gardening. You can move plants around at will to put color just where you want it. Try to combine container color with nearby flower borders, or brighten a shady corner with hot-pink wax begonias and sprightly rose impatiens. Think of potted plants as easy accent tools for garden color in any season.

Potted plants are useful, also, to screen out or divert attention from faltering garden flowers. Cascading petunias can hide a multitude of sins and leave the garden visitor none-the-wiser. In fact, you can convert all ground-level space to durable ground covers, then grow flowers exclusively in pots, boxes, and hanging baskets, where care is relatively easy and daily watering is just a simple routine.

A green-gold background of shrubs and new trees or a brick-paved patio surrounded by climbing vines are ideal settings for a container garden. To make your groupings harmonious and cohesive, choose various-sized pots of similar colors in clay, wood, or plastic. And, select plant colors that blend with each other so that a change in pot groupings is never dissonant.

Plan, also, to have an off-to-the-side holding area where you can nurture new plants through the seedling and bud stages and grow replacements. Make it a sunny place, perhaps with a planting bench and—to meet the needs of individual plants—a variety of soil mixes in convenient bins.

Cluster your pots all in one place for maximum show, or divide them between the terrace and a clearing near the rear of the garden. This gives you a near and distant view, and an excuse to wander out for a closer look. Potted plants make good devices for manipulating a party crowd, directing people toward an open lawn area, or keeping them away from a new bed of freshly-seeded wildflowers.

And—another great advantage—whenever your container plants want to reach out or cascade, you can always provide

A lath trellis protects impatiens and other shade-loving plants from strong sunlight.

A low, curved patio wall makes for comfortable seating and a great showplace for tulips, pansies, geraniums, and lilies.

them with the space to grow their merry way.

Give your container plants a well-rounded appearance by grouping four to six plants to a medium-sized pot. Set three to five seedlings on the slopes of a little hill of soil, leaning toward the rim, and one on the top of the mound, reaching straight up. If you want the tall-look, pot up foxglove, lupine, or delphinium seedlings in sturdy containers sheltered from high winds. Or, for both flowers and a

crop, try scarlet runner bean seeds set in a big pot with tall stakes for future plant support.

Try some exciting plant combinations, too. Plant up bright pink geraniums in a 12-inch pot edged with sweet alyssum or blue lobelia seedlings to drape over the rim. Consider spring-flowering bulbs for a special spring show. You'll need to pot up the bulbs in the fall and season them in a cold frame outdoors through the winter, but by spring those clusters of crocus,

daffodils, and tulips will make it all worthwhile.

Grow one or more hybrid morning-glories from seed in a pot fitted with bamboo trellising, or try growing cherry tomatoes within a cylinder of chicken wire set into the pot itself. The opportunities are endless. With pots and planters brimming with colorful flowers, it's possible to turn an otherwise sterile-looking patio into a beautiful, bloom-filled garden in just a few short weeks.

Strawberry Jars

The pocketed strawberry jar still gets occasional use as a container for strawberry plants and their luscious fruit. But each year, more gardeners are using these jars to display many other kinds of plants, including petunias, lobelia, and succulents. In fact, any cascading or semi-trailing plant is a candidate.

Strawberry jar-gardening is simple—mostly a matter of selecting plants that harmonize well with the red clay surface of the jars. Trailers and small bouquet shapes fit best in the tiny compartments, and are generally preferred to larger plants that would overwhelm and hide their interesting containers.

Candytuft or sweet alyssum make a pleasing contrast, and primrose polyanthus pockets well in a cool, moist, and somewhat-shaded place. A mix of pansies and violas, peeking out in all directions, is an amusing sight. And impatiens or fibrous begonias also lend themselves to strawberry jar treatment. Fuchsia and Rieger begonias make a particularly spectacular mild-climate display. And any pocketed jar is ideal for showing a special succulent collection or a gathering of cacti.

If you stay with strawberries, try both the June- and everbearing varieties. Surecrop and Fairfax are outstanding in the first category, and Ogallala and Ozark Beauty in the second. Then there is Fraises des Bois, a tiny French strawberry of exceptional sweetness and flavor.

The plants do best in light-textured soil that is well-drained. The June- and everbearing varieties prefer full sun; the French strawberries, woodland half-shade.

Set plants in the pockets so crowns are level with the surface of the soil. Fan the roots out and down, firming soil over them. Apply 10-10-10 fertilizer about six weeks after planting.

On June-bearers, pick off blooms before they set fruit the first year to channel the plant's efforts into becoming well established and sending out runners.

After the season's growth, move the jar to a sheltered spot and mulch each pocket and the top with straw or snippets of pine branches.

In spring, top-dress with well-rotted cow manure or other fertilizer.

1 To plant a pocket jar, first spread a thick layer of broken crockery or potshards. Cover it with a circle of screening mesh or a layer of nylon hose discards. If the jar is more than 2 feet tall, add a 3-inch cylinder of screening mesh as a central core to assure deep watering. Then, a little at a time, put rich potting soil around the cylinder and in the pockets. Keep the soil lightly textured, and don't hard-pack.

2 After the jar is filled with soil to 1 inch from the top, add the plant seedlings in groups of two or three to each pocket opening. It's a bit easier to plant from bottom to top, turning the jar as each section is completed. On larger jars, some gardeners plant each pocket as the soil is layered in, making it easier to evenly spread out the roots. Be sure to save enough plants to evenly fill out the jar top.

3 Your pocket jar can become a gay ornament almost immediately if you select seedlings that are already in flower or bud. Keep these flowers coming by watering the jar well at the onset and keeping the container lightly moist most of the time. To maintain an equal display on all sides, turn the jar a quarter turn every two or three days (use a turntable or casters under large, heavy strawberry jars).

Trailing lobelia makes an attractive addition to any strawberry jar.

Hanging Baskets

There's a special pleasure in growing plants overhead. They can enclose you in a canopy of flowers, *without* robbing you of vital outdoor living space. If you have a wide roof overhang, an arbor, a pergola, or a pretty gazebo, you have the framework for an overhead garden. So plant your flowers high up, to enclose your yard with color.

All you need is a handful of screw eyes or clothesline hooks screwed into the roof beams, a few wire baskets or clay bowls, and some lightweight chain or rope to use for hanging. Sphagnum moss or lightweight perlite or vermiculite mixed with standard potting mix will make the pot burden lighter.

If your climate is nicely humid most of the time, your plants will grow well in moss-lined baskets. In drier situations, plants do better in clay or plastic pots, saucered to hold moisture. It's true that hanging pots take more attention, frequent primping, and generally almost-daily watering. But this is no great chore if you have the plants concentrated in one place. And it's a small price to pay for showpiece plants that are viewed close-up by visitors.

You also can bring some of your houseplants outdoors for a cool summer under the eaves. Ferns, Swedish ivy, and tradescantia all do well in a sheltered corner with half-light. If you don't want to transplant them to baskets, drill three holes in the rims of their saucers and use chain to hang the saucers and pots together. But be aware of the weight of each pot, and keep the heaviest ones on a rack or table.

In moss-filled baskets grow any of the cascading petunias. Chiffon or Pink Cascade are beauties. Try the cup flower, nierembergia Regal Robe. It retains brilliance in strong sunlight. Start semi-trailing Gleam nasturtiums from seed planted in somewhat-dry soil in a sunny location, and have blooms in six weeks. In filtered sunlight, grow the unusual Amethyst browallia for sheer grace. Plant ivy or scented geraniums by themselves, and the self-branching Carefree with cascading Sapphire lobelia. Combine Button, Lilliput, or Thumbelina zinnias with Linearis, the basket plant zinnia. Or, do a basket with nothing but verbena in a bright color mix—Regalia or the red, white, and blue Spirit of '76.

1 To start a hanging basket, assemble a wire basket frame, a sack of sphagnum moss, a bag of potting mix, and several flats of seedlings—pansies, alyssum, and wax begonias. Then soak the moss in a pail of water (overnight, if you have time), drain off the surplus water, and shape the moss into flat cakes.

2 Line the interior of your wire frame with the moss layers, working the moss around the wires to disguise it. Thicken the moss lining until you have a quart-size cavity in the center. Recheck the lining for thin spots and make the necessary additions, interlocking the moss fibers well throughout.

3 Finish the basket with a cushion of moss around the wire rim. Then carefully fill the cavity with a good planting mix, shaking the mix into all the nooks and crannies as you go. Fill this center soil cavity to the top, then strike the basket on a tabletop until soil settles to 1 inch below the rim.

4 Tilt your basket on its side, then begin planting the seedlings between the wires in dimpled depressions you make with your fingers. Run three ribs of alyssum bottom to top, adding wax begonias between. Round out the arrangement with pansies, planting the remainder on top. Hang the basket with chains and water well.

Hang a basket of sunshine overhead—a dappling of sweet-smelling alyssum and fibrous begonias, with sparks of pansies.

95

Problem Areas

Granted, few of us have perfect garden plots. Some are too hot and dry; others, too wet and shady. Our soils can range from sticky clay to runny sand or coarse gravel. And our sites can vary from windswept hilltops to peaty bogs. We cannot hope to quickly remake the soil into an ideal mix with the right pH. Nor should we expect to grow shade trees overnight or to clear a thickly wooded plot without considerable effort. It's better that we recognize our gardens for what they are and select plants that survive or flourish with the conditions we have to offer.

Too much shade may be the steadiest source of annoyance and concern. We love our trees, but they hide the sun. The plants shown on these pages can come to the rescue. Fancy-leafed caladiums have foliage in reds, pinks, whites, and silver, and prefer moist soil and semi-shade. Wax begonias prosper under shrubs or beside shaded walks, their luminous blooms shining out from the darkest corners. Impatiens also are prime shade plants, covering the ground with gay flower colors, spring to fall.

In very bright sun grow zinnias, big sunflowers, and hollyhocks. And the prerequisites for nasturtiums are a sunny location and dry—even poor—soil.

If you crave privacy, start a tall barrier row of tithonia, the bushy Mexican sunflower with red-orange dahlia-like flowers. Or on wide plains or hilltop sites, grow asters and cosmos for their flexible stems.

Brighten the gloomy pockets of your garden through the summer with caladium—the most brilliant of our shade plants.

Plant pink Carmen and red Indian Maid wax begonias under taller plants and beside a shaded garden walk.

Elfin impatiens—low-growing, self-branching, and shade-loving—offers prolific bloom all summer in a corner that's moist and cool.

Problem Areas

Don't let garden problems get you down. Take it easy and approach them one at a time. In solving your first problem, you may well solve a few others, too. If your land slopes away too steeply, modify the angle with intermediate terraces or a graceful flow of steps. To remove abrupt changes in grade, reshape the land with earth fill or a structure framed with railroad ties, redwood timbers, or concrete slabs. Once the angle of repose is established, plant evergreens and flowering shrubs nearby, to mark the way in time. Meanwhile, resort to flowering annuals for instant enhancement of the scene.

A slope planted with spreading juniper is, meanwhile, graced with sweet alyssum.

Heavy timbers serve here to unify steps and retaining walls. While shrubs mature, petunias and marigolds contribute instant color.

An informal planting of petunias, marigolds, caladiums, and sedum fill a curved rock outcropping between a driveway and entry.

Problem areas can well be creative challenges if we learn to think of them as opportunities instead of hindrances. With such devices as retaining walls, fencing, steps, and storage sheds, we can develop stable slopes and privacy.

It's been said that if the task is too easy, we come up with dull solutions. Tough problems, however, lead to exciting solutions. We need to be flexible and willing to make some drastic and irrevocable changes. And the momentum of change can have a valued effect on

other problem areas: early success generates new confidence in tackling other garden problems.

There's an excitement in shaping gardens to human needs, in carving terraces into hillsides, in constructing a small deck on a rise of ground, or in pushing back the weeds to make room for a cutting garden. We should look for lively solutions to our problems—an earth berm embankment covered with flowers on a heavily trafficked street corner, or a rooftop haven or balcony retreat where no land is

available. Many of us might reconvert the raw, scarred land of a new suburbia to a country landscape awash with flowers.

Don't be afraid to experiment with something radically new or different: sunken gardens filled with bright-flowering annuals and durable perennials, tall hedgings to enclose and enfold, or fast-growing vines to clamber up the walls of a small areaway. And always remember the rumor that the world's best gardens occupy the most difficult sites.

Climbing Annuals

A generous planting of annual vines can teach us much about gardening in a single year. These vigorous and quick-growing plants demonstrate the abilities of vines to screen out an unpleasant view, to shade a bald plot, or to enliven a dull corner. They've been labeled the quick-change experts of the garden, and rightly so.

Once you're convinced of the value of vines, you can rely on annuals to continue as temporary foliage while newly-placed perennial vines mature. Sow a fresh packet of seeds, and in a few short weeks, you'll have cover and color just where you wish.

Most packets contain more seed than you'll ever need. This allows you the gamble of an early planting. If these seeds fail, plant again. If you still have a surplus, plant the remainder in a place where you can use a trailing ground cover, preferably in full sun. Annual vines expend most of their energies producing lavish blooms, probably because they don't have to plan for their own survival. Woody perennial vines more often have good leaf-green and less color.

All annual vines climb upward by twining, so it's necessary to give them strings or garden nets to twine upon. Experienced gardeners find it wise to set the strings or nets as they plant the seed, and to sow seeds right where they're to grow. Vines don't like to be moved, especially morning-glories. Soak the hard-shelled seeds overnight in warm water to hasten germination, or shake them in a glass jar that has been lined with a piece of sandpaper. The scraping will wear down the tough cover, and is easier than notching the seed one-by-one.

Annual vines are invaluable in small gardens where space is limited. They can clothe harsh walls, or soften unattractive fencing. Used on an arbor, pergola, or trellis, they interrupt a neighbor's overhead view. They're also good as summer cover on a sunny porch or patio, but pull them down in the fall to reopen the space to the warming winter sun. Vines can be useful in many ways—as cover for a dead tree, screening for an ugly storage structure, or to scale an airy cage or a new gazebo. Design a series of pillar plantings, or hang vines over a concrete retaining wall.

The choices are many. Still most favored are the morning-glory and the climbing nasturtium. But others deserving your attention are the cup-and-saucer vine *(Cobaea scandens),* the black-eyed susan vine, the cardinal climber (known also as the scarlet star glory), the moonflower, and the colorful ornamental gourds.

You can grow sweet peas for their flowery cover or for the cutting bouquets they offer. Start these and scarlet runner beans when the weather is cool. The sweet peas grow to 6 feet; the scarlet runners, to 12. Runner beans are also edible.

Grow hops *(Humulus japonicus)* for good green foliage, or its fancier green-and-white variegated cousin. Look for the tricolor morning-glory in purple, white, and yellow.

Reach up to pick nasturtiums from your climbing vine; picking fosters bloom.

Moonflowers offer giant, evening blooms all summer long.

Cobaea scandens, known both as the cup-and-saucer vine and cathedral bells, is a delightful oddity. Its flowers change from green to purple-blue as they mature, and it can reach heights of 25 feet under optimum conditions.

Heavenly Blue is a proper name for this outstanding morning-glory. Other winners include Pearly Gates (white), Scarlett O'Hara (scarlet-red), and the Early Call (rose or blue). Plant all in full sun and in well-drained soil.

Annuals for Special Situations

Flowers solve problems—problems either overlooked in the original landscape plan or problems inherited with your remodeling or your site selection. To solve them, rely heavily on annuals for their dependable, long-lasting color. Most will bloom from late spring till frost.

There's an annual for every need, and maintenance isn't at all demanding. For an average of just a few minutes each day, you can hide a strip of foundation, fill bare spots where nothing has grown before, erect living screens for privacy, or blanket a small rocky expanse.

A packet of flower seeds is still the great American bargain. Nowhere else can you get such immeasurable beauty in such a small package to produce such a lasting impression.

For Shady Spots

Annual aster
Calendula
Centaurea
Clarkia
Cleome
Dusty miller (foliage plant)
Feverfew
Larkspur
Lobelia
Nemophila
Phlox drummondi
Snapdragon
Sweet alyssum
Tassel flower
Wax begonia

For Dry Soil

Browallia
California poppy
Celosia
Cleome
Coreopsis
Cornflower
Cosmos
Four-o'clock
Gaillardia
Gypsophila
Portulaca
Rudbeckia
Scarlet sage
Sunflower
Zinnia

For Moist Soil

Annual forget-me-not
Baby-blue-eyes
Blue lace flower
Butterfly flower
Calendula
Mallow
Monkey flower
Nemesia
Nicotiana
Phlox drummondi
Sweet pea
Torenia

For Poor Soil

California poppy
Celosia
Cleome
Coreopsis
Four-o'clock
Gaillardia
Marigold
Morning-glory
Nasturtium
Portulaca
Sweet alyssum
Zinnia

For Tall Borders

Celosia
China aster
Cleome
Cornflower
Marigold (giants)
Tithonia
Sunflower

For Edging

Ageratum
Alyssum
Browallia
Candytuft
Dianthus (dwarf pinks)
Marigold (dwarfs)
Nasturtium
Nemophila
Pansy
Petunia
Portulaca
Sweet alyssum
Torenia
Wax begonia

For Drying

Baby's-breath
Bells-of-Ireland
Celosia
Bachelor's-buttons
Everlasting (helichrysum)
Gaillardia
Globe amaranth (gomphrena)
Statice
Verbena
Zinnia

For Trellises and Screens

Cup-and-saucer vine (cobaea)
Moonflower
Morning-glory
Scarlet runner bean
Sweet peas

For Early Planting

Baby's-breath
Calendula
California poppy
Candytuft
Clarkia
Coreopsis
Cosmos
Gaillardia
Marigold
Petunia
Phlox drummondi
Stock
Sunflower
Sweet alyssum
Sweet pea
Verbena
Zinnia

For Window Boxes

Button zinnias
Creeping sanvitalia
Gazania
Geranium
Impatiens
Lobelia
Marigold
Nasturtium
Petunia
Sweet alyssum
Wax begonia

For Fragrance

Annual carnation
Candytuft
Heliotrope
Moonflower
Nasturtium
Nicotiana
Petunia
Stocks
Swan river daisy
Sweet alyssum
Sweet-sultan
Verbena
Wallflower
Woodruff (annual)

For Night Gardens

Candytuft
Canterbury-bells
Cleome (white)
Evening stocks
Feverfew (white)
Four-o'clock
Iceland poppies
Larkspur
Marguerite (white)
Moonflower
Nicotiana
Petunias (white)
Sweet alyssum

For Privacy Hedges and Screens

Amaranth
Balloon vine
Balsam apple
Cardinal climber
Castor bean
Crimson star glory
Cup-and-saucer vine (cobaea)
Cypress vine
Dahlia
Hyacinth bean
Moonflower
Morning-glory
Ornamental gourd
Rainbow corn

For Strawberry Jars

Blue lobelia
Dusty miller
Impatiens
Pansy
Petunia
Sweet alyssum

For Hanging Baskets

Cascading petunia
Ivy geranium
Trailing lantana
Trailing lobelia
Wax begonia

For Cutting Gardens

African daisy
Annual carnation
Bells-of-Ireland
Calendula
Canterbury-bells
China aster
Clarkia
Cleome
Cornflower
Cosmos
Felicia daisy (blue)
Feverfew
Gaillardia
Gazania
Gloriosa daisy
Godetia
Gypsophila
Larkspur
Lupine
Marigold
Pansy
Petunia
Plumed celosia
Statice
Stock
Swan river daisy
Sweet william
Sweet pea
Wallflower
Zinnia

For Wild and Prairie Gardens

Bird's-eyes
Black-eyed susan
Blazing-star
California poppy
Chinese-lanterns
Cornflower
Corn poppy
Lupine
Mountain garland
Painted daisy
Purple coneflower
Queen-anne's-lace
Tahoka daisy

Annual Basics

To grow beautiful annuals well, you need friable soil or a nutritious soilless substitute. Friable soil crumbles in your hand, and is a combination of humus and minerals, mostly sand and clay. But *combination* is the key word. If a soil is all sand, it drains too quickly and retains too few nutrients. But if it is all clay, it holds water so well that it can drown your plants. Soil also contains incidental trace elements, fungi, and bacteria.

The quickest way to analyze your soil is to pick up a handful and squeeze it lightly. If it runs through your fingers too fast, it contains too much sand; if it remains in your hand as a sticky mass, it's heavy with clay. But if the soil falls apart in your hand in crumbling bits and pieces, it should be good to use. Improve any soil by incorporating humus materials annually.

SOIL PREPARATION

Most soils contain enough food elements to last for many years. But for one reason or another, some soils do not contain these elements in a form readily usable to plants. The natural processes that make these elements available can be accelerated by the addition of peat moss, compost, and other organic materials. But because this process may take considerable time, plant foods should be added periodically to supply nutrients for immediate plant needs.

If your soil is heavy with clay, you will need to improve the soil structure, either by adding a thin layer of leaves, grass clippings, and spent annuals, or by aerating the soil by spading or tilling. It's best to do both. Spread compost, peat, and other decomposed organic matter in a thin layer over the surface and work the materials into the soil. Rent a rotary tiller for a weekend to complete the job with less effort, breaking up remaining clods and leveling the ground as you go.

Apply your additives at the rate of 2 or more bushel per 100 square feet. Not only will these organic materials stimulate root development, but they also can help hold water and maintain a more even moisture level in the ground.

When breaking up the soil on a new annual bed, use a garden fork rather than a spade. The fork tines tend to break up clods vertically as well as horizontally, thereby eliminating one chore in the process.

Tilling the soil with the help of horsepower greatly cuts down on labor, and permits you to do a better job. Cross over your tracks for another run—it helps further.

Rake beds repeatedly until you have leveled the ground and removed all weeds, twigs, and stones. Then level with final raking.

FERTILIZERS AND AMENDMENTS

A soil amendment is anything that makes up for deficiencies. Examples are organic matter, balanced plant foods, lime, manures, and other waste matter. Organic matter includes decomposed leaves, dried grass clippings, straw, sawdust and wood ashes, corn or cane stalks, fruit pomace, spent hops, seaweed, banana skins, cocoa hulls, cottonseed, wood chips, and even sludge. The last two, combined under forced aeration and cured for 30 days, produce a finished product that looks and smells like ground bark, and has a pH factor of 6 to 7.

Balanced plant foods include many commercial products that contain nitrogen, phosphorus, and potash. Most of these sacked fertilizers contain lesser amounts of calcium, sulfur, and magnesium. Of the chemical fertilizers, ammonium nitrate should be used exactly as per directions. Because it has a high nitrogen content (33%), it needs sufficient dilution to avoid burning plant material. Super-phosphate contains 20% phosphorus, and muriate of potash, 60% potassium. All should be applied with care.

Animal manures are good all-around fertilizers because of the humus they contain; dried manure is safer to use than fresh manure. Bone meal is a good additive for plants that prefer a slightly alkaline soil. It also contains some nitrogen and phosphoric acid, but no potash. Cottonseed meal helps acid-loving plants. Lime modifies both the physical and chemical properties of the soil. It pulls together small particles of clay, and thereby makes the soil more porous.

Perlite and vermiculite can be used to lighten soil and keep the particles apart. Urea formaldehyde is a synthetic organic fertilizer that contains a very high amount of nitrogen (38%). But since it has a built-in release control, the nitrogen is available to the plants over a longer period of time, virtually eliminating the danger of burning plant tissues. Other additives that should be widely available soon are wood and coal ashes.

NITROGEN

Nitrogen combines both protein and chlorophyll molecules—and thus stimulates vegetative growth. Deficiency symptoms are pale green or yellow-green leaves and dwarf or stunted plants. Too much nitrogen can often result in no flower.

POTASH

Potash helps form stronger stems and roots and deepens the flower color. Acute deficiencies are noted by weak stems and a yellowing and browning of leaves at tips and margins. Also, leaves often turn under at the edges. Grasses may become yellowed.

PHOSPHORUS

Phosphorus is very necessary for maximum fruit formation. Essential at seeding time to favor rapid root and stem growth. Leaves that are stunted with purple or red discoloration are sure signs of deficiency. On fruit trees the entire leaf stem discolors.

The importance of nitrogen, phosphorus, and potash to the growth of your new annuals cannot be overemphasized. The hyphenated numbers on a bag of fertilizer indicate the pounds of nitrogen, phosphorus, and potash per hundred pounds of fertilizer.

Nitrogen is necessary for the formation of new cells in all plant parts, and stimulates the growth of stems and leaves. It is the soil nutrient most often lacking, and hence, the one most often replaced.

Phosphorus strengthens both stems and roots. It also stimulates food storage and increases seed and fruit production. Next to nitrogen, phosphoric acid is the most valuable fertilizer constituent.

Potash, the third major element in fertilizer compounds, is needed for normal plant growth to protect plants from the ravages of disease. It also aids and stimulates the growth of sturdy roots, and is essential for good flower color. Potash is a soluble mineral found in several compounds, including potassium carbonate and potassium hydroxide.

Good fertilizers for annuals include manure, superphosphate, and mixed fertilizers in combinations such as 4-12-4 or 5-10-5. Apply manure at the rate of about 4 bushels per 100 square feet, and superphosphate at about 5 pounds per 100 square feet. With formula fertilizers, apply according to the manufacturer's directions. Work them into the top 6 inches of soil every other year.

For an added boost, you can apply inorganic fertilizer to your annuals just before they start flowering. Apply at the rate of 1 pound per 100 square feet. For flowers with a long blooming period, give beds a second treatment halfway through the season.

The best time to apply commercial fertilizers is a day or two before you put the seeds in the ground. Because the minerals are sacked with sand or some other inert and inexpensive material, they may not be thoroughly mixed. By raking them in, you ensure a more even distribution. Intermediate applications should be applied to rows as top-dressing. They will seep down with sprinkling. Keep the fertilizer 6 inches from the base of plants to avoid possible burning.

105

Annual Basics

COMPOSTING

Homemade compost is one of the most valuable soil builders you can use; it's inexpensive because you can make it from waste materials that would otherwise be carted away. Compost is vegetation that has been decomposed by bacteria and fungi. A compost pile is a kind of factory where millions of microbes are at work making a product that can yield virtually everything plants need.

Locate the pile on fairly level land in an out-of-the-way corner. A shady spot is best, as it won't require watering as often. Don't crowd it against a fence or the garage.

HOW TO BUILD A COMPOST PILE

For an average suburban lot, plan on a pile about 5-feet-square. If you have a lot of trees, make two piles. The pile may be started at ground level, or from a pit about 18 inches deep. A pit makes the pile somewhat less conspicuous and keeps the level of moisture more constant. You can erect side walls on two or three sides to better hold the pile within bounds. Two-inch planking makes good walls, as do brick or concrete blocks. Make walls about 3 feet high.

Fallen leaves probably will be your chief composting material, but grass clippings spread out in thin layers together with green weeds also should be included. The trick is to pull the weeds before they go to seed. Make a practice of saving vegetable and apple parings, dry bread crusts, lettuce, carrot tops—in fact, any kitchen discards that don't contain fat or grease that might attract rodents.

However, do not include eggshells or citrus fruit rinds, which decompose too slowly and leave the pile looking untidy. Top the kitchen wastes with leaves or soil.

After the leaves fall in autumn, mow the lawn one more time, crushing the dried leaves as you go. Then dump these materials onto the pile in 4-inch layers, topped with thin layers of soil. The soil keeps the moisture in, prevents blowing, and adds bacteria to the stack. Soak the pile well after each major addition. Adding a pint of lime or plant food to the layer speeds decomposition.

The process of decomposition may take six months, a year, or longer, depending upon the moisture the pile receives and the air that reaches it. Techniques and methods vary from region to region. Californians have evolved a platform base surrounded by snow fencing to allow for the free flow of air and water. They turn or stir the pile frequently, and in some cases, compost is finished and ready to use in two months.

HOW TO USE COMPOST

It's fine to have a big pile of rich compost stashed away in a far corner of the garden—a stack so completely decomposed that you can't recognize any of its parts—but it does your garden no good at all unless it's spread around.

Compost is particularly useful when you're starting a new flowerbed. If you make your plans and diagram the bed in the fall, you can add a 2-inch layer before you turn the soil. Do this before winter and let the clods lie open to the snow and freezing rain. This will break down the lumps and freeze out some weed roots in the process. Then turn the soil once more in the spring, adding a second layer of compost if your soil is poor, and your bed will be ready to plant. As the annuals reach maturity and begin to bloom, you can add a top-dressing of compost around each plant. The extra nutrients will keep the flowers blooming longer, and will enrich the soil for subsequent plantings.

In the spring, combine compost with garden soil for your seedling plantings if you don't want to spend the money for a sterile mix. To make your concoction sterile, you need to bake it in an oven or barbecue along with a potato. When the potato is baked soft, the plant mix should also be sterile and free of weeds. If you are reusing old pots or planting trays, be sure they are clean and free of disease. A soapy scrubbing can work wonders. But if you value your time, potting mix bought sacked and sterile costs much less.

Compost also can help in the renovation of an old garden or the making of a new one. Old gardens usually benefit from a grand cleanup, and the resulting heaps of leaves and other debris are often partially decomposed already. Pile these materials in a stack in the fall, water the pile well, and by spring, you should have compost good enough to scatter as a top-dressing around old trees and shrubs and new flowerbeds.

If you're starting with raw, bulldozed, suburban land, you may have to gather your compost materials elsewhere. Strike up an acquaintance with local tree-trimming crews and leaf rakers in older sections of town. Also, scrounge spent hops from the nearest brewery, pomace from a fruit-canning factory, or topsoil from a road construction crew. If your soil is mucky clay, add sand and gypsum sufficient to modify the problem, but not so much that you end up with something closely akin to concrete.

As you plant your garden, add the scrounged compost to each heap of soil as you return it to the ground with planting of trees and shrubs. If you crave privacy, plant castor beans and tithonia, the Mexican sunflower, in a boundary-line trench laced with compost. These two annuals will grow 4 to 5 feet high as a summer foliage barrier.

For overhead color, combine compost with perlite or vermiculite to fill hanging pots of petunias. Or fill containers with compost and soil to grow marigolds and zinnias beside your doorstep. If you still have leftover compost, plant it with zucchini in a large-sized tub.

PESTS AND DISEASES

There are two ways to approach pest and disease control. First, you can make your annuals as strong and healthy as possible with good soil, protection from the elements, and a steady and assured water supply. It is the plants that have been weakened by wind, drought, and insufficient nutrients that fall prey to bugs and disease. And second, you can hand-pick and kill the bugs, caterpillars, beetles, and cutworms that show up to threaten your plants.

As long as you concentrate on annual flowers, pests and diseases are a small threat. Your best defense is to pull out and destroy any plant that becomes deeply infected with aphids or leaf-miner. Beetles and caterpillars can be pulled off one by one and dropped in a can of kerosene for quick extinction. Cutworms are most often a threat to new seedlings set out on open ground. They feed on young, succulent stems, sometimes felling several seedlings in a single night. Young pansies, cineraria, and geraniums are their most common prey. Unfortunately, tomato and cabbage starts are a cutworm delicacy. Wrap a 2-inch protective collar around these seedlings.

The aphid is perhaps the greatest pest for annual-growers. A sucking insect, it attacks dahlias, dianthus, ageratum, petunias, snapdragons, and zinnias, just to mention a few. Not only do aphids rob plants of vigor and deform buds and flowers, they also carry mosaic and other virus diseases. Small colonies should be cut out and destroyed. You can detect their presence by the accumulations of honeydew they secrete. Rotenone and pyrethrum, botanical poisons, are effective against these insects. Nicotine sulphate is an old-time remedy, and malathion is a modern help.

Diseases, on the other hand, afflict annuals less than trees and perennials. Powdery mildew, the mosaics, and ring spot are the most damaging. Your best bet is simply to plant disease-resistant varieties.

Annual Basics

Get the jump on summer color by starting your annuals indoors on a warm windowsill or under artificial lights. Whether you want many plants or just a few, you can get your summer beds growing early with the starter kits available at most nursery houses and supermarkets. The kits come complete with everything you need. Just follow the simple package instructions and, with a bit of diligence, you'll be setting out seedlings well ahead of your garden neighbors. As you watch the seedlings grow from day to day, you'll have time to plan their outdoor placements carefully.

These seed-starting kits are almost one-step affairs—quick, clean, and efficient. The individual planters are net-enclosed peat packets that swell to pot-size when soaked in water. Plant 2 or 3 seeds in each pot and return to the tray of moist peat or vermiculite, which is kept damp by a wick in a plastic reservoir. Only occasionally do the pots and plants need overhead watering. When the seedlings show their first true leaves, thin out the plants, leaving the strongest one to mature. You don't need to fertilize, because the growing medium contains enough plant food to sustain the seedlings until they are moved to their place in the garden.

If you grow your kits in a sunny window, you'll need to turn the flats occasionally to avoid developing spindly plants. Turn the trays every time the shoots start leaning toward the light. Most common bedding annuals now are available in kits.

COLD FRAMES

Want a part-time greenhouse to extend your gardening seasoning? With a cold frame, it's as easy as building a box. The same basic structure you use as a cold frame also can double as a hotbed with the addition of a soil-heating cable (see page 110). Some cables come equipped with built-in soil thermostats, preset for 70 degrees.

Both structures use the heat of the sun to warm the enclosed soil. The hotbed provides supplemental heat during the nighttime hours, a key requirement for easy seed-starting.

Locate the frame facing south and give it some shelter against harsh winds. Choose a level site and see that the soil has good drainage.

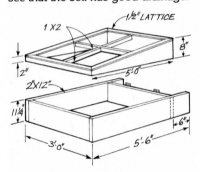

The sloping top of the frame will ensure easy runoff of rain. Turn the soil within the frame and rake even. If you plan to grow plants in pots, add sand as a top surface. If plants are to grow in the ground, add a top layer of good soil. The ideal temperature for seed-starting is 70 degrees, so buy an inexpensive thermometer to aid in maintaining the sufficient heat. When the frame temperature rises, prop the lid open. At night, if heavy frosts are due, add insulated covers to hold heat. Temperatures below 45 degrees can damage delicate seedlings. Water only with a sprinkling can; the excessive pressure from a garden hose can uproot the little plants.

Don't use fertilizer in the seedbed, as small seedlings can't tolerate plant foods. And water whenever the soil feels dry, or whenever you notice signs of plant-wilting. Be ready to plant seedlings in early spring.

For the base of a cold frame or hotbed, use 2x12 rot-resistant lumber, preferably redwood or cedar, to make a 36x66-inch box. If you use non-resistant wood, treat it with a wood preservative other than creosote, which is known to be hard on plants.

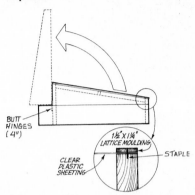

Build the top to measure 36x60 inches, and taper the sides from 2 to 8 inches. Inside the top, fasten a piece of 1x2 lumber side-to-side and flush with the top edge. Add another piece front-to-rear, also flush with the top. Use a lap joint where the strips cross. This grid supports the plastic sheeting. Hinge the top to the base with 4x4 butt hinges.

The top, fully open, is supported

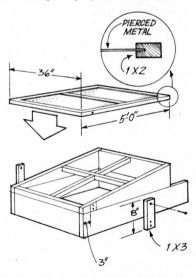

on the expansions of the side base boards. Stretch and staple clear plastic (6 to 8 mils thick) to the lid edge, and top with molding strips to prevent tearing in the wind. Also build a frame of 1x3s to hold a sheet of pierced metal for use as a sun filter. When freezes are due, cover lid with blankets or building boards

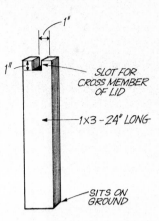

weighted with bricks.

A number of products are available that will insulate against cold air. A lid of rigid composition board that is impregnated with a tar-like substance works well. Cut a piece of 1x3 wood 24 inches long to serve as a prop for the lid. Stand it on the ground inside the frame and rest a crossmember of the lid into the notched top. Move prop to adjust for air.

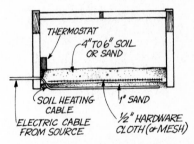

Use the cold frame for early crops of radishes, lettuce, and onions (all quick-growing), and for starting seedling vegetables or annuals.

Pot up cannas, dahlias, and tuberous begonias to start in the frame about 6 weeks before the last frost date. When the weather is frost-free, set the plants out for summer blooming. Use the frame with the sun filter to harden-off greenhouse-grown plants, or to condition small houseplants to an outdoor environment.

In late summer or fall, sow the seeds of biennials and perennials for use in the garden the following year. Or, as days cool, plant fall crops of parsley, radishes, and lettuce to harvest from the frame.

Annual Basics

COLD FRAME

In the fall, move plants that aren't reliably winter-hardy in your area into the cold frame. Chrysanthemums can be established in the frame in the fall, then saved for cuttings or divisions to use in the spring. Canterbury-bells, English daisies, foxgloves, and forget-me-nots also may be carried safely through the winter for early spring planting.

If you move some of your houseplants outdoors for the summer, use the frame (with the sun filter) for the more delicate plants that need protection from sun and wind during the hottest months.

Take advantage of the micro-climates in your garden when you locate your box. Place it against a south wall or a building where it's protected from the prevailing wind. The lower side of the box should face south to admit the most sunlight. For your own convenience, place it near the house for easy winter-tending, and near an outside faucet for the necessary watering year-round. During the bitterest winter months, cover the frame with blankets and an old tarpaulin; uncovering it only on bright sunny days. It's a privilege to harvest fresh parsley or crisp lettuce, or to grow flower seedlings for spring.

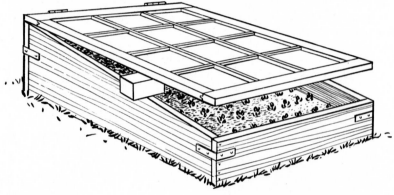

HOTBEDS

With a little bit of adjustment, the same cold frame can be used as a hotbed. Lay a coated soil cable on the ground in an even pattern, and then cover over with dirt. Next, spread a mesh layer across the entire box area, and cover with 4 to 6 inches of good garden loam.

In this little hothouse, you can plant seed and grow young plants that will be ready to set out in the garden as soon as the danger of frost has passed. To make your life easier, select a cable with a built-in thermostat so you don't have to tend the hotbed as often. In two or three months, this very small space can enable you to grow 20 or more trays of seedling varieties that otherwise might not be available.

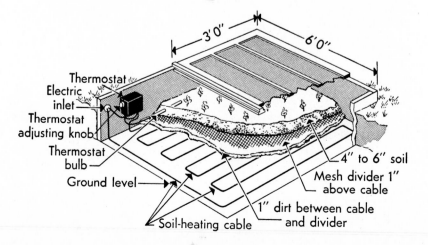

Thermostat
Electric inlet
Thermostat adjusting knob
Thermostat bulb
Ground level
Soil-heating cable
3' 0"
6' 0"
4" to 6" soil
Mesh divider 1" above cable
1" dirt between cable and divider

STARTING SEEDS OUTDOORS

The hardier annuals can be planted out as seeds—not as seedlings half-grown in a hotbed, on a windowsill, or under artificial lights. With the proper planting, good soil, and the right amount of moisture, you can go seed-to-bloom in just one step.

First, scatter seeds over a raked area. Do not cover with soil, but rather firm the seed in place with a board or your hand. Water the bed well by misting so as not to wash the seed away, and keep it moist until the seedlings show green.

Sow large seeds in shallow troughs to a depth of about three times the diameter of the seed. For climbing vines, install a trellis before you plant, raking soil over seeds.

Your main obligation for the next week or two is to keep the area just moist enough—and never soggy—while the sprouts are germinating and taking hold.

On a hot, windswept location, temporarily cover the seed with thin-mesh cloth—old window curtains or cheesecloth will do—and tie down the corners. As the seedlings start showing their second and third sets of little leaves, carefully thin out the weaker plants without damaging the select ones.

About one month after seed planting, pinch off the top shoots with your thumbnail and forefinger to encourage good branching. Some seed plants are bred for such branching; the pinching process will not be needed on these. Initially, weed the bed by hand to encourage plant growth. Do not endanger the young sprouts with hoe-cultivation.

Strive always for good foliage and bushy plant forms. The abundant show of flowers will follow naturally. Keep the blooms coming by proper watering whenever natural rainfall is not enough. And cut out all faded flowers as they appear to keep them from going to seed. This will result in the development of a new crop of flowers.

Add handfuls of compost or mulching material around the growing plants to keep them from suddenly drying out in the hot sun. When flower bloom slows, renew by cutting back leggy stems and adding fertilizer around the stalks. Then water in well.

Plant sweet peas in a freshly dug trench laced with nutrients. Backfill to 2 or 3 inches from the top, and place the seeds according to packet instructions. Return the surplus soil to the trench as needed to give cover. Keep the trench moist.

THINNING

The practice of thinning involves the sacrifice of some plants for the benefit of others, and should be practiced whenever quality is desired over quantity.

Some gardeners find the thinning process a bit disturbing, and prefer to salvage the plants they lift to use elsewhere. This operation is usually called pricking out, and it works better with sturdy vegetable starts than with flowers.

The hardier annuals are generally not offered in pots or flats by nursery houses or supermarkets since they grow easily from seed.

Annual Basics

SEEDLING KNOW-HOW

You can avoid a lot of fuss and muss by buying started plants in flats or trays at your local nursery supplier. These seedling plants also are available in individual peat pots.

The small expanding peat pots can be set out just as they are, or you can peel off the nylon net wrapping and quickly put them in the ground. If you use fiber mix containers, break off the pot rim before you set the plant in the ground. With large flats, break away one side of the box and lift out the individual plants with a putty knife.

Space the plants 6 to 8 inches apart—less for pansies and alyssum, more for tall marigolds. And pull up weeds when they first appear so they won't compete with the annuals for sun, space, water, and nutrients.

Water-in the seedlings with a soaker hose, or with a soft all-night rain, if you can schedule it. The object is to ease the garden soil closely around the young roots, leaving none exposed to the air. If the days are hot and sunny at planting time, stick a wooden shingle on the south side of each plant for a week or so to give the plant some shade and time to adjust to the brighter situation.

Gently sprinkle entire bed; if you just water the individual plants, dry soil nearby will leach away the moisture. As the plants mature, with some reaching heights of 3 to 4 feet, raise your sprinkler onto a stool so its stream will arc over plants, rather than hitting them full-force.

If you don't like to use your fingernails to pinch out young annuals, snip them out instead. But either way, trim leggy plants by removing three or four upper leaflets just above a leaf joint. Do this when the plants are about 6 inches tall, unless they are already branching well on their own. Information on seed packs usually indicates if the plant is self-branching.

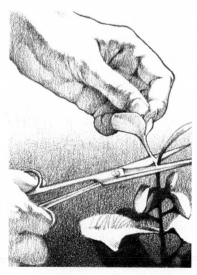

For low plant maintenance, spread an inch or more of mulching material around bases.

The mulch insulates surface soil from the sun, protects against drying winds and beating rains, and also retains soil moisture.

MULTIPLICATION KNOW-HOW

To get more mileage out of certain garden plants, simply root cuttings that you clip in midsummer. But don't get carried away—take only as many cuttings as you can carry through the winter easily. Then you'll have new plants to enjoy indoors during cold weather, plus sizable starts for next spring. Such plants as coleus, geranium, and wax begonia are easy to manage.

Regardless of which of these plants you want to increase, the procedure is the same as shown here for coleus. Take about 4 inches of stem, making a cut just below a leaf stem. Remove lower leaves and insert in a rooting medium of peat and perlite or all sand. You can root cuttings in water, but later the transfer to soil may be tricky.

After you insert cuttings in the rooting medium, water well and put the container in a tightly closed plastic bag that's out of direct sun. In about ten days, check for roots by pulling gently on a cutting. When you are sure of roots, pot up the cuttings in a porous mix in 3-inch pots. Set in good light and water whenever surface soil dries.

With geraniums, you can shape your garden plants to smaller mounds in August for another surge of bloom. Use the cuttings to start new potted plants for winter bloom in your sunniest room. Come spring, you can return the plants to the frost-free garden beds to begin the cycle again.

Take cuttings from three or four of your favorite coleus plants and nurture them as above. They'll repay you with a showy display of color throughout the winter months. Then, ready new trays of bright cuttings in moist sand for eventual return to the garden.

Try the Victorian custom of planting a stand of cosmos in a big tub or container for a feathery accent on a summer terrace. Then when frosts threaten, bring the tub indoors to a sunny window and enjoy continuing bloom through Thanksgiving.

As summer ends, rescue wax begonias, verbena, and impatiens to use indoors.

A large planter full of soil weighs more than you might expect. Move such a load easily with three poles or lengths of broomstick. As the rear pole is uncovered, move it around to the front of the line.

113

ABCs of Annuals

Of the top ten flowering plants in the United States, at least half are annuals—and for good reason. Annuals are economical to buy and grow for quick summer color, and bloom all season to frost. They require no winter care or storage, and are heat- and drought-resistant, as well as relatively disease- and insect-free. With their wide range of colors and heights, they permit great freedom in garden design, and adapt to various planting times. And, most important, annuals will bloom for even the most inexperienced gardener. Here, in easy-to-find alphabetical order, are all the annuals, along with details on colors, heights, preferred environments, and culture.

African daisies make fine companions for taller Iceland poppies.

A

ACROCLINIUM
(helipterum)

DESCRIPTION: Double and semi-double blossoms are 2 to 3 inches across on slender 2-foot stems; oval pointed leaves are gray-green. Mixed seed includes shades of pink, white, and beige. Flowers resemble daisies and asters, but are usually slightly smaller and more delicate than strawflowers.
SOIL AND LIGHT: Acroclinium grows best in well-drained, average-to-dry soil that receives full sun.
PLANTING: Sow seed outdoors after all danger of frost. It should germinate in about 15 days and bloom about 6 weeks later. Seedlings may be thinned to 6 to 12 inches apart; they are often difficult to transplant.
SPECIAL HELPS: Flowers may be used in fresh arrangements and are excellent additions to dried bouquets. To dry, cut the whole stem before the flower is fully open; strip foliage. Hang upside down in a cool, airy, shady place so that stems will be straight. The flowers should be dry enough to use in two to three weeks. If desired, spray with hair spray or clear acrylic to help prevent shedding or humidity damage. Keep dried flower arrangements out of direct sunlight to prevent fading.

AFRICAN DAISY
(arctotis)

DESCRIPTION: Daisy-like blooms grow 2 to 3 inches across on stems 1 to 2 feet tall. Arctotis is available in shades of yellow, pink, and brown; but the most common variety has gold-edged blue centers with white petals that are a light purple underneath. Plants have sparse but attractive gray-green foliage. Flowers close at night.
SOIL AND LIGHT: These do best in sandy, light soil with full sun, and adapt to dry conditions. Plants like hot days and cool nights.
PLANTING: Start seeds indoors 6 to 8 weeks before last frost, or sow directly in the ground after all danger of frost. Seedlings may be thinned to 6 to 12 inches apart; prune plants to keep bushy. In mild climates, the seed may be sown in late summer, if desired.
SPECIAL HELPS: Arctotis are effective in mass plantings and in front of borders, especially when planted to receive reflected heat from sidewalks or walls. Attractive flowers and long stems make them desirable for fresh bouquets. Plants are native to South Africa.

AGERATUM
also called flossflower

DESCRIPTION: These 3- to 6-inch dome-shaped plants are almost constantly in bloom. The small fuzzy blooms are most commonly seen in shades of blue-violet, but are also available in white and pink.
SOIL AND LIGHT: Plants are easy to grow and are tolerant of all soil conditions. They prefer full sun, but will adapt to some shade.

PLANTING: Start seeds indoors 6 to 8 weeks before last frost. They germinate in 5 to 10 days and grow slowly. Seedlings are also quite tender, so you may prefer to buy started plants. Plants may be propagated from stem cuttings. Set plants 5 to 9 inches apart; in some areas, they may self-sow.

SPECIAL HELPS: Their mounding, compact shape makes these plants excellent for edgings, borders, and rock gardens, either alone to form a solid mass of color, or in combination with other border plants. Tall varieties make good background plantings. Snip faded flowers to assure constant bloom. Ageratum doesn't tolerate drought conditions, so keep evenly watered. Plants were originally found in Mexico; in 1822, the seed was taken to England where it was first cultivated. Painter's brush and tassel flower are other names sometimes used in referring to this plant.

ALCEA ROSEA
see hollyhock

ALYSSUM

DESCRIPTION: Delicate white, pink, or purple flowers cover these compact plants from spring to frost, scenting the air with honey-like fragrance. Most varieties grow only 3 to 4 inches tall; others may reach up to 9 or 10 inches. Plants tend to spread, making them wider than they are tall. Popular varieties include Rosie O'Day, Carpet of Snow, Royal Carpet, and Violet Queen.
SOIL AND LIGHT: These do best

115

in full sun, but will adapt to some shade. They're tolerant of all soil conditions.

PLANTING: Sow seed as soon as the ground can be worked, or set out started plants when weather is warm. Space plants 6 to 8 inches apart. Dig up with a clump of dirt around the roots in the fall for a showy houseplant. Plants self-sow in many areas.
SPECIAL HELPS: These fragrant, spreading plants are excellent choices for borders, edgings, rock gardens, bulb gardens, hanging baskets, and window boxes. In warm climates, they will often bloom all year. If flowering decreases toward the end of the summer, trim plants back to encourage new growth. Alyssum is native to the Mediterranean area.

AMARANTH
also called love-lies-bleeding

DESCRIPTION: Tall plants (3 to 6 feet) with vibrantly colored foliage and long, red tassel-like flowers. The drooping flower heads may last up to 8 weeks before fading. Foliage of some varieties changes color in the fall. Often-planted varieties include Illumination, Early Splendor, Aurora, Molten Fire, and Joseph's Coat. Amaranth also is called summer poinsettia.

SOIL AND LIGHT: These plants tend to grow taller in rich soil, and to develop brighter colors in poor soil. Amaranth is drought resistant, and prefers full sun.
PLANTING: Get a head start by planting seed indoors about 6 weeks before the last frost. Space plants about 18 inches apart; they are relatively easy to transplant. Stake the plants, especially in windy locations.

SPECIAL HELPS: Grow amaranth in a spot where you want a temporary hedge, or use them as background plantings or against a wall. The name amaranth is from the Greek, and means "does not wither."

AMMOBIUM
also called winged everlasting

DESCRIPTION: These fairly tall plants (about 3 feet) are characterized by raised ridges on the stems and clusters of yellow-centered white flowers, 1 to 2 inches across. Leaves are soft and silvery.
SOIL AND LIGHT: Plants do best in full sun and light, sandy soil, explaining their Latin name, ammobium, which means "living in sand."
PLANTING: Sow outside as soon as the ground is workable; or start indoors 6 to 8 weeks before the last frost is due. Set out started plants

about 9 inches apart when evening temperatures stay above 50° F. Plants usually survive transplanting at any stage, if it's carefully done.
SPECIAL TIPS: Flowers are traditionally dried for winter bouquets. Cut before flowers are fully opened, and hang upside down in a dry, shady place. Ammobium is native to Australia.

ANCHUSA
also called summer forget-me-not

DESCRIPTION: Similar to true forget-me-nots (see myosotis), this annual features clusters of tiny five-petaled flowers on stiff, hairy stems, 1½ to 2 feet tall. Flowers are usually blue with white centers, but also may be all white. Best-known varieties are Blue Bird and Blue Angel. Another common name for anchusa is cape forget-me-not.
SOIL AND LIGHT: Although they'll tolerate shade, anchusa prefer full sun. They also like rich soil that's more often moist than dry.
PLANTING: Start seeds indoors 6 to 8 weeks before the last frost is due. When it's dependably warm, set plants 10 to 12 inches apart in a prepared bed. Seeds also may be sown directly after all danger of frost has passed. Because of its moderate height, anchusa is good for middle-of-the-bed location in borders.

116

SPECIAL HELPS: Excellent for window boxes and massed beds, anchusa also can be grown as container plants. To stimulate vigorous flowering, cut plants back to about 6 inches after the first bloom fades. Anchusa specimens were first found in South Africa and then taken to England.

ANTIRRHINUM
see snapdragon

ARCTOTIS
see African daisy

ASTER
(callistephus)

DESCRIPTION: Plants range from about 8 inches to nearly 3 feet in height, with blossoms from 1 to 5 inches across. Flowers may be double or single, and shaggy or shaped like a daisy, mum, or pompon in a rainbow of colors. Frequently, centers are yellow. Some varieties of annual asters include Early Bird, American Branching, California Giant, Extra Early, Totem Pole, Perfection, Milady, and Powderpuff. Plants also are called China asters, as a Jesuit missionary found them in China in 1731.

SOIL AND LIGHT: Choose a sunny or lightly shaded location for asters. A rich, well-drained soil is best, but you may need to add a little lime if soil is too acidic. Mulching with peat or grass clippings will help maintain moisture and protect the shallow root system.

PLANTING: Start seeds indoors about 6 weeks before last frost, then space seedlings 12 to 15 inches apart (check seed packages for the correct spacing of specific varieties). Seeds also may be sown outdoors after frost danger. Be careful not to plant asters in the same location 2 years in a row, as they are susceptible to a fungus disease that lingers in the soil. For a continuous show of color, plant some of each of the early, mid-season, and late varieties. Or plant the mid-season and late varieties at 2-week intervals. If flowers fail to develop and foliage turns yellow, the plant may have a virus disease that is commonly spread by leaf hoppers. To reduce this possibility, look for varieties labeled "wilt-resistant."
SPECIAL HELPS: Choose a size, color, and shape to mix with other annuals in any part of the flower bed, but stake tall varieties that may get leggy. Cut flowers are good for fresh bouquets.

B

BABY-BLUE-EYES
see nemophila

BABY'S-BREATH
see gypsophila

BACHELOR'S-BUTTON
see cornflower

BALSAM
see also impatiens

DESCRIPTION: Also known as garden balsam, touch-me-not, and lady slipper, this member of the impatiens family has two varieties. Bush balsams average 8 to 10 inches in height with flowers at the tops of the plants. Other varieties have flowers growing along the stems, which can be as tall as 15 to 24 inches.

The camellia-like blossoms may be double or semi-double in shades of pink, red, salmon, purple, white, or combinations. Flowers are usually 1½ to 2½ inches across.
SOIL AND LIGHT: All kinds of balsams do best in rich, well-drained soil that is kept slightly moist and receives full sun. They will adapt to grow in shade.

PLANTING: Seeds should be soaked in water for 24 hours before planting. Sow outdoors after all danger of frost, or start inside 4 to 6 weeks earlier. For best display of flowers, space plants about 18 inches apart. If you transplant seedlings, dig up a small ball of soil with each plant.
SPECIAL HELPS: This native of Asia is often grown in old-fashioned

117

gardens. Although both types work well in beds and for edging, the varieties with flowers along the stem instead of at the ends make a unique addition to borders.

The common name touch-me-not refers to the plants' seed pods that burst open with the slightest touch, a characteristic they share with other members of the impatiens family.

Cuttings may be taken in the fall for winter houseplants.

BEGONIA
wax begonia or fibrous begonia

DESCRIPTION: Single and double flowers normally cover these rounded plants that average 6 to 9 inches tall. The clusters of flowers are usually white or shades of pink and red. Foliage ranges from glossy green to red to bronze.
SOIL AND LIGHT: Plants will grow under almost any light conditions, and will bloom in shady areas. Soil should be rich and kept moist. Water plants regularly to help them resist hot weather.
PLANTING: Seed is very fine and should be started indoors 4 to 6 weeks before first frost, so it's often easiest to purchase started plants. Space starts 6 to 8 inches apart. Start seed in September for winter houseplants, or dig up plants in the fall. Cuttings root easily.
SPECIAL HELPS: This annual is best in a massed bed of its own or as an edging for a shady perennial border. Begonias do well in pots year round, but may need an occasional trimming to keep bushy.

BELLS-OF-IRELAND
(moluccella)

DESCRIPTION: This old-fashioned plant is named for the green bell-shaped calyxes which grow along the 2- to 3-foot stems. Tiny white flowers are almost hidden inside. Some varieties have a white veining pattern on the 1- to 2-inch-long bells.
SOIL AND LIGHT: Bells-of-Ireland can be grown in average soil, but they'll do even better in rich, well-drained soil. Plant in a sunny location and keep evenly moist.
PLANTING: Although plants occasionally sow their own seed, you'll do better to toss in a few seeds after frost danger is past. Later, space plants about 12 inches apart. In warm climates, sow again in August. Transplanting is not easy, so it's better to sow directly where you want plants.
SPECIAL HELPS: Native to the eastern Mediterranean area rather than to Ireland, these plants make an unusual addition to winter dried bouquets. Cut the whole stalk when flowers are in bloom, then tie stalks together and hang upside down in a cool, dry place. When dried (in 2 to 3 weeks), remove the small flowers from inside bells.

BLANKET FLOWER
see gaillardia

BLUE LACE FLOWER
(trachymene)

DESCRIPTION: Similar to the wild Queen Anne's lace, these plants bear umbrella-shaped clusters of flowers on slender 1½- to 2½-foot stalks; flowers usually are blue. A white-flowering variety is called Lace Veil; trachymenes may also be pink. Each cluster of tiny flowers is 2 to 3 inches across and sweetly scented. Foliage is finely cut and sparse.
SOIL AND LIGHT: Plants grow in well-drained soil and full sun, but they prefer cool regions and do not do as well where summers are hot and dry.

PLANTING: Start seed indoors 6 to 8 weeks before the last frost is due, or sow outdoors as early as the ground can be worked. Space plants about 12 inches apart. Each plant blooms for only about 3 weeks, so sow at intervals for continuous color. When plants are about half grown, you may want to insert brush or stakes in the rows to keep them from toppling in the wind.
SPECIAL HELPS: Use in borders or cut the delicate flowers for a graceful addition to fresh bouquets. Plants originated in Australia.

BRACHYCOME

see swan river daisy

BROWALLIA

DESCRIPTION: Compact, sprawling plants may cover a 10- to 15-square-inch area, displaying their small petunia-like flowers till frost. Blossoms have a velvety texture in shades of blue, violet, and white. Size of plants and flowers varies with the variety. Choose from Blue Bells Improved, Silver Bells, or Velvet Blue, among others.

SOIL AND LIGHT: Plants tolerate all soil types, especially if kept moist. They may be grown in full sun or partial shade.

PLANTING: Seeds tend to be slow to germinate; start indoors 6 to 8 weeks before last frost, or buy started plants. For best display, space plants 8 to 10 inches apart. They will usually start to bloom about 12 weeks after sown. May self-sow in warm areas.

SPECIAL HELPS: Pinch plants for bushier growth. Browallia is an excellent choice for hanging baskets, window boxes, or edging plants. It may be cut back in the fall and potted for all-winter bloom on a sunny windowsill.

BURNING BUSH
(kochia)

DESCRIPTION: Also known as fire bush and summer cypress, these plants are known for globe-like, dense foliage. The delicate green,

finely cut leaves turn bright red in fall. Plants average 2 to 3 feet in height. One common variety is Childsi.

SOIL AND LIGHT: Kochia is especially tolerant of hot weather and appreciates full sun. Soil may be of any type as long as it is kept on the dry side.

PLANTING: Sow seed outdoors when weather is warm, or start indoors 4 to 6 weeks earlier. Space plants 18 to 24 inches apart so they can develop into a full, solid shape.

SPECIAL HELPS: Excellent for hot, windy areas, Kochia is sometimes grown in pots on balconies to give privacy; they may be used anywhere as temporary hedges. The plant's origins have been traced from France across Asia to Japan.

BUSH BALSAM
see balsam

BUTTERFLY FLOWER
(schizanthus)

DESCRIPTION: Fragile and lipped flowers with spotted petals resembling butterflies give the plant its name. The bicolored blossoms are predominantly pink, red, yellow, purple, and white. The pale green

foliage is delicate and fernlike. Plants vary from 1½ to 4 feet in height, depending on where they are grown.

SOIL AND LIGHT: This uniquely flowered annual prefers cool regions and does not do well where summers are hot. Give it a garden spot that receives full sun to partial shade. Keep the rich, well-drained soil moist.

PLANTING: Start seed indoors 6 to 8 weeks before last frost. Seed also may be sown directly. Make fall plantings in warmer areas. Each plant blooms profusely, but only for a few weeks; make plantings every 2 weeks for 6 weeks to extend the blooming season. Set plants about 12 inches apart.

SPECIAL HELPS: Show off the gaily colored and deeply cut flowers by letting them tumble over hanging baskets or window boxes. Taller varieties benefit from brush or stakes inserted in the row for support when plants are about half grown. When plants are about 3 inches tall, start pinching to develop more bushy, less straggly plants. These plants also bloom well in a cool-temperature greenhouse. Plants are originally from Chile, and are also called the poor man's orchid. Blooms may be cut for flower arranging.

119

C

CALIFORNIA POPPY
(eschscholzia)

DESCRIPTION: Silver-green, finely cut foliage provides the background for these silky, cup-shaped flowers on long stems. Single and double varieties are available. The 2- to 3-inch blossoms were originally bright yellow, but now may be found in shades of orange, gold, bronze, red, and white. Petals may be crinkled and edged with a darker shade. Varieties include Ballerina, Mission Bells, Aurantiaca, and Sunset.

SOIL AND LIGHT: Give these a slightly sandy soil in a sunny to partially shady location.

PLANTING: Seed is hardy and usually not hurt by frost, so plant as soon as the ground can be worked. However, germination is slow and the first blooms may not appear for 2 months. Space individual plants 6 to 12 inches apart to allow for spreading. Plants often self-sow.

SPECIAL HELPS: Originally found on the Pacific Coast by Russian explorers, this poppy now is the state flower of California. The brightly colored, open-faced flowers show to advantage in planters and window boxes. Flowers usually don't last when cut.

CALLIOPSIS
see coreopsis

CALLISTEPHUS
see aster

CANDYTUFT
(iberis)

DESCRIPTION: Choose either the brightly colored, dwarf plants with flat top clusters of tiny flowers, or the taller, sweetly scented type with white blossoms in dense hyacinth-like clusters. Heights range from about 6 inches to nearly 2 feet. Two of the varieties are Umbellata Dwarf Fairy and Giant Hyacinth Flowered Iceberg.

SOIL AND LIGHT: Both types do well in average soil and a sunny location. But if it's hot, they appreciate a little shade.

PLANTING: Plants do best in cooler weather; to give plants a chance to develop before it gets too hot, sow as soon as the ground can be worked. And, to provide continuous flowering, make successive plantings every 2 to 3 weeks. Plants are not easily transplanted, so discard seedlings after you thin plants to about 7 inches apart. Flowers should appear 8 to 10 weeks after seed is sown.

SPECIAL HELPS: The smaller, globe-shaped types add bright colors to rock gardens, borders, and edgings. The taller ones add a dramatic highlight to borders. Trim back both types after the first

flowering to stimulate a second bloom. Both the white and colored varieties are a good choice for fresh bouquets.

CAPE DAISY
(dimorphotheca)

DESCRIPTION: Masses of 3- to 4-inch daisy-like flowers characterize these clumping plants which average 12 to 15 inches in height. Petals come in shades of yellow, orange, rose, salmon, and white, usually with a blue- or lavender-shaded underside. Slender stems support the flowers and narrow leaves. Aurantiaca is one popular hybrid variety.

Cape daisies are often called cape marigolds, but actually they are not related. Cape daisies are tender perennials, native to Africa, which can be easily grown as annuals in colder climates. True marigolds originally were found in America.

SOIL AND LIGHT: Plants must have sun or the flowers won't open. Plant in well-drained soil that is kept dry; they thrive in heat.

PLANTING: Sow outdoors after all danger of frost, or start inside about 5 weeks earlier. Flowers appear 7 to 8 weeks after seeded. In warm areas, seeds may be sown again in the fall for winter and spring bloom.

SPECIAL HELPS: Save cape daisies for a sunny, hot spot in the garden or along a border. Flowers close at night and on cloudy days, so they are not recommended for fresh arrangements.

CARNATION
(dianthus)

DESCRIPTION: These pink, yellow, red, and white flowers rival those from the florist's greenhouse. Blossoms are 1 to 3 inches across with a spicy fragrance on 12- to 24-inch stems. Foliage is blue-gray. Some favorite varieties for home gardens include Chabaud, Dwarf Baby, Giant Enfant de Nice, Giant Marguerite, Juliet, and Pixie Delight.
SOIL AND LIGHT: Give plants full sun and a light soil mixture that's kept moist.
PLANTING: About 10 weeks before the last frost, start seeds indoors. They should germinate in about 10 days, but they'll need about 5 months to produce flowers. In mild areas, the plants may last for many seasons.
SPECIAL HELPS: Snip faded flowers for continuous bloom. Plants are dramatic when massed in the garden or border. Cut them for long-lasting arrangements.

CASTOR BEAN
(ricinus)

DESCRIPTION: Looking like they belong in the tropics, these exotic plants often grow to 10 feet in one season. Each palmlike leaf may be 1 to 3 feet in length. On some varieties, the leaves will change from red to brown or green as they grow older. These are sometimes called castor oil plants or palm christi. Flowers are nearly hidden by the foliage, appearing on the top and side stems of plants as reddish-brown clusters with no petals.
SOIL AND LIGHT: Plants thrive with plenty of heat, moisture, and sun.
PLANTING: Seeds have a hard outer covering; soak in water or nick with a file before planting. Start seed indoors 6 to 8 weeks before the last frost, or wait to sow outdoors after the weather has warmed. Space about 3 feet apart.

SPECIAL HELPS: Castor beans make an excellent choice for a quick-growing, background screen that may last for several years in mild climates. Seed pods are poisonous and should be clipped before they mature, especially if plants are in an area where children may be playing. Be aware, also, that some people are allergic to both the seed pods and foliage. Plants are grown commercially in India for castor oil.

CELOSIA

DESCRIPTION: Cockscomb (or crested) and plumosa (or feathered) are the common names for the two most typically found celosias. Both names describe the shape of the brilliantly colored flowers that appear in red, yellow, orange, and pink; blooms measure 2 to 12 inches across. Dwarf forms average about 8 inches in height, while taller varieties may reach 18 to 24 inches. Favorite plumosa varieties include Lilliput, Crusader, Golden Torch, Red Fox, Forest Fire Improved, and Golden Triumph. Some top cockscomb varieties are Extra Dwarf, Jewel Box, Empress Gladiator, Fireglow, Floradale, and Toreador.

SOIL AND LIGHT: Plants will tolerate nearly all soil types, and even survive drought; but they must have full sun and usually don't grow in partial shade. They do best in well-drained soil.
PLANTING: Start seeds indoors 6 to 8 weeks before the last frost is due; space plants 8 to 12 inches apart. Seed may also be sown directly in the ground after the weather has warmed. Started plants are generally available.
SPECIAL HELPS: These ornamental beauties are impressive in massed plantings, but should be used with discretion in mixed annual beds lest their strong colors steal the show. Dwarf varieties may be used for edging. Flower heads are extremely long-lasting when cut, and also make excellent dried specimens. To dry, cut when mature, before the black bead-like seeds appear. Hang in bunches, head down, in a dry, airy place. Pot individual plants in tubs for movable accents on patios.

CENTAUREA
see cornflower, dusty miller, sweet sultan

121

CHINESE FORGET-ME-NOT

see cynoglossum

CHRYSANTHEMUM

DESCRIPTION: Yellow, purple, scarlet, orange, salmon, or white usually color these daisy-like flowers. Varieties may have a dark eye, or a contrasting ring of color near the center. Both single and double flowers may be 2 to 3 inches across, on 2-foot stems. Dwarf types grow only to about 10 inches with 1-inch flowers. Popular varieties include Rainbowl, Paludosum, and Golden Raindrops. Leaves are generally smaller and more succulent than perennial types.

Annual chrysanthemums often are called painted daisies.
SOIL AND LIGHT: Plants do best in rich, moist soil with full sun, but they will tolerate some shade. Cool summers are preferred.
PLANTING: Sow outdoors as soon as the ground can be worked. They grow rapidly and can later be thinned to 12 to 18 inches apart. Seedlings are easily transplanted. Pinch back young plants to encourage bushiness.
SPECIAL HELPS: Utilize dwarf varieties as a colorful edging, or plant taller varieties as borders. Both provide long-lasting cut flowers.

CIGAR PLANT

see cuphea

CLARKIA

also called Rocky Mountain garland; see also godetia

DESCRIPTION: Originally a wildflower in the western United States, these have been cultivated to produce double-flowered varieties in shades of pink, rose, scarlet, purple, orange, and white. The delicate 1-inch blossoms appear at every joint along the slender stems, forming spikes 1 to 2 feet tall. Flowers have a deep, penetrating fragrance.
SOIL AND LIGHT: Plants do best in light, sandy soil, and seem to bloom most profusely when soil is low in nitrogen. Set them in a semi-shady location, although they will tolerate full sun.

PLANTING: Sow seeds outdoors as early as the ground can be worked. Don't bother with trying to start them inside; they prefer the cooler outdoors. Plants will thrive where summers are cool, often blooming from July until October. Thin seedlings to about 9 inches apart.
SPECIAL HELPS: These make long-lasting cut flowers, but they do not do well in hot climates. Plants were named for Captain William Clark of the Lewis and Clark Expedition ordered by President Jefferson in 1804.

CLEOME

also called spiderplant, spiderflower

DESCRIPTION: Cleome is a tall plant with an unusual appearance and a pungent scent that some people find disagreeable. At the end of each 3- to 6-foot stem is a rounded flower cluster measuring about 8 inches across. Long, thread-like stamens and pistils extend from the pink, rose, orchid, or white flower clusters. As the flower matures, slender seed pods dangle on 4-inch wiry stems, looking very much like spider legs and giving the plant its common name. Flowers appear continuously, usually from June through August. Three of the most commonly found varieties are Ruby Queen, Helen Campbell, and Rose Queen.
SOIL AND LIGHT: Sometimes described as a "rough and tumble garden plant," these thrive in poor, sandy, or average soil; but rich soil is okay if kept on the dry side. Full sun is best, but plants will tolerate some shade.
PLANTING: Sow seeds outdoors after all danger of frost; thin to 18 to 24 inches. Self-sowing is common.
SPECIAL HELPS: Most people prefer to use cleome as background

or screen plantings, especially along a fence or wall. Flowers show up well at a distance, and the strong scent is not as noticeable. They also may be used in tubs, in massed plantings on banks, or in front of tall shrubs. Seed pods add a handsome touch to dried arrangements.

COLEUS

DESCRIPTION: Colorful foliage is the trademark of these plants, with multicolor patterns of chartreuse, yellow, pink, white, red, and green covering the often-ruffled leaves. The white or blue flower spikes are usually pinched off. Plants range from 6 to 24 inches in height. Some of the common varieties are Carefree, Rainbow, Color Pride, Pink Sensation, Red Velvet, Salmon Lace, Sunset Glory, Volcano, and Candidum.
SOIL AND LIGHT: Plants do best in average to rich, well-drained soil that is not allowed to dry out. Give them indirect light or partial shade; they'll tolerate full sun if it doesn't last all day.
PLANTING: Seeds will produce a variety of colors and leaf patterns. Start indoors very early; young plants develop slowly. Started plants are commonly available and allow you to choose desired colors; space them 8 to 10 inches apart. Stem cuttings root quickly in water and make attractive houseplants.
SPECIAL HELPS: Plant coleus wherever you want an attractive foliage accent. Keep plants pinched back to encourage bushiness.

CONEFLOWER
see rudbeckia

CONSOLIDA
see larkspur

CONVOLVULUS
also called morning-glory

DESCRIPTION: Also known as the dwarf morning-glory, these plants do indeed have similar leaves and flowers. But instead of vines, plants are bushy mounds about 12 inches tall and 18 inches wide. The 2-inch trumpet-like flowers show their colors (blue, pink, lilac, and red) all day. Some double-flowering varieties are available. Others are striped or "tricolor" with a white band separating the yellow throat from the colored petals.
SOIL AND LIGHT: For constant bloom, plant in a dry, sunny location. Almost any type of soil is suitable if it is kept dry.

PLANTING: Seeds have a hard outer shell which should be chipped or soaked to speed germination. Sow outdoors after frost danger, or start inside 4 to 6 weeks earlier. Space seedlings about 12 inches apart.
SPECIAL HELPS: Enjoy these all-day bloomers in window boxes, hanging baskets, borders, or edgings.

COREOPSIS
(calliopsis)

DESCRIPTION: These are hardy plants, despite their feathery, light-green foliage and wire-thin stems. Flowers are daisy-like with toothed petals often appearing in

double layers. Blooms show rich shades of golden yellow, mahogany, crimson, maroon, and orange, often with small brownish-yellow centers. Dwarf varieties grow to 12 inches, while taller ones may reach 3 feet.

SOIL AND LIGHT: Sun is the only definite requirement for these plants; soil can be of any type. Plants are especially adaptive to smoky city air.
PLANTING: Seed should be sown as soon as the ground can be worked in the spring. Plants should flower in about 40 days. Seeds were once used to dye cloth. Coreopsis are self-sowing in many areas.
SPECIAL HELPS: This easy-to-grow annual also has a perennial form. Staking will help support the flowers. Use both varieties in borders where they are easy to reach for cutting flowers.

CORNFLOWER
(centaurea); also called bachelor's-buttons

DESCRIPTION: Most commonly found with blue fringe-petaled flowers, these graceful, easy-to-grow plants are an old-fashioned favorite. Flowers also have been developed in shades of pink, white, red, and lavender. Plants average 1 to 3 feet tall with fine, lacy, light-green or gray-green foliage. Popular varieties include Blue Boy, Pinkie, Snowman, Jubilee Gem, and Red Boy.

123

SOIL AND LIGHT: Choose a sunny location for planting. Average soil is fine, if well-drained.

PLANTING: Seeds are hardy and can be sown as soon as the ground is workable. Seed also may be sown in fall for flowers the following year. Plants often are self-sowing, although flowers tend to become gray-white in succeeding years.
SPECIAL HELPS: Keep faded flowers snipped to encourage continuous bloom. Plants show well in massed groupings since individuals are fine-textured and graceful. Use flowers in fresh arrangements, or hang to dry.

COSMOS

DESCRIPTION: Wide, serrated petals in shades of pink, rose, yellow, red, and lavender surround a yellow-gold center to form these delicate 3- to 4-inch flowers. Foliage is lacy and fernlike, adding to the airy quality of the plants—even though they average 4 to 6 feet tall. Common single and double flowering varieties include Dazzler, Radiance, Sensation, Bright Lights, and Diablo.
SOIL AND LIGHT: Flowers will appear earlier if soil is fairly dry and not very fertile. Full sun is best, although plants are somewhat shade-tolerant.
PLANTING: Start seeds indoors 5 to

6 weeks before the last frost is due; or wait and sow when weather has warmed. Space seedlings about 12 inches apart. Plants grow rapidly. If you live in an area of the country that normally receives a killing frost before the first of October, don't bother with the late-blooming cosmos unless you start the seeds early indoors.
SPECIAL HELPS: If set in a windy spot, plants will benefit from staking. When flower buds first appear, fertilize with a little wood ash from the fireplace to help produce an abundance of bloom. Cut flowers, combined with a little foliage, make a delightful bouquet.

CUPFLOWER
see nierembergia

CUPHEA
also called cigar plant

DESCRIPTION: The common name of this plant comes from the ¾-inch tubular flowers which have black and white tips that resemble cigar ash. Flowers are fiery red in the most familiar variety; others are pink, lavender, or rose. Plants are 10 to 12 inches tall, erect, and bushy with lance-shaped leaves. Other common names are cigarflower, firefly, and firecracker plant.
SOIL AND LIGHT: Cuphea do well in average soil that receives full to partial sun.

PLANTING: Plants are usually purchased, but seed may be started in mid-winter. Set plants about 9 inches apart.

SPECIAL HELPS: Although most widely known as an everblooming houseplant, cuphea make a striking addition to rock gardens, sidewalk edgings, window boxes, and hanging baskets. Plants are perennial in their native Mexico. Young plants should be pruned to encourage bushiness. Make cuttings in the fall for winter houseplants.

CYNOGLOSSUM
also called Chinese forget-me-not

DESCRIPTION: Taller than the conventional forget-me-not (myosotis), these have similar tiny flowers on graceful branching stems that are 1½ to 2 feet tall. Flowers are usually blue, although pink and white varieties are available. A common compact variety with blue flowers is Firmament. Blanche Burpee is taller with different colored flowers.
SOIL AND LIGHT: Plants thrive in light, sandy soil where summers are hot and dry. They're adaptable, however, and will tolerate any type of soil in sun or shade.
PLANTING: Plants grow quickly from seed, so there's little advantage to starting them indoors. Sow as soon as the ground can be worked. Make consecutive plantings for

continuous bloom. Plants often self-sow and may become a nuisance. Seeds are described as "stick-tights" because they adhere to clothing and animals. Set about 12 inches apart.

SPECIAL HELPS: Flowering branches add airiness to fresh bouquets and to mixed annual borders. Plants are sometimes called hound's tongue because of the shape of their petals.

D

DAHLBERG DAISY
(dyssodia)

DESCRIPTION: Also known as golden fleece, these attractive, compact plants feature aromatic, feathery foliage that is almost hidden by bright yellow ½-inch flowers. Plants are 8 to 12 inches tall.
SOIL AND LIGHT: Characteristic of their native Mexico and Texas, plants do best in full sun and light, sandy soil. Hot weather doesn't bother them.
PLANTING: Unless you live in a warm climate, it's best to start seeds

indoors 8 to 10 weeks before last frost, since plants often take 4 months to bloom. Seed also may be sown outdoors as early as the ground can be worked. Space plants about 6 inches apart.
SPECIAL HELPS: Cut flowers make attractive small bouquets. Use plants for accent color in rock gardens, edgings, and borders.

DAHLIA

DESCRIPTION: These bushy plants have dark green foliage and 2- to 3-inch flowers in brilliant shades of yellow, orange, red, lavender, purple, and white. The single, double, and semi-double flowers appear on 12- to 24-inch plants. Taller varieties with

larger flowers are usually grown as perennials. For annuals, choose from these: Coltness, Early Bird, Redskin, Sunburst, Cactus-Flowered, Pompon, and Unwins.
SOIL AND LIGHT: Plants need at least a half-day of full sun and prefer well-drained soil that is kept moist during hot, dry weather.
PLANTING: Started plants are generally available in nurseries, or you can start your own. Sow indoors 6 to 8 weeks before the last frost. Seeds should germinate in 5 to 10 days and be of flowering size in 8 to 10 weeks. Set plants 10 to 15 inches apart.
SPECIAL HELPS: If desired, tubers may be dug in the fall and stored over winter for the next season. Use dahlias in borders where you can easily cut the flowers for fresh bouquets. Give taller varieties extra support by staking.

DELPHINIUM
see larkspur

DIANTHUS
see carnation, pinks, sweet william

DIMORPHOTHECA
see cape daisy

DUSTY MILLER
(centaurea)

DESCRIPTION: The principal reason for growing this 12- to 15-inch annual is its silvery white, fernlike foliage. Flowers are insignificant and seldom seen.
SOIL AND LIGHT: Plants need full sun and tolerate dry soil.

PLANTING: Since they're slow-growing, it's usually best to buy started plants. Set them about 8 inches apart.

SPECIAL HELPS: Dusty miller is an excellent choice for combination plantings with brightly colored, flowering annuals, or as an accent against shrubbery. Since they prefer dry soil, plants do well in window boxes and other hard-to-water locations.

DYSSODIA
see dahlberg daisy

E

ESCHSCHOLZIA
see California poppy

EUPHORBIA
also called snow-on-the-mountain

DESCRIPTION: White-edged green foliage, with an occasional all-white leaf, characterizes these 18- to 24-inch plants. Flowers appear on spikes, but are generally insignificant. Another variety has red-edged leaves and is also known as annual poinsettia, Mexican fire plant, and fire-on-the-mountain.

SOIL AND LIGHT: Euphorbia adapt to any soil, including that usually considered "poor." Full sun is best.

PLANTING: Plants grow easily from seed sown in early spring. Self-sowing habits can make the plant

a "noxious weed" in some areas.

SPECIAL HELPS: Euphorbia provide a showy background or border filler, either alone or with other annuals. Cuttings enhance fresh bouquets, but should be seared in flame or dipped in boiling water to keep the sap from coagulating and clogging the stem, causing it to wilt. When cutting, be careful not to get any of the milky sap in your eyes, mouth, or on skin cuts; it is poisonous. Plants are sometimes called ghost weed.

EVERLASTING
see strawflower

F

FAREWELL-TO-SPRING
see godetia

FEVERFEW
(matricaria)

DESCRIPTION: Sprays of button-like gold, white, and yellow flowers appear on branching but compact plants 8 to 30 inches tall. A member of the chrysanthemum family, feverfew resembles some of the perennial mums; flowers can be single or double. Foliage is generally feathery with a tangy fragrance.

False chamomile is another common name. Good varieties include Golden Ball, Lemon Ball, Snowball, and Capensis.

SOIL AND LIGHT: Plants thrive in cool climates with rich, well-drained soil and plenty of sun. In warmer areas, give them partial shade and a light mulch, especially if it's dry.

PLANTING: Scatter seed outdoors as soon as the ground can be worked; or start indoors 4 to 6 weeks earlier. Space plants about 6 inches apart.

SPECIAL HELPS: Flowers are often used by florists, since plants generally bloom all summer. Plants act like perennials in warm areas.

FLAX
(linum)

DESCRIPTION: These 18- to 24-inch plants have grasslike foliage and white, pink, blue, or bright red flowers that last only 1 day, but are replaced with new ones.

SOIL AND LIGHT: Give flax a sunny location with well-drained, light sandy soil. Where strong winds are common, set plants in a protected spot or add trimmed branches for stakes.

PLANTING: Start seeding as soon as the ground can be worked; repeat

126

every 3 to 4 weeks, if continuous flowering is desired. Thin seedlings to 8 inches. Plants do best where summers are cool.

SPECIAL HELPS: Plan flax into your cutting garden for a charming addition to fresh bouquets. They'll give the same airy quality to annual beds and borders.

FLOSSFLOWER
see ageratum

FLOWERING TOBACCO
see nicotiana

FORGET-ME-NOT
see myosotis

FOUR-O'CLOCKS
(mirabilis)

DESCRIPTION: True to their name, these bright, trumpet-shaped flowers appear in late afternoon, usually staying open until the next morning. Colors are lavender, pink, white, salmon, yellow, and violet. Dense foliage gives the 2- to 3-foot plants a shrub-like appearance. Another name is marvel-of-Peru.

SOIL AND LIGHT: Plants thrive best in a sunny location with average, well-drained soil.

PLANTING: Sow when soil is warm, or start indoors about 5 weeks earlier. Space plants about 12 inches apart. Self-sowing is common.

SPECIAL HELPS: One of the more hardy annuals, these are treated like perennials in warm areas. Colorful and quick-growing, they make a good, low hedge. If desired, dig the fleshy tuber-like

roots in the fall; store over winter and set out again the following spring. The resulting plants will probably have larger flowers.

GAILLARDIA
also called blanket flower

DESCRIPTION: Sunset shades of red, yellow, and cream grace these 2- to 3-inch daisy-like flowers. Both single and double, as well as shaggy, ball-shaped flowers, are available. Plants are 14 to 24 inches tall. Common varieties include Tetra Fiesta, Gaiety, Lollipops, and Primrose.

SOIL AND LIGHT: These tough plants can take dry conditions and almost any type of soil. They thrive in full sun.

PLANTING: Seeds are slow to germinate, but plants grow fast and will usually bloom 9 to 10 weeks after planting. Start indoors 4 to 6 weeks before the last frost, or sow outside as soon as the ground can be worked. Seedlings are hardy and can usually survive a late spring frost. Space plants 8 inches apart.

SPECIAL HELPS: Since these annuals like hot, dry conditions, they're a good choice for planting in window boxes, tubs, and other quick-to-dry places. Flowers work well in fresh arrangements.

GAZANIA

DESCRIPTION: Single 4-inch flowers in shades of cream, red, bronze, gold, orange, bright yellow, and pink—often with dark-rimmed contrasting centers—grow on 6- to 12-inch stems. The thick leaves are usually dark green on top and white underneath, often with a felty texture.

SOIL AND LIGHT: Windy, hot and dry days with summer temperatures in the 80s and 90s are the ideal conditions for the gazania. Sandy, light soil is best, and, of course, full sun.

PLANTING: Sow seed outdoors a couple weeks after the last frost, or start inside 5 to 7 weeks earlier. Space plants 8 to 12 inches apart.

SPECIAL HELPS: Gazania are an excellent choice for hot, dry locations; but flowers close at night and on cloudy days, so they don't make good cut flowers.

GERANIUM
(pelargonium)

DESCRIPTION: This versatile group includes nearly 600 different varieties. The most common colors are shades of red, pink, and white. Flowers vary in size, with some strictly individual and others growing in clusters. Foliage may be green or variegated, large-leaved or small. Plants range from 4-inch miniatures to 5-foot "trees." Most commonly found are the zonals, with their bush-like structure; the trailing ivies, with their smaller flowers; and the scenteds, whose leaves smell like peppermint, apple, lemon, or rose when rubbed. Other fragrances are also available. Familiar names to look for are Sprinter, Carefree, Colorcade, and Martha Washington.

SOIL AND LIGHT: Geraniums will grow almost anywhere with minimal care. They like full sun, but will adapt to partial shade. For best results, pot them in well-drained soil that is only of medium richness. They especially like warm days and cool nights.
PLANTING: Seeds can be slow to germinate, so allow at least 4 months to produce a flowering-size plant. Started plants are readily available and should be set about 12 inches apart. Sprinter varieties reach maturity faster than others.
SPECIAL HELPS: Although popular as container plants, geraniums also do well set in the ground. Pin the stems of ivy geraniums to train them to grow close to the ground. In fall, take stem cuttings for winter windowsill plants. Ivy varieties, particularly, do well in hanging baskets.

GLOBE AMARANTH
(gomphrena)

DESCRIPTION: These mounding plants, 6 to 24 inches tall, are continuously covered with ¾-inch clover-like blossoms in red, pink, yellow, purple, and white. Common varieties include Cissy, Buddy, and Rubra.

SOIL AND LIGHT: Plants will tolerate all soil types, but need full sun. They usually stand up well in wind and rain.

PLANTING: Germination takes 12 to 14 days, so start plants indoors 6 to 8 weeks before the last frost. Or, sow seed outside when warm. Set plants 8 to 12 inches apart.
SPECIAL HELPS: Flowers are an unusual addition to fresh and dried arrangements. To dry, cut flowers just as they're fully opened; hang upside down. Since they don't mind wind or dry conditions, plants are a good choice for window boxes and tubs, as well as beds and borders.

GLORIOSA DAISY
see rudbeckia

GODETIA
also called satinflower, farewell-to-spring, clarkia

DESCRIPTION: Satin-petaled and cup-shaped flowers 3 to 5 inches across grow in shades of pink, rose, lilac, red, salmon, and white on 10- to 30-inch stems. Flowers may be single or double; foliage is gray-green and tends to form mounds. Top varieties are Sybil Sherwood Double, Duke of York, Sutton, and Dwarf Gem.
SOIL AND LIGHT: Plants do best in areas where nights are cool and the air is dry. Give them full or partial sun, and light, sandy loam. Soil that is too rich will produce more foliage than flowers.
PLANTING: Sow seeds as soon as the ground can be worked in spring. Later, thin to 6 to 12 inches apart.

Seed may be fall-sown in mild climate areas.

SPECIAL HELPS: These plants are a showy addition to both indoor flower arrangements and garden borders. They adapt well to cool greenhouses. Give tall varieties brush support or staking.

GOMPHRENA
see globe amaranth

GYPSOPHILA
also called annual baby's-breath

DESCRIPTION: Plants are generally larger than perennial forms, but with similar delicate flowers scattered on many-branched stems that range from 15 to 24 inches tall. The finely cut foliage does not detract from the white, pink, or rose flowers. Covent Garden and King of the Market are two popular varieties.
SOIL AND LIGHT: Typical of their name (gypsophila means "chalklover"), these plants do best in poor soil. Adding lime or wood ash from the fireplace will help them in acid soil. Although plants will grow in richer soils, they will not be as sturdy, making them less resistant to wind and rain. Full sun is best.

128

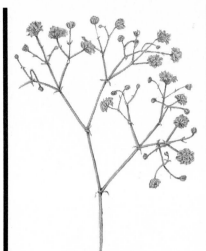

PLANTING: Although it is easiest to buy plants, seed may be sown in mid-winter (in a warm place) for summer flowers. Space plants about 12 inches apart, and try root or stem cuttings to increase your supply.

PLANTING: Save your indoor seed beds for other annuals—these plants grow rapidly when sown outdoors as early as the ground can be worked. Blossoms don't last long, so repeat sowings to ensure a continuous supply of flowers. Space plants 8 to 12 inches apart.

SPECIAL HELPS: Plan a few rows of gypsophila in your cutting garden for a light, airy contrast. Sprays of the tiny starlike flowers also add grace to fresh and dried bouquets.

H

HELIANTHUS
see sunflower

HELICHRYSUM
see strawflower

HELIOTROPE

DESCRIPTION: A Victorian favorite, these 12- to 24-inch plants bear clusters of 6- to 12-inch lilac-like flowers in dark violet, white, or heliotrope blue. Depending on the variety, flowers may be scented. Choose from Marine, Regale, Mme. Bruant, Cherry Pie, or Pacific, among others.

SOIL AND LIGHT: Plants do best in rich, well-drained soil. Give them full sun or light shade, and keep evenly moist.

SPECIAL HELPS: Fragrant as well as colorful, heliotrope can be grown in window boxes, tubs, and borders. Bring the pots indoors, or make cuttings for winter windowsills. Blossoms may be dried for sachets or enjoyed fresh in an old-fashioned bouquet. A native of Peru, heliotrope means "constantly turning face to sun."

HELIPTERUM
see acroclinium

HOLLYHOCK
(alcea rosea)

DESCRIPTION: Two- to six-foot spikes bear single, double, semi-double, and occasionally frilled flowers that are 3 to 4 inches across. Red, rose, pink, and yellow are the most common colors. Some of the variety names are Silver Puff, Majorette, Summer Carnival, Indian Summer, and Triumph Supreme.

SOIL AND LIGHT: Full sun is this annual's only requirement; soil may be of any type.

PLANTING: Start seed indoors 6 to 8 weeks before the last frost, and set outside when night temperatures have warmed. Plants do best when sheltered from the wind and placed 12 to 24 inches apart.

SPECIAL HELPS: Hollyhocks can be annual, biennial, or perennial, depending on their variety and location. They are often suggested as a backdrop for flower beds or as a row of color along fences and walls. But you may want to cut them after the first bloom to encourage another crop of flowers in fall.

I-J

IBERIS
see candytuft

ICE PLANT
(mesembryanthemum)

DESCRIPTION: These creeping 6- to 8-inch plants have dark green, succulent leaves. Foliage sometimes has tiny ice-like flecks, giving the plant its common name. Flowers are daisy-like and usually about ½ inch across in shades of pink, yellow, white, lavender, and red. They close at night and on cloudy days.

SOIL AND LIGHT: These will grow nearly anywhere, and even flourish on dry, rocky banks. They do less well in shady, moist locations.

PLANTING: Start plants indoors about 10 weeks before the last frost is due, or sow directly when the weather is dependably warm. Space seedlings about 2 inches apart. Plants started outdoors will bloom later, but tend to last longer.

SPECIAL HELPS: Rock gardens and window boxes are a natural habitat for these dry-loving plants. They also do well in windy locations.

IMPATIENS
see also balsam

DESCRIPTION: These compact plants—usually 6 to 18 inches tall—mound to cover a wider area. The flat blossoms look like violets and appear all over the plant in shades of pink, red, purple, orange, and white, plus some bicolor varieties. Choose from hybrids

such as Zig-Zag, Elfin, and Imp, or standards such as Glitters and Sultani.

SOIL AND LIGHT: Partial shade is the first choice of these flowering beauties. Rich, moist soil is preferred.

PLANTING: Sow seed indoors 6 to 8 weeks before the last frost is due. When weather warms, set plants outside, but be forewarned that they are quite sensitive to cold. Started plants are usually readily available; they may also be propagated by cuttings.

SPECIAL HELPS: Also known as busy lizzie and patient lucy, this plant has a seed pod that easily breaks and scatters seed at the slightest touch. Pot them in hanging baskets or planters for easy transport to a sunny window in the fall. For bushier plants, pinch back the tips of young plants. Before a killing frost, take some cuttings inside to grow in water during the winter.

K

KOCHIA
see burning bush

L

LANTANA

DESCRIPTION: Lantanas are available in both bushy and trailing varieties. As a stiff-branched shrub, the common lantana averages about 3 feet in height; dwarf varieties are 12 to 18 inches tall. Clusters of tiny flowers appear in pink, yellow, white, red, and bronze. Trailing varieties usually have yellow-centered rosy flowers that grow in clusters.

SOIL AND LIGHT: Both varieties prefer rich, well-drained soil and full sun, although they will tolerate partial shade.

PLANTING: Seeds are slow to germinate and develop, so new plants are more easily propagated by cuttings from established plants. Or, buy nursery-started bedding plants. Space plants 12 to 18 inches apart in the garden.

SPECIAL HELPS: With both bushy and trailing varieties available, you can use lantanas nearly anywhere in the garden—from hanging baskets and tubs, to borders, edgings, and rock gardens. In warmer areas, the trailing variety can be used as a ground cover. You can bring plants inside for the winter, too. Cut them back 6 to 8 weeks before the first fall frost is due, and pot. You can leave them outdoors for several weeks to allow them to adapt to their container.

LARKSPUR
(Consolida regalis)

DESCRIPTION: This old-fashioned favorite is often identified as the annual form of the perennial delphinium. Predominantly known for their spikes of purple or blue flowers, larkspur also comes in shades of rose and white; flowers may be single or double. Plants can either be branching with a flower spike on each stalk, or hyacinth-like with only one large flowering stalk. The foliage is bright green and lacy. Common varieties are usually 3 to 5 feet tall, but a dwarf variety that averages 12 inches is also available. Look for Dark Blue Spire, tall, vigorous Supreme Mixed, and White King All-American winner.

SOIL AND LIGHT: Light, well-drained fertile soil is preferred, but plants adapt to other types. Full sun is best, but plants need a little shade in hot climates.

PLANTING: Larkspur seed can be planted in the late fall or very early spring (as soon as the ground can be worked) because seeds need cool temperatures to germinate. For continuous bloom, do a second planting in 3 weeks. Seedlings are not easy to transplant, but thin them to 8 to 15 inches apart.
SPECIAL HELPS: If you have a wall or fence to conceal, larkspur will cover it with a mass of color. Taller varieties may need staking to help support the flower weight. Keep faded flowers trimmed to encourage later bloom.

LINARIA
also called toadflax

DESCRIPTION: This 9- to 12-inch plant presents a mound of dainty ½-inch flowers that resemble snapdragons in shape. Flowers are mostly bicolor, with reds, yellows, and lavenders predominant. A popular variety is the dwarf Fairy Bouquet which blooms in abundance.
SOIL AND LIGHT: Give these an open sunny position, and they will adapt to nearly any soil type. They do, however, prefer cool summers.
PLANTING: Plants are not heat-resistant, so seed should be sown in the fall or very early spring.

Transplanting is not recommended. Thin seedlings to about 6 inches apart.

SPECIAL HELPS: If possible, give linaria a spot where they can be mass planted to show off their colors. They also make attractive edgings and spots of color in rock gardens. Arrange cut flowers in a small vase for indoor enjoyment.

LINUM
see flax

LOBELIA
(Lobelia erinus)

DESCRIPTION: Both compact and trailing varieties of this popular edging plant are available. Plants grow to 6 inches tall and are covered with ½-inch flowers. Blooms are usually blue, although they may be white, pink, or lavender. Trailing varieties vine up to 2 feet. Foliage tends toward a dark metallic green color with toothed edges. Good edging varieties are Bright Eyes, Crystal Palace, Blue Stone, and Cambridge Blue. For trailing, plant Blue Cascade or Sapphire.
SOIL AND LIGHT: For best results, give lobelia full sun and rich, moist soil. They will adapt to other soil types, but will not flower as lavishly. If summers are hot, give this plant some shade.

PLANTING: Seeds are quite small and often slow to germinate, needing 2 months to reach flowering size. Start seed indoors 8 to 10 weeks before the ground is warm, or buy started plants. Set plants about 6 inches apart.

SPECIAL HELPS: Depending on the variety, lobelia may be used in hanging baskets, window boxes, or borders. The trailing variety is sometimes used as a ground cover. Potted plants may be kept through the winter in a sunny window. After the first blossoms have faded, cut the plant back to encourage a second blooming.

LOVE-IN-A-MIST
see nigella

LOVE-LIES-BLEEDING
see amaranth

LUPINES

DESCRIPTION: Also known as the Texas bluebonnet, this annual is smaller and shorter than perennial forms. The 1- to 3-foot plants branch from the base, and feature spikes of clustered flowers in blue, pink, lavender, yellow, and white. Bicolored forms are also available.
SOIL AND LIGHT: Lupines thrive in the cool temperatures of spring and early summer; they are not heat-resistant. Give them a rich, moist, well-drained soil and plenty of sun. In climates where summers are intensely hot, plant lupines

varieties. Plants range from 6 to 7 inches (dwarfs) up to 2 to 3 feet. All sizes are erect and bushy in nature, with many flowers per plant. A few of the many dwarf double varieties available are Goldie, Bolero, King Tut, and Gypsy. Naughty Marietta is a reliable dwarf single. Taller varieties include Gay Ladies, Toreador, Golden Climax, Golden Jubilee, Senator Dirksen, and Alaska.

SOIL AND LIGHT: Full sun is the only requirement of these hardy plants. They'll adapt to any soil.

MIGNONETTE
(reseda)

DESCRIPTION: Fragrance is the best reason for planting mignonette; the flowers are rather drab, appearing in shades of greenish-yellow to brownish-red on 6- to 12-inch spikes. Plants are 12 to 18 inches tall.

SOIL AND LIGHT: Mignonette prefers fertile soil, but will adapt to other types if kept moist. Partial shade is desirable especially where summers are hot, since these plants flower best when temperatures are on the cool side.

PLANTING: Sow outdoors after the last frost, repeating at 3-week intervals to ensure continuous bloom. Seedlings don't transplant well, so it's risky to replant them when you thin; thin to about 10 inches apart. If they are too crowded, the flowering spikes will not show to their best advantage.

SPECIAL HELPS: Plant mignonette where you can enjoy their strong pleasant fragrance—near the patio or doorstep, underneath an often-opened window, or in pots on the windowsill. And as the blossoms are attractive to bees, they'll help garden pollination.

where they'll get shade for at least half a day.

PLANTING: Plants do not transplant easily, so start them outdoors in early spring. Later, thin to 8 to 10 inches apart. Seed usually needs to be treated with a legume bacteria culture like that used for sweet peas; follow the package directions.

SPECIAL HELPS: Keep faded flowers trimmed, or cut early to enjoy in bouquets.

M

MARIGOLD
(tagetes)

DESCRIPTION: This easy-to-grow annual is known for its flowers of bright orange, yellow, and recently, white and cream. Depending on the variety, flowers may be shaped like a globe, carnation, or mum, and can be either single or double. Foliage is deep green and finely cut. Most have a pungent scent, although this has been bred out in some newer

PLANTING: Sow seed outdoors after the last frost, or start inside about 6 weeks earlier. Started plants are readily available and seedlings are easily transplanted. Give them a chance to develop their full bushiness by spacing 12 to 15 inches apart, depending on the type.

SPECIAL HELPS: Plant marigolds in beds, borders, and tubs—either singly or massed—as well as in vegetable gardens.

MATRICARIA
see feverfew

MATTHIOLA
see stocks

MESEMBRYANTHEMUM
see ice plant

MEXICAN SUNFLOWER
see tithonia

MIRABILIS
see four-o'clocks

MOLUCCELLA
see bells-of-Ireland

MORNING GLORY
see convolvulus

MOSS ROSE
see portulaca

MYOSOTIS
also called forget-me-not

DESCRIPTION: This favorite spring flower may be an annual, biennial, or perennial, depending on the species and the region of the country. Most bloom only in the spring; others may bloom all summer. The small flowers are usually blue, but also may be white or pink. Plants are generally 8 to 12 inches tall and compact in nature. Blue Bird is a reliable annual variety.
SOIL AND LIGHT: As long as temperatures are cool, myosotis will adapt to nearly any soil and either sun or shade.
PLANTING: Seed should be sown in early spring or late fall. Self-sowing is common.
SPECIAL HELPS: This plant is a graceful contrast to spring-flowering bulbs in beds and borders. Use it for indoor arrangements also. Annual varieties of myosotis will often reseed themselves and quickly naturalize a rock garden or woodland setting. They make an especially striking display mixed with English daisies, sweet williams, pansies, or violas.

N

NASTURTIUM
(tropaeolum)

DESCRIPTION: Shiny shield-like leaves and single or double flowers, often with a tart fragrance, identify this annual. It blooms in shades of red, yellow, pink, and white. Bush varieties are usually 8 to 15 inches tall; climbing varieties may reach 6 feet or more. Good double varieties include Cherry Rose and Dwarf Jewel. Dwarf Single is a reliable single form, and Single Climbing is a fine trailer.
SOIL AND LIGHT: A spot with full sun and sandy soil is your best choice for bush-type nasturtiums. Other soils will usually suffice if they are kept dry. Water only if plants become dry enough to droop; too much water will produce all leaves with few flowers. Vining varieties prefer a moist soil and shade from the midday sun.
PLANTING: Seedlings are not easily transplanted, so it's usually simpler to sow seed outdoors after the last frost. Seed should germinate in 8 to 13 days and be of blooming size in 7 to 8 weeks. Thin bush types to about 6 inches and climbers to about 10 inches.
SPECIAL HELPS: If you'd like to have some flowers around the house but don't want to spend much time on their care, nasturtiums may be the answer; they thrive on neglect, including poor soil and little water. Climbers usually want

more water than bush-types; try them on a trellis, fence, or to cover a tree stump. Leaves of both types may be added to salads; they have a taste similar to watercress.

NEMESIA

DESCRIPTION: These compact plants reach about 10 inches in height and bear 3- to 4-inch flower clusters on 2- to 3-foot spikes. The ¾-inch flowers are cuplike and come in shades of yellow, pink, lavender-blue, crimson, and white.
SOIL AND LIGHT: Cool, damp areas of the country are best suited for nemesia, since these plants cannot tolerate heat. They'll thrive in full sun (or partial shade in warm-weather areas) in any kind of soil if it is kept moist. Plants benefit from humus added to the soil.
PLANTING: In early spring, sow seed where plants are to stay, or start them indoors 4 to 6 weeks earlier. Seedlings are delicate, so take extra care if you transplant them. Thin to about 6 inches apart.
SPECIAL HELPS: Nemesia make charming cut flowers. If you don't use them all for bouquets, be sure to cut plants back after the first bloom fades to encourage later flowering. This is also a good time to feed them. Use nemesia as edging plants in the garden.

NEMOPHILA
also called baby-blue-eyes

DESCRIPTION: Clusters of white-centered sky-blue flowers on the tips of delicate stems give this plant its common name. Five rounded petals form a cup shape about 1 inch across. Plants mound in 6- to 8-inch heights, about 12 inches across. Foliage is pale green with a hairy texture.
SOIL AND LIGHT: Sun or partial shade and light, well-drained soil are recommended for nemophila. They'll thrive where soil is kept moist and summer nights are cool. Hot, dry days discourage flowers.
PLANTING: Nemophila is hard to transplant, so it's best to sow seed as early as the ground can be worked, even if it's still 1 or 2 weeks before the last frost is due.
SPECIAL HELPS: Try nemophila as a ground cover or edging around flowering bulbs. They'll also make a good showing in a moist area of a rock garden or display bed. Flowers look nice in cut flower arrangements, but they don't last long.

NICOTIANA
also called flowering or ornamental tobacco

DESCRIPTION: Delicate flowers with a pleasant, though heavy, fragrance characterize this plant. Most varieties bloom only in the evening; newer day-bloomers often are much less fragrant. Clusters of trumpet-shaped blooms appear at the ends of branches; take your pick of red, lavender, pink, rose, chartreuse, or white flowers. Plants are generally 1 to 3 feet tall, although some varieties may reach 5 feet. Leaves are very large with a soft texture and grow mainly at the base of the plant. Try richly-colored Crimson Bedder, Compact Dwarf, White Bedder, day-blooming Daylight, Sensation, or extremely

fragrant Lime Green.
SOIL AND LIGHT: Heat does not hurt these plants, although they prefer partial shade in very warm areas. Full sun is desired elsewhere. Nicotiana tolerate almost all soils.
PLANTING: Seed is very fine and slow to germinate, so you may find it easier to buy started plants. In warm areas, seed may be sown directly into the garden. Space plants about 9 inches apart.
SPECIAL HELPS: Plant nicotiana where you can enjoy the evening fragrance. They look especially attractive when set in front of tall shrubs or perennials.

NIEREMBERGIA
also called cupflower

DESCRIPTION: Dense and spreading in character, these 6-inch mound plants are covered almost continuously with bright violet, cup-shaped flowers. Blooms have a yellow center and measure about an inch across. Purple Robe, a compact, densely blooming variety, is the most widely grown.

SOIL AND LIGHT: For best results, plant in a location that's sunny but not too hot, and where the well-drained, rich soil can be kept moist. In hot areas, give plants some shade and plenty of water.
PLANTING: Start plants indoors 8 to 10 weeks before the last frost; seeds develop slowly so you may wish to buy started plants. Set them about 8 inches apart where they can be sheltered from strong winds.
SPECIAL HELPS: Found wild in Argentina, these plants can be used in rock gardens, window boxes, or edgings. When cut, the flowers make delightful miniature bouquets.

NIGELLA
also called love-in-a-mist

DESCRIPTION: Also called fennel flower and devil-in-a-bush, this 12- to 24-inch plant features very fine pale green foliage and 1½-inch cornflower-like blossoms in blue, rose, pink, purple, or white. The popular variety Persian Jewels has light, feathery foliage.
SOIL AND LIGHT: As long as they get plenty of sun, these plants will tolerate any type of soil.
PLANTING: Seed can be planted in the fall in mild climates, or very early in the spring elsewhere. Seedlings are hard to transplant but should be thinned to about 8 inches apart. Make 2 or 3 plantings about a month apart to increase the blooming period.
SPECIAL HELPS: Flowers are attractive in fresh arrangements, but don't cut them all or you'll miss the large balloon-shaped pods that

follow. The pods, pale green with reddish-brown markings, add a unique touch to dried-flower arrangements. To dry, cut stems when pods mature and hang upside down in a dry, shady place.

O

ORNAMENTAL TOBACCO

see nicotiana

P

PAINTED TONGUE

see salpiglossis

PANSY

(*Viola* sp.)

DESCRIPTION: Face-like markings on large, open flowers characterize this old-fashioned favorite. The five overlapping petals of each flower combine variations of stripes and blotches in shades of purple, blue, yellow, dark rose, and white. Plants average about 8 inches in height and tend to spread out. A host of interesting varieties are available; some of the best known are cardinal-red Alpenglow, large-blossomed white Moon Moth, vigorous Paramount, clear yellow

Coronation Gold, and heat-resistant Imperial Blue.

SOIL AND LIGHT: Plants do best in cool spring weather. Give them full sun and a rich, well-drained, moist soil.

PLANTING: For late spring blossoms, start seed indoors about 10 weeks before planting, or buy started plants. In most areas, seed can be sown in mid- to late summer and the plants kept in a cold frame over the winter for early spring bloom. Space them about 6 to 8 inches apart in the garden.

SPECIAL HELPS: A favorite for edging beds, pansies also make a good show in rock gardens and around spring-flowering bulbs. They adapt well to containers and window boxes. Flowers should be cut to stimulate further blooming; use fresh for charming bouquets. Pinch back young plants to encourage branching. But even with continuous pinching, the plants may look quite leggy and straggly by summer. When this happens, cut back to within 1 or 2 inches of the base and fertilize; or dig out and replace with another low annual. If extra large flowers are desired, allow only four or five flower stalks to develop on each plant.

PELARGONIUM

see geranium

PERIWINKLE

see vinca

PETUNIAS

DESCRIPTION: A number of colors, shapes, and sizes are offered by this popular annual. One main type is classified as multiflora, indicating that it blooms freely. It produces 2- to 3-inch single and double flowers on branching plants 12 to 15 inches high. Many gardeners find that this is the easier type to grow. A second type is classified as grandiflora. These plants are generally about the same height, but bear flowers that measure up to 5 inches across, often ruffled and fringed, and either single or double. Petunias are available in both bush and cascading varieties.

SOIL AND LIGHT: Petunias like at least a half-day of full sun and rich, well-drained soil that is kept on the moist side. For the best display, feed regularly during the summer.

PLANTING: Seeds are small and sometimes hard to start, so most people find it easier to buy started plants. Set plants 8 to 16 inches apart, depending on the variety.

SPECIAL HELPS: Pack petunias into sunny spots in borders, window boxes, hanging baskets, tubs, and planters. To encourage branching, pinch plants back after the first blossoms fade. When the weather turns cold, bring some of the potted plants inside and set them in a sunny window. Good varieties to try are the trailing grandiflora Red Cascade; the hybrid grandifloras Malibu (blue), Happiness (pink), and Sunburst (yellow); and the multiflora hybrids Comanche (red) and Sugar Plum (lilac).

135

PHLOX

DESCRIPTION: Clusters of flowers show well above the foliage on these 15- to 18-inch plants. Dwarf varieties are available in 6- to 8-inch heights. Flowers may be lavender, red, pink, blue, or white; bicolors are sometimes available. Some favorites include vigorous salmon Glamour, dwarf Blue Beauty, and Twinkle.
SOIL AND LIGHT: Almost any well-drained soil is suitable for phlox. Full sun is desirable, although they'll adapt to light shade. Water during dry periods.
PLANTING: Seed should germinate in 8 to 17 days, depending on conditions. Blossoms generally appear about 65 days later. Plant outside after the last frost, or start inside about 5 weeks earlier. Set plants about 6 inches apart.
SPECIAL HELPS: Keep old flowers clipped to encourage further growth. If plants get too straggly, cut back to about 2 inches above ground. In a few weeks, the plants will be covered with vigorous new branches. Use plants in rock gardens, beds, and flower borders.

PINCUSHION FLOWER

see scabiosa

PINKS

(dianthus)

DESCRIPTION: The common name of this annual refers not to the color, but to the fringed (pinked) edges of the flower petals. Many popular varieties do produce pink flowers, but reds, whites, and bicolors also find favor with gardeners. Plants are usually 8 to 12 inches tall. Try scarlet red hybrid Queen of Hearts, white-edged China Doll, or early-flowering Magic Charms for starters.

SOIL AND LIGHT: Full sun and a light, well-drained soil should give you good results. Lime or wood ash is often added to keep the soil alkaline. In dry weather, be sure to water plants regularly—perhaps even daily.
PLANTING: Sow outside after the last frost, or start seed indoors about 7 weeks earlier. Seed should germinate in 6 to 10 days, producing blooming plants in about 3 months. Space seedlings about 8 inches apart. Mature plants tend to be frost-resistant, and may overwinter in moderate-climate areas.
SPECIAL HELPS: Use the shorter varieties for attractive edging plants or in rock gardens. Save the taller ones for borders, flower beds, and massed plantings. Seed forms quickly after flowering, so keep plants trimmed; this also encourages new flower formation. Some pinks are very fragrant, but these are usually the perennial forms.

POPPY

(papaver)

DESCRIPTION: The four most popular varieties feature bright, crinkled flowers on wiry stems above clumps of foliage. Flowers may be single or double, and are often fragrant. Alpine is the shortest, averaging 6 to 10 inches. The others usually range between 1½ and 3 feet. The two perennial types are Iceland and Oriental; Iceland has a wide range of colors, while Oriental poppies have the showiest blooms. Shirley, an annual, is the tamed offspring of the black-centered red poppies common in the fields around Flanders. California poppies are the easiest to grow. A popular Iceland poppy is the vigorous Champagne Bubbles; you'll also have good luck with the Oriental poppies Brilliant Red and Queen Alexandria. Try deep pink Sweet Briar or bicolor Double Donna Shirley poppies. Mission Bells, a double and semi-double poppy, and orange Aurantiaca are popular California poppies.
SOIL AND LIGHT: Poppies require full sun, but will adapt to most soil conditions. Cool, moist weather is

136

best, and wind protection helps preserve the fragile blossoms.

PLANTING: For easier planting, mix the fine seed with sand first. Sow in late fall or very early spring. In areas where summers do not get too hot, make consecutive plantings about 6 weeks apart. Space seedlings 6 to 12 inches apart, but don't try to transplant. Some varieties will self-sow each year.

SPECIAL HELPS: Massed plantings are the most effective way to show off these colorful annuals. To use in bouquets, cut just when the buds start to split open; sear stem ends immediately to conserve their moisture. Keep faded flowers trimmed back.

PORTULACA
also called moss rose or rock moss

DESCRIPTION: This creeping succulent will spread a carpet of brightly colored single and double blossoms over the poorest, driest soil. Foliage is needle-like and usually dark green. Plants are usually only 3 to 6 inches tall. Some of the available types include vigorous, long-blooming Sungalo, colorful Claudia, and double Day Dream.

SOIL AND LIGHT: Full sun and well-drained soil are the only requirements.

PLANTING: Seed is very fine and may be mixed with sand to give better coverage. It needs warm weather to germinate, so sow outdoors after the ground has

warmed. If you want to start earlier, sow indoors in a warm place; they transplant easily and may be thinned, if desired. In most areas plants will self-sow. The flower size and color quality will be diminished the second year, so it's best to start over annually.

SPECIAL HELPS: Rock gardens, planters, and problem areas will support these neglect- and drought-loving plants.

RICINUS
see castor bean

ROCK MOSS
see portulaca

ROCKY MOUNTAIN GARLAND
see clarkia

RUDBECKIA
also called gloriosa daisy or coneflower

DESCRIPTION: Hybridized from the wild black-eyed susans, these plants have similar large, daisy-like flowers on stems 18 to 36 inches tall. Petals are usually shades of yellow, orange, or bronze with brown centers, although one variety has a green center. Some of the common

varieties are bright yellow Golden Daisy, green-centered Irish Eyes, and bicolor Pinwheel.

SOIL AND LIGHT: Rudbeckia are quite undemanding as to soil type. Plant them in full to partial sun and they'll thrive.

PLANTING: Plants are very hardy and can be sown in late fall or very early spring. They are also easy to transplant and will usually self-sow, although the colors of resulting plants may not be as strong. Allow 12 to 18 inches between plants.

SPECIAL HELPS: For the best display, plant in clumps along a fence row or in the back of the flower bed or garden. Flowers are long-lasting in cut arrangements and should be kept trimmed to encourage continuous flowering.

SALPIGLOSSIS
also called painted-tongue

DESCRIPTION: Salpiglossis is also known as velvet flower because of the texture of its petunia-like flowers. They appear in muted shades of pink, purple, yellow, orange, and red covered with an intricate pattern of veining in a contrasting color. Foliage is sparse on the slender-stemmed 2- to 3-foot plants. Bolero is a vigorous variety that bears large quantities of huge blooms. Also try the dwarf-like, bushy Splash and Colorful Emperor.

SOIL AND LIGHT: Plant in a rich, well-drained soil that is kept moist until the plants are mature, after which it can be allowed to dry between waterings. Full sun is preferred, and protection from the wind with added brush supports is advisable.

PLANTING: Plants develop slowly, so it's a good idea to start them indoors 6 to 8 weeks before the last frost. If you don't mind late-blooming plants, wait and sow seed outdoors after the last frost. Space 10 to 12 inches apart.

SPECIAL HELPS: These richly colored and marked flowers make interesting fresh arrangements and good border or background specimens. Pinch back young plants to encourage branching.

SALVIA

DESCRIPTION: Spikes of intense red flowers characterize scarlet sage, a traditional foundation planting. Plants are usually 12 to 30 inches in height, although dwarf varieties may grow from 6 to 10 inches. Foliage is deep green. Among scarlet sage varieties, try scarlet Blaze of Fire; long-blooming Red Blazer; dwarf, early Scarlet Midget; and early-blooming St. John's Fire. Besides red, you now have a choice of pink, white, and blue varieties that are quite adaptable to lightly shaded sites. Also grow Lavender Love, White Fire, or coral Rose Flame.

SOIL AND LIGHT: Salvia needs full sun for at least a half-day. A rich, well-drained soil is best.

PLANTING: Since the seed needs heat to germinate and grows best under controlled temperature conditions, most people find it easiest to buy started plants. Space bedding plants about 12 inches apart in the garden.

SPECIAL HELPS: Salvias usually bloom from July till frost, making them a good choice for nearly every yard spot as well as balcony and patio tubs. Choose plants in a specific height range for the desired location. But be careful in mixing them with other flowers; some colors—especially bright red—can be overpowering. Flower spikes may be cut for drying; cut them at their peak and hang upside down.

SATINFLOWER
see godetia

SCABIOSA
also called pincushion flower

DESCRIPTION: Flowers are sweetly scented, large, and showy, in white or shades of blue, rose, lavender, red, and coral. Long silvery stamens cover the blossoms. Plants are usually 2- to 3-feet tall, with dwarf varieties to 14 inches. Compact Dwarf Double and double Giant Imperial are two top varieties.

SOIL AND LIGHT: Plants will do best when soil is well-prepared and enriched with humus. Water regularly during dry weather. Full sun is preferred.

PLANTING: Seed germinates in 15 to 20 days and should be of blooming size in 3 months. Sow outdoors after all danger of frost, or start inside about 6 weeks earlier. Space plants 8 to 12 inches apart, depending on the variety.

SPECIAL HELPS: Plan these into a mixed bed, or give them a massed spot of their own. Flowers are especially good for fresh bouquets; keep faded ones snipped.

SCHIZANTHUS
see butterfly flower

SEA LAVENDER
see statice

SNAPDRAGON
(antirrhinum)

DESCRIPTION: Plants range from 6-inch miniatures to 3-foot giants. Each features spikes covered with clusters of tubular flowers in an assortment of colors. Some of the hybrids are the popular heat-tolerant Rocket and Topper varieties, and the semi-dwarf Little Darling. Also try the bedding Coronette Mix and Sweetheart. Giant Ruffled Tetra snapdragons produce stocky plants that bloom later than other types, but with larger flowers.

SOIL AND LIGHT: For best results, plant in rich, well-drained soil that receives full to partial sun.

PLANTING: Plant early enough so plants are well established before hot weather. Buy started plants, or start seed indoors 6 to 8 weeks before the last frost. Transplant outdoors as soon as the ground is workable, setting 6 to 12 inches apart (depending on the variety). Growth is not as good if seeds are sown directly in the garden.

SPECIAL HELPS: Rust can be a problem in older varieties, but most of the newly developed ones are rust-resistant. Early pinching will help promote bushier plants. Dwarf varieties are especially good in rock gardens and borders. Larger ones make attractive backgrounds; staking is recommended.

SNOW-ON-THE-MOUNTAIN
see euphorbia

SPIDERPLANT
see cleome

STATICE
(limonium); also called sea lavender and thrift

DESCRIPTION: This 1- to 3-foot plant features a rosette of scalloped leaves that lies flat on the ground.

Stems holding tiny, papery-textured flowers in shades of blue, lavender, rose, white, and yellow rise from this base.

SOIL AND LIGHT: Statice is found naturally in salt meadows, so it does especially well in seaside gardens. Give it full sun. Plants will adapt to most well-drained soils, but they prefer cool weather.

PLANTING: If the seed you have is enclosed in a husk cluster, break it up before planting. Sow outdoors after all danger of frost, or start inside about 7 weeks earlier. Space plants about 10 inches apart.

SPECIAL HELPS: Flowers work well in both fresh and dried arrangements. To dry, cut when flower is fully opened; hang upside down in a shady place. When dried, flowers will last several months.

STOCK
(matthiola)

DESCRIPTION: Plants are 1 to 3 feet tall with attractive foliage and spikes of tiny, delicately scented flowers. Blooms usually are deep blue, but lilac, white, and pink varieties are available. Try the vigorous, large-flowered Giant Imperial, the early-blooming Early Cascade Blend, or the extremely early-blooming Trysomic Seven Weeks.

SOIL AND LIGHT: Cool temperatures and moist, moderately rich soil will satisfy these plants. Give them full sun unless summers are excessively hot—then give them partial shade.

PLANTING: Start early for best results. Sow outdoors as soon as the ground can be worked, or start indoors about 6 weeks earlier. In warm areas, sow seed in the fall.

SPECIAL HELPS: Remember this fragrant flower when planning the beds and borders around your porch, patio, or near the front entry. Cut for indoor enjoyment.

STRAWFLOWER
(helichrysum); also called everlasting

DESCRIPTION: The daisy-like double "flowers" are actually stiff, modified leaves surrounding the true flower in the center. The colorful petals show shades of red, purple, yellow, or white.

SOIL AND LIGHT: Full sun is preferred, and nearly any soil is tolerated if it is kept on the dry side.

PLANTING: Sow outside after the last frost, or start indoors about 6 weeks before. Set plants about 8 inches apart.

SPECIAL HELPS: Flowers hold their color especially well when dried, but may also be used in fresh arrangements. To dry, cut when half open, strip the foliage, and hang upside down in a dry, shady place.

139

SUMMER FORGET-ME-NOT

see anchusa

SUNFLOWER

(helianthus)

DESCRIPTION: Most commonly thought of as the 10-foot giant with single flowers that grow 8 to 14 inches across, sunflowers also come in a 2- to 4-foot variety with 3- to 4-inch single and double flowers. Yellow, orange, and mahogany, and bicolored flowers are available. Popular varieties include Teddy Bear (2 feet), Sungold (5 feet), Dwarf Sungold (2 feet), and Mammoth (10 feet).

SOIL AND LIGHT: Sunflowers will tolerate all soil conditions, although the shorter ones need more moisture. Full sun is required.

PLANTING: Plants develop quickly, so there's no advantage to early indoor starting. Sow outdoors after the last frost. Seedlings may be transplanted, but they'll grow taller and bloom earlier if left alone.

SPECIAL HELPS: Tall varieties often are used for temporary hedges; smaller ones may be planted into borders. Flowers may be cut for indoor arrangements, but be sure to leave some in the garden, as they attract birds. Squirrels like the seeds, and you may even want to save some for yourself.

SWAN RIVER DAISY

(brachycome)

DESCRIPTION: Many fragrant ½- to 1½-inch flowers cover this compact 12-inch plant. Bloom colors include blue, rose, violet, pink, and white.

SOIL AND LIGHT: Full sun and rich, well-drained soil is best, and wind protection is recommended.

PLANTING: Seeds should produce flowering plants in about 6 weeks, but the blooming season is short so plant at weekly intervals starting after the last frost. Space about 6 inches apart.

SPECIAL HELPS: Plants do best where summers are cool. Use them in borders, rock gardens, or movable pots. Flowers are short-stemmed, but make attractive arrangements in small containers. Keep the faded blossoms snipped.

SWEET PEA

(lathyrus)

DESCRIPTION: This old-fashioned favorite has enjoyed increasing popularity with the development of hardier varieties. Most are climbers, stretching as high as 8 feet. Bush types, growing 15 to 30 inches, are also available. The fragrant, bonnet-shaped flowers have ruffled or plain petals in nearly every color. Varieties to try include 12-inch bush Bijou, 30-inch climbing Knee-Hi, heat-resistant Cuthbertson Floribunda, and vigorous Summer Flowering Spencer.

SOIL AND LIGHT: Sweet peas do best in cool temperatures, although breeding has given new varieties more heat resistance. Give them full to partial sun and rich, well-drained soil that is kept moist. A light mulch will help protect roots from heat and dryness.

PLANTING: Soak seed before planting, and check the seed packet to see if they need to be treated with a nitrogen-fixing bacteria. Sow as soon as the ground can be worked. Seed should germinate in 2 to 4 weeks and bloom in 2 months.

SPECIAL HELPS: Although new varieties are more hardy, they also may be less fragrant. Vining types make attractive screens and backdrops, while bush types are good in beds or borders. For continuous bloom, pick all faded flowers.

SWEET-SULTAN

(*Centaurea moschata*)

DESCRIPTION: Pleasantly fragrant, these tassel-like flowers are fluffy and soft, and bloom in shades of

140

yellow, pink, lavender, and white. Plants grow 2 to 3 feet tall with deep green, finely cut foliage. Seeds are usually in mixed color assortments.
SOIL AND LIGHT: Sweet-sultans do well in any soil that receives full sun.
PLANTING: Plants do best in cool weather, so make two sowings about three weeks apart beginning in very early spring.
SPECIAL HELPS: Use flowers in fresh arrangements, or plant in mixed borders. Keep faded flowers snipped to encourage bloom.

SWEET WILLIAM
(dianthus)

DESCRIPTION: Often grown as a biennial, this compact plant may be as short as 4 inches or as tall as 2 feet. Flowers are in flat clusters in shades of red, purple, pink, and white. Reliable varieties include scarlet-red Queen of Hearts, 4-inch Wee Willie, quick-blooming Red Monarch, and richly colored Pink Beauty.
SOIL AND LIGHT: Full sun and moist, light soil are recommended.
PLANTING: Buy started plants, or sow seed indoors about 7 weeks before the last frost. Space 8 to 10 inches apart. In milder climates, sow seed in late summer and cover the seedlings with a layer of mulch during the winter. Plants started in this manner will bloom much earlier than spring-sown plants. Plants usually bloom a second summer where winters aren't severe.
SPECIAL HELPS: Flowers usually aren't fragrant, but they add much color to borders and rock gardens.

T

TAHOKA DAISY
(*Machaeranthera tanacetifolia*)

DESCRIPTION: These bushy 1- to 2-foot plants have wispy, fernlike foliage and long-lasting, yellow-centered, blue-violet flowers.
SOIL AND LIGHT: Plants resist drought and will tolerate all soil types. Give them full to partial sun.
PLANTING: Seeds need 4 months to produce flowering plants, so they do best in warm climates. Sow in very early spring, or start indoors 6 to 8 weeks earlier. Space plants about 6 inches apart.
SPECIAL HELPS: Blooming continuously from midsummer till frost, these plants are a good choice for borders and beds in areas where the warm season is extended. Flowers also keep well in fresh arrangements.

THRIFT
see statice

TITHONIA
also called Mexican sunflower

DESCRIPTION: Also called the "golden flower of the Incas," this bushy 4- to 6-foot plant features red-orange flowers that are gold on the underside. Foliage is gray-green and velvety in texture. Orange-red Torch is a common variety.

SOIL AND LIGHT: Resisting both drought and heat, plants need full sun and will adapt to any soil.

PLANTING: Plants grow rapidly but often need 4 months to flower. Sow after the last frost or start indoors about 5 weeks earlier. Set about 24 inches apart.
SPECIAL HELPS: Since they're bushy in habit, they make an excellent temporary hedge, especially in hot, dry areas. Flowers last well if they're cut in the bud, seared, and placed in warm water.

TOADFLAX
see linaria

TORENIA
also called wishbone flower

DESCRIPTION: This 1-foot plant displays trumpetlike flowers with flattened enlarged lips and blotches of blues, purples, yellows, and whites. The common name comes from the appearance of the crossed stamens. Foliage is dark green.
SOIL AND LIGHT: Torenia thrive in partial shade, and warm, moist soil.
PLANTING: Seed is very fine and germinates slowly, but plants grow quickly. Sow in the garden after the last frost, or start inside about 10 weeks earlier. Set plants about 8 inches apart. In warm areas, torenia are often self-sowing.

141

SPECIAL HELPS: Torenia are best suited to tropical and subtropical areas. Cuttings make unusual houseplants on a sunny windowsill in any climate.

TRACHYMENE
see blue lace flower

V

VERBENA

DESCRIPTION: Both a creeping type and an upright mounding type are available. Each bears flat clusters of tiny, fragrant flowers in many colors, usually with white centers. Heights range from 6 to 15 inches. Look for 8-inch Dwarf Sparkle, bush-type Spirit of '76, early-blooming Ideal Florist, and scarlet-flowered Blaze.

SOIL AND LIGHT: Verbenas like full sun and rich, well-drained soil. Most are heat-resistant.
PLANTING: Seeds need two weeks to germinate, so sow outdoors after the last frost, or start inside three months earlier. Started plants are generally available. Space 6 to 12 inches apart.
SPECIAL HELPS: Creeping varieties are especially good ground covers as well as potted specimens in window boxes and hanging baskets. Use others in rock gardens. Keep faded flowers snipped.

VINCA
also called periwinkle

DESCRIPTION: Shiny green leaves and five-petaled open flowers in shades of blue, pink, and white characterize this bushy, 1- to 2-foot plant. Foliage also may be a variegated green and white. Bush types are usually about 1½ feet tall. Annual varieties include dwarf bedding Little Pinkie, Little Blanche, and Little Bright Eye; ground cover Polka Dot; and the standard bush varieties.
SOIL AND LIGHT: Vinca likes full sun if soil is kept moist. In hot areas, give plants some shade. Any soil will be tolerated, but a rich type is preferred.
PLANTING: Seeds are slow to germinate; start indoors 3 months before the last frost, or buy started plants. Set 8 to 10 inches apart.
SPECIAL HELPS: Borders, pots, tubs, and window boxes are all good spots for vinca. Shear plants if growth lags. Plants are perennial in warm areas, where they make a good ground cover.

W

WAX BEGONIA
see begonia

WINGED EVERLASTING
see ammobium

Z

ZINNIA

DESCRIPTION: This favorite annual comes in a variety of heights, colors, and flower shapes. The tallest may reach 3 to 4 feet, while the shortest are only 6 to 12 inches. Among the many types are 2-foot Scarlet Ruffles; 2½-foot green-flowering Envy; 3-foot large-blooming State Fair; cactus-flowered Blaze and Snow-Time; and miniature Thumbelina, Pink Buttons, and Cherry Buttons.
SOIL AND LIGHT: Zinnias like hot weather and full sun.
PLANTING: Sow seed outdoors when temperatures are warm; they should germinate in 4 to 5 days and grow quickly. Space 6 to 12 inches apart, depending on the type.
SPECIAL HELPS: There's a size and flower shape for nearly every sunny spot. Remove faded flowers.

Bright-colored portulaca thrives in dry, sunny spots, and tolerates even the poorest soil.

143

The Wonder of Roses

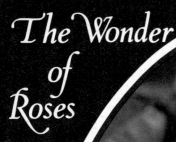

Unchallenged elegance, pure radiance, thorned vitality, and delicate petals simulating silk and satin make the rose the unequaled "Queen of the Garden Flowers." No other flower gives such an array of shape, size, fragrance, and color.

More than any of the world's flowers, the rose has captured the esteem of man and captivated the hearts and souls of all. No other flower has so magnificently passed the tests of time. No other flower so beautifully says, "I love you."

Throughout history, no flower has been so loved by man, so revered, so renowned, or so admired as the rose. It is older than the human hands that first drew pictures of it; fossils of roses from our Northwest date back 35 million years. The rose apparently originated in Central Asia about 60 million years ago, spreading over the entire northern hemisphere (no wild roses have ever been found to grow below the equator). Five thousand years ago, the Chinese appreciated its value and cultivated it widely, as have many other past civilizations.

Ancient history is filled with references to the rose. It is said to have grown in the Garden of Eden, ancient Persia, and the Hanging Gardens of Babylon. Frescoes with roses have been found, some dating back to 1,600 B.C. Cleopatra welcomed Marc Antony in a room filled with rose petals, and legend says that Nero once spent the equivalent of $150,000 for roses to use at a party. Emperor Heliogabalus is reputed to have had so many rose petals in one room that his guests suffocated in them.

In ancient Greece and other countries, the rose had a powerful mystique. The symbol of the city Rhodes was this revered flower, which still grows in abundance on that island today.

The Romans loved roses in a more physical way, using them in candy, wine, pudding, garlands, and rose water. For them it became a symbol of debauchery and secrecy—the origin of the term "sub rosa." Rose growing was a profitable living in pre-Christian Italy, and the Romans also imported many cut roses from Egypt.

In Greece and Rome, the rose was the flower of Aphrodite (Venus in Rome), the goddess of love and beauty. Even today, the rose characterizes womanly perfection and the mysteries of love.

Early historians, scientists, and men of the arts wrote of its beauty and charm. During the Middle Ages, the rose became valued for extracts used in various medicines and ointments. Its petals have been used for potpourri and its hips as a source of vitamin C.

Early on, the rose was an intricate part of the Christian religion. Chris-tians used roses to symbolize the Trinity, chose the white rose for the Virgin Mary, and gave its name to the rosary. A legend claims the brier rose sprang from Christ's blood as he wore the crown of thorns. The Vatican used the rose as a model for a papal award given to men who had done a service for the Church. The rose's petalled shape contributed to the magnificent stained glass windows in many cathedrals.

Soldiers throughout history have followed banners decorated with the rose. In his epic work, the *Iliad,* Homer tells us that the rose adorned the shield of Achilles and the helmet of Hector. A well-known historical event, England's War of the Roses, started in 1455 when the house of Lancaster feuded with the house of York. The red rose of Lancaster *(R. gallica)* and the white rose of York *(R. alba)* soon became the symbols of this war that ended in 1486 when Princess Elizabeth of York married Henry Tudor, a Lancastrian. In 1551, the red and white, two-tone rose, York and Lancaster *(R. damascena versicolor),* was so named to memorialize the war.

No flower is more steeped in folklore and legend than the rose. In the United States, the American Indians tell several tales about the Cherokee rose and its origins. The Grant rose, which has a heavy and unpleasant odor, is said to have sprung from the blood of a Mrs. Grant, a Florida pioneer who was killed by Seminole Indians during an uprising. Columbus reportedly picked up a rose bush floating on the water the day before he discovered America in 1492, and the Virginians say their rose will die if transplanted to foreign shores.

The perfect flower of the rose has influenced fashion, interior design, and architecture. Sculptors, artists, and craftsmen have used it more than any flower; the most popular bloom adorning silver, china, and wallpaper is the rose. The rose has contributed its pure beauty to coats of arms, awards, currency, coins (some dating to Asia in 4,000 B.C.), emblems, medals, and stamps of some 42 countries. Four states, the District of Columbia, and England have chosen the rose as their official flower.

Roses have been immortalized in the arts for centuries. The earliest known painting of a rose dates to a 16th-century-B.C. rendition of *R. gallica.* Medieval tapestries are adorned with roses, and for Renaissance and impressionist artists, the rose was a favorite subject.

Poets and playwrights have used the rose in their romantic language of love. Sappho, the Greek poetess, first named the rose the "Queen of Flowers" in 600 B.C. Shakespeare, Omar Khayyam, Gertrude Stein, Robert Burns, and countless others have glorified the rose. Composers and balladeers have given the world thousands of songs romanticizing this most precious of flowers. Children reading "Alice in Wonderland" or "Beauty and the Beast" learn early of the role of roses in tradition and folklore.

Kings, queens, and presidents have long been associated with the rose. Legendary King Midas is said to have grown roses, as did Alexander the Great. In 1272, Edward I used the rose as a badge. Henry IV chose the red rose as his symbol; Queen Elizabeth placed the white rose on her banner. George Washington grew roses at his home; and after Franklin Roosevelt died, members of Congress wore white roses in mourning.

Modern history will long remember the story of Peace, hybridized by Meilland in France during the early days of World War II. He managed to ship budwood to the United States on the last plane before the fall of France in 1940. Bouquets of Peace were presented to delegates of 50 nations at the first U.N. conference in San Francisco—the day a truce was signed in Europe. The following August, on the day Peace was announced as an All-America Rose Selections (AARS) award winner, a cease-fire with Japan was signed.

Cut roses have always been used to mark special moments. A bouquet of red roses on Valentine's Day says, "I love you," and many a bride walks down the aisle with a bouquet of pure white roses.

Men have revered the rose so much they have named their children, their homes, and their colleges for it. This flower is the ultimate in beauty and perfection—this is the charisma and wonder of roses.

145

Eglantine, named for the flower of poets, was the 19th-century literary hostess who rewarded her writers with a gold rose.

The Eglantine or sweetbrier rose, Rosa eglanteria, with its apple-scented foliage, is the wild rose of lyric and legend still growing in gardens old and new.

146

The History of the Rose

The basic ancestor of all modern roses is *Rosa gallica,* the French rose, the oldest known rose and one that once bloomed over the entire Mediterranean area. Its origins are unknown. From *R. gallica* came *R. damascena,* the damask rose, whose well-known fragrance has been a part of rose history since it first appeared about 500 B.C. Autumn damask, *R. damascena semperflorens,* thrilled Romans about the time of Christ because it was the first to bloom twice a year. *R. alba,* a cross of *R. damascena* and *R. canina,* dates to before the second century.

After the fall of the Roman Empire and before the Renaissance, the history of the rose is incomplete and clouded. The Christians of the Middle Ages, unlike their earlier counterparts who shunned the rose because it reminded them of pagan Rome, kept the rose alive in their gardens and in the symbolism of their religious beliefs.

Once considered an ancient rose, the cabbage rose, *Rosa centifolia,* is now thought to be a product of 17th-century Dutch rose growers. Its exact background is not known but is probably a complex hybrid of many ancient roses, including the gallicas, damasks, and albas. Its most famous sport is *R. centifolia muscosa,* the moss rose, which appeared about 1700 and is still grown and used in hybridizing.

A revolution in rose growing took place in Europe in the late 18th and early 19th centuries with the importation from the Orient of *R. chinensis,* the China rose and its close relative, *R. odorata,* the tea rose. Laying the foundation for today's roses, they exhibited continuous repeat bloom, a phenomenon then unknown in Europe. The foliage of the Chinas is almost evergreen; that of the tea rose is mildew-resistant. The most unfortunate characteristic the tea rose bestows upon its descendants is a lack of hardiness.

The China rose has also been called the Bengal rose because in 1789 it was found growing in Calcutta by a sea captain who afterward took a plant home to England.

The Empress Josephine did more to popularize and foster rose growing and hybridizing than anyone of her time. An ardent lover of the rose, she started a rose renaissance by attempting to grow every rose known to man in her garden at Malmaison. In the ten years between 1804 and 1814, she collected 250 different roses—gallicas, centifolias, moss roses, damasks, and Chinas. The reputation of this garden spread across Europe, igniting an interest that would eventually lead to the birth of the modern roses.

Pierre-Joseph Redouté, the Raphael of the rose, created exquisitely detailed watercolors of the roses in Josephine's garden. His work "Les Roses" is an unsurpassed reference work still used today.

The portlands were a new class of rose that came into existence about 1800, probably derived from a cross of the autumn damask with the China rose and *R. gallica.* Named for the Duchess of Portland, it was one of the first good garden hybrids and one of the first to show repeat bloom. Also known as the damask perpetuals, the portlands remained popular until the hybrid perpetual was introduced almost 40 years later.

Rosa x borboniana, the bourbon rose, was brought to Europe in 1817 from the island of Réunion (Bourbon) in the Indian Ocean. Its background is uncertain, but it is probably a natural hybrid of *R. chinensis* and *R. damascena semperflorens* (autumn damask). The bourbon rose quickly became the most popular rose of the time because of its recurrent bloom and because it was one of the first to combine the best of both the European and Oriental roses. The original bourbon, now lost, was a bright pink; one of its hybrids is a primary source of red in today's roses.

Other plants that arose from the Chinas and European roses were called the hybrid Chinas. Unlike their contemporaries, the bourbons, the hybrid Chinas were very tall and did not exhibit repeat bloom.

The American contribution to rose history is *R. noisettiana,* called the noisette rose, a cross between *R. moschata* and *R. chinensis* made by Champneys in Charleston, S.C., in 1812. Seedlings of it were sent to France by Noisette, whose family raised it and gave the new rose its name. Typical noisettes are usually tender, vigorous climbers or very bushy plants.

The line of modern roses began in 1838 with the introduction of the hybrid perpetual rose. A hybrid it truly was, for it had in it the blood of almost every rose known at that time—bourbons, damasks, Chinas, portlands, teas, and noisettes. The plants were extremely hardy; the flowers, large and very fragrant. Unfortunately, the bloom was not perpetual, but it was more frequent than other roses of the day. Hybrid perpetuals reached their height of popularity during the Victorian era in England, and, sad to say, most have disappeared from the scene, having given way to the hybrid teas and their more dependable repeat blooming cycle.

The beginning of a new era occurred in 1867 with the introduction of La France, the first hybrid tea. This crossing of a tea rose with a hybrid perpetual happened by chance in the garden of J. B. Guillot in France. The new roses were of a neater growing habit than the hybrid perpetuals, plus they were definitely more everblooming.

By the end of the 19th century, all the elements of the modern rose were present but one—there was no attractive yellow rose. In 1900, after 13 years of trying, Pernet Ducher introduced Soleil d'Or, a cross between a hybrid perpetual and persian yellow, a form of *R. foetida.* A range of colors never known before in modern roses came into being—gold, copper, orange, apricot. For 30 years, these roses formed a separate class known as the pernetianas, now merged with the hybrid teas.

Unfortunately, bad characteristics accompanied the good; with the new colors came foliage susceptible to disease and plants unable to withstand pruning. However, some of these faults gradually have been bred out.

The new hybrids resisted cold weather but had weak and spindly roots and no vigor. Grafting onto wild rose roots—especially *R. multiflora,* the Japanese rose, which had been

147

brought to Europe from the Orient prior to 1868—helped to solve the problem.

Climbers are a category rather than a class of rose. The first of the rambler type was Crimson Rambler (1893). Many ramblers grown today were produced from *R. wichuraiana* (1891); others descend from *R. multiflora*. Large-flowered types are sports of bush roses or have wide and varied parentage, with many recent kinds coming from *R. kordesi* (1952). The hybrid musks, introduced in the 1920s, are hardy shrubs and moderate climbers that are crosses between noisettes and *R. multiflora* ramblers.

In 1862, a famous French nurseryman and rose grower, Jean Sisley, received seeds of *R. multiflora*, which he grew and crossed with the Dwarf Pink China *(R. chinensis),* producing a new class of roses known today as the polyantha. The first of these low-growing plants, smothered in clusters of small (one-inch) flowers, were Paquerette (1875) and Mignonette (1880).

In the beginning of the 20th century, a Danish rose breeder, Poulsen, crossed the polyantha and the hybrid tea and produced what is now known as the floribunda. Else Poulsen was the first of these new roses (1924) and, as the name implies, was covered with an abundance of flowers. From its hybrid tea parent, the rose inherited its height and long-cutting stems, characteristics that created a stir in rose circles.

In 1954, the grandiflora class was created for the rose, Queen Elizabeth, a cross between the hybrid tea and the floribunda. Grandifloras are taller and hardier than hybrid teas, with clusters of flowers exhibiting the classic hybrid tea forms, fragrance, and long-cutting stems.

The popular miniature rose of this century derives from *R. chinensis minima (R. rouletti),* the fairy rose that reached Europe in 1815 from the island of Mauritius in the Indian Ocean. For some unknown reason, it disappeared and was thought lost until a rose of its type was found growing in a window box in Switzerland in the 1920s. Recent breeding has produced many new varieties of this tiny favorite by crossing it with both polyanthas and floribundas, also descended from the China strain. These new varieties, though small, are just as hardy and colorful as their taller cousins.

Bahia shows its prizewinning style with exuberant displays of ruffled, orange-red flowers.

149

Roses' Role in the Garden

If your garden is bathed in at least six hours of sun a day, you should find a place in it for roses. Used alone or intermingled with other plants, the rose is unsurpassed in beauty and abundance of flowers.

No room for a formal rose garden? Don't worry. Roses don't need a special place for themselves but can be dotted here and there in many parts of the landscape. Shrub roses form the perfect backdrop for lower-growing plants in the border. Try them and floribundas, instead of other, more commonly used flowering material. You'll be pleased with the long season of colorful results.

Try roses in the perennial bed to bring a continuity of color from one blooming season to another. Low-growing floribundas or miniature roses are sensational finishing touches as edgings to perennial or shrub borders. Or mingle roses with bright annuals for a full season of color.

A bare slope can become a bank of flowers with roses as a ground cover. There's no more colorful way to bring life and beauty to dull spaces, to prevent erosion, or to smother weeds. If a sun-loving ground cover is what you need, try Max Graf, *Rosa wichuraiana,* Sea Foam, the miniature Red Cascade, or one of the ramblers. Many of these will root along their canes as they sprawl, making them seem more like vines than roses.

Imagine long slender buds gradually unfolding into exquisite, high-centered flowers whose perfectly arranged petals glisten in the morning dew. Imagine watching this miracle of nature while starting the day over a cup of coffee. Imagine resting at twilight watching the roses reflect the brilliance of the sunset. Roses not only enhance the beauty of the garden, they also enhance the view from within your home, so select their location carefully, with both places in mind at planting time.

No cut flower is more loved than the rose. Why not use your rose garden as a source of long-stemmed beauties for home or office bouquets and arrangements? The flowers' fragrance will fill and enrich the air of garden or home.

You don't need a lot of room to create beauty. Roses can be effective even in small places—surrounding the base of a flag pole, accenting a mailbox, decorating an outdoor light. Rock gardens are ideal spots for small polyanthas, floribundas, and especially minis, welcoming the season-long color so often lacking in this type of garden.

A traditional rose arbor, *opposite,* remains the perfect choice for a sun-filled garden. Both breezy and romantic, the lath shelter offers some shade itself; when embellished with a variety of climbers, it can be an old-fashioned focal point in the garden. Cautious gardeners cover the lathing with hardware cloth to protect the blooms from wind, rain, or hail damage.

The use of climbers extends far beyond the rose arbor. Train them along a split rail or picket fence to brighten up the wood and curve the straight lines. Espalier them against the side of a stockade fence or the wall of the house. Climbers can cover eaves and outline windows and doors, adding graceful color to the outside of the home and softening hard corners. Let climbing roses ramble up posts, cover old tree stumps, or spill over from the tops of stone walls.

Some climbers grow tall and erect: perfect for trellises, arches, and pergolas. Handel, Coral Dawn, and many of the Kordesi shrubs are among these pillar roses that also may be used in rose beds to break the monotonous pattern plants the same height can produce, if they are planted alone.

Roses are being used more and more in landscape design to define curves and soften harsh, modern lines. An informal grouping of roses can brighten up a corner of the garden that would otherwise receive little attention.

Tree roses bring needed height and accent to the garden. They may be used as formal specimens or underplanted with floribundas or annuals for a more informal look. If you plant them against a wall of a contrasting color, the beauty and form of the tree rose will stand out.

Plant roses in unlikely places, like along the driveway or behind the garage. Then collect their petals to make candy, wine, sachets, and potpourri.

If room permits, a formal rose garden is most striking. The shape is up to you and your imagination and may be round, square, rectangular, triangular. Keep it simple and it will be very dramatic. Edge it with boxwood, teucrium, annuals, or miniature roses, and use a statue, pottery, a pool, a fountain, or a tree rose as a focal point. Border the formal garden with evergreens, place it against a simple background, trim it with spring bulbs, and your picture is framed.

Miniature roses are playing a new and important role in the garden scene. Plant them in drifts to enhance the vista from the living areas; use them in mass instead of bedding plants. Children in your family? Give them a few plants and watch them thrill to cutting flowers from plants their size for friends, teacher, or grandmother. It's also one of the best ways to get them interested in gardening at an early age.

Using Roses

Barriers can be beautiful when they're alive and clothed with the constant color of roses. If a tall privacy screen is what you need to keep out intruders or block the view of motorists, neighbors, and nearby buildings, plant a hedge of shrub roses. All this and beauty, too—no other hedge can even begin to compete.

Plant a low-growing hedge of floribundas, polyanthas, or miniature roses to separate the patio from the lawn, creating a strip of color that will contrast with the sea of green. Their dense habit of growth makes them an ideal choice for framing the path to the front door, paralleling the driveway, or making a mark between your property and the sidewalk strollers. A hedge of roses between you and your next door neighbor is more attractive than a fence and has the advantage of being equally beautiful from both sides.

Unless your property is extremely large, avoid planting living hedges of *Rosa multiflora,* which become much too large and hard to control.

Nor is a hedge the place for a variety of colors. Stick to the planting of the same variety or at least varieties of the same color and size.

Roses for hedging purposes should be planted closer together than normal to ensure dense, floriferous growth. When they are lining paths or sidewalks, be sure to set them back far enough to protect passersby from thorny branches. Two to three feet back from the walkway is an acceptable distance. To insure uniform color and height, don't mix varieties in a hedge.

Outline your lawn with the beauty of F. J. Grootendorst. Dense and thorny, it helps to detour wandering pets.

A hedge of white floribundas, like Saratoga, extends a gracious invitation to wander down the garden path and beyond.

153

Using Roses

Roses at the entryway to a home are a cheery way to say, "Welcome" and "Come in." Whether it be one large plant or several smaller bushes, roses teamed with evergreens at the front door outline an inviting portico.

For an informal, asymmetrical look to your entryway, place a tree rose on only one side of the front door. Complement it with smaller-growing roses on the opposite side.

If you have a front porch or a back deck, let roses tie your garden to the house. Climbers can sprawl across the roof or overhang, spilling over into the outdoor living area, while lower levels can be filled with color from bush roses.

If slopes or large areas around your home are carpeted with evergreen ground covers, mix roses in with them to break up the single color and add a change in texture.

If you have a garden gate, spark it up with a planting of roses. Your family and friends will pass by and admire it every day.

The spot where the driveway swings into the street is ideal for a welcoming group of roses. Plant it with white or other light-colored roses, and it will stand out at night. A small brick wall and a spotlight will finish off the entrance planting.

Line a walk with a row or two of roses—a perfect path to stroll along. The bordering may be in a straight line or, for a more informal look, in scallops or gentle curves. Use one variety or choose two whose colors complement each other. In a two-deep border, the plants may be of the same height. Or place a low-grower (like Accent) along the walk, backed up by one that grows taller (like Sunsprite).

Tree roses are also effective lining a walk. Standing straight and tall, they give the path direction. To tone down their stiffness, combine them with mounds of lower-growing roses, annuals or perennials, or both. Or scatter them here and there for a change of pace.

Steps to the house or from one level of the garden to another are more than just useful when roses

Climbing Golden Showers creates an alluring archway of yellow.

highlight them with color. If the ground is level around steps leading to the front or back door, deck, or gazebo, plant taller roses at the rear and shorter ones at the front to follow the line. If the ground slopes with the steps, choose roses of the same height to create a wave of color. Sea Foam is a sight to behold, spilling its flowers over the ground and the steps.

Brighten a dark retaining wall by planting climbers atop it and letting them hang over. Train them down and help keep them in place by pegging the canes to the wall. For summer-long color, be sure to choose one of the everblooming varieties.

If you're building a brick or stone wall around your property or patio or next to your driveway, allow room to plant roses. Red Cascade, a climbing miniature, will be spectacular and graceful and will not obstruct the view.

Garden by the sea? Roses tolerate drying winds and salt spray. Those

that do best are the species and shrub roses: they are vigorous, easy to care for, and thrive in sandy soil.

Trailing roses such as Max Graf, *Rosa wichuraiana*, or the hybrids of *Rosa rugosa* are perfect scrambling over ledges, holding sand dunes in place, or flanking steps to the beach.

Combine them with other seaside plants like bayberry, juniper, and pine to create irregular drifts of richly textured and contrasting foliage. Because these roses grow dense and thorny, they provide protection from trespassers along property lines.

Every home has the same problem—hiding eyesores like gas tanks and trash receptacles. A rosy solution is to place a trellis in front of the area and let climbers do the screening job. Planted in this manner, climbers will make taking out the trash a more pleasant burden. One or two shrub roses will also substitute nicely and be just as attractive.

And if you have a bare, unsightly, hard-to-plant slope, use miniatures as a hardy ground cover.

154

Bordering this walk with color are Sonoma, left, a salmon-pink floribunda, and Medallion, a hybrid tea of rich apricot.

Using Roses

Planting beds overflowing with the richness of roses can highlight any segment of the home or garden. When designing planting beds, place them where they will catch and hold the eye. Their uses are endless, from emphasizing the good features of a garden or house to camouflaging nearby eyesores.

Rose beds need only to be in sun and within reach of the garden hose. If possible, keep them away from competing large trees and shrubs. Soil near the foundation of the house is often dry because eaves and overhangs prevent rainwater from hitting it, so keep this in mind and plan to supplement natural moisture.

The shape of rose beds is up to your taste, ingenuity, and the land available to you. Formal beds blend best with period architecture; informal beds are in keeping with the more modern design of today's homes. Allow the beds to follow the lines of the house or curve them to break rigidity. So long as space isn't limited, place two or three rows of roses in your beds, particularly freestanding ones. Any less, and the resulting effect will be skimpy; any more, and it will be difficult to work or view the roses in the middle of the planting. There may be space for only one row of roses against the wall of a house or fence, but the background will still make it a startling sight.

To keep the colors from appearing spotty, plant varieties in pairs or trios.

When you use more than one variety, keep your eye on color harmony and place plants accordingly. Also, keep in mind the color of the wall or the fence the bed may be against, and choose roses whose hues will best stand out against it.

Height is another factor that must be considered when designing rose beds. If beds are planted against a backdrop, be sure to place the taller varieties in the back and work down to the shorter varieties in front. In freestanding rose beds, place the taller varieties toward the center so there will be an even view from all sides.

Planting beds around the house will dress it up and show everyone how much you care for the beautiful things in life. High traffic areas (the corners of a garage or the path to a patio) merit special attention and should be spotted with roses, if only a few. Your friends will do a double take when they walk by the luxurious blooms.

Just a couple of rose bushes can make the back or side door inviting. And with the plants so close to the house, it's easy to reach out and snip a few blooms for the guest room to make your visitors feel equally welcome inside.

Use a bed of roses to enliven a narrow strip of land between driveway and fence. Espalier climbers along the fence, or plant one or two tall tree roses. Lower-growing roses can be placed in front and the bed edged with minis or annuals. The fence will be turned into a wall of beautiful color.

Garden sheds storing tools, bicycles, furniture, and the like are often stark and unattractive. They needn't be. Transform them into rose-covered "cottages" by planting informal beds of roses around their perimeters. Soon after, you'll be rewarded with a tapestry of flowers that will brighten even the ugliest of buildings. This is also a good way to perk up a dull neighborhood.

First Prize and Smoky fill a corner.

Blooms of red Pharaoh contrast with salmon-pink of Laura.

Blue violas, assorted roses, and pots of gay petunias and geraniums give vertical color, interest, and life to a fence.

Using Roses

Roses naturally imply fragrance. Lovely to look at and lovely to smell, roses are perfect in beds near patios and terraces. But not all roses are fragrant, and some are much more so than others, so check descriptions carefully before buying roses of any kind.

If drainage is a problem in your area (and even if it isn't), raised beds are most attractive and come with built-in finished edging. For an informal, casual, and natural look, design them in flowing curves. Add a bench or two along the bed where you can sit and reap pleasure from your plantings.

When laying out planting beds, be sure to make provisions for paths in between them, whether of grass, brick, gravel, flagstone, or other paving material. Make paths wide enough so garden equipment such as lawnmowers and wheelbarrows will fit through the beds comfortably. Set the rose bushes far enough back from the edge of the beds so they do not entangle visitors (two feet is a good rule of thumb for most roses). Within the beds, rose plants are displayed most effectively when they are staggered within the rows, rather than lined up straight like a rank of toy soldiers.

Sit back on your terrace, relax, and enjoy the sight and fragrance of luminescent pink Electron and golden El Dorado.

Plant hybrid teas, like Secret Love, along a walk or drive, and enjoy the individual flowers as you stroll by each day.

Movable Roses

Rose gardening using containers reflects the movable and changeable ways and whims of today's society. Portable rose planters are not only a decorative addition to any part of the outdoor living area, they are also a perfect way to change the look of the landscape as quickly as you change your mind.

Movable roses extend the scope and possibilities for gardening spots. Wide paths and walkways can be highlighted with tubs of roses spotted here and there along them. If you have steps leading up to the front or back door, place a pot of roses on each tread to bring it to life.

Dress up windows with boxes of miniature roses. Rather than plant the roses directly into a soil-filled window box, fill the box with individual flower pots of minis. In that way, the roses can be easily moved indoors in winter or replaced quickly if something goes awry.

Patios, decks, and terraces have become favorite spots for entertaining and relaxing on warm summer days and evenings. Add to the pleasure of these moments with planters teeming with the color and fragrance of roses, such as the bicolor Snowfire and the orange-red Gypsy, *right.* Or let containers dress up a porch.

Brick or paved areas around swimming pools are often filled with lounge chairs and tables—but no color. Bring beauty right down to the water's edge with container planters of your favorite roses.

If you have a spot to hang a basket, fill it with miniature roses for a continuous display of summer color (and then move the basket indoors for the winter). The best varieties for baskets are Red Cascade, Green Ice, and Sugar Elf. Let their flowers cascade from lamp posts, tree limbs, gutters, overhangs, and brackets attached to fences or house.

If you have the space, grow movable roses in an out-of-the way place.

Should the plants in your containers lose their bloom or look less than ideal, they may easily be replaced by these fresher ones held in reserve.

Garden without a garden? Container plantings make it possible to grow roses on balconies, terraces, and roof tops high above city streets. The limited gardening space that comes with so many brownstones and town houses can be multiplied with portable planters.

Movable roses should be limited to shorter hybrid teas, floribundas, polyanthas, and miniatures. When planted in pots, these more compact roses look better than the tall hybrid tea or grandiflora. Shorter varieties produce flowers below eye level in height. Besides, the flowers on most of these roses appear in clusters, thereby covering the plant with more color at one time.

Tree roses, whether full size or miniature, are perfect choices for containers and should be placed wherever an accent is needed. Plant colorful geraniums or other annuals at the base of the tree rose to fill in the void and create two levels of interest.

Containers can be round, square, or any other shape so long as they are at least 18 inches across and deep. They can be made of plastic, clay, terra-cotta, ceramic, or one of the decay-resistant woods, like redwood, cypress, or cedar. And because they may be heavy and hard to move about, mount them on casters or on a dolly.

Although all roses, even those in containers, need at least six hours of sun a day, place movable roses in a spot where they receive morning sun

and some protection from the heat of the midday rays. Also try to keep them out of drying winds. Because the containers are exposed on all sides, they will dry more rapidly if overexposed to sun and wind. If roses in planters receive uneven sun and start growing in one direction to reach the light, be sure to rotate them every few days so they will grow straight.

Roses in containers need more watering than the same roses in the ground do. Not only are all sides of the container subject to drying wind and heat, there is also no ground moisture for the roots to rely on. So watch planters carefully, and water when the medium starts to dry out, never letting it become bone dry. Water until moisture runs from the bottom of the container. A mulch at the top of the planter will help keep the roses moist.

Planting medium for containers must be rich and well-drained. One of the packaged soilless potting mixes may be used, or mix your own soil, using equal parts of garden loam, sand, and peat moss or vermiculite. The high humus content will help to keep the medium moist.

The best fertilizer for movable roses is water soluble. Feed once a month, following label directions, or, for more even growth, every other week at half strength.

When winter comes, move the planters indoors (often impractical) or into an unheated porch, garage, or basement. The containers may also be sunk into the ground or placed in a cold frame. Check now and again to be sure the medium is slightly moist. If you choose to sink the planters in the ground, always add winter protection as suggested for garden-grown roses. See page 181. Then, in the early spring remove the planters from the ground, and place them in their previous locations. Prune away any winter-killed branches.

Movable Roses

Miniature roses are versatile movable plants, happy to spend the winter indoors after vacationing outside all summer. They can also be grown indoors all year or brought to life outdoors in summer and allowed to go dormant when cold weather comes.

Inside, minis need a lot of light, so grow them in an unobstructed south window or under ten to 14 hours of high-intensity, fluorescent lights per day. They thrive at normal household temperatures but like more humidity than most homes offer when the heat is on. To remedy this, grow minis on trays of pebbles, or mist them only on the morning of sunny days to limit the possibility of disease.

Indoors, the best planting medium for minis is a soilless mix of peat moss and perlite or vermiculite, although the same mixture used for outdoor movable roses can also be used with good success inside.

Miniature roses are thirsty plants and must be watered frequently enough to keep the medium evenly moist, neither soggy but not bone dry. Plastic pots are best for miniatures indoors because they don't dry out as quickly as clay pots do.

Start new miniature rose plants in four-inch pots, gradually working them into larger pots as they grow. One mini will fill out a small hanging basket, but for the ten- or 12-inch hanger, three plants are needed so the basket doesn't look skimpy.

Let fresh air reach your indoor miniature roses, but keep them out of cold drafts. Don't let the pots or plants touch each other; it will hamper air circulation and invite disease problems.

The major enemy of the miniature rose indoors is the spider mite; the best preventive and cure for this pest is water. Once a week, hold your plants upside down at the kitchen sink and spray away your problems with a stream of water. If mites should get away, spray the plants with water every day for ten days, or dip them into a warm detergent solution and rinse. Don't spray pesticides inside.

Fertilize movable roses indoors with a soluble plant food just as you would fertilize outdoor container plantings of roses.

You don't need to talk or sing to your miniature roses indoors, but they do benefit from being picked up every day. You can tell when they need watering and will be able to spot any troubles at the outset. Turn them around every so often so light strikes them evenly and they grow straight and uniformly. Pruning becomes an easy task if you regularly cut flowers for bouquets and boutonnieres.

Movable roses outdoors are cared for in the same way as roses planted into the garden, except for the differences already mentioned. Because they are planted in "up close" spots, they should always be picture perfect and may need a little extra attention. If you have an out-of-the-way garden corner, be sure to keep a few rose bushes growing in reserve to take over for any that aren't in peak bloom. In some ways, care of portable roses is easier because you can get to all sides of the plants to prune, spray, disbud, or cut flowers without becoming entangled in other bushes. Move the containers out of their spots for maintenance, and then move them back into place when finished. It's easy!

Enjoy the fragrant flowers of Mr. Lincoln, a popular hybrid tea.

Rev up an entry planting of evergreens and ground covers with a container of the low-growing floribunda, Puerto Rico.

163

Companions for Roses

If you want to show off your roses, don't let them stand alone. Giving them companions in the garden will complement and emphasize their beauty and charm.

Rose beds don't have to be unattractive expanses of bare ground and canes during the winter and early spring. Perk them up with colorful borders of snowdrops, crocus, squill, chionodoxa, and species tulips. Between the plants, clumps of golden daffodils glisten in the sunshine as the new foliage opens into bronze tones. By the time these bulbs have finished and the foliage disappears, the roses are ready to take over the limelight. As an added plus, fertilized roses will make the bulb flowers extraordinarily large.

Scads of spring perennials bloom before the roses. Use these freely without being concerned with color clash or interference. Try alyssum, creeping phlox, anemones, candytuft, or primroses for low-growing edgings to the rose border. Many of these will remain neat and attractive even when not in bloom.

Once roses come into bloom, they can rub shoulders with all sorts of other plants and together earn their place in the sun. These plants will provide color should the roses be between blooming periods. Choose the companions carefully, and practice a little caution when deciding on colors and sizes. They should complement the beauty of the roses but not dominate the scene.

Companion plants to roses in beds will most likely be used as borders and interplantings. Most low-growing annuals fill this role perfectly and do not compete for water and food, as do the heavy-rooted perennials.

Color is not the beginning and end of gardening, but it is used to create accent, emphasis, balance, and rhythm and is important in the selection of companions for roses.

Blue is a popular companion color because there are no blue roses. The deep blues of cornflower, anchusa, and clematis blend beautifully with soft yellow and red roses. White, orange, and pale pink roses can be used with the clear blue of delphinium. Veronica, asters, bellflower, verbena, and petunias are also good sources of blue contrast —just don't try to mix them with most mauve roses which will look washed out in comparison.

Red as a color in the garden is too much if it predominates, but it shouldn't be omitted either. For attention and accent, red can't be beat, but use it discreetly. Red companions go best with white, soft yellow, or clear-pink roses. Annual phlox, verbena, aster, balsam, petunias, and portulaca all have red flowering forms.

Orange companions bring brilliance and warmth to roses and are used most effectively with dark red, yellow, or pure white roses. Gazania, portulaca, marigolds, calendula, and lantana are good orange choices; but they'll clash with pink rose petals.

Yellow is the light and life of the garden, always adding a touch of gaiety to the scene. Deep yellow roses are intensified with a light, almost cream-colored zinnia. The yellow of celosia, sanvitalia, or linum brings a harmonious accent to orange, red, pink, mauve, or white roses. Yellow will make delicate shades sparkle and add warmth and cheer to darker roses. Use it thoughtfully, trying, in most settings, to match pale with pale and strong with strong.

Pink is a color that, used in the garden alone, is not strong enough unless varying shades of it are combined (right). Many pink flowers are beautiful in plantings of roses with contrasting tones. Pink geraniums appear even pinker next to white roses. Clear pink is striking next to mauve roses and red ones, too, if the hue is just right. Harmonize pale yellow roses and yellow blends with pink snapdragons, or bring pink to the garden with sweet william, verbena, or petunias.

Though you might think it is, white isn't always easy to use in the garden. White is often used as a foil between two strong colors. No problem, so long as it does not disturb the unity of the scheme. But too much of it will make the garden seem spotty. Bold masses of white produce a dignity hard to beat. Interspersed with strong colors, white softens; used among paler tints, it strengthens.

White flowers come from many sources—begonias, sweet alyssum, portulaca, balsam, or geraniums. They can be combined with nearly every rose.

Violet is often difficult to use effectively in the garden. Deep shades will stand out against mauve roses and blend well with pink roses so long as they do not have much red in them. Violet also is very attractive with soft yellow; with white, it brings a pleasant, cooling effect. Think twice before combining violet with roses of red, orange, or strong yellow. Violet, purple, and magenta tones are found in asters, sweet alyssum, heliotrope, nierembergia, or verbena.

Don't think of flower color only when choosing companions for roses. Plants with silver or gray leaves add a charm independent of their blossoms and, while lightening heavy colors, bring conflicting colors into a pleasing relationship. Good choices include dusty miller (centaurea) and either Silver King or Silver Mound artemisia.

Companions for Roses

Roses should be thought of as perennials and combined with them in planting beds. Golden coreopsis and daylilies are striking next to the hot orange of Tropicana or Fragrant Cloud. After they bloom, the flowers of yarrow leave behind delicate, fern-like foliage. The burst of color with which roses herald the beginning of fall is heightened by chrysanthemums.

A touch of white for here and there in the perennial rose bed is achieved easily with shasta daisy or phlox, plants that also will benefit from exposure to the sun. If you want blue, interplant roses with scabiosa, delphinium, cornflower, bellflower, aster, anchusa, balloon flower, flax, or nierembergia.

Lilies are perfect companions for roses, they like the same growing conditions and, with proper selection, will bloom all summer in many complementary colors. Don't forget the other bulbs, especially the tender ones, to fill in spots of color among the roses. Gladiolus, dahlias, canna lilies, freesia, and many others are perfect for instant companionship and for filling in unsightly bare spaces in the garden. If the soil beneath your roses is cool and shady, try a mass planting of tuberous begonias.

Geraniums, too, will find a place wherever roses grow. Should a favorite rose not survive the winter, its spot can quickly be filled in with pink, red, or white from these common garden favorites.

Roses that climb on trellises or against houses should have annual or perennial plants below them. Vines such as clematis look and perform better with a rose bush set in front of their base. Roses are also a good choice in front of other climbers such as thunbergia, morning glory, or Dutchman's pipe.

Tall growers used for the back of the border, such as delphinium, hollyhock, or cosmos, will stand out even more with roses of contrasting colors set in front of them. Miniature

Marigolds reflect colors of Lemon Spice and Seventh Heaven.

roses or ground-hugging annuals can blanket the area between and in front of the roses. They will also help keep weed growth choked out.

Instead of planting roses in containers to add interest to flower and shrub beds, try the opposite. Portable planters of marigolds, zinnias, geraniums, petunias, or annual phlox can add a contrast in color and texture to rose beds. If your roses are near the house or patio, dress the sky above them by hanging baskets of annuals from nearby posts and overhangs. These containers, strategically placed, not only lend a colorful

touch, they also create a line leading the eye to the focal point of the garden, the rose bed.

Companions for roses don't have to be alive. If you have a red climber on a fence, give it a coat of white paint to create a dazzling effect. If the climber is a softer tone of pastel pink, yellow, or apricot, a naturally weathered, gray split-rail fence provides a subtle combination.

A statue, sundial, bird bath, garden light, small pool—these are only a few of the items that when combined with roses make interesting garden features.

166

Bermudiana's two-toned buds open to a pleasing clear pink, combining with the blue of Belladonna delphiniums.

Companions for Roses

Companions for roses need not be limited to flowering annuals, bulbs, or perennials; shrubs also make good neighbors. Use roses with shrubs in two different ways: to extend the blooming period of spring-flowering forsythia, spirea, azaleas, lilacs, viburnum, or beautybush, or to provide a colorful complement for summer-flowering shrubs. For beds of this type, plant weigela, mock orange, abelia, rose-of-sharon, vitex, or hydrangea.

A small, decorative tree is a lovely companion for the rose garden. In spring, blooms from cherry trees, magnolia, dogwood, flowering peach, crab apple, or hawthorn fill the air before the roses show off theirs. Later on, the tree provides a pretty place to rest under. Place the tree so the roses are in its shade during the afternoon, and put a bench under it so you can sit and enjoy the rose garden. Don't plant the roses too close to the tree, or they will fight for sun, food, and water.

Let's go one step further. Don't think ornamentals are the only companions for roses. Think of planting edibles, too, in rose and mixed flower beds.

Vegetable gardens are usually put off by themselves, and they shouldn't be. Many edibles are attractive. They can easily mix with roses, and they love the same things roses do—sun, food, rich soil, and water. Roses can be planted in front of trellises bearing cucumbers, beans, or squash; they can go between tomatoes and peppers. To save space, grow underground crops such as beets, carrots, and onions between the rose bushes. To edge rose beds, try sage, thyme, or parsley.

The one thing you must watch when mixing roses and edibles is the use of pesticides. Read labels carefully to make sure the material is suitable for crops and to find out how long you must wait between spraying and harvesting. Many of the commonly sold rose pesticides are harmful to vegetable crops.

Edgings of white alyssum complement dazzling Sunsprite.

COMBINATIONS TO TRY

With red roses . . .
Yellow portulaca
Pink wax begonias
Dwarf white snapdragons
Peter Pan Orange zinnia
Amethyst verbena

With pink roses . . .
Blue salvia
Dwarf coreopsis
Sprinter Scarlet geranium
Rosie O'Day sweet alyssum
White Cascade petunia

With orange roses . . .
Showboat marigold
Crystal Palace lobelia
Dwarf calliopsis
Silver dusty miller
White gypsophila
Canary Bird zinnia

With yellow roses . . .
Pink Beauty phlox
White TomThumb balsam
Purple Robe nierembergia
Petite Orange marigold
Old Mexico zinnia
Blue Blazer ageratum

With white roses . . .
Baby-blue-eyes
Saint John's Fire salvia
Gaillardia Lollipop
Pacific Beauty calendula
Blue Picotee petunia

With mauve roses . . .
Yellow dwarf dahlias
Gray santolina
Pink bachelor's-buttons
Snowflake dianthus
Blushing Maid petunia

168

The royal color of violas strikingly contrasts with the subtle pink of Gay Princess.

Color Schemes

There are those who think shades of color will not clash naturally. They plant their gardens in every color of the rainbow. But unfortunately, the beauty of many subtle tones is lost in the confusion. The proper color scheme will bring out the best of everything.

Monochromatic color schemes may be dull and uninteresting; those using a dominant color with a contrasting secondary color are more striking. The lesser color will not compete with the main one but instead will accentuate it. If you like yellow, roses in various shades of gold will dominate, tied together by blue, orange, scarlet, or pink.

Another color scheme uses two dominant colors, softened by a touch here and there of a third. Deliberately putting two strongly contrasting colors together creates drama in the garden. Look at Heat Wave and Pascali, *right.*

Another principle allows for many colors in a logical gradation or progression; they can be pale to dark or a central focus of strong colors leading through transitional shades to lighter tones. The many different colors can be unified with a border of white or soft pastel.

Designing the garden is not the same as flower arranging or interior decorating, because you must take into consideration the effects of sunlight and the competitive contrast of a green landscape and blue sky. The principles of color harmony have less impact in the great outdoors where weather conditions play more of a modifying role.

Look to nature, however, for ideas on color schemes for roses. She combines some opposite hues in a startling manner. There are daisies of pink and white, violet asters with yellow centers, red and yellow gaillardia, marigolds of orange and gold, red and white impatiens, or red and pink phlox. Borrow from these natural palettes to get ideas for the rose bed.

When planning the garden, remember that solid colors are more difficult to harmonize than blends. They have no contrasts on their flowers, no tones to be picked up by a neighbor. On the other hand, put too many blends together and the delicacy of their subtle colors will be lost. Following the same theory, too many pinks together will wash each other out. A good rule of thumb is to place blends next to solids to make the better qualities of each stand out. Light-colored blends are easy to mix with most any color.

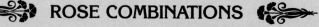 **ROSE COMBINATIONS**

Garden Party and Electron
Rose Parade and Oregold
Spanish Sun and Angel Face
Duet and Lady X
Tiffany and Lemon Spice
Neue Revue and Red Lion
Ivory Fashion and Peer Gynt
Anabell and Irish Gold
Europeana and Bahia
Royal Highness and Christian Dior
Gene Boerner and Apricot Nectar
Fragrant Cloud and Saratoga
Sunsprite and Accent
Iceberg and Sundowner
Chrysler Imperial and King's Ransom
Peace and Pink Peace
Orangeade and Sarabande

Matador and Summer Sunshine
Mister Lincoln and Pascali
Fire King and Woburn Abbey
Pristine and Granada
Seashell and First Edition
Evening Star and Heirloom
Queen Elizabeth and Susan Massu
Red Masterpiece and Paradise
Portrait and Mt. Shasta
Chicago Peace and Promise
Mojave and American Heritage
Big Ben and Century Two
Prominent and Redgold
Medallion and Matterhorn
Blue Moon and Michele Meilland
Double Delight and White Masterpiece
Sunset Jubilee and Portrait

Color Schemes

Another difference between flower arranging and choosing a color scheme for the garden is that you have to make your plans without having the flower to look at. This requires early planning, a good memory, or good notes. As you see something you like in a friend's or public garden, jot down the name and the color. It will make things easier later on.

Use color to provide accent. Relieve large masses of one color with a smaller group of plants of a complementary color—or by the sparing introduction of white. Color accents along a border produce movement, rhythm, and sequence. They carry the eye along to the climactic point.

Climax is important for every garden, no matter what the size. The point of climax should be stressed in the design, and the roses with the strongest colors should be placed near this focal point.

Placement of color is also very important in the scheme of things. Don't concentrate the color of roses in one bed and not use it elsewhere. Spread color all about the garden to create the illusion of abundance. Correct placement of colorful roses will also lead the eye away from unattractive eyesores.

Choice of color is vital. Warmtoned roses in shades of red, yellow, or orange convey boldness and make the garden appear smaller. White and mauve roses give a cool feeling and make the garden seem larger. Rarely, however, is limiting the garden to either warm or cool roses an effective technique. Both should be used, and each will help the other.

The color scheme you choose for your garden may also depend on whether you're a man or a woman. In the past, some men seem to prefer the strong reds and oranges while women often favored the pastels.

However, this tradition shouldn't limit you in choosing colors for your garden. Today's trend is definitely a bold one. Contemporary gardeners crave color in large masses and in forceful combinations. Don't be afraid to put strong contrasts together, and use the easy-to-mix creams, buffs, light yellows, and pink and yellow blends to buffer strong colors and tie the color scheme of the garden together.

The most effective way to use the colors you choose is to plant them in masses. Whether it be a dominant color scheme or one using two or three colors, it is a much more forceful technique to have the colors in blocks, rather than scattered about like a checkerboard. To achieve this, at least two and preferably three of a variety should be planted together. This goes for the annual or perennial companions as well as the roses. Drifts of individual complementary colors are far more effective than a crazy-quilt pattern of scattered colors.

One final but important considera-

Lavender Angel Face with White Knight has a timeless quality.

tion in choosing a color scheme is taking a hard look at what is already there. What color is the house? The fence? The driveway? The deck? Unless you are willing to change the color or buy something new, you will have to work your color scheme around what you already have. This background color is so obvious it is often overlooked, but it shouldn't be because it can mean the difference between a spectacular garden and a lackluster one.

If the house is green or one of the earth tones, any color scheme will do. After all, these are the colors of nature. Against a red house, concentrate yellow or white; a blue house looks special with plantings of red, pink, white, or yellow. If the house is yellow or gold, try orange or pink. White on white can be sterile, but with the right accents, the combination can be breathtaking.

No one can tell you what color scheme you should be using. Only suggestions and guidelines can be given. Response to color is a very private thing, a reflection of the personality. Some people prefer the warm tones; others are lovers of cool colors. Taste is as different as night and day, as black and white. Only a purist will plant only one color in his or her garden. As for you, it's your garden. You decide.

The deep, velvety red of Proud Land forms a stunning partnership in the garden with the pinks and coral of Vin Rose.

173

Basics of Rose Care

When do you plant roses? Bare-root roses are planted at times when they are dormant and the ground is not frozen. In warm areas, this is in late winter. Where winter temperatures do not go below 0° Fahrenheit, planting may be done in early spring or late fall. In areas of extreme cold, roses should be planted in spring only. Where possible, fall planting is preferred, because bushes are freshly dug and the roots will grow for much of the winter, leading to strong top growth in spring.

Bare-root roses, usually bought from mail order nurseries, should be planted as soon as possible after they arrive. If they have to be stored for several days before planting, put them in a cool place, and keep the roots moist by wetting them down and wrapping them in damp newspaper or plastic. If several weeks will pass before they can be planted, heel the roses in by burying the entire plant, canes and roots, in a trench in a cool, shaded spot.

Before planting, soak bare-root roses in a bucket of water or mud for six to 24 hours. This will restore moisture to the canes lost during shipping.

Before you place roses in the ground, think ahead. Place them where they can stay put and will not have to be moved in two or three years. Set your roses where they will receive at least six hours of full sun a day, preferably in the morning. Where summer heat becomes intense, help them gain relief from high temperatures and glare by placing them in a spot that gets light afternoon shade. Miniatures will tolerate a little more shade than their larger cousins and are very happy in the dappled shade of an ornamental tree.

Don't plant roses where their roots will compete with roots from other trees and shrubs. If this is impossible, install underground barriers made from impenetrable and durable material, such as an asbestos shingle or aluminum siding. Place it so the competing roots will stay away from the roses, yet give the rose roots room to grow.

If at all possible, keep roses out of drying winds by using a fence, living hedge, or other break. High winds will also damage or destroy open flowers. And as pretty as a ground cover may look, don't put it in a spot near the roses where it might steal food and water.

HOW TO PLANT A ROSE

Locate the bud union, which is the point where the rose was grafted to the understock. It is easy to recognize as a knob on top of the root shank at the base of the canes. It should be placed just above ground level after planting because sun helps in the formation of basal breaks. In areas with cold winters, it will need to be protected from freezing.

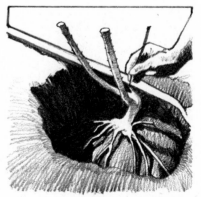

After the planting hole is dug, place a mound of improved soil in the bottom of it. Set the plant on top of the cone of soil, spreading out the roots evenly on all sides. Lay a broom or shovel handle across the rim of the hole, using it to position the bud union correctly. Place it slightly above ground level; it will sink. Be sure to keep the roots moist as you work.

A rose is no better than the soil it is planted in, so take a few minutes to improve the good earth. Drainage is of utmost importance; roses do not like wet feet. Dig a hole large enough to hold a gallon of water. Fill it. If it drains in an hour, don't worry. If it doesn't, improve the drainage by adding perlite, vermiculite, or coarse sand, setting drainage tiles or terracing.

Soil should be light and rich to guarantee good growth, so improve it by adding organic matter such as peat moss, leaf mold, compost, or well-rotted manure. Organic enrichment should be a quarter of the total soil volume. Heavy clay soils should be loosened with gypsum.

The pH is also important. For good roses, it should be between 6.0 and 6.5, a slightly acid reading. To get the soil to this level, use lime if your soil is more acidic and sulfur if it is on the alkaline side. Have a soil test done to be sure where you stand.

Good root growth is a sure thing if superphosphate is incorporated into the soil at planting time, but use no other fertilizer when planting. Prepare the soil deeply, to a depth of 24 inches, and you are ready to pick up your shovel.

Dig a hole about 18 inches deep and around, and plant the rose as illustrated below. Don't be afraid to prune away any broken roots or roots that are too long to fit into the planting hole without crowding.

In most climates, 24 inches between hybrid teas, grandifloras, or floribundas will be just right. Where winters are very mild and the roses have little dormancy, if any, plants may be spaced farther apart as they grow larger. For dense edging and hedges, space a little tighter. Shrub and old garden roses are spaced according to their size, about four to six feet apart in most cases. Climbers to be trained horizontally along a fence should be given a distance of eight to ten feet between plants. Miniatures are laid out depending on their height. Microminis can be as close as four inches; taller varieties should have 12 to 18 inches between plants.

If leaves are falling when you are planting your roses, add a border of crocus at the edge of the bed and clumps of daffodils between the plants. They will bring early color, and by the time they fade, the roses are almost ready to bloom.

The advantage of buying roses in containers is that the planting season is extended throughout the summer, allowing you to fill in bits of color whenever or wherever it is needed.

Dig a hole larger and deeper than the container, and prepare the soil the same way as for bare-root roses. Place soil back in the hole so the bud union will be on the correct level after planting. Carefully remove the container, peel it away, or slit it with a knife, disturbing the root ball as little as possible. Holding the rose in place, firm soil around the roots by hand or with the help of a spade. Water well, stand back, and watch your rose grow.

Planting a rose into a decorative container is the same as planting it into the ground. Be sure the container has drainage holes, and for best results, use a soil-less potting medium. Commercial potting medium will provide all the nutrients your roses need and will be light enough to make all your containers extra portable.

After the rose is in place, remove the name tag if it is attached with wire. The wire might damage the cane. Even if it doesn't, the cane will one day be pruned away, and the tag may go with it. Use a plant label, and keep a record of what you plant.

Holding the rose straight and at the right level, back-fill the planting hole about two-thirds full. Gently tamp down the soil around the roots by hand or by stepping on it lightly. Fill the hole with water and allow it to drain, which will eliminate air pockets. After all the water is gone, fill the hole to the top with the improved soil mixture.

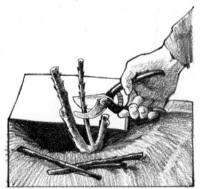

Prune the new roses back by a third, removing any dried or broken wood at the same time. The first few weeks of the rose's life are the most important, and it should never be allowed to dry out from sun or wind. Mound soil over the rose's canes approximately two-thirds of the way up the plant, and leave it in place until new growth is one to two inches long.

After the new growth is well developed, wash the soil mound away with a gentle stream of water from the garden hose. Be careful not to accidentally damage any new shoots that may be developing under the soil protection. Check all the plants one more time while waiting for bloom, and prune back any canes that may not have grown.

175

Pruning

It is sometimes difficult to take pruning shears in hand and cut away live wood from a rose bush. If you don't however, it will soon become tall and rangy and produce few good flowers. Pruning is needed to control the size and shape of a plant and keep it healthy, vigorous, and covered in bloom.

Pruning time comes when the buds begin to swell—but before they show signs of becoming a leaf. Depending on where you live, this will vary between midwinter and midspring. If forsythia grows in the neighborhood, prune your roses when yellow blooms show.

The correct tools of the trade are most important. A curved edged pruning shears, as large as your hand can comfortably hold, should be used, rather than the straight-edged, anvil variety that can crush the stems as it cuts. The only time anvil shears can be used, without damage, is in the removal of dead wood. Also, have on hand a long-handled lopping shear to cut out thick branches or tackle old garden and shrub roses and climbers. A pruning saw is a great aid in cutting out thick canes.

Make sure your pruning shears are sharp! If they become dull, sharpen the blade yourself, have it professionally sharpened, or buy a replacement blade. Jagged cuts from dull shears do not heal quickly and are prone to insects and disease.

Prune hybrid teas, floribundas, and grandifloras as illustrated below. In climates where winters are severe, the pruning height may be determined for you, depending on how much winterkill the plant experienced. If you can choose your heights, prune hybrid teas and floribundas to a height of 12 to 18 inches and grandifloras about six inches higher. Another good way to measure is to cut off a third to a half of the plant. There is no advantage to pruning a plant very low (six inches); it will not produce larger blooms. The higher a plant is pruned, the earlier it will bloom, but don't let this lead you to believe it should not be pruned—it must be, to keep it well groomed.

To control the spread of disease from one plant to another, swish your pruning shears in a half-and-half solution of household bleach and water each time you make a cut.

HOW TO PRUNE A ROSE

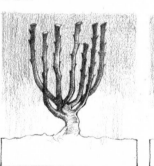

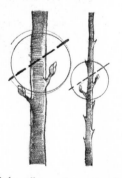

The first step in pruning rose bushes is to remove the winter protection, so you can see what you are dealing with. Cut away all dead and diseased wood first, pruning all dead canes flush with the bud union. Any branches that are broken, wounded, or have cankers should be pruned below the injury to the point where the pith is white and completely healthy.

Next, cut out weak or spindly branches, which generally will be smaller in diameter than your little finger. Canes that are growing into the center of the plant are removed next, along with those that crisscross each other. Keep the middle of the plant open to let in sunshine and allow air to circulate freely through the plant to discourage diseases.

By this time, you should be left with several good, strong canes. Select three or four of the newest and strongest canes to remain on the plant, removing all of the others flush with the bud union. Never leave short stumps on the bush, because insects and disease then have an entryway. For the same reason, do not leave short spurs higher on the canes.

Make all pruning cuts at a 45-degree angle, about ¼ inch above a bud and sloping downward from it, so water will run off freely. If too much cane is left above the bud, it will die back; if the cut is made too close, the bud may not survive. Wherever possible, prune to an outward facing bud, to keep the plant open and nicely shaped and to avoid tangled centers.

Blackspot spores spend the winter in the canes of a rose bush. If the disease was a problem last season, this is the one time you should prune your bushes lower than usual. You will cut away and discard many of your problems. Never leave cuttings lying between the roses. They, too, may carry disease.

Pruning cuts that are ½ inch or more in diameter may be sealed with a pruning compound, orange shellac, or grafting wax if boring insects are a problem in the area. Otherwise, sealing should not be necessary. White glue, which is often recommended as a sealant, is water soluble and will wash away in the first rain.

Floribundas used for hedges and masses of color may be pruned higher, with more canes remaining. Hybrid perpetuals should be taller than hybrid teas, and, because they bloom heaviest on last year's wood, should have only the oldest canes removed. Shrub and old garden roses are pruned primarily to remove old, weak, or dead wood or to correct misshapen growth. Leave them as large and natural as space permits.

Miniatures should be pruned ac-cording to how you are going to use them. If you like them petite, they may be pruned as low as three to four inches. If used as hedges and edgings, they may be left as tall as six to eight inches. Follow the same guidelines as those for larger bush roses. Remove dead, diseased, or weak wood; take out any crisscrossing canes; and open up the center of the plant. Up to six new and strong canes may be left on the plant after pruning.

Tree roses are pruned much the same way as bush roses, but keep in mind they are unattractive if they are not symmetrical. Prune canes to 12 inches in length, and leave them as evenly spaced around the plant as possible.

Polyantha roses are fairly hardy and seldom suffer any winter dieback. Prune them to about half their former height. They are vigorous plants, sending up many new canes each year. Prune the oldest ones each spring, leaving as many as eight on a plant. Like shrub roses, they are primarily grown for landscaping effect, so should be left on the full side.

Go easy in the first few years of a rose bush's life, pruning it on the light side until it is well established. In the first spring after it is planted, it will rarely be necessary to do more than remove weak, dead, or diseased wood; shape; and cut to size. In following years, old canes may be removed as new ones grow.

Pruning can be a scratchy chore, especially if large bushes and long canes are involved. For protection against marked arms and thorned fingers, wear long sleeves and a pair of heavy gloves. Watch what you wear, too, for some fabrics (nylon for one) catch on the thorns much easier than others do.

Several weeks after you have pruned, take a walk through the garden with your shears. A late spring frost or other unexpected mishap may have caused some minor dieback on one or two canes. There might be a dead branch or two you missed the first time through. Just snip it off down to a good bud.

Although you will need the shears throughout the summer (to cut flowers from the plants), clean and oil them after pruning.

HOW TO PRUNE A CLIMBER

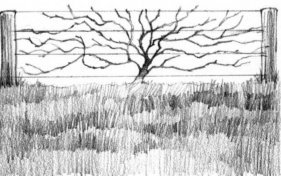

Climbers are pruned somewhat differently than bush roses. The majority of climbers bloom on old wood; the canes which grew the year before. Spring pruning chores should be limited to cutting out any wood that might have died over the winter or some last-minute shaping. Pruning done in early spring only results in cutting away all the flower buds.

After the climber has bloomed, remove one or two of the oldest canes to make room for new ones to grow. Thin out dense growth and shorten canes if the plant is too large. A rose grows where it is cut, so prune it back further than you want its final size to be. To get maximum bloom from most climbers, train canes horizontally along a fence, and secure them with plant ties.

How to Care for Roses

If you take care of your roses, they will reward you all summer with beautiful blooms. Take water as an example. Roses will survive with only a little but will do so much better with the right amount. Blooms will be larger, have more substance, better color, and last longer.

There is more than one way to water your roses. Sub-irrigation pipes may be installed underground, but this is not a method recommended for the home garden. Soaker hoses may be laid on the ground and the water allowed to trickle from their tiny holes. Because it may require the skill of an acrobat to move them around, they should be left in place all summer. The garden hose may be laid on the ground and the water allowed to run from it, or the roses may be watered by hand with a watering can or wand.

One of the easiest ways to water is with an overhead sprinkler. So long as it runs in the morning (wet leaves at night may become diseased), it is an excellent way to give needed moisture to your roses. There are also a few nice side effects of overhead watering. Spray residue is washed off the foliage, as is dust, and the high moisture will discourage spider mites.

Roses should be watered regularly, throughout the growing season, if the skies do not cooperate by providing rain. The equivalent of one inch of rain should fall on the rose garden each week. This will mean enough moisture for the entire root area to become wet. Sandy soils, which drain quickly, will need to be watered more often, and clay soils, which hold great amounts of water, will need watering less frequently. Soils that have had organic matter mixed in with them, as they should, will also retain moisture better than unimproved ones and do not need to be watered as often. Mulched gardens will also need less water than unmulched gardens.

Frequency of watering also depends on the weather. When the thermometer skyrockets, extra water will have to be applied. These rules apply to all plants and not just to roses, so don't think you have to be a slave to the garden hose. Water the roses when you water other flowers or the lawn, and they will respond.

If you are not sure when your roses need water, stick your finger into the soil as far as you can; if your fingernail hits dry soil, it's time to water. A rain gauge can also be installed as a guide. Whatever you do, water deeply; light sprinklings do more harm than good.

HOW TO CARE FOR ROSES

Spring is a time spent preparing for the roses of summer. As soon as weather permits, remove winter protection, prune, clean up, and apply a dormant spray of lime sulfur for insect and disease control.

Water is the most essential element you can give to your roses. If you have the time, water by hand with a wand, as illustrated. This is also an excellent way to relax and enjoy the rose garden on a summer evening.

Next to water, fertilizer is the best thing you can give to your roses. A balanced fertilizer, such as 5-10-5, or a prepared rose food, is the best bet. The first digit represents the percentage of nitrogen needed for growth and good, green leaves. The second is the amount of phosphorus, which ensures sturdy root growth and better flowers. The last number stands for the amount of potash, which is essential for plant vigor and food production.

Roses should be fertilized at least three times a year—right after pruning in early spring, just before the plants show their first bloom, and again two months before the first frost is expected. An alternative to this schedule is to fertilize once a month during the growing season, observing the same cutoff date for last feeding.

Apply the fertilizer, following label directions for the amount to use and spreading it over the entire root area, but not on the bud union. Lightly work into the top of the soil or the mulch, and water in well. Use twice the recommended amount for large shrub roses or climbers and a quarter to a half the amount for miniatures. Newly planted bushes should not be fed until they bloom.

Relatively new, slow release fertilizers give food to the plant when the soil is warm and stop feeding when temperatures drop. They may be used at the second feeding, eliminating the need to do further fertilizing that year. The mulch must be pushed aside, the fertilizer lightly scratched into the soil, and the mulch restored.

Liquid feeding is a marvelous way to give an instant boost to your plants, especially when they are coming into their first bloom. Mix one of the soluble fertilizers with water, and apply the solution with a watering can. If you have a lot of roses, a proportioning sprayer will be a great time-saver. You can apply the liquid to the roots or spray it on the leaves. Foliar feeding is recommended at any time the temperature is not over 90° Fahrenheit. Soluble food can also be mixed in with your fungicide or insecticide spray, thereby letting the spray do double duty.

Several other elements are needed for good growth. One is calcium, which you get with lime if you are raising the pH or from gypsum if the acidity does not need adjusting. Another is magnesium, present in dolomitic limestone. If leaves turn yellow, it might be a lack of iron.

It's possible to grow roses without mulching them, but they will be much better if you do. A mulch is simply a layer of material spread on top the soil. It keeps the soil cool and even tempered, conserves moisture, and keeps away the back-breaking chore of weeding. As it decomposes, it enriches the soil. Left in place all winter, it prevents the heaving of plants from the soil due to alternate freezing and thawing. Mulched roses will also be cleaner because the mulch prevents any soil from splattering the foliage during rainstorms.

Any number of organic mulches may be used; the only requirements are that they be light, permeable, and attractive. Try wood chips, pine needles, buckwheat hulls, cocoa bean shells, sawdust, or chopped oak leaves. Peat moss is not a good choice, because it gets crusty and is hard to wet; straw and hay are weedy; grass clippings, unless thinly dried, are slimy and mat down. If the material is fresh, apply extra nitrogen. Otherwise, the roses will be robbed of it as the mulch decomposes.

Once mulch is in place, it does not have to be removed in winter. If necessary, you can add to it the following year.

Besides mulch, another way to control invading weeds is with metal edgings. The metal will help keep grass and other weeds out of beds, making garden maintenance easier.

Spread fertilizer evenly around the root area, and work it lightly into the soil. If you have doubts about the condition of your loam, have a soil test done to see if it is lacking in any of the essential elements.

In mid-spring, after the ground is warm but before the weather becomes hot, apply a layer of mulch two to three inches thick. Do not let the mulch come in contact with the canes. Mulch will keep the soil cooler in summer.

How to Care for Roses

Keep an eye out for suckers, canes that grow from the understock beneath the bud union. They are easy to recognize because their foliage is quite distinct from that of the top part of the plant. If they ever reach the blooming stage, you'll see tiny white flowers (*Rosa multiflora*) or blooms of red (Dr. Huey). On tree roses, suckers can come from two locations—from the root stock or from the stem. Miniatures and some old garden and shrub roses are grown on their own roots, so suckers are not a problem and should not, of course, be removed.

DISBUDDING

If you want large flowers, one bloom to a stem, you will have to disbud. As soon as tiny buds are visible around the central bud or down the stem, remove them gently with your fingers or with the help of a narrow, pointed implement, a toothpick, for example. If you wait too long before disbudding, you will have a big black scar.

For a more attractive floribunda

spray, remove the central bud as soon as it forms. If you don't, the middle flower will be past its peak while the other flowers are in bloom or just opening; removing it then will leave a hole in the spray.

Some of the old garden roses—

albas, centifolias, and moss roses in particular—can be pegged or pinned down at the end of the long canes. Not only will this make these large plants easier to control and more shrubby in appearance, it will also encourage the formation of more basal breaks.

DEADHEADING

Deadheading is the term applied to the removal of spent blooms from the rose bush. A good rule to follow is to cut the stem down to the first leaf with five leaflets, the point from which the next stem will grow and bloom. First-year plants, in particular, should be cut back only slightly at this time to encourage sturdy and vigorous growth.

When deadheading, taller and more vigorous plants may have a longer stem cut off, if you wish to shorten the bushes. Remember, though, that every time you cut off an extra leaf, you are cutting off a food-producing factory. Don't overdo it, or you will weaken the rose. Allow at least two leaves to stay on any cane—and preferably more.

Old blooms past their peak should be removed from the plant as soon as possible. Not only does this show off your good gardening and keep your beds free of fallen petals, it also encourages the plant to repeat its bloom more quickly.

Every rule has an exception and this one is no different. Shrubs, old garden roses, and climbers that bloom only once don't have to be deadheaded. Attractive hips of red or orange will form that will lure the birds and be used in recipes.

To keep climbers in bloom all

summer, prune them as soon as their first flush of flowers is finished. Cut the lateral canes back, leaving two five-leaflet leaves on each. A new stem topped with a bloom will grow from each leaf axil.

Roses cut in bud or bloom, to be brought inside the house for flower arrangements, are handled in the same way as deadheaded flowers. Roses for arrangements should be disbudded. Cut the stems as long as you want, so long as two leaves are left on the main cane.

To keep those flowers large and beautiful and the plants vigorous and healthy, don't forget the soil. Roses grow best in a soil that is just slightly acid. Every few years, make sure the pH is at the right level.

PROTECTION

If you live in an area where winter temperatures drop below 20° Fahrenheit, take steps to protect your roses, especially the tender varieties.

Most climbers will withstand temperatures even lower than 20° without suffering severe damage. In sections where the cold reaches 0° Fahrenheit or lower, take climbers off

their supports, lay the canes on the ground, peg them down, and cover them up with oak leaves or soil, for example. In early spring, remove the protection and tie the climbers back up. An alternative to this is wrapping the canes in burlap while they are still attached to the supports, but this method can be cumbersome and much more difficult to manage.

Miniatures are tough plants and rarely need much protection, even in the coldest of climates. Raking leaves around and in between minis is the most they will ever need to get them through the winter. Shrubs and many of the old garden roses are very hardy and need no winter protection. This is a good thing, because most of them grow so large they would be impossible to protect. Polyanthas, too, are very hardy, withstanding the rigors of most any winter.

But the hybrid teas, grandifloras, and floribundas are not so independent and need your help to survive the cold if the thermometer reads below 20° Fahrenheit. This does not mean an occasional plunge in the temperature will harm your roses. Great fluctuations in temperature, extended periods of severe cold, and drying winds cause winter dieback. A deep layer of snow lying over the roses all winter is one of the best protections nature can provide.

Right after the ground has frozen is the perfect time to apply winter mulch. Use one of the methods illustrated below, or try something different. Rose cones made from plastic foam fit over the plants and keep out wind and cold. They should be saved for very cold areas or very tender plants, because the bush will have to be cut back severely for the cone to fit over it. Cones can also act like a greenhouse and cause premature growth during January thaws or other warm spells, growth that will undoubtedly die later.

Another good method of protection is evergreen boughs, and these are readily available in the form of unsold Christmas trees after the holidays are over.

Roses are not generally pruned in the fall. But if they grow particularly tall during the summer, cut them back before applying protection. This will prevent them from whipping in the wind or breaking under the weight of snow.

Protection during the winter is often not needed. If you are not sure which way to go because you live in a borderline area, protect those roses listed as tender. Most of the yellow roses, plus many pastel pinks and whites need protection.

Remove the protection when growth starts in the early spring, just before pruning. That prevents the new shoots from growing through the soil mound and becoming soft and brittle. But remember don't get itchy and remove winter mulch too early; a late frost may unexpectedly cause damage.

Remember that strong, healthy, well-cared-for bushes will fare better in winter than weak or neglected ones. Lush growth from the previous season that has not been hardened off is also susceptible to attack by the cold. This is why you shouldn't apply fertilizer after midsummer. By halting your rose bush feeding plan in midsummer, you will allow plenty of time for the rose bushes to harden off and ready themselves for winter.

Move container roses to a frost-free spot. Wrap tree roses in burlap, lift, and move them indoors for the winter.

HOW TO OVERWINTER ROSES

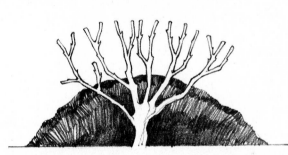

The traditional way to protect roses is to mound up soil over the canes, to a height of about 20 inches. The most important thing to do if you use this method is to bring soil in from another part of the garden. Don't take soil from around the plants, because this will expose delicate feeder roots to the cold air. In the spring, the soil will have to be removed from the plants and the beds and stored somewhere during the summer. Be sure to remove the soil from around the plants before the next season's growth begins. Young shoots are extremely tender and are easily damaged by rough treatment. To keep damage to a minimum, it's a good idea to first wash the soil mound away from the immediate vicinity of the crown of the plant with a gentle stream of water from the garden hose. Then, carefully scrape away the rest of the mound with a trowel or small spade. When the soil mound is removed, the bud union of the rose should be visible just above the ground level.

Once the soil has been removed, it's time to add several inches of mulch to increase soil moisture.

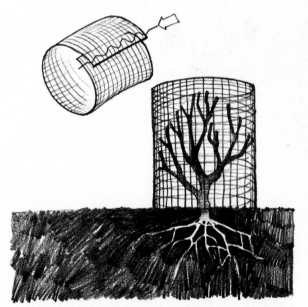

Another effective method of protecting your roses is to wrap a wire mesh cylinder around them and fill it with leaves. Make sure you choose a type of leaf that will not mat down and will allow water to drain through it. Oak leaves are perfect; maple leaves are to be avoided, at all costs. This rule also applies when you're raking leaves into rose beds to protect them during the winter. It's an easy method if you have the right trees.

181

Pests and Diseases

Unfortunately, pests and diseases enjoy our roses as much as we do. However, you don't have to let the garden become their home. The effectiveness of today's chemicals, the ease with which they're mixed, and the availability of modern equipment have made pest and disease prevention and control easy tasks.

Don't let the illustration on the opposite page alarm you. It shows all the pests and diseases that could possibly attack a rose. The chances of every one appearing at the same time in one garden are very small.

The question of spraying vs. dusting often arises. If you have only a few bushes, dusting is more convenient because no mixing is needed. Place the powder in the duster, and use when needed, without cleaning in between. On the other hand, spraying is more effective because coverage is more uniform.

What type of sprayer should you use? If you have a small number of plants, use a small bottle of the type used to mist indoor plants. Proportioning sprayers attach to the end of the garden hose and automatically dilute a concentrate as they spray, although the spray is coarse and not always uniform. There are sprayers that pump up; they're good but heavy. Electric or battery powered sprayers deliver a very fine mist but are impractical, except in large gardens. Whatever you use, clean it after every spray.

Spray to control insects. To prevent diseases, on the other hand, you must spray every ten days. Choose the right material for the job, handle it with care, and read the label. Rather than spraying twice, combine insecticides and fungicides in the same spray, or buy one of the combination sprays.

Systemics are great labor-saving materials that are absorbed by the plant to do their work from within. Apply them less often.

Starting at the lower left (opposite) and proceeding clockwise around the rose are potential pests and diseases and the recommended prevention or control:

Spider Mite This tiny creature is not an insect. It sucks life from the undersides of leaves. Foliage turns a dull red, and webs appear in advanced stages. If they become a problem, spray every three days with a rose miticide to kill new mites as they hatch. Mites also hate water, so mist or hose the plants frequently.

Rose Scale This insect hides under a crusty white or gray shell and sucks sap from plants so they eventually wilt and die. Cut out infested areas, and apply a dormant lime sulfur spray in early spring. Use a commercial rose insecticide.

Fuller Rose Beetle This gray-brown insect munches on rose leaves, doing most of its damage while in the larval stage. Use a commercial rose insecticide.

Rose Slug This soft, yellow-green insect is actually the larva of one of the flies. It eats holes in the leaves and in time skeletonizes them. Use a commercial insecticide.

Rose Chafer A spiny-legged beetle with a grayish-brown cast, it feasts on flowers and leaves in early summer. Use a commercial insecticide.

Tarnished Plant Bug Not a frequent visitor to roses, this green to brown insect lays eggs along the stems and sucks juices from them. They can also carry disease.

Aphids Also called plant lice, they are green or brown sucking insects that colonize along buds and young shoots in spring. Luckily, they are easy to control with soapy water or a commercial insecticide.

Leaf Rollers These caterpillars roll themselves up in the foliage and eat through it from the inside out in spring. They also bore small holes into the base of the buds. Use a commercial insecticide.

Thrips These microscopic insects squirm between the petals of the bud and suck juices from it. Buds fail to open or produce distorted, brown flowers. Thrips favor white and pastel roses. Remove infested buds; use a commercial insecticide.

Midge A minute maggot causes sudden blackening of buds and young shoots, which should be cut off. Use a commercial insecticide.

Japanese Beetle Shiny copper and green insects eat holes in the flowers in midsummer, especially the varieties with lighter colors. Hand pick or spray with commercial insecticide. Grubs can be stopped with a rose insecticide applied to the soil.

Spotted Cucumber Beetle A yellow insect with 12 dark spots on its wing covers, it feeds on rose blooms from time to time. It also is a carrier of bacterial disease. Use a commercial insecticide.

Leaf Cutting Bee This bee bites neat, perfect circles in the margins of the leaves but luckily does not bother the blooms. Use a commercial insecticide.

Mildew This fungus disease is characterized by a white powder coating the leaves, which curl and become distorted in severe cases. Mildew occurs when days are warm, nights cool, and air circulation poor. Use a commercial fungicide.

Harlequin Bug A brightly colored red and black insect, mostly found in the South, sucks the leaves, leaving calico markings and causing wilt. Use a commercial insecticide.

Black Spot As the name suggests, this fungus disease causes round, black spots on the leaves. The leaves turn yellow and eventually fall off. The disease is spread by splashing water, so run sprinklers only in morning. Use a commercial fungicide.

Canker This fungus disease usually enters through wounds and causes canes to turn brown, purple, or white. Prune to below the canker in early spring, and apply a spray of dormant oil.

Rust Primarily confined to the Pacific coast, it causes orange spots on the undersides of leaves to appear in wet and mild weather. Use a commercial rose spray.

Cane Borer Boring insects can tunnel into canes or under bark. Where this is a problem, seal canes after pruning. Use a commercial insecticide.

Not illustrated, but potentially lethal, are nematodes, which are tiny animals that cause swellings on roots and cause stunted growth. Use an all-purpose rose spray that specifically mentions nematodes. Crown gall is another underground problem, a bacterial disease that causes rough, round growth on the roots or bud union. Sorry, but remove the plant.

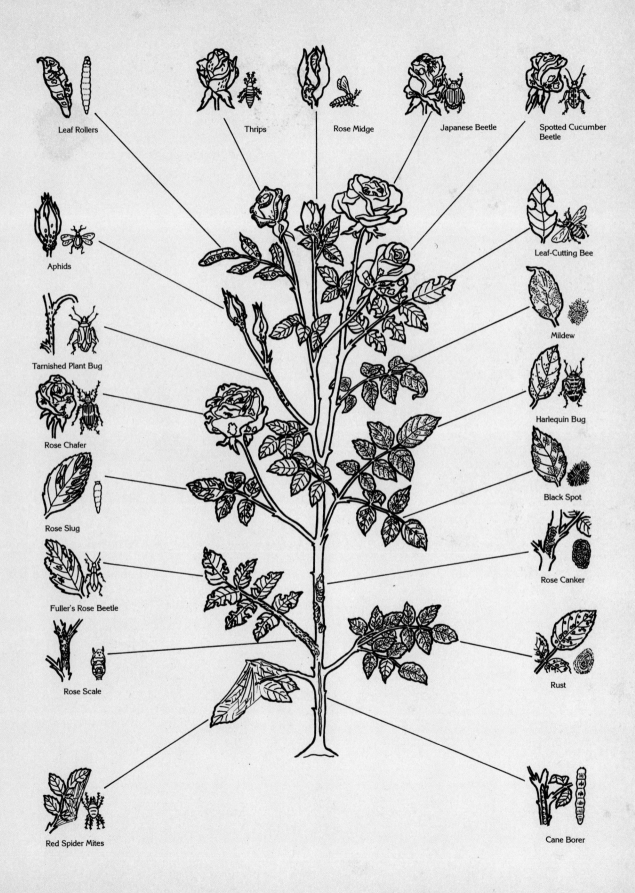

Leaf Rollers

Thrips

Rose Midge

Japanese Beetle

Spotted Cucumber Beetle

Aphids

Tarnished Plant Bug

Rose Chafer

Rose Slug

Fuller's Rose Beetle

Rose Scale

Red Spider Mites

Leaf-Cutting Bee

Mildew

Harlequin Bug

Black Spot

Rose Canker

Rust

Cane Borer

A Rose is a Rose

Is a Rose

Shakespeare once wrote that a rose by any other name was still a rose and smelled as sweet. Whether they're fragrant or not, roses come in sizes, forms, and colors to win any heart. Choosing roses is as easy as A,B,C — alba, bourbon, centifolia, damask, eglanteria, floribunda, grandiflora, hybrid tea. . . .

When you plant roses, you plant for years of beauty. To make sure you achieve it, plan ahead; later you can sit back and enjoy the garden. Choose your roses with care, looking at color, form, height, and hardiness before buying. With success come satisfaction, happiness, admiration.

Old Garden Roses

It's more than nostalgia or historical significance that makes all of the roses in grandmother's garden so popular. They stand on their own virtues—beauty, fragrance, hardiness, low maintenance, charm, long life. Flowers of all colors vary in form—from delicate singles to robust doubles. Old garden roses are a welcome contrast to the styles of today, a not-to-be-forgotten link with yesterday. By definition, any rose belonging to a class in existence before hybrid teas (1867) is an old garden rose.

ALBA

Albas are tall, dense, hardy, and disease-resistant roses characterized by blue-green foliage. Medium-size flowers are in tones of pink or white, borne in clusters and deliciously fragrant. Like so many of the old fashioned roses, they bloom only once a year.

KÖNIGIN von DÄNEMARK
Flesh pink, very double, quartered flowers have a darker center and unfold from a peachy bud.

MAIDEN'S BLUSH
Blush pink, globular flowers fading to white bloom on long arching canes.

BOURBON

Vigorous, shrubby plants have glossy, bright green leaves and clusters of fragrant double flowers. Bourbons are moderately hardy and exhibit good repeat bloom.

LA REINE VICTORIA
This slender, upright rose has cup-shaped, rich pink flowers that deepen in tone with age. Its famous sport, Mme. Pierre Oger, is identical in all respects, except the flower is blush pink, developing a rosy cast as it opens. Both varieties are hardy and relatively disease resistant. The flowers are deeply fragrant and long lasting when cut.

SOUVENIR de la MALMAISON
Large, flat, quartered blooms of flesh pink with a rosy center appear freely on a dwarf, compact plant.

VARIEGATA di BOLOGNA
One of the finest striped roses. This tall-growing plant has globular white flowers, striped in purplish-red shades.

CENTIFOLIA

These are the cabbage roses, so named for the 100 or more petals that overlap like leaves of a cabbage. They are also called Provence roses for the part of France where they were once widely grown. Globular flowers of white through deep rose bloom once a year on slender, arching branches that carry wrinkled leaves. The blooms have a sweet fragrance; the plants are very hardy.

PETITE de HOLLANDE
Small, double, rose-pink flowers bloom in clusters on a medium-size, bushy plant.

ROSE de MEAUX
This is the miniature of the old garden roses. Tiny, double, light pink flowers are like pompons and give a charming, airy grace to this short plant. Although hardy in most areas of the country, this variety is susceptible to black spot disease. Flowers are about 1½ inches wide and come in either red or white. Plants will grow 2 feet tall.

CHINA

The Chinas, with delicate-textured small flowers of pink or red, have played an important role in the development of modern roses. Their reliable and consistent repeat bloom coupled with glossy, almost evergreen foliage is a definite plus; unfortunately, they are extremely tender.

GREEN ROSE
An oddity in the rose world is the green rose, *Rosa chinensis viridiflora.* The flowers are very small; the green "petals" are actually a multitude of sepals.

HERMOSA
High-centered, fragrant, double, blush-pink flowers that bloom in clusters are set off by blue-green leaves.

OLD BLUSH
Two-tone pink, semi-double flowers appear in large clusters on an upright plant and have only a slight fragrance.

DAMASK

Known for their fragrance, these roses are medium to large in size, with drooping or arching branches. They're extremely hardy and disease resistant. Except for the autumn damasks, they bloom just once.

CELSIANA
A graceful, slender plant with gray-toned foliage bears large, semi-double blooms of pale pink that fade to a warm blush. The petals are crinkled, giving an interesting appearance to the flower. Gold stamens set off the center of the flower. The loose, informal flowers are flat and once blooming.

MADAM HARDY
One of the most splendid white roses of all time is this very double, cup-shaped flower that opens flat to reveal a green eye in the center. A tinge of pink often appears on the buds of these spring bloomers.

ROSE de RESCHT
Rosettes of bright fuchsia to deep pink flowers bloom over a long season on dwarf, compact bushes.

GALLICA

The French rose, and the oldest one known, has flowers of red, pink, or purple over dark green, rough-textured leaves. The plants are hardy but occasionally will look spindly; the flowers may be single or double, with tremendous fragrance or none at all, and bloom once in spring.

CAMAIEUX
Low-growing plants have semi-double flowers of white, striped with rosy purple; they have a spicy fragrance.

CARDINAL de RICHELIEU
Dark, wine-red to purple flowers are large, fragrant, and double. The bush is medium in height and about as wide as tall.

CHARLES de MILLS

Rounded, cup-shaped blooms packed with petals give this variety an almost crepe paper-like appearance. Flowers are deep red with purplish undertone. A very popular and vigorous variety.

ROSA MUNDI
This rose, known botanically as *Rosa gallica versicolor,* is striped pink, red, and white, every petal different from the other. The flowers are semi-double and accented with bright yellow stamens. It is often confused with York and Lancaster.

HYBRID FOETIDA

This class of roses contributed its beautiful yellow color to modern hybrids. The plants are vigorous, tall, once blooming, but susceptible to black spot. The name comes from the offensive odor found in the species.

HARISON'S YELLOW

Clouds of small, semi-double, open, very fragrant, bright yellow flowers cover this plant and almost hide its small, rich green, ferny leaves. Early American settlers took this rose with them wherever they went.

HYBRID PERPETUAL

This class is the transition between old and modern roses. The plants are tall, vigorous, hardy, and bloom repeatedly all summer. Flowers are large, double, and colored white, pink, red, or mauve.

BARONESS ROTHSCHILD
Stiff, erect plants are graced with large, fully double, cupped flowers of soft rose, tinted with white.

FRAU KARL DRUSCHKI
Pointed buds open into sparkling snow white flowers, often touched with pink. It's one of the best. Plants easily grow six feet tall and flower repeatedly all season long.

GÉNERAL JACQUEMINOT

Long stems made this an early florist's rose. Blooms are cupped, bright, clear red, and distinctively fragrant.

MRS. JOHN LAING

Low-growing for its class, this rose is covered with soft pink flowers that are strongly fragrant.

PAUL NEYRON

Cupped flowers of rose-pink tinted lilac bloom on long stems over rich green foliage.

ROGER LAMBELIN

This rose is very distinct, with wavy petals of maroon, edged in white. A medium-size plant, its flower is slightly fragrant.

HYBRID SPINOSISSIMA

Hybrids of the Scotch rose are mostly modern additions to the shrub border, valued for their bloom.

FRÜHLINGSGOLD

Although it blooms only once, this rose is worth the space if you want a large, vigorous plant with arching canes filled with good-sized, single, very fragrant flowers of pure golden yellow.

STANWELL PERPETUAL

Blush-pink flowers are medium-size, sweetly fragrant, double, and repeat blooming on this large but graceful plant.

MOSS

Mutations of the centifolias, the moss roses have small, hairy glands covering the sepals (and sometimes the stem and leaves) that look like moss and produce a marvelous fragrance. The plants are hardy and, for the most part, medium in height, ranging from six to eight feet. The flowers are large, double, and globular, blooming later in the spring than most roses. Most varieties of moss roses bloom only once a year. Others will bloom sporadically throughout the summer and early fall.

ALFRED de DALMAS

Called Mousseline by some, this rose is a compact grower with pale pink flowers that bleach to white in the heat of the sun. It shows some repeat bloom.

COMMON MOSS

Globular flowers open flat to reveal a button center amid clear pink petals. This very popular moss rose is also called Communis.

CRESTED MOSS

Summer clusters of pink flowers open from tri-cornered, mossy buds, giving the rose its other name, Chapeau de Napoléon.

GLOIRE des MOUSSEUX

Midsummer blooms are a clear, bright salmon pink, deeper in the center and appearing in clusters.

SALET

Flowers of rosy pink open flat and show some repeat bloom.

NOISETTE

Mild-climate-only plants are tall, making good climbers, and bear clusters of white, red, pink, purple, or yellow flowers throughout summer.

MARECHAL NIEL

Large double flowers of golden yellow bloom profusely, with a strong fragrance.

PORTLAND

Sturdy, erect bushes produce double, very fragrant flowers all season.

JACQUES CARTIER

Light pink flowers with a dark button center are large and full, often quartered, blooming atop light green leaves. Not winter hardy.

SPECIES

Species roses are wild roses, but many deserve a place in the garden. All are single-flowered, and most grow into very large plants.

AUSTRIAN COPPER
Rosa foetida bicolor

Arching canes are smothered in late spring with masses of coppery-red flowers that are golden yellow on the reverse of the petals.

CHESTNUT ROSE
Rosa roxburghi

Gray branches shed their bark, and the flower bud looks like a chestnut burr, making this rose unique. The flowers are double, flat, and medium pink; the bush repeats its bloom and grows close to the ground.

FATHER HUGO'S ROSE
Rosa hugonis

This rose is one of the first to bloom and should be grown as a climber. The masses of flowers are sunny yellow, blooming on drooping branches over small, dark green leaves.

TEA

Translucent, pastel flowers that give color to the garden all summer also emit a delicious, fresh-tea-leaf fragrance. The teas are graceful but tender plants of medium height.

CATHERINE MERMET

Double flowers of soft flesh pink with lilac edges and creamy overtones have perfect form. The stems are long and perfect for cutting.

MAMAN COCHET

Very double, large flowers have classic form and petals of soft pink with a yellow base. Flowers are scented and appear all season long. It will grow four feet tall.

Shrub-Like Roses

So often and unjustifiably neglected in the landscape setting is the shrub rose. Few plants in a mixed border are so tough, hardy, and tolerant of neglect and poor growing conditions. Use shrub roses singly or in mass for a bold effect. They vary in height, from ground covers to hedges and screens, and bloom in all colors and flower forms for a longer period than any other shrub. Large yet luxuriant, the shrub rose, whether old fashioned or modern, deserves to be in every garden.

EGLANTERIA

Hybrids of the Sweetbrier rose have a large, dense, thorny habit of growth and leaves that are scented like apples. Small single or semi-double pink flowers bloom in spring on hardy plants that will often grow from eight to 12 feet high. Colorful hips appear after each bloom.

LADY PENZANCE
Small, single flowers of coppery pink with yellow centers bloom on large, arching plants that look almost scarlet from a distance. Foliage and flowers are fragrant, but plants are susceptible to black spot.

LORD PENZANCE
Clusters of small fawn flowers, tinted lemon-yellow, bloom on strong stems. This variety does not bloom as early or as long as Lady Penzance.

HYBRID MOYESI

Hybrids of *Rosa moyesi* are large, stiff, hardy plants. Most will reach about six feet in height. All have uniquely attractive red hips following each bloom. Most are very disease resistant.

NEVADA
Pink buds open into creamy-white, large, single flowers that are often splashed with red. Each flower has attractive, prominent, golden-yellow stamens. The plant is vigorous and shows repeat bloom. Most will grow five to seven feet tall.

HYBRID RUGOSA

Hybrids of *Rosa rugosa* show the same characteristics as their parent—hardiness; disease resistance; easy care; large, dense growth; and deep green, wrinkled foliage. Their hips are a valued source of vitamin C.

BLANC DOUBLE de COUBERT

Large, double, very fragrant, snow-white blooms appear all summer on large, spreading plants that grow to five feet in height. Flowers are sweetly fragrant and are followed by attractive red hips in the fall. Mature hips are an excellent source of vitamin C. This variety is one of the best white shrubs.

DELICATA

This rose is anything but delicate. It will thrive where winter temperatures drop to 50 degrees below zero (Fahrenheit); it will do equally well on coastal sand dunes where the air is salt laden. The three-inch blooms appear repeatedly; hips are the size and color of crab apples, and they are high in vitamin C.

F. J. GROOTENDORST

Tiny, double flowers are frilled like carnations and bloom in clusters throughout the summer on tall, upright plants. Well-known sports of this rose include Pink Grootendorst, a medium dusty pink, and Grootendorst Supreme, a bright medium crimson, identical in all respects except for flower color. All three can reach six feet tall.

MAX GRAF

This rose is valuable as a ground cover or trailer. It has large, single, bright pink flowers with golden centers. Bloom is profuse and fragrant but appears only once per season. Good choice for problem slopes where other ground covers will not thrive.

KORDESI

These modern shrubs and semi-climbers are very hardy and offer a variety of flower forms and colors. All have glossy foliage.

DORTMUND

A vigorous climber, this rose has large, single, striking crimson flowers with white eyes. The blooms grow in clusters and repeat profusely. Bright orange hips form after flowers fade. This variety will eventually grow 15 feet long.

HEIDELBERG

Clusters of large, scarlet and crimson flowers bloom on a bushy plant. Use as either a shrub or climber.

MUSK

Musks, or hybrid moschatas, will grow in less sun than any other rose. They bloom all season in large clusters or trusses; their fragrance is heavy. Some varieties have double or semi-double flowers but most are singles. Plants are tall, disease resistant, and moderately hardy.

BELINDA

Wavy petals of soft pink grace semi-double, white-centered flowers. Plants flower repeatedly on trusses ten feet in length.

BUFF BEAUTY

A beauty it is, with double flowers of pale apricot-yellow. Plants grow six feet tall and are a good choice for planting along a fence.

CORNELIA

Coral-pink flowers are flushed with yellow and are small, double, and fluffy. Blooms appear all summer, even in partial shade. Plants will grow eight feet long.

WILL SCARLET

Semi-double flowers of scarlet are a delight on this landscape plant. It blooms repeatedly throughout the season, with colorful orange hips.

SHRUB

This class is a "catchall" for roses that don't fit into the other categories. Shrubs are of varied parentage but are generally large, hardy, and disease resistant.

GOLDEN WINGS

Large, single blooms of sulphur-yellow are graceful, slightly fragrant, and flower again and again. Stamens are prominent; attractive.

SEA FOAM

A sea of double, slightly fragrant, creamy-white flowers borne in clusters envelop this trailing plant all summer. The flexible, normally arching canes can climb a medium-size trellis, weep down an embankment, or form a handsome ground cover.

SPARRIESHOOP

Large, single, light pink flowers bloom off and on all season on an upright plant. It can grow 12 feet tall.

Sea Foam is versatile enough to fit into any landscape plan.

Belinda will easily produce masses of spectacular color, even in partial shade.

Hybrid Tea Roses

The classic beauty of the rose is defined in the hybrid teas. As the long pointed buds open, they reveal swirls of petals and elegant, high-centered blooms in every color but blue. There's hardly one that doesn't emit that fine and famous rose fragrance from flowers on plants two to five feet high. Alone or by the dozen, the hybrid tea is the perfect flower for a vase, perched proudly upon a long cutting stem. Pick one of the following and you won't be disappointed.

AMERICAN HERITAGE
Large and long double flowers of creamy yellow tickled with pink bloom on tall, upright plants. Slightly tender.

ANTIGUA
The blooms are double, golden apricot, and fragrant; the petals are wavy; the plant, tall. Like most varieties this color, it is tender.

APOLLO
Medium yellow, loose, fragrant flowers cover this tall plant. It's good for garden display, and the foliage is disease-resistant.

BEWITCHED
Large, silky pink flowers with a damask fragrance bloom profusely on a vigorous plant. This variety will commonly grow to 4 feet tall.

BIG BEN
Large, perfectly formed, heavily fragrant flowers are dark, velvety red and bloom freely on a tall bush.

BLUE MOON
Like all mauves, Blue Moon is very fragrant. The flowers of lilac blue cover an upright, medium-size plant.

CANDY STRIPE
This sport of Pink Peach has large, fully double, cupped-shaped, and fragrant blooms that are streaked in shades of pink and white on a plant of medium height. Use Candy Stripe with other roses or alone as a unique specimen plant.

CARLA
Soft pink petals with salmon undertones form a double, fragrant flower gracing a medium plant. Tender.

CENTURY TWO
Large, pale pink flowers are fragrant and shaded slightly darker on the outside of the petals; they're borne on a medium-height plant.

CHARLOTTE ARMSTRONG
A famous parent of many roses, this is a tall, bushy plant with full, loose, fragrant flowers of deep pink to light red.

CHICAGO PEACE
Identical to Peace except for the flower color, which varies in shades of yellow, bronze, and deep pink.

CHRISTIAN DIOR
All plants are adorned with double, glowing, cherry red blossoms that are slightly fragrant. Plants are compact and tall.

CHRYSLER IMPERIAL
A classic among reds, this very fragrant, large, perfectly formed rose blooms on a medium-size plant. At its best in warm weather. Hardier than other varieties.

COLOR MAGIC
Never the same twice, the petals of this rose change color from ivory to pink, coral, and rose. The blooms are large; the plant is medium size. Tender in cold climates.

COLUMBUS QUEEN

This well-branched, vigorous fragrant variety easily produces masses of 4- to 4½-inch pink, cupped flowers. Petals are slightly darker on the reverse side.

COMMAND PERFORMANCE

Reflexed petals give a star shape to this fragrant, orange-red rose that blooms on a very vigorous and tall plant.

CONFIDENCE

Large, sweetly fragrant blooms of pearly light pink are shaded in peach and yellow. Of medium height, it prefers warm climates. Stems are long and slender.

CRIMSON GLORY

Cupped, large flowers are deep, velvety red and extremely fragrant. The plant is low-growing and spreading.

DAINTY BESS

This single, 5-petalled flower is fragrant, soft rose pink, and set off by maroon stamens. Vigorous and free-blooming.

DIAMOND JUBILEE

Large, double, fragrant flowers are buff yellow to apricot on a plant of medium height. Growth is upright and compact; foliage, dark green and leathery. A good choice for mass planting or mixed rose border.

DOUBLE DELIGHT

A delight to look at and smell—with white petals edged in raspberry red to form a perfect flower on a low, spreading plant.

DUET

A rose of medium height that almost never stops producing fragrant, sparkling pink flowers with a deep pink reverse.

ECLIPSE

This rose first bloomed on the day of an eclipse in 1932 and is at its best in its golden yellow bud stage.

EIFFEL TOWER

The plant towers over others in the rose garden; the flowers are high-centered, very fragrant, and medium pink. The bushes are upright, vigorous, and very free-flowering.

ELECTRON

Thorny stems are topped with glowing pink, fragrant blooms, produced freely on a bushy, medium-size plant.

FIRST LOVE

Long, slender buds and flowers of pearly pink are attractive and fragrant on a tall plant or in a vase. A tender variety in cold areas.

FIRST PRIZE

Perfection in flower form is found on this fragrant rose with ivory pink centers, deeper pink outside.

FRAGRANT CLOUD

Clusters of orange-red flowers carry a heavy fragrance and bloom freely on a low- to medium-growing bush.

FRIENDSHIP

Friendship has sweet, fragrant, flesh-colored flowers.

GARDEN PARTY

This white, floriferous plant produces large, high-centered flowers.

GRANADA

Fragrant flowers are a luscious mix of red, gold, yellow, and pink over crinkled foliage. Slightly tender.

GRAND SLAM

Vigorous and bigger than average, this variety has superb form from bud through bloom. Excellent for cutting and can provide a source of long-stemmed flowers.

GYPSY

Buds almost black in color open into dark orange-red, fiery double flowers with a spicy fragrance. The plants grow tall.

HEIRLOOM

Semi-double, magenta flowers lighten to lilac as they age. Richly fragrant and decorative.

HELEN TRAUBEL

Tall plants produce apricot-pink, fragrant flowers often troubled by a weak neck.

IRISH GOLD

Fragrant, medium-yellow blooms are pointed and often tinged with pink. The plant grows low and tender.

ISABEL de ORTIZ

Well-formed flowers of deep pink with a silver reverse are large, double, and fragrant. Borne on long stems on a tall plant. Tender.

JADIS

Slender, very fragrant blooms of rose-pink top an upright, tall plant.

JOHN F. KENNEDY

Large, graceful, pointed buds appear on the tender plants all summer long, opening to reveal 3- or 4-inch dazzling white flowers. Foliage is dark green and disease-free. With good growing conditions the upright plants will grow to 4 feet tall.

Columbus Queen is a shapely, orchid-tinted pink with handsome foliage. Its long stems are almost thorn-free.

KING'S RANSOM

Almost perfect golden yellow, fragrant blooms sit atop long cutting stems. Tender in cold climates. Foliage is glossy green.

KORDES' PERFECTA

Creamy-white petals, tipped with crimson, on a fragrant, double flower grace this tall plant. The color darkens as the temperature climbs.

LADY X

High-centered blooms of pale pinkish lavender are slightly fragrant on this, the tallest and most vigorous of the mauve roses.

LEMON SPICE

The name says it all—lemon yellow blooms with a spicy fragrance. The plant is tall and spreading; the stems, weak and often thin.

MATTERHORN

Yellow, tinted buds open into high-centered, large, ivory-white flowers atop this very tall plant.

MEDALLION

Tall, robust plants produce equally large, light apricot blooms with a fruity fragrance and a crepe paper texture.

MICHELE MEILLAND

As feminine as its name, this creamy-pink, perfectly formed flower is shaded salmon in the center. It's a medium grower and a vigorous bloomer.

MIRANDY

This old-timer in rose gardens has an old-fashioned fragrance and double, deep red flowers on a compact, bushy plant. At its best where the weather is warm and humid.

MISS ALL-AMERICAN BEAUTY

So dark pink it's almost red, this large, cupped, double, very fragrant rose blooms on a plant of medium height.

MISTER LINCOLN

This tall, long-stemmed, high-centered fragrant beauty is one of the best of the dark reds.

MOJAVE

The colors of the desert shine red, apricot, and orange on a tall, slender flower and plant of the same shape.

NEUE REVUE

The plant's tall and so thorny you can hardly touch it; the flower is chalky white, edged in bright red. Double and fragrant.

OKLAHOMA

So dark red it's almost black, Oklahoma is tall and sturdy with velvety, very fragrant flowers.

OLDTIMER

Oldtimer produces masses of yellow-bronze flowers all summer long. Blooms are large, often reaching 7 inches in diameter.

OREGOLD

The blooms are large, loose, and deep gold that does not fade. Fragrant on a medium-size bush.

PAPA MEILLAND

Very fragrant, dark, velvety crimson blooms open slowly and adorn an erect, medium-growing plant.

PARADISE

Magnificent, perfectly shaped blooms of silvery mauve are shaded to pink at the center and highlighted by petals with red edges. The flowers are fragrant on tall, strong stems.

PASCALI

The bloom is small but perfectly formed, creamy white, and dependable, with a touch of fragrance on a tall plant.

PEACE

This timeless favorite is very full, light to golden yellow, and flushed with pink on the edges of a medium-size, spreading plant.

PEER GYNT

Tall and husky, this bush has large, full, golden yellow flowers with a touch of red on the edges of the petals as it ages. It's tender but bounces back quickly.

PERFUME DELIGHT

As the name says, the rose is richly fragrant with intense, old rose pink flowers of classic form on a medium-size plant. Plants are very disease resistant.

PHARAOH

Brilliant red, velvet-like flowers on long stems perfect for cutting. The plants are vigorous and tall.

PINK PEACE

The name is misleading, because this is not a pink duplicate of Peace but is tall and bushy with very fragrant flowers of deep, dusty pink.

PORTRAIT

The bush is tall and never without medium-size, fragrant blooms of blended pinks and ivory.

PRISTINE

Feminine purity best describes the delicate white with pink picotee, lightly fragrant flowers that bloom on a slightly tender plant of medium height. Use Pristine alone as a specimen plant, or mix with other hybrid teas.

Perfume Delight is all its name implies. A delightful, spicy fragrance escapes when the bright pink flowers unfold.

PROMISE

Pure, clear, dawn-pink flowers are large, high-centered, and lightly fragrant on a tall plant.

PROUD LAND

This brilliant red, flowering rose easily grows 6 feet tall. Blooms are fragrant and often measure 6 inches in diameter. Stems are long.

RED DEVIL

Large, very double blooms of bright, medium red have a silvery reverse and a pleasing fragrance on a plant of medium height.

RED LION

Thick, cherry-red petals form a perfect, high-centered flower on a medium tall bush.

RED MASTERPIECE

The flowers on this medium to tall rose are double, high centered, very fragrant, and deep red, marred only by petal edges sensitive to sunlight.

ROSE GAUJARD

Plant grows tall and very wide. Double, fragrant flowers of cherry red with a reverse of pale pink and silvery white. Here's one hybrid tea that likes a little shade.

ROYAL HIGHNESS

It's very tender but has perfectly formed, soft pale pink, very fragrant flowers that make it worth the effort to grow this tall plant.

RUBAIYAT

A hardy, vigorous bloomer, Rubaiyat produces large rose-red flowers all season. Foliage is dark green and attractive.

SEASHELL

The flowers are small but very numerous in luminous shades of shrimp pink, peach, and coral; they're strongly fragrant. The plant is of medium height and branches heavily. Slightly tender.

SILVER LINING

Very fragrant blooms of silvery pink have darker pink edges and a slightly cupped form. The tender plant is a medium grower.

SNOWFIRE

Bright scarlet petals are a blaze of color on a pure white reverse. The flowers are large, double, and open; the plants, compact and tender.

SOUTH SEAS

Large, frilled flowers open flat and fragrant in shades of soft salmon to coral pink on long stems and on a spreading plant.

SPELLBINDER

As ivory buds unfurl, the roses begin to take on a pink blush that grows deeper and deeper, until the large, double flowers end up a rose-red. A tender plant of medium height.

STERLING SILVER

The original lavender rose, Sterling Silver produces medium-size, slightly fragrant flowers. Foliage is dark, glossy, and attractive. Stems are long.

SUMMER SUNSHINE

The brightest of the yellow roses is large, full, and fragrant and on a medium to tall plant. Tender in cold climates. The color doesn't fade.

SUNSET JUBILEE

Very large, high-centered blooms of coppery pink with light yellow tints become more brilliant as the weather warms up. The medium-tall plant is almost never out of bloom.

SUSAN MASSU

Long thorny stems are clothed with fragrant, high-centered blooms of light yellow, tipped with a blush of light pink.

SUTTER'S GOLD

Orange and rust-red buds open into very fragrant, large, golden orange flowers with scarlet veining and petal edges. In cool weather, the tall plant produces blooms of more vibrant color.

SWARTHMORE

Tall, somewhat tender plants have slightly fragrant, high-centered flowers of cherry pink to dusty rose, with petals edged in gray. Plants are vigorous, bushy, and free-flowering.

TIFFANY

Long buds open to reveal delicate pink flowers with a yellow base. Famous for their heavy fragrance and long-cutting stems. Foliage is dark green and attractive.

TORO

Many say this is the same rose as Uncle Joe. Both have enormous buds that unfurl slowly into large, strongly perfumed, dark red flowers on long, strong stems.

TROPICANA

The first of the fluorescent coral-orange roses is still one of the most popular, with perfectly formed, fruity-scented flowers on a tall, spreading plant.

WHITE KNIGHT

Large, pure white, high-centered flowers appear on long stems all season long. Plants are vigorous and upright with attractive light green foliage.

WHITE MASTERPIECE

Compact, spreading plants produce very large, ruffled pure white double flowers on a very thick penduncle. Slightly tender in cold climate areas. Very disease resistant.

WINI EDMUNDS

High, reflexed flowers are strawberry colored, with a straw yellow reverse and moderately fragrant on a tall plant. Tender.

YANKEE DOODLE

Large, globular flowers of light yellow are flushed with apricot and salmon, fragrant, and produced on a upright, bushy plant. Tender in cold climates. Plants are vigorous and hardy with attractive olive-green foliage. A good specimen plant in almost any location.

A sure favorite in any garden, Double Delight is hardy, long-stemmed, and fragrant, with disease-resistant foliage.

Grandifloras

A compromise in the rose garden is the grandiflora, which exhibits the best traits of its parents, the hybrid tea and the floribunda. From the hybrid tea it inherits flower form and long cutting stems; from the floribunda it receives hardiness, continuous flowering, and clusters of blooms generally at the same stage of development. The unique thing about most members of this class is that they grow taller than either parent. You can plant the grandiflora at the back of the border, or use it as a screen.

AQUARIUS
Long, tight buds open into perfectly formed flowers that are blended in pinks and mildly fragrant. The blooms are produced one per stem or in clusters on a tall, slender plant.

ARIZONA
Large, double flowers are the colors of an Arizona sunset—orange, gold, copper, and pink—very fragrant and blooming on a medium-size, upright, and slightly tender plant.

CAMELOT
Double, cup-shaped, decorative blooms are coral-pink and bloom in clusters on a vigorous bush.

CARROUSEL
Because this plant is very tall, place it in the background. The vivid flowers are semi-double, dark red, and lightly scented in small clusters.

COMANCHE
Bold, brick-red to orange blooms are large, double, and well formed. The flowers appear singly and in clusters, are quick to repeat, and have a slight fragrance.

JOHN S. ARMSTRONG
Slightly fragrant, double, cupped flowers are vivid dark red and bloom freely on a tall plant.

MONTEZUMA
Coral-orange and terra-cotta in color, double, high-centered blooms have a slight scent. The plants are tall and do best in moist climates.

MOUNT SHASTA
Seemingly as high as a mountain, this rose has blooms as beautiful in bud as they are when the large, fragrant white flowers are open. It is not at its best in midsummer heat.

OLÉ
The double, orange-red blooms are ruffled and frilled and look like a camellia. The fragrant flowers appear profusely above dark green, holly-like foliage.

PINK PARFAIT
Pastel pink, double blooms, teamed up with abundant foliage, are together so thick you can barely see the canes of this medium-size plant.

PROMINENT
It's short for a grandiflora, but the bright orange-red, star-shaped flowers more than make up for it.

QUEEN ELIZABETH
The symbol of perfection among grandifloras is this tall rose with radiant carmine to dawn pink, fragrant blooms in clusters.

SCARLET KNIGHT
Large, slightly fragrant, velvety crimson to scarlet, high-centered flowers bloom heavily on a medium size, bushy plant.

SONIA
The flowers are satiny, small, and on the coral side of pink; the plants are low-growing and tender in cold climates.

Floribundas

The floribunda, or landscape rose, is a cross between the flower form of the hybrid tea and the abundant blooms of the polyantha. Sprays that flower nearly all the time contain every stage of bloom, from tight buds to fully open flowers, on long cutting stems. Floribundas are hardier, lower-growing, and bushier than most hybrid teas, making them a perfect choice for hedges, massing, or borders. On top of all this, the mounded plants show every rose color available and are relatively free of disease.

ACCENT
Sprays of medium, decorative flowers bloom profusely on a low-growing, compact plant, perfect for low hedges and edgings.

ANABELL
Fragrant, rich orange-salmon, showy flowers bloom all summer in large sprays on a low to medium plant. This variety is slightly tender.

ANGEL FACE
Deep lavender, wavy flowers are fragrant and semi-double, opening quickly to show off golden stamens on a low, mounding plant.

APACHE TEARS
Scarlet edges tint the classically formed white flowers that appear one per stem or in clusters on short, upright plants. This variety is slightly tender.

APRICOT NECTAR
Large sprays of double, cupped, creamy apricot flowers are touched with pink and gold and have a very fruity fragrance. The plants are medium-tall, bushy, vigorous, and will not fade out in bright sun.

BAHIA
Double, cupped, orange-red flowers have a golden yellow reverse and a spicy fragrance. Good for massing, the plants are upright and bushy. Plants bloom in large attractive clusters and can be grown as a showy hedge, barrier plantings, or property dividers.

BETTY PRIOR
Growing tall and wide, the plants produce sprays of single, carmine pink, fragrant flowers.

BON BON
Flowers of hybrid tea form are rose-pink with a silvery reverse, blooming in trusses on low-growing plants. Blooms are slightly fragrant and appear all summer long, until the first frost.

CATHEDRAL

Wavy, open flowers on a medium-size bush are vibrant orange with a touch of yellow. They're sweetly fragrant.

CHARISMA
Brilliant orange and gold tones jump from the sprays of flowers that bloom continuously on very low-growing plants. They're excellent for massing or bedding. Flowers are long-lasting and weather resistant.

CIRCUS

Fragrant double flowers are yellow with red edges, becoming more and more red as the blooms age. The plant is low-growing and spreading.

CITY OF BELFAST

Small, double, cupped blooms of metallic orange-red flower in large trusses on a low-growing plant. Ideal for a hedge or foreground.

ELSE POULSEN

Semi-double, slightly fragrant flowers are bright rose-pink, blooming in sprays on a medium-size, bushy plant.

EUROPEANA

Blooms are dark crimson, large, double, and decorative in very large and heavy trusses. New red foliage adorns low, spreading plants.

EVENING STAR

These flowers look like a cross between the bloom form of the hybrid tea and the spray of the floribunda. Flowers of pure white glisten on tender plants of medium height.

FABERGE

Neat, compact plants are clothed in small, warm peach-pink flowers in tight sprays. This one will even stand partial shade.

FASHION

Lively coral and peachy-pink flowers are double and fragrant, opening flat in large sprays on a low, bushy plant that will grow 3 feet tall. Blooms are long-lasting, storm-resistant, and about 3½ inches in diameter.

FIRE KING

Tall, vigorous bushes are clustered with fiery orange-red to scarlet flowers that are free-blooming and musk scented.

FIRST EDITION

Large, double, bright coral blooms are held on good-sized but short-stemmed trusses. The plants are of medium height and spreading.

GENE BOERNER

The medium pink flowers are petite replicas of a perfect hybrid tea, with a slight luminescence and a sweet fragrance. Plants are upright of medium height, with blooms in small inflorescences.

GINGER

Tropicana coral-orange-colored blooms are large, cupped, fragrant, and openly decorative on a low, compact, bushy plant.

ICEBERG

About the tallest of the floribundas, it has pure white, open, double, very fragrant flowers in loose, carefree sprays, set off by light green foliage.

A good choice for edging a walk, driveway, or evergreen planting.

IVORY FASHION

Long buds open slowly into flat, semi-double, fragrant flowers of ivory white on a short to middle-size plant.

LITTLE DARLING

The flowers are little and darling, a blend of yellow and soft pink, with a spicy fragrance. The plants, on the other hand, are large and spreading, bearing flower sprays on arching stems.

MATADOR

Small, startling blooms are a blend of orange and gold, slightly ruffled on a compact, dense plant.

ORANGEADE

Bright, pure orange, semi-double flowers bloom in large sprays on husky and slightly spreading plants.

PICNIC

Here's a vigorous, free-blooming plant of medium height, with flowers of coral that have a yellow base and a tinge of pink.

REDGOLD

Medium, double, slightly fragrant flowers are, as the name implies, gold, edged in red. Plants are neat, low- to medium-growing, and tender. An effective landscaping plant, even though the flowers are slightly smaller than other floribundas. In some locations, Redgold may occasionally look a bit rangy. Blooms appear singly, as well as in large clusters, and turn darker with age.

206

A good choice for most any landscaping situation, Redgold produces masses of long-lasting, showy flowers.

ROSE PARADE

Masses of shrimp pink, large, open, cupped flowers are fragrant and bloom in small sprays on a round and compact, medium-size bush. The double flowers will bloom up to 4 inches across. Rose Parade is very hardy, disease-resistant, and well shaped. Plants will bloom continuously.

SARABANDE

Semi-double, orange-red flowers open flat to show off bright yellow stamens on a low-growing, sprawling plant. Sarabande blooms continuously all season long, with flowers that measure up to 4 inches across. A good choice for larger gardens.

SARATOGA

Low-spreading plants with many branches are smothered in gardenia-like, very fragrant white flowers. Plants will grow 3 feet tall and are hardy in most areas.

SEA PEARL

Buds of pastel pink open into flowers of pearly pink, diffused with peach and yellow. The tall plants generally produce one bloom per stem. Foliage is dark green and attractive; plants upright, bushy, and hardy. Blossoms open to 4½ inches.

SPANISH SUN

Deep golden yellow blooms are large, hybrid tea-shaped, extremely scented, and excellent as cut flowers or as a garden display on a bushy

plant. Blooms measure 2½ to 3 inches across and will often appear on stems up to 10 inches long. Foliage is dark green and shiny.

SPARTAN

Small sprays of orange- to coral-colored, high-centered, very fragrant blooms appear on vigorous plants of medium height. Many blooms are borne singly on slender graceful stems.

SUNSPRITE

Deep, bright, sunny yellow flowers are large, fragrant, and early-blooming on a tidy, very disease-resistant plant. Blooms will measure 3 inches across.

TAMANGO

Disease-resistant, tall- and wide-growing plants are covered with carefree, massive sprays of velvety crimson flowers.

VOGUE

Slender buds open to fragrant, cherry-coral flowers.

WOBURN ABBEY

Bushy, tall-growing plants produce large sprays of orange, fragrant, medium-size flowers that are shaded with red and gold.

POLYANTHA

If you're looking for a rose that is low-growing, compact, blooms continually, and is very hardy, the polyantha is for you. The flowers are small and of informal shape, like pompons, and massed over the plant in very large clusters. Try polyanthas for bedding, low hedges, and foregrounds. Although many polyanthas have been replaced in the rose garden by their larger-growing and showier relatives, the floribundas, several are still worth growing. Blossoms rarely get over 2 inches across, but when in flower, this group of roses is famous for colorful display.

CECILE BRUNNER

This is the original "Sweetheart" rose, with small, double, perfectly formed, light pink-on-yellow flowers of moderate fragrance.

CHINA DOLL

Dense clusters of bright pink, tiny flowers bloom continually and almost hide the low-growing bush that's perfect for a border. Most specimens will grow 18 inches tall. Foliage is leathery and attractive.

MARGO KOSTER

Double, salmon flowers are globular and shaped like tiny ranunculus. The low-growing bushes make good potted plants or edgings. Flowers are slightly fragrant, borne in small clusters. A good choice for greenhouse culture.

THE FAIRY

Use this bushy plant of medium height as a hedge or in the shrub border for everblooming, cone-shaped clusters of delicate, light pink flowers. It grows 2 to 3 feet tall and quickly forms a hardy, compact bush. It's very resistant to insects and disease and will even flower abundantly in partial shade. The Fairy is a good variety for low-maintenance gardens.

One rose no garden should be without is Spartan. It's always spectacular, with a truly delightful fragrance.

Tree Roses

Tree roses, otherwise known as standards, are the crowning glory of the rose garden. If you want to view your favorite blooms at eye level, plant them in the form of tree roses. They will accent a bed, dress up an entrance, or decorate a patio. Formal gardens are perfect sites for tree roses, as is any spot needing a certain air of distinction. You will have to see the beauty of a tree of roses for yourself to appreciate what it can do as a highlight in your garden.

Tree roses are the man-made plants of the rose garden. Onto a root understock is grafted a stem of *Rosa multiflora, R. rugosa,* De la Grifferaie, or a similar strong grower. Onto the stem is budded any bush rose there is—hybrid tea, floribunda, grandiflora, polyantha, miniature, climber. The process is a long one, which makes tree roses more expensive than other roses, but their well-proportioned, full, and wide heads of color make them worth the price.

Tree roses vary in height. Most have trunks three feet tall, but there are others only two feet tall that are perfect for patios, garden apartments, and small terraces. Minis are usually grafted onto an 18-inch trunk, forming an 18-inch ball of color atop it. And occasionally you will see a six-foot tree rose with the canes of a climber tumbling down from the top.

Flowers of tree roses are the same as the flowers of the original bush roses—and better. The color is the same, the blooms larger, of better form, and more freely produced.

Roses available as standards vary from year to year. When choosing yours, pick one of the spreading, rather than upright, varieties for a full, round head three to four feet across. One of the floribundas would be most colorful, and a tree rose of The Fairy or of Sea Foam is spectacular as a light and graceful cloud of blooms.

When planting tree roses, place a stake next to the trunk, and secure the trunk to it in three places with soft ties that will not damage the bark. The stake should extend into the head; it will be hidden by the flowers. Supports can be of metal or decay-resistant wood. Because the bark of the tree is very sensitive to the sun, place the stake on the sunny side, or wrap the trunk in burlap.

When planting a tree rose, remember it is a specimen of beauty, so choose its home carefully. Because the eye will be drawn to it, the background must be complementary and at least as attractive. A light-colored rose against a dark background will make the tree stand out even more. After you have the tree rose in place, especially if warm spring weather is fast approaching, wrap the canes in moist sphagnum moss, or pop a plastic bag over the tree's head. This will prevent the canes from drying out and will help them to sprout more quickly. Just be sure to remove either as soon as the buds break into leaf.

Consider planting tree roses in decorative containers. Not only will you be able to move your specimens around, it will also be easier to protect them in winter. Simply bring the containers indoors into a frost-free area. High in the sky as they are and therefore even more exposed to the rigors of winter, tree roses are the most sensitive to cold and wind and must be heavily protected in all but the mildest of climates.

Climbing Roses

Climbing roses are not climbers in the true sense of the word; they do not send out tendrils and need to be tied to their supports (with a few exceptions). Climbers are really long caned, pliable roses that will usually produce many more flowers if trained horizontally. The class includes climbers that produce loose clusters of large flowers on fairly hardy plants and climbing sports of hybrid teas, grandifloras, floribundas, and polyanthas. The climbing sports have flowers identical to their parents' (sometimes of better quality), but the bushes are not so hardy.

Some climbers are referred to as pillar roses, because they grow smaller, more upright, and with stiffer canes.

ALOHA
Long-stemmed clusters of large, cup-shaped, fragrant, medium rose-pink flowers (with a deeper reverse) bloom recurrently on a climber that grows best on a pillar. A climbing hybrid tea, not a sport of a bush rose.

AMERICA
Slow to climb, easy to train, this large-flowered climber is a bright coral pink, opening from salmon buds. The flowers are large, pointed, spice scented, and seem to glow all summer. The plant is easy to keep just where you want it.

BLAZE
Most nurseries sell the improved strain that blooms heavily in June and fairly regularly all summer. Flowers are medium, semi-double, bright scarlet, cupped, and slightly fragrant. They form in large clusters on an easy grower. Large-flowered climber.

CHEVY CHASE
Chevy Chase is a fine addition to fence or garden wall. This rambler rose carries masses of dark red bloom at the end of each cane. Plants are very vigorous but bloom heavily only once a season. With good growing conditions, mature specimens will grow 15 feet tall.

CORAL DAWN
Large, coral to rose-pink double, the cupped flowers have satiny petals and a pleasing fragrance.

DON JUAN
Slightly stiff stems make this large-flowered climber a good pillar rose. Blooms are dark velvety red, very fragrant, and perfectly formed on long-cutting stems. Tips freeze in cold winters but snap back fast.

DR. J. H. NICOLAS
Large, globular flowers of medium rose-pink are borne in small sprays that give the plant an airy look. The large double blooms are fragrant, and the plant does well on a pillar or trellis. Large-flowered climber.

GOLDEN SHOWERS
Stems of this large-flowered climber are so strong and stiff that it can stand unsupported as a large shrub. Try it on a trellis, too, but it's a little too upright for a fence. Repeating, semi-double flowers are loose, fragrant, and daffodil yellow.

HANDEL
Clusters of wavy, frilled, double flowers are ivory edged in deep rose-pink to red. The strong plant grows quickly and repeats fairly well all summer. Large-flowered climber.

HIGH NOON
Bright, sunny yellow flowers are tinted with red in a double, loose, cupped form. Blooms bear a spicy fragrance and recur on a large and rampant climbing hybrid tea. Individual canes will grow 8 feet or more in length. Foliage is glossy, dark green, and, with good care, is attractive all season long.

JOSEPH'S COAT

Multi-colored, like the Biblical garb for which it was named, this large-flowered climber has buds of orange and red opening into yellow blooms that pass through shades of orange and scarlet as they age. The small fluffy flowers are showy all season on a vigorous pillar rose. Tender.

NEW DAWN

This sport of Dr. W. Van Fleet is identical to it in all respects, except that it blooms repeatedly. Flowers are of the palest pink, double but opening fast on a very large and vigorous plant.

PAUL'S SCARLET CLIMBER

This large-flowered climber is similar to Blaze, its offspring, except that it rarely repeats bloom. The plants are very vigorous, with bright scarlet, weather-resistant flowers borne in large clusters. Foliage is dark green, glossy, attractive, and disease resistant. Plants can grow 16 to 20 feet tall.

PINATA

Similar to Joseph's Coat, but with large flowers, this large-flowered climber has sunshine-yellow blooms, diffused with orange and red. The plant repeats consistently and is so neat and strong it can stand alone as a shrub.

RED FOUNTAIN

Arching canes are filled with sprays of velvety, dark red, ruffled, and cupped double blooms. The fragrance is reminiscent of an old-fashioned rose. Plants are strong and may be trained against supports or left without staking. Large-flowered climber.

RHONDA

Clusters of large, double, salmon-pink flowers bloom heavily on a strong, large-flowered climber.

ROYAL GOLD

Deep yellow, non-fading flowers are moderately fragrant, blooming heavily in June and showing some repeat during the summer. The large-flowered climber is stiff and compact. Tender.

ROYAL SUNSET

Hybrid tea-shaped flowers are large, double, and a deep, rich apricot, fading to light peach in summer heat. The large-flowered climber has a fruity fragrance. Tender.

TALISMAN

Medium-size, yellow-bronze flowers appear on long, slender stems. Blooms open flat, with a strong, pleasant fragrance. The foliage is light green, glossy, and attractive all season. Talisman is easily trained and makes a good choice for arbor or trellis. A vigorous grower in most areas.

TEMPO

Very double, high-centered, deep red flowers bloom in clusters on a tidy, large-flowered climber. An early bloomer, this variety will often be the first climber in the garden to show bloom. Flowers vary between 3 and 4 inches in diameter and are extra showy. Blooms are long lasting and weather resistant. Tempo is a vigorous grower and very disease resistant.

WHITE DAWN

Gardenia-like, snow-white, semi-double flowers are everblooming, fragrant, and clustered on this, the first and still the best white, large-flowered climber. It's hardy, vigorous, and will quickly spread over a large area. Foliage is glossy and attractive.

In addition to these climbers, many popular bush roses have sported to produce climbers. These include Charlotte Armstrong, Chrysler Imperial, Crimson Glory, First Prize, Peace, Queen Elizabeth, Sutter's Gold, and Tropicana.

RAMBLERS

Decades ago, the climbing roses of the garden were the ramblers, descendants of *Rosa wichuraiana* and *R. multiflora*. They are huge and rampant growers, with small flowers appearing in one gorgeous flush of spring bloom. Many ramblers produce supple canes up to 30 feet long that must be pruned back after each bloom period to keep the plants in good condition. Ramblers are also very hardy, but because of their vast size, high maintenance, and limited bloom, they have all but disappeared from the rose marketplace. Replacing them are the large-flowered climbers and climbing hybrid teas of today, which bloom freely, continually, and easily from early spring, right up until frost. Some ramblers are still popular, however, in far northern latitudes.

Enjoy the beauty of Chevy Chase added to fence or garden wall. It carries red flowers at the end of each cane.

Miniature Roses

There is something very precious about a tiny reproduction —whether it be a baby, a dollhouse, or a rose. It won't take long for the charm and attraction of miniature roses to get to you. On a mini, everything is small—the flowers, the leaves, the plant. Plant sizes range from 3 to 4 inches for a micro-mini to 18 inches for a tall grower, with all heights in between. For growing minis in an indoor garden, best results are achieved with one of the lower growing and more compact plants.

BABY BETSY MCCALL
Beautifully formed, dainty, light pink buds and flowers, with just a hint of cream at the base of the petals, grace a mid-size plant.

BABY DARLING
Tulip-shaped buds and free-flowering apricot blooms top this easy-to-grow plant of medium height. There is also a climbing form.

BABY MASQUERADE
Blooms on this mini change from yellow to orange and red as the flowers open and mature. The plant grows tall; there is also a climbing form.

BEAUTY SECRET
This one is vigorous, upright, and tall, with long, pointed buds and medium-red, large, fragrant blooms.

BO-PEEP
This is a micro-mini with double soft pink flowers, always in bloom on a neat and compact plant, at times looking like an old-fashioned rose. Foliage is small, glossy, and very attractive.

CHIPPER
This tall, yet compact and bushy, mini is a blooming fool, with large, coral-pink flowers of excellent form and substance.

CINDERELLA
Dainty white flowers with a hint of pale dawn-pink sit atop this neat and compact micro-mini. There's also a climbing form. It's a good choice for both indoor and outdoor culture,

producing its fragrant flowers all year long if the plants are kept under grow-lights.

CUDDLES
Fully double, high-centered, reflexed, coral-pink blooms stand on a tall, vigorous plant. The foliage is small, glossy, and attractive.

DWARFKING
Dark red, well-shaped buds open flat into double flowers on a strong and bushy plant. Mature plants will grow 10 inches tall and bloom all season.

EASTER MORNING
Very double, fragrant, ivory-white flowers bloom abundantly on a bushy plant. Easter Morning will easily grow 16 inches tall.

FAIRY ROSE

This variety rarely gets over 1 foot tall but still manages to produce a profusion of attractive, rose-red, double flowers. Foliage is glossy and delicate.

GLORIGLO

Magnificent, glowing, fluorescent-orange, high-centered blooms have a white reverse and flower on an unusual and tall bush.

GOLD COIN

Blooms are yellow and open quickly to an attractive, flat, decorative form. The plant is a neat grower of medium height.

GREEN ICE

Apricot buds open into double white flowers that turn light green with age. It blooms in heavy clusters, which make it excellent for hanging baskets.

HULA GIRL

A fresh orange fragrance and a bright, orange-yellow double bloom remind one of a South Pacific sunset. Small, firm foliage covers a bushy, medium plant.

JANNA

Flowers are white with pinkish-red edges; the plant is tall and vigorous.

JEANIE WILLIAMS

Small red and yellow bicolor blooms make this an excellent plant of medium height.

JEANNE LAJOIE

Medium-pink, double flowers have hybrid tea form and bloom repeatedly on this climbing miniature that also doubles well in a hanging basket or window box.

JUDY FISCHER

Profuse flowers have perfect exhibition form and are a medium rose-pink. The plant is tall and strong.

KATHY

Fragrant blooms are rich red with white at the base of the petals on a plant of medium height.

KATHY ROBINSON

Pink with buff reverse flowers top this mini whose blooms repeat well on a tall, bushy plant.

LAVENDER LACE

Very double, fragrant, large flowers of lilac decorate a plant of medium height.

LITTLEST ANGEL

This micro-mini has fragrant, medium-yellow flowers blooming continually on a compact bush.

MAGIC CARROUSEL

One of the best, the plant is tall, the flowers double-white with red edges, the petals pointed and lacy.

MARY ADAIR

Soft, apricot flowers have excellent form and substance and bloom on a plant of medium height.

MARY MARSHALL

A perfect bud and high-centered exhibition flower of coral-orange with a yellow base make this mini a garden favorite.

OVER THE RAINBOW

This mini is tall, blooms profusely, and has striking, high-centered blooms of a unique blend of red and gold.

PIXIE ROSE

Small, very double, delicate flowers of deep rose-pink bloom freely on a dwarf, compact plant.

RED CASCADE

Hundreds of dark red flowers cover this spreading miniature. At home in a hanging basket or covering the ground.

ROSMARIN

A double micro-mini in a blend of pinks is a tiny replica of the perfect hybrid tea.

SCARLET GEM

Pointed petals of clear orange-red top this tall, upright plant. The flower is cupped and very double.

SEABREEZE

Cone-shaped clusters of medium-pink flowers have a hint of yellow at the base and a light, airy appearance.

SHERI ANNE

Good substance and form characterize the orange-red blooms that have a yellow base and flower on a tall plant.

SIMPLEX

Delightful and charming, this medium-size mini has only five petals of white, set off by bright yellow stamens.

STARINA

The favorite of them all has glowing, orange-red, fragrant flowers of classic form.

TOP SECRET

Deep red and fragrant flowers are almost identical to Beauty Secret (of which it is a sport) but with a few more petals.

TOY CLOWN

This high-centered and fragrant mini has white blooms with red edges, much like Magic Carrousel but with fewer petals and not as tall. Foliage is glossy and attractive.

The pale pink, Lavender Lace, resembles its floribunda cousins in shape of bloom and bushiness of foliage.

How that Perfect Rose Happens

The top quality roses introduced every year are not just accidental finds made by rose growers. These new and improved varieties are products of years of observation, patient research, skill, and hard work by hybridizers in the United States and Europe. Luck plays a certain part in the development of an outstanding new rose, but few rose growers can depend on it. Research personnel must have intimate knowledge of which roses make good parents, which good (and bad) traits are passed on most frequently, and which combinations are most apt to produce the desired result.

These traits are the ones most gardeners want their roses to have: disease resistance, vigorous growth, long buds, a color breakthrough, abundant flowering, good foliage, hardiness, fragrance, perfect form. One quality doesn't make a good rose; the entire ensemble does. It sounds like a tall order for even one variety of rose. Yet hybridizers have accomplished the task time and again to give rose lovers satisfaction every year.

The road from creation to eventual introduction of a new variety is a long one, one demanding patience and perseverance. First, some of the crosses may not take. Those that do are sown and grown in the greenhouse where they are evaluated. The promising ones (about one percent) are chosen to be budded for further testing, and the rest are discarded.

The newly budded seedlings are then grown outdoors in field trials for at least two years and usually more. These new roses are viewed in the grower's own field, in public gardens, and often by homeowners in a diversity of climates.

Little by little, through the process of elimination, the field is narrowed to that special rose or roses that will be placed on the market. For every 30,000 seeds planted, chances are only one rose will ever be worth marketing. The odds are staggering to say the least.

Once a selection is made and a decision reached to introduce a new rose, it takes another two years to produce enough plants to sell. So, from the time the initial cross is made, through the greenhouse and outdoor testing, to the ultimate sale, at least seven, and more likely ten, years have passed.

Roses sold in this country are known as two-year plants, meaning that two years have gone by from the time the understock was planted to the harvesting of the new variety. Understock is planted one year, budded the next, and dug the following season. Although the understock is two years old, the new variety has been budded onto it for a little more than one year.

The exception to this process is the miniature rose. Although methods of crossing varieties to make new hybrids are essentially the same, minis are not budded but are grown on their own roots. For this reason, reproduction is quicker, and the testing and waiting period are not so long. Miniatures are propagated by stem cuttings taken after the flowers fade and the wood is hard. Minis will root in several weeks and bloom a few weeks later.

Like tends to beget like in the breeding of plants. When breeders set out to create a new rose, they have a definite goal in mind and select the parent plants with meticulous care. A great deal of time, money, and work will be involved, so they cannot afford a haphazard approach.

Breeding roses is an art, not a science, and involves an infinite number of possible offspring. For example, Charlotte Armstrong is a cross of Soeur Therese x Crimson Glory. You could cross these same roses forever and never come up with another Charlotte Armstrong. In fact, four seeds from the same hip could grow into four entirely different roses.

Charlotte Armstrong was widely used as a parent, however, and produced some famous offspring. Many other roses are used extensively as parents because they pass on desirable traits such as vigor, disease resistance, or fragrance. The offspring may appear with all the possible combinations of characteristics in the parents' backgrounds, but the hybridizer is after that one combination of traits that will give him the perfect rose. He may have to grow 30,000 seedlings to find it.

Below is a hypothetical example of breeding a perfect rose. There is no certainty this combination of parents will produce this rose, but it is possible. The uncertainty also breeds excitement.

Although it's highly unlikely that a home gardener could spare the time or the space needed to develop a new rose variety, it is possible to breed your own roses on a small scale. You might not develop a prizewinning rose, but you will learn a lot about your roses, their life cycle, and their genetic makeup. And most of all, by taking an active part in your rose growing, you will be better able to appreciate the magnificent accomplishment of the rose hybridizers and the modern rose. But before you start, be sure to read through the breeding guidelines shown on the following page.

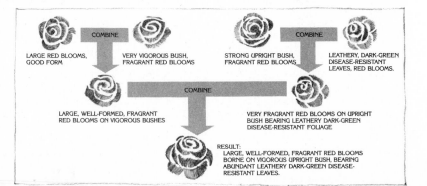

COMBINE

LARGE RED BLOOMS, GOOD FORM

VERY VIGOROUS BUSH, FRAGRANT RED BLOOMS

COMBINE

STRONG UPRIGHT BUSH, FRAGRANT RED BLOOMS,

LEATHERY, DARK-GREEN DISEASE-RESISTANT LEAVES, RED BLOOMS.

COMBINE

LARGE, WELL-FORMED, FRAGRANT RED BLOOMS ON VIGOROUS BUSHES

VERY FRAGRANT RED BLOOMS ON UPRIGHT BUSH BEARING LEATHERY DARK-GREEN DISEASE-RESISTANT FOLIAGE

RESULT:
LARGE, WELL-FORMED, FRAGRANT RED BLOOMS BORNE ON VIGOROUS UPRIGHT BUSH, BEARING ABUNDANT LEATHERY DARK-GREEN DISEASE-RESISTANT LEAVES.

The first step in hybridizing consists of removing the yellow pollen-bearing stamens from the male parent. This is done with tweezers after removing the flower petals. Pollen is placed in a metal box or glass jar for drying and should be stored in the refrigerator. Stamens are removed from the female (seed-bearing) parent, and the rose head is bagged to avoid unintended pollination by insects or wind. When the stigma of the female parent is receptive, or sticky, pollen from the metal box is gathered on the tip of a camel's-hair brush or finger and is dusted on to induce the setting of seed. The bag is replaced for a week, and a record of the cross is made.

After the seed pod swells, matures, and turns red or orange, it is cut from the plant. Seeds are taken out of the hip and placed in a tightly closed can or plastic bag with a moistened germinating medium. They are then placed in the refrigerator to ripen for up to three months. Examine the seeds every two weeks, in case any start to sprout before the three months pass. If any do, remove them and plant them in a light soil mix. When the three months have passed, sow the seeds. When the new seedlings start to bloom (often within six weeks), the poor ones are culled, and the few good ones are saved and grown on—with high hopes.

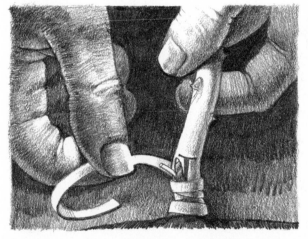

To multiply a promising seedling, a flowering stem is cut from the bush. This is known as budwood. Foliage is removed, leaving a short piece of leaf stem for a "handle." At the leaf axil (where the leaf joins the stem), there is a growth bud. The bud and the handle are both sliced from the stem and slid into a T-shaped slit that has been made in the bark of the understock plant near the soil level. This grafting process is referred to as budding. The bud is held firmly in place by a rubber band that keeps out air and prevents the bud from drying out. Budding is a delicate process, usually performed after the first flush of bloom is complete. If the bud fails to swell and turn green after being budded, a new bud can be added to the understock.

If the bud stays plump and green, the hybridizer knows it is alive and capable of growing (if it dries and shrivels after a week, he tries again). After the seedling bud is knitted in or making growth on its own, the whole top of the understock is cut back to within about ½ inch of the graft. From then on, the understock nurses the developing bud, which grows into a new bush that may eventually find its way into your garden. Test seedlings and commercially produced roses are budded onto understock, primarily of *R. multiflora* or Dr. Huey, to give them greater strength, vigor, and winter hardiness than they would have on their own roots. Then, only if the plants produce the expected results consistently in the field will it be grown commercially.

221

Hardy Bulbs

What are they and
what can they
do for you?

For all who
live in a cold
wintry climate,
few spring sights can
excel the first colorful
appearance of bright crocus. Coming along a bit later to splash clear
blue on a barren garden bed are
scillas and grape hyacinths.

Monarchs of
the spring bulb
parade are tulips
and daffodils which
hybridizers have developed in
a breathtaking variety. Tulips are
available in early-, mid-, and late-
season types to help prolong the
bulb season well into May.

The hardy bulb family also counts glory-of-the-snow, bulb iris, snowdrop (galanthus), and Roman or wood hyacinth among its spring array. And then there are the relatives, such as lily-of-the-valley, grown from "pips," and eranthis, grown from corms, to add to spring color and fragrance.

All spring-flowering bulbs (and relatives) must be planted in the fall. Most are rather easygoing about the soil type, but all need good drainage, so avoid low spots.

A good rule of thumb about planting depth for various bulbs is that it should equal three times the diameter of the bulb. So tiny bulbs, like crocus, need to be planted only 2 to 3 inches deep. A hyacinth bulb will need a hole 8 to 10 inches deep.

The best fertilizer for hardy bulbs is bone meal, and some should be added to the soil when planting.

With the exception of standard tulips, all spring-flowering hardy bulbs listed here may be "naturalized"—or grown in grass, on hillsides, under trees, and allowed to multiply naturally each year. But such plantings **must** stay unmowed until bulb foliage yellows. This allows the bulb to build up

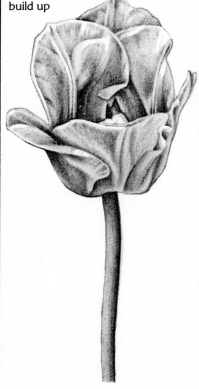

strength for bloom the next spring. Easily suited to natural plantings are most varieties of narcissus or daffodils (daffodils are, in fact, members of the narcissus family). Avoid bulbs of questionable hardiness in your growing zone if you're planning to naturalize.

If you live in zone 9 southward, you will have to treat tulips as annual plants, for they need a long dormant period of cold weather in order to bloom in spring. But it would be a shame to miss the show entirely, and southern gardeners can purchase cold-treated bulbs or may do their own cold-treating by refrigerating bulbs for at least 6 weeks at 40° F. Plant bulbs after the first of December for spring bloom.

In addition to their uses in beds and borders, many hardy bulbs are fine subjects for forcing (bringing into bloom weeks ahead of outdoor flowering dates, to be enjoyed indoors).

Hyacinths and narcissus are the easiest, but if you pick the right varieties, there are many tulips that force very well.

Rules for forcing all bulbs are to plant bulbs in pots in the fall; place where temperatures of 40 to 45° F. will be maintained for approximately 12 weeks (in bottom of refrigerator, in root cellar, or in an outdoor trench). Soil must be kept fairly moist during this time, but not so wet that rot occurs.

If you choose to set pots into an

outdoor trench, dig it 18 inches deep and line it with hay or straw, tucking some in between pots as you set them in place. Cover tops of pots with more straw or hay; then add soil and leaves to reach soil level.

In January, check to see if good roots have formed. If so, bring indoors to a cool, dark place until the foliage is up from 4 to 5 inches. Then bring into warmth and strong light to watch flower buds shoot up.

If you choose to force tulips, the single early and darwin classes are easiest. Among single earlies, try Bellona (golden-yellow), Coleur Cardinal (crimson), or Princess Irene (salmon). Good darwins, include Apeldoorn (orange-scarlet, black base) and Paul Richter (red).

How to Use Bulbs

A massed planting of hardy spring-flowering bulbs is by far
the most spectacular way to use them—even if there are no
more than 20 or 30 bulbs in the "mass." It will heighten
the visual impact to use all one variety and color in a
group. Mixing colors and kinds tends to give a patchwork
look. In a mixed border, space bulbs among the perennials
that will bloom later, counting on perennial foliage to
hide ripening bulb foliage. Plant at least five to a group.

*For a cool green-white scene, set White
Triumphator tulips (lily-flowered) next to
white azaleas and a green box hedge.*

Trumpet daffodil Unsurpassable, above, produces colossal flowers of gold-yellow, and is easy to force (see forcing instructions on page 223). Pots decorate brick ledges flanking a garden fountain and pool. Berlioz, below, of the kaufmanniana group, teams well with daffodil Jack Snipe. Star magnolia, right, backs narcissus Mrs. Ernst H. Krelage.

HARDY BULBS
Tulips

Tulips form such a varied and gorgeous tribe that they deserve your study. Consult bulb catalogs and get to know the species or botanical tulips—they're closer to being perennial than the darwin or cottage types. Included in this group are fosterana, greigi, and kaufmanniana tulips.

Bunch-flowered tulips, as their name implies, send up several blooms on a branched stem. In the May-flowering group are cottage and darwins. Others you should know include graceful lily-flowered, parrot (Gay Presto, above, is one of the parrot group), peony, and fringed tulips.

Remember that all tulips must have excellent drainage and full sun in spring. Let foliage ripen naturally, helping bulbs to bloom the next spring.

Kaufmanniana tulips bloom early on stems 4 to 8 inches long.

Tall stems and cup-shaped blooms are typical of darwin tulips.

For late bloom on very tall stems, plant cottage tulips.

HARDY BULBS
Daffodils

Grow narcissus (daffodils) for many years of spring pleasure. Mostly hardy from zone 4 south, they self-propagate to make big clumps of small ones in a few years' time. To encourage spreading, plant 5 to 7 inches deep in a well-drained location. Plant in fall.

The wide variety of forms in which this bulb is available includes: flatcup, poeticus, trumpet, miniatures, triandrus or bunch-flowered, split-cup (shown above), and cyclamen-flowered.

Remarkably good for naturalizing are trumpet variety narcissus.

Cyclamineus narcissus.

Triandrus narcissus are among the late-flowering varieties.

229

HARDY BULBS
Other Favorites

Earliest spring color is the gift of the little hardy bulbs, like the vivid blue, 6-inch grape-hyacinths above. Muscari (their botanical name) thrive in sun or shade.

There is also a white variety of muscari. Both will multiply rapidly over the years and are a good choice for naturalizing. They bloom in early March. Zone 4.

Eranthis or winter aconite sends up yellow flowers on 5-inch stems in February. It likes shade and a moist location.

Chionodoxa or glory-of-the-snow: starry blue or pink flowers with white centers. Blooms in March, in sun or shade.

Hyacinths White Carnegie, Pink Pearl, and King of the Blues

Hardy through zone 5.
Anemone blanda shows its 6- to 9-inch blue or rose daisy-like blooms in March; it is a handsome companion for early daffodils. Soak bulbs in water overnight, then plant in shade. Most varieties not hardy north of zone 6.

Galanthus, or snowdrop, puts up a nodding white bell-shaped bloom before frost goes out. Plant 3 inches deep and 3 inches apart in light shade.

Inexpensive to buy, they multiply quickly. Zone 4.

Puschkinia: creamy white flowers touched with blue. Blooms March and April; sun or shade. Flower stems 8 to 12 inches. Plant 3 inches deep. Zone 4.

Hyacinths for Scent

Hyacinths can perfume the air of your spring bulb garden, besides adding their colors of blue-purple, rose-pink, white, and yellow.

Larger than the bulbs

we've been discussing previously on these pages, hyacinths need to be planted deeper—about 8 inches. Be sure planting site is well drained.

Besides their outdoor uses, hyacinths are easy to force. Buy top-size bulbs, and see instructions for forcing on page 223. Good varieties for forcing include Jan Bos (red), Lady Derby (pink), Bismark (blue), Perle Brillante (blue), Carnegie (white), and L'Innocence (white).

Other Favorites

Allium giganteum puts up huge ball-like blooms on 5-foot stems.

Chrysantha tulip, 8 inches tall. March.

Six-inch hoop-petticoat narcissus. March.

232

Little-known bulbs could easily join your list of favorites if you choose those hardy to your zone and suited to your soil. Some are tiny, some huge; some bloom in spring, others in summer, and a few in autumn.

Across the page are pictured three bulb plants you may never have grown. All would make excellent additions to your mixed perennial border, or could be grown in beds of their own.

Related to Allium giganteum *and also blooming in summer, is* A. christophi; *its ball of bloom less dense and bearing lavender star-shaped flowers on a 2-foot stem. It, too, is June-flowering. Zone 4.*

Camassia, *which thrives in sun or shade, sends up tall bloom spikes that produce hundreds of blue-purple, star-shaped flowers; May. Zone 4.*

Dogtooth violet, or erythronium, *is probably better called by its other, less-widely-used common name—trout lily. Some varieties, such as* E. multiscapoideum, *bloom early and are more heat- and drought- resistant than the native trout lily—* E. americanum. *All varieties have slim, mottled foliage, and most have yellow flowers with recurved petals. Plant in light shade. May bloom. Zones 4 through 8.*

Snowflake, or Leucojum aestivum, *puts up tall scapes, 8 to 10 inches, bearing a white bloom that is reminiscent of lily-of-the-valley, much enlarged, and with green dots at the tips of the scalloped edges. Blooms April through May. Plant in fall, 4 inches deep and the same distance apart. Snowflake prefers rich, sandy soil, and is effective in plantings coupled with chionodoxa. Zone 4.*

Summer and Fall Bloom

Although it is true that most of the hardy bulbs bloom in spring, there are a few—in addition to the alliums and hardy lilies already discussed—that are of interest for summer-fall bloom.

Eremurus, *fox-tail lily or desert-candle, actually grows from a corm rather than a bulb. Hardy through zone 5. It will need a heavy winter mulch when grown farther north. In June, flower scapes growing as high as 8 feet arise from low-growing foliage rosettes. Flowers are borne on half the length of the stem and stay in bloom for weeks. Foliage disappears after bloom period; may be over- planted with annuals. Shelford hybrids of this plant reach only 3 to 4 feet, and come in mixed hues of pink, orange, yellow, cream, and rose.*

Hardy cyclamen *is from 4 to 6 inches tall, with attractive foliage that, on a miniature scale, closely resembles the potted greenhouse specimens we associate with Christmas. Most varieties bloom in fall—early September.* Cyclamen purpurascens *has crimson flowers in autumn. Hardy in zone 6, and in zone 5, if protected.*

Lycoris, *or spider-lily, a member of the amaryllis family, sends up strap- shaped foliage in spring. This dies and disappears. Then fragrant pink lily- like blooms on 2-foot stems appear in August.* Lycoris squamigera *should be planted 8 inches deep in part-shade. Reliably hardy in zones 4 through 9.*

Colchicum *bulbs come on the market in late summer and should be planted immediately. The big vase-shape lavender bloom appears within weeks after planting. The next year dense foliage appears in the spring. This ripens slowly, so choose a location where other foliage will disguise the unsightly leaves. Plant 4 inches deep in part-shade. Bulbs multiply rapidly. Zone 4.*

Bulb Know-How

Spring-flowering bulbs must be planted in autumn, before deep frost hardens the ground. Once in the earth, roots begin to grow and flowers start to form inside the bulbs, continuing even when heavy snows come and temperatures plummet. In northern gardens and in Canada, planting times range from September to November. In southern states, planting time will begin a month or so later.

In the deep South, where no true winter occurs, tulips and hyacinths must be treated as annuals—they will not bloom the following year. And the bulbs—if not already cold-treated—must be pre-cooled before planting. Do this by storing bulbs in the bottom of your refrigerator at 40° to 50° F. for 6 to 12 weeks.

Flowering times vary depending on season (early or late), placement of bed (plants facing south flower earlier), shade or sun (tulips in part-shade flower later), and other environmental factors.

Be sure the site you've selected is well-drained, for if water stands, bulbs will rot. In soil with too much clay, use peat and vermiculite to lighten the consistency. Work bone meal into the soil at the bottom of the hole or bed where you'll plant the bulbs, and topdress with balanced fertilizer after blooming. Do *not* cut off foliage, but allow it to ripen naturally. You should, however, clip off all flower stems as soon as bloom is spent.

If any amount of time elapses between purchase and planting of tulips, be sure to store bulbs in a dark, cool place—temperatures not over 70° F. And if you plant on a warm, sunny day, *never* leave bulbs in the sun. Even a short time under such conditions will noticeably reduce the size of bloom.

Field mice are a menace to newly planted tulips in some areas. To reduce such danger, don't plant bulbs next to garden walls or house foundations where mice make runs. And before planting, clean beds of all garden waste that could make ideal mice nests.

For your convenience in planting bulbs near each other which will bloom at about the same time, use the following chart. It also lists height at maturity, depth to plant, and space to allow between bulbs.

A GUIDE TO BULB CULTURE

Flowering Period	Genus and Species or Variety	Average Height at Maturity (Inches)	Depth of Planting (Inches)	Space Between Bulbs (Inches)
Very Early *March 15-30*	Crocus chrysanthus	3-4	4	2-3
	Crocus sieberi	3-4	4	2-3
	Crocus tomasinianus	3-4	4	3-4
	Eranthis species	3-4	4	2-3
	Galanthus species	3-4	4	2-3
	Iris reticulata	4-5	4	2-3
	Scilla tubergeniana	4-6	4	3-4
Early *March 31-April 20*	Anemone blanda	3-4	4	2
	Chionodoxa species	5-8	4	2-3
	Crocus flavus	3-4	4	3-4
	Crocus vernus	4-6	4	3-4
	Muscari azureum	4-5	4	1-2
	Narcissus cyclamineus	10-14	6	4-6
	Puschkinia scilloides	4-6	4	3-4
	Scilla siberica	4-6	4	3-4

Flowering Period	Genus and Species or Variety	Average Height at Maturity (Inches)	Depth of Planting (Inches)	Space Between Bulbs (Inches)
Mid-Spring April 21-May 15	Erythronium 'Pagoda'	8-12	4	3-4
	Fritillaria imperialis	25-30	6	8
	Fritillaria meleagris	6-8	4	3-4
	Muscari armeniacum	6-8	4	4
	Muscari botryoides album	4-5	4	1-2
	Narcissus jonquilla	10-14	6	3-4
	Narcissus triandrus Thalia	10-14	6	4-6
	Narcissus W. P. Milner	8-10	6	4-5
	Hyacinth Blue Jacket	10-12	6	9
Late May 16-June 5	Allium aflatunense	26-30	4	4
	*Allium elatum	32-40	6	6
	Allium karataviense	8-10	4	6-8
	*Allium rosenbachianum	40-48	6	6
	*Camassia quamash	12-16	6	4
	*Ixiolirion tataricum	15-17	4	6
	Narcissus Baby Moon	10-14	6	4-5
	Ornithogalum umbellatum	8-10	4	3-4
Very Late June 6-July 1	*Allium caeruleum	20-26	4	2-3
	Allium christophi	20-26	4	6-8
	Allium giganteum	40-48	6	6
	Allium moly	10-14	4	2-3
	Allium oreophilum	10-14	4	2-3
	Allium sphaerocephalum	22-26	4	3-4
	*Triteleia laxa	12-16	4	4

*Not reliably winter-hardy north of zone 5.

TIPS ON PLANTING TULIP VARIETIES ACCORDING TO SEASON OF BLOOM

For earliest spring tulip bloom, choose the botanical or species types. These include the fosterana, greigi, and kaufmanniana types, as well as Tulipa clusiana, T. praestans (variety Praestans Fusilier), and T. pulchella (variety Violacea). This last-named variety will bloom with late crocus; all others can be expected to bloom in mid-April with narcissus. The botanicals also have the virtue of being more nearly perennial than the more hybridized varieties such as the cottage, darwin, and parrot tulips. Most of the botanicals are close to the tulips that first sent Hollanders into the frenzy called "tulipomania" when early travelers brought home bulbs from Turkey. Today, native varieties are imported from Russia to cross with others in a never-ending search for something new.

The enormously popular tall darwin tulips which bloom in May are followed by the cottage tulips.

The darwin hybrids, including such well-known varieties as Parade, Oxford, Gudoshnik, and Apeldoorn, are the result of crossing darwins with Red Emperor, and can be counted on to bloom about a week ahead of the darwins.

Darwins such as The Bishop (violet with a blue throat), Queen of the Bartigons (salmon-pink), Balalaika (red), and Glacier (white), bloom slightly later in May than do the cottage tulips: Halcro (red), Mrs. J. T. Scheepers (yellow), Spring Snow (white), and Blushing Bride (yellow and rose).

Bulb Know-How

Tulips, hyacinths, and the other spring-flowering bulbs must all be planted in the fall. Depth of planting is related to the size of the bulb, as the chart below shows.

SOIL PREPARATION

Dig soil for all bulbs to full spade depth. If soil is heavy, turn under a thick layer of compost to improve drainage. For bulb beds, it's also wise to spade in a fertilizer high in phosphorus and potash at the same time, such as 3-18-18. Level and rake smooth.

Proper tillage can go a long way toward improving the structure of your soil. On the other hand, improper tillage can do your soil great harm.

Never till your soil when it's too wet. If you can take a handful of soil and squeeze it together to form a sticky, compact mass, then it's too wet to be worked. Heavy clay soils that are tilled when they're too wet become hard and lumpy.

But even when the moisture content is right, it's possible to overwork your soil. Avoid working it so finely that it will crust after a rain. Instead, try to break up the clods and level the surface without destroying the structure of the soil.

PLANTING

For a bed of several types of bulbs, outline the area for each group with the end of a rake handle. Space tulips and other big bulbs fairly close (5 or 6 inches) to make a splashy color effect (wide spacing weakens their impact). Set bulbs inside outlines before you plant, and print varietal names on stakes set at the center of each group. Plunge garden trowel full depth, as shown above; pull toward you to open pocket; and set bulb firmly in place. Then cover with soil. Very deep planting of tulips (10 to 12 inches) inhibits offset formations that weaken main bulbs.

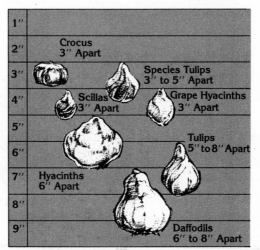

Use the chart at left to determine proper planting depth for a wide variety of spring-flowering bulbs. Also note recommended distances for spacing them.

REPLANTING

Although digging up tulips after blooming is not recommended, it can be done. However, it's best to leave the bulb in place during the period when foliage is yellowing and dying down. It is in this period that the bulb makes the most use of strength gained through foliage

to help form bloom for the following season.

If tulips must be dug before foliage ripens, dig a shallow trench and heel-in bulbs with foliage attached. Mark the variety, and lift later to replace in a permanent garden location.

MAINTENANCE

In addition to applying plant food to tulips when you plant them, you also should add it immediately after the blooming period ends. Water beds liberally during every drought, but try to keep water from getting on the leaves; hose-soak the root areas. A 2-inch layer of good mulch, such as cocoa bean hulls, straw, or ground corncobs, will conserve soil moisture and will also help keep down weeds.

Always snap off seed heads when bloom fades. The plant's energy will

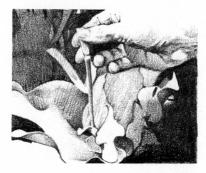

then go into the formation of larger bulbs for the next season of bloom. Flower stems may be left standing.

Even though you plant fine bulbs and give them good care, you'll find that the hybrid tulips tend to throw smaller bloom after a few years, and finally disappear except, perhaps, for a few shoots of foliage. Species or botanicals, however, are much more nearly perennial by nature. This group includes the fosterana, the greigi, and the kaufmanniana groups—all well worth exploring. Most bloom on fairly short stems, and many bloom considerably earlier than do the hybrid varieties.

MICE PROTECTION

Mice and chipmunks can be a real source of trouble if you plant bulbs in quantities. The only sure way to protect newly planted bulbs against this kind of damage is to place them in baskets fashioned from hardware cloth, their tops left open. This technique, unfortunately, is too time-consuming and expensive except in smaller gardens.

NATURALIZING BULBS

Hybrid tulip varieties are not good subjects for "naturalizing"—that is, planting on slopes, in grass, or under trees to give the effect of natural growth.

Narcissus are among the showiest and most satisfactory of bulbs to grow in this manner, and many growers offer either a mixture of bulbs just for this purpose, or greatly reduced prices on varieties purchased in large quantities—by the thousand. These bulbs produce bulblets that, left undisturbed, will eventually form a clump of blooming narcissus where you originally planted a single bulb.

To gain the natural look, some gardeners favor standing still and casting a handful of bulbs into the air, letting them fall where they will, then using a trowel to make an appropriately deep hole for each bulb where it lies. For the same effect sooner, plant bulbs in groups of three, fairly widely spaced.

Don't avoid planting in areas under trees. The early spring-

blooming bulbs will have bloomed and their foliage will have ripened in the sun that comes through branches of deciduous trees at this season. In fact, blooms will last longer and retain a deeper color in a planting site covered by light shade during the warmest part of the day. The one area to avoid in naturalizing—or, for that matter, in planting any bulbs—is one that constantly stays wet or moist. Bulbs will rot if roots are kept wet.

WINTER PROTECTION

Applying several inches of mulch over perennial beds that include spring-flowering bulbs is a wise precaution in areas where sudden thaws and freezes might cause the ground to heave, damaging bulbs and roots. The best materials are those that let rain and melting snow come through easily, keeping moisture levels adequate. Straw, hay, and the prunings from evergreens are best.

As important as applying the mulch either just before or just after a killing frost is knowing when to remove it. Left in place too long, it will damage tender foliage shoots when you take it off. Taken off too soon, it renders plants vulnerable to a sudden frost that could nip and "brown" tips of leaves, as well as flower buds.

Since the arrival of spring varies widely from area to area—and even from week to week within the same area in different years—the safest way to decide when to lift mulch is to make frequent checks as weather begins to warm. Usually when tulip foliage is 2 inches above soil, it's time to take off the mulch.

DISEASES AND PESTS

Quality bulbs are subject to few pests or diseases. But if a plant should show signs of disease, such as misshapen foliage, it's wise to lift and destroy the entire plant so that the disease will not spread. Healthy bulbs should feel firm and solid to the touch; don't plant those that seem soft or spongy. If you buy your bulbs through reliable dealers, you probably needn't worry about diseases or their treatment.

237

TENDER BULBS

Gladiolus

Plant gladiolus and you'll soon know why they're garden favorites of beginners and experts alike. Their dramatic solid and two-toned flower spikes—in all colors but true blue—are just-right accents in any garden location. Use glads alone, or in perennial or annual borders.

The unique form and startling colors of gladiolus appear two to three months after the corms are planted. Set them out every two weeks from the last frost until midsummer for constant bloom, or plan your planting for concentrated color when the rest of the garden is not at its peak.

Gladiolus grows easily in slightly acid, well-drained soil that's in a sunny spot. Flowers range from the large, exhibition, florists'-type to the small, airy, less-formal miniature. Both make magnificent cut flowers, and their strong vertical lines and sword-like foliage are good garden accents.

1 Glads should be planted in rows or clumps of four, eight, or more, and set out about 6 inches apart. Plant jumbo corms 6 inches deep; medium-size (2-inch-diameter) corms are laid down 4 inches; and small ones are put 2 inches into the ground. New corms that form over the summer can be dug and stored. Few insects or diseases bother glads.

2 Staking may be necessary to prevent plants from falling over. Choose inconspicuous stakes, such as bamboo, and use string to support plants. Run it down each side of plants, or around clumps if you've planted in groups. For extra support, mound soil around plant bases. After flowers have bloomed, fertilize to encourage strong corms for next year.

3 Mulching is a good practice with all tender bulbs. Covering the ground with leaf mold, grass clippings, wood chips or other organic matter lessens the need for weeding and allows the ground to stay moist and cool. After blooms fade, leave foliage until it matures. Dig corms, cut off tops, and cure in a warm place. Store where it's cool and dry.

TENDER BULBS

Dahlia

Dwarf dahlias, above, border an entrance walk to brighten this garden with everblooming plants all summer long.

These dwarfs are ideal bedding plants—they're small-flowered, low-growing, and need no staking or disbudding.

Like their larger cousins, dwarf dahlias blossom in many forms and in every rainbow color but clear blue.

STARTING DWARF DAHLIAS FROM SEED

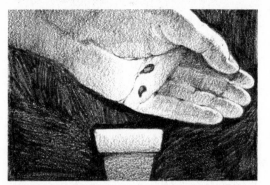

1 Bushy, dwarf dahlias, which grow only 1 to 2 feet tall, are commonly and easily started from seed. Sow three seeds per pot in sterile soil, then pull all but the largest seedling. It should grow rapidly, quickly setting flower buds and developing its fat, fleshy tuber. In addition to the dwarf dahlias, there are the larger single, anemone, peony, cactus, miniature, and pompon varieties. Blooms range from 1 inch to 1 foot across, while the plants themselves can stretch from 6 inches to 10 feet in height. Buy tubers for larger types.

2 When the soil is warm and all danger of frost is past, transplant tubers outdoors into a sunny spot. Soil should be rich and well-drained. Dahlias need lots of water and fertilizer to stay in bloom, and should be mulched to keep their roots cool and the ground moist and free of weeds. Dwarf dahlias should be spaced 18 inches on center; intermediate-sized miniatures and pompons, 2 feet apart; and the tall, exhibition varieties, 3 to 4 feet apart. Use dahlias for borders, in perennial beds, with annuals, and as screens.

STARTING STANDARD DAHLIAS FROM TUBERS

1 Before planting a tall tuber, push a stake in the ground to support the stem. Make holes 4 inches deep, set tubers horizontally, and fill in the holes as your plants grow.

2 Allow only one shoot per tuber to grow, and when two pairs of leaves form, pinch off the growing tip. The bared stem then should be tied to the stake to keep plant upright.

3 As each stem matures, cut off side flower buds as they form to produce large central blooms. Dahlias make magnificent cut flowers. Dig tubers in fall after frost darkens foliage.

TENDER BULBS
Tuberous Begonia

Choose upright plants for pots, edgings, and borders, and use trailing types atop low walls and in hanging baskets.

Elegant tuberous begonias belong on your "must-have" list if you want spectacular color for semi-shady spots.

A gorgeous palette of red, pink, yellow, orange, and white provides beauty from midsummer until frost.

Tuberous begonias display a colorful variety of flower forms—formal, ruffled, rose, carnation, and camellia.

How To Grow and Store Tuberous Begonias

 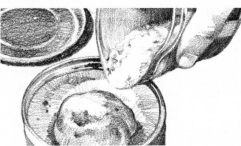

1 Buy hard, round tubers in April or May and grow them indoors so they'll bloom earlier. In a shallow flat of barely moist sphagnum moss, sand, and vermiculite, plant the tubers, round side down. Don't overwater or the begonias may rot. Keep them warm (at least 65° F.) in bright light, but avoid burning sun. When roots are well-established and the tops near 3 inches tall, pot up tubers 1 inch below the surface of the soil. Shift outdoors after all danger of frost is past.

2 Outdoor tuberous begonias need rich soil and perfect drainage. Water frequently to keep surface roots moist. The foliage also benefits from frequent misting. Fertilize every week or two with soluble plant food for an array of vibrant color and good year-round growth. Before frost comes in the fall, dig plants and dry two weeks or until stems and soil easily drop from the tubers. Store dry, out of frost's way, in a holder of peat, sand, vermiculite, or sphagnum moss.

TENDER BULBS

Caladium

Let tropical-looking caladiums brighten up a shady corner of your patio or garden with their jewel-like, heart-shaped foliage of vivid red, green, pink, white, and silver. You can use them in planters on terraces and patios, plant them directly in the garden, or sink potted tubers into the ground. Their bright colors make them increasingly popular.

Caladiums like well-drained soil that's rich in organic matter. Water them frequently to keep the soil damp, and treat the foliage to a misting on hot days. Caladiums may be grown in full shade, although a little sunlight gives them a more intense color. They thrive in warm temperatures and high humidity, and should be fed every month. Three weeks before frost in fall, stop watering. Dig when foliage dies.

1 For fewer plant losses, start caladiums indoors four to six weeks before moving outside. A good rooting mixture is half-and-half peat and perlite. Space tubers round side up 1 inch apart in a shallow box. Cover lightly with mixture, water, and place in a warm spot draped with clear plastic.

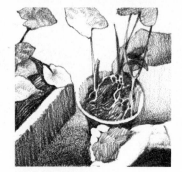

2 Transplant from flats to 4-inch pots when rooted, whether you'll bed them or use in containers. Firm a loose potting mix around the plants, allowing ½ inch at the tops for water. After watering, locate plants in a bright, warm spot. Transfer outdoors when all danger of frost is past.

Canna Lily

If you still think of cannas as tall Victorian plants, you're in for a nice surprise. The new dwarf cannas grow to just 2 or 3 feet, but bloom with spectacular color in sunny locales.

Cannas like a rich, moist soil, and should be fed several times during the growing season. Start them inside one month before the last frost in spring, or plant horizontally in the ground 1 inch deep after frost is past. Dig rhizomes in the fall after tops blacken.

Large, bright flowers of apricot, orange, red, white, pink, and yellow stand proudly above bronze or green foliage. Cannas flower in the heat of late summer, and are excellent in beds or patio tubs.

TENDER BULBS
Calla Lily

The calla lily's spathe-shaped flowers of pink, yellow, and white bloom 2 feet above its arrow-shaped and often spotted foliage. Callas are perfect in pots or beds.

Known primarily as a greenhouse or indoor plant, the calla lily deserves more recognition as a tender outdoor bloomer, happy in full sun or light shade.

Start calla lilies indoors in March or April to fill the garden with delicate flowers by May and June. Or plant outdoors 3 inches deep when soil warms.

Calla lilies need rich, organic soil, lots of water, and liquid feeding every two weeks. Dig rhizomes after frost has darkened the foliage and store for next year.

Exotics

Aptly called the pineapple lily, the eucomis sends up flower spikes that mimic the fruit—complete with topknots. The spikes of cream-and-green star-shaped flowers appear less than two months after bulbs are started. Give them rich soil and feed monthly.

The climbing gloriosa lily presents exotic red and yellow blooms starting in July, and makes an excellent cut flower. Give the lily a trellis to climb on, or provide support stakes. Plant tubers 4 inches deep in good soil. Dig both plants and store before hard frosts.

For a touch of the very unusual, try eucomis, the pineapple lily, left, or the gloriosa lily, above. Both need full sun and do equally as well in beds or containers.

TENDER BULBS

Exotics

Flowers of orange, red, yellow, or copper and narrow, sword-shaped leaves adorn the montbretia from late summer until frost. For best effect, plant in clumps of twelve, with corms 4 inches deep and 4 inches apart in a light, sandy soil.

Fragrant white flowers with black centers sit atop the acidanthera two months after they are set out. Also called sweet-scented gladiolus, they should be planted 2 inches deep and 5 inches apart in coarse soil. Lift both in fall.

Corms of montbretia, left, and acidanthera, above, grow into 2-foot plants filled with graceful flowers. Both need full sun and should be watered freely.

Perfect double-flowers of ranunculus bloom in many colors in early summer. Lift them after they flower.

Intermingle blue agapanthus with hardy daylilies to achieve a burst of midsummer color in sun or light shade. Plant agapanthus 2 inches deep in rich, moist soil.

Summer Bulb Storage

If you plant recommended varieties of summer bulbs "by the book" and you still don't reap the promised glorious harvests of color, you should check your bulb quality. Examine your storage area first, because quality usually depends on correct storage more than on any other factor. Just as dampness, extreme temperature, and pests can make your dinner inedible, the same factors render these bulbs' carefully-built reserves of "food" unusable for starting new blooms.

Gladiolus Dig corms anytime after foliage begins to yellow. You can wait until frost to dig late plantings, but don't wait until a hard freeze. Leave about 1 inch of growth on corms, then cure for two to four weeks at 75 to 80 degrees in a well-ventilated room.

Before placing the corms in winter storage, dust them lightly with an all-purpose garden or rose dust. The best storage temperatures range from 35 to 45 degrees. Make certain that the temperature never drops below freezing. Break off the 1 inch of the top growth left on the corm for curing, then store corms in old nylon hose or onion bags hung from a ceiling or wall. You also can store them in shallow flats with screen wire bottoms.

You'll probably want to save the smaller corms—called cormels—for propagation of some of your favorite varieties. Some are as small as buckshot, so dig carefully to avoid losing them in the soil. Separate them immediately from large corms and store in barely dampened sand or peat moss. Examine them every few weeks to make sure they're still healthy, but not sprouting. If sprouting occurs, your storage medium is too moist.

Dahlia Wait until after a light frost, then cut plants back to 4 to 6 inches above the soil. Dig carefully to avoid damaging or breaking off the tubers. Hose off as much soil as possible, and allow to dry only slightly in a shady area before storing. Do not divide at this time—wait until spring when bud growths show you where to cut.

Ordinary cartons make good storage containers. Place the still-moist tubers in the boxes and cover with dry vermiculite, sawdust, or sphagnum moss. Tie a label to each clump or write the name on the stem with an indelible pencil. Check monthly and sprinkle on more packing material if the roots begin to shrivel. Store at 35 to 45 degrees.

Tuberous begonia A light frost is not too harmful, but dig the tubers before frost, if possible. Leave about 4 inches of top attached. Then dry for several days in the sun—long enough so that stem stubs detach easily. Store tubers as you do dahlia roots, but at a slightly higher temperature—45 to 60 degrees. Keep the packing dry to avoid decay.

Canna After the first killing frost, cut off tops to within 14 inches of soil level. Dig roots and dry in a warm room for two to three weeks. Dust the undivided clumps with a fungicide, and store, stem side down, at a temperature of 45 to 50 degrees. Packing material is optional, but roots must be kept dry during storage.

Caladium Tubers are very sensitive to frost, so dig them in early fall while weather is still warm. Carefully remove most of the clinging soil, then dry for a week or so in a warm, dry place. Store as you would dahlias, but at 60 degrees, and never at temperatures over 80 degrees.

Ismene Dry the bulbs, with fleshy roots attached, in an inverted position for two weeks. Store at 60 degrees.

Calla lily Store rhizomes just as you would dahlias, but keep the packing medium-dry, since callas are prone to rot. Store at 45 to 55 degrees.

Galtonia Lift bulbs anytime before frost. Dry, and store at 60 degrees.

Gloriosa Dig in the fall before frost, then store at 45 to 50 degrees.

Hymerocallis Bulbs should be lifted before frost and dried upside down. Store at 60 degrees.

Tigridia Treat the same as gladiolus, although they are somewhat more hardy. In some areas, they can be mulched and left outdoors through the winter. Or, store indoors in a dry place at 40 to 50 degrees.

Tritonia Also similar to gladiolus, these bulbs should be dug before frost. They, too, can be left to winter outdoors in warmer climates after they have been mulched. Store indoors at 45 to 50 degrees.

Coraldrops In northern climes, dig up after foliage dies back and store at temperatures of 55 to 60 degrees for the winter.

Tuberose In the North and South, dig up bulbs in the fall and replant in the spring when both days and nights are warm. Cut off frost-nipped stems and dry thoroughly. Store in peat at 55 to 65 degrees.

Oxalis In warmer climates, leave the Chilean variety in the ground through the winter, with at least a 2-inch layer of soil and some mulch in wind-plagued areas. Other varieties serve well indoors as winter pot plants.

Sprekelia Also known as Aztec lily and as a form of amaryllis, this bulb should be lifted before frost and dried fully. Then take off dried foliage and store in perlite or vermiculite through the winter at a steady 55 to 60 degrees.

Achimenes After flowers fade, pack rhizomes in vermiculite and store in a cool place through winter.

Allium Leave in the ground and mulch each year until they overcrowd. Then dig up and replant in the spring or fall.

Anemone Leave poppy anemone in the ground, but in northern states, lift and store Greek (blanda) and apennine varieties in the fall.

Freesia Bulbs remain in the ground in the South, but elsewhere, they must be lifted and stored in a dry place until time for replanting.

Foxtail lily This tuberous-rooted plant prefers to remain in the ground, and should not be disturbed. Mulch it each fall with straw or wood chips.

Ranunculus Dig bulbs in the fall after foliage dies back and store through the winter in peat or perlite at 50 to 55 degrees.

Lilies This is a large family, but most prefer to remain in the ground.

Specialties

Gardeners who cultivate wildflowers help to preserve our American heritage of natural beauty. Many a wood has been robbed by thoughtless passersby who plucked or pulled up wildflowers by the roots. But today, almost every garden magazine lists experts who specialize in cultivating wildflowers. Order plants suited to the shady or partly shady spots you can offer, or grow from seed.

Bloodroot (Sanguinaria canadensis), one of spring's early charmers, thrives in partial shade.

Jack-in-the-pulpit (Arisaema triphyllum) shoots up in late spring in shady, moist areas. The plants multiply rather slowly; and produce red berries in late summer.

Hepatica, its blue flowers at center of planting, above, is named for its liver-shaped leaves. Here it's hidden by the foliage of Dutchman's-breeches, pink-flowered neighbors. Both need shade.

Marsh marigold, when given the very moist location it needs, rewards you with a yearly springtime show of glossy gold bloom. Difficult to grow from seed; best started from purchased plants.

Dog-tooth violet, left, belongs to the lily tribe. A spring bloomer, it is best grown in moist soil with good shade.

Trillium, below, needs moisture and shade. This showy variety (Trillium grandiflorum) will increase yearly.

Virginia bluebells (Mertensia virginica) bloom a bit later in spring than most other wildflowers pictured. They flower in sun or shade, and spread rapidly. Fine companion to spring bulbs.

Shooting-star (Dodecatheon) gets its name from its cyclamen-like bloom. Give this spring bloomer good drainage in a shady or part-shady location in moderately rich soil that's not too dry.

253

WILDFLOWERS

Name	Description	Light and Soil	Propagation	Special Helps
Alumroot (heuchera)	Tiny blossoms on stems 16 to 36 in. tall; May to August	Shade Well-drained, dry soil	Seeds Division	Leaves mottled when young
Anemone, rue (anemonella)	Early blossoms on stems 5 to 9 in. tall; white and pink from March to June	Shade Well-drained, dry soil	Seeds Division	Divide after plant has died back in the fall
Arbutus, trailing (epigaea)	Tubular blossoms on 3-in. plants; white and pink with white berries, March to May	Partial shade Well-drained, dry soil	Seeds Stem cuttings Stem layering	Keep well-mulched
Baneberry (actaea)	Small white blossoms on 24-in. plants; red or white berries in April and May	Shade Well-drained, dry soil	Seeds Division	Sow seeds in the fall
Bellwort (uvularia)	Yellow blossoms on graceful 4- to 12-in. plants, April to June	Shade Well-drained, moist soil	Seeds Division	Fleshy winged seed capsules
Bishop's-cap (mitella)	Tiny white flowers on 6- to 12-in. plants from April to June	Shade Well-drained, moist soil	Seeds Division	Keep well-mulched
Black-eyed susan (rudbeckia)	Flat, daisy-like flowers on 2-ft. wiry stems; July and August	Sun Well-drained soil	Seeds Often self-sows	Often grown as a biennial
Bloodroot (sanguinaria)	Large-leaved plants 8 to 10 in. high; single white flowers in April and May	Shade Well-drained, dry soil	Seeds Division	Multiplies rapidly; forms thick mat
Bluebells (mertensia)	Tall 2-ft. stems of blue flowers on plants in April and May	Sun or partial shade Well-drained, moist soil	Seeds Division	Plants disappear during the summer
Butterfly weed (asclepias)	Clusters of red-orange flowers on 2-ft. plants; July and August	Sun Well-drained, dry soil	Seeds Root cuttings	Brilliant color
Cinquefoil (potentilla)	Tiny white flowers on 3- to 6-in. plants that turn red in the fall; June to August	Shade Well-drained, dry, acid soil	Seeds Division Stem cuttings	Good ground cover
Columbine, wild (aquilegia)	Finely cut, pendulous flowers on 1- to 2-ft. plants from April through July; yellow and red	Shade Well-drained, dry, slightly acid soil	Seeds Often self-sows	Very showy
Coneflower, prairie (ratibida)	Large yellow flowers on plants up to 6 ft. tall from June to August	Sun Well-drained, dry soil	Seeds Division	Graceful and showy
Coneflower, purple (echinacea)	Large, single purple flowers on plants 3- to 4 ft. tall from June to October	Sun Well-drained, dry soil	Seeds Division	Tall and impressive

Name	Description	Light and Soil	Propagation	Special Helps
Crowfoot, buttercup (ranunculus)	Small yellow flowers on plants 6 to 24 in. tall from April to August	Shade or partial shade Tolerant of most soil types	Seeds Division	Can become invasive
Dog-tooth violet (erythronium)	Solitary white flowers on plants 6 in. tall in April and May	Shade Well-drained, moist soil	Offsets Seeds	Forms a dense mat; leaves are mottled with brown
Dutchman's-breeches (dicentra)	Unusually shaped white flowers clustered on stems from plants 6 to 12 in. high, April to May	Shade Well-drained, dry soil	Division Seeds	Disappears after flowering
Evening primrose (oenothera)	Pale yellow fragrant flowers on plants 2 to 4 ft. tall in July and August	Sun Well-drained, dry soil	Seeds	Flowers open only at night Treat as a biennial
Flag, blue (iris)	Large, purple blossoms on plants 2 to 3 ft. tall in May and June	Sun Moist-to-wet, slightly acid soil	Division Seeds Often self-sows	Forms a dense colony
Foamflower, False miterwort (tiarella)	Small white flowers clustered on stems from plants 6 to 12 in. tall	Shade Well-drained, moist soil	Division Seeds	Effective in mass
Forget-me-not (myosotis)	Pale blue flowers with yellow centers on 6-in. plants all summer long	Sun Well-drained, moist-to-wet soil	Division Seeds	Keep very moist
Gentian, closed, blue (gentiana)	Tubular violet flowers on plants 1 ft. tall in August and September	Sun or partial shade Well-drained, moist-to-wet, slightly acid soil	Division Seeds	Flowers remain closed
Geranium, wild (geranium)	Large, red-violet flowers in clusters on plants 24 in. tall	Shade Well-drained, moist soil	Division Seeds	Effective in mass
Ginger, wild (asarum)	Inconspicuous tubular violet-brown flowers at the base of plants 4 to 8 in. tall in April and May	Shade Well-drained, moist soil	Division Rhizome cuttings	Interesting ground cover
Hepaticas (hepatica)	Showy rose, white, or blue flowers on short 6-in. plants from April to May	Shade Well-drained, dry, slightly acid soil	Division Seeds Often self-sows	Valued for early color
Jack-in-the-pulpit (arisaema)	Unusual vase-shaped greenish-brown flowers on plants 2 ft. tall from April to June. Red berries follow later in the season	Shade Well-drained, moist soil	Seeds Often self-sows	Very showy and attractive
Jacob's-ladder (polemonium)	Small clusters of blue flowers on 3-ft. plants in June and July	Shade Well-drained, moist soil	Seeds Division	Fine border plant
Lady's-slipper, yellow (cypripedium)	Very showy yellow flowers, often veined in blue, on plants to 30-in. tall in May	Shade Well-drained, moist soil	Division	Give an annual top dressing of compost

WILDFLOWERS

Name	Description	Light and Soil	Propagation	Special Helps
Lobelia, blue (lobelia)	Tiny blue flowers on plants 2 to 3 ft. tall from August to October	Sun or partial shade Well-drained, moist soil	Offsets Division Stem cuttings Seeds	Valuable for late-summer color
Mallow, rose (hibiscus)	Large red, pink, or white flowers on plants 6 ft. tall from July to September	Sun Well-drained, moist soil	Division Stem cuttings Seeds	Use as a background plant
Marigold, marsh (caltha)	Brilliant yellow flowers in small clusters on plants 2 ft. tall in April and May	Sun Moist-to-wet soil	Division	Plants disappear in summer
Mayapple, mandrake (podophyllum)	Single white daisy-like flower on 12- to 18-in. plants in April and May Unusual umbrella-like leaves; this plant bears yellow fruit in August	Partial to full shade Well-drained, moist soil	Division Seeds	Rapid spreader Good, quick ground cover
Meadow rue, early (thalictrum)	Inconspicuous greenish-violet flowers on 2-ft. plants in April and May	Shade Well-drained, moist soil	Division Seeds	Handsome, dainty foliage
Meadow rue, tall (thalictrum)	Large clusters of white flowers on plants to 10 ft. tall from August to September	Sun Well-drained, moist-to-wet soil	Seeds Division Stem cuttings	Use as a background plant
Partridgeberry (mitchella)	Small white flowers on plants to 6 in. tall in June and July Small red berries follow later in the season	Shade Well-drained, moist, acid soil	Stem cuttings Seeds	Effective ground cover
Pasqueflower (anemone)	Large showy, purple flowers on 16-in. plants in March and April	Sun Well-drained, dry soil	Seeds Root cuttings	Very early and attractive
Phlox, blue (phlox)	Pale blue flowers on 6- to 15-in. stems in April and May The nonflowering part hugs the ground	Partial shade Well-drained, dry soil	Division Stem cuttings	Often form large clumps
Phlox, downy (phlox)	Red-violet flowers on stems from 6 to 15 in. tall in May and June The nonflowering part hugs the ground	Partial shade Well-drained, dry soil	Division Stem cuttings	Plant in sandy soil
Poppy, California (eschscholzia)	Brilliant orange cup-like flowers on plants 10 to 20 in. tall from April to June	Sun Well-drained, dry soil	Seeds	Vigorous and hardy
Prairie rose (rosa)	Handsome pink flowers in small clusters on spreading branches up to 15 ft. long from May to July	Sun Well-drained, dry soil	Seeds Stem layering	Branches are thornless

Name	Description	Light and Soil	Propagation	Special Helps
Sand verbena (abronia)	Small pink, yellow, or lilac flowers on 12-in. plants from May to September	Sun Well-drained, dry soil	Seeds	Trailing stems
Shooting-star (dodecatheon)	Small, attractive red-violet flowers in clusters on 1 ft. stalks in May and June	Light shade Well-drained, moist soil	Division Seeds Root cuttings	Plant disappears in summer
Snakeroot (cimicifuga)	Tiny white blossoms in spike clusters on plants 8 ft. tall from July to September	Shade Well-drained, moist soil	Division Seeds	Use as a background plant
Solomon's-seal (polygonatum)	Inconspicuous greenish-white, bell-shaped flowers appear under the leaves on plants 1 to 2 ft. tall in May and June Bluish-black berries follow later in the season	Shade Well-drained, dry, slightly acid soil	Seeds	Interesting leaf arrangement Good ground cover in shady areas
Spiderwort (tradescantia)	Blue or white flowers in small terminal clusters on 1- to 2-ft. grass-like plants from June to August	Sun or partial shade Well-drained, moist soil	Division Seeds Stem cuttings	Vigorous and quick-growing
Spring-beauty (claytonia)	Delicate pinkish-white blossoms on plants 4 to 6 in. tall from March to May	Shade Well-drained, dry soil	Division Seeds Often self-sows	Good ground cover in shady areas
Sunflower, sawtooth (helianthus)	Large yellow blossoms with brown centers in clusters on plants 10 ft. tall from July to October	Sun Well-drained soil	Seeds Division	Showy background plant
Toothwort (dentaria)	Tiny pinkish-white flowers in small terminal clusters on plants 6 to 12 in. tall in April and May	Shade Well-drained, moist soil	Seeds Division	Valued for early spring color
Trillium (trillium)	Showy white or purple blossom on erect terminal stems on 12-in. plants from April to June	Shade Well-drained, moist soil	Seeds Division	Effective in mass
Turtlehead (chelone)	White or pink terminal flowers on plants 3 ft. tall from July to September	Shade Well-drained, moist soil	Seeds Division Stem cuttings Often self-sows	Interesting and handsome
Violet, blue (viola)	Blue flowers on small 6- to 8-in. plants from April to June	Partial to full shade Well-drained, moist soil	Seeds Division Often self-sows	Can become invasive
Wood aster, blue (aster)	Small, light purple flowers in open clusters on plants 4 ft. tall in August and September	Partial to full shade Well-drained, moist soil	Division	Good background plants

Ground Covers

In sun, ajuga bears spires of purplish-blue bloom during the spring; in shade, less bloom. Its glossy leaves and low-growing habit make it attractive.

Count on ground covers to add beauty to bare spots beneath shrubs and trees. Those pictured here are well known and widely used, but less conventional ground covers include mass plantings of such annuals as dwarf marigolds or portulaca (in sun); hosta; and perennial ferns (in shade). Do not use annuals as a ground cover on slopes. The soil will be subject to erosion during winter months when the plants are dead.

Once planted and established, perennial ground covers require little attention from you. The thick foliage smothers most of the weeds, and they are, in general, drought resistant and hardy.

Perennials protect slopes from erosion year round. As with most pe-rennial plants you expect to grow in the same area for a number of years, careful preparation of soil is important. Be generous with compost and peat moss, spading them deeply into the garden soil. Spacing of new plants depends on how big they'll get. As a rule, low-growing kinds (ajuga, for example) are best spaced eight to 12 inches from each other. Taller kinds, such as Hall's honeysuckle and polygonum, may be spaced from two to three feet apart.

Many ground covers, though they may seem expensive when you buy them, will spread rapidly. And you can increase your supply. Take cuttings and root them in moist vermiculite (*Vinca minor* lends itself well to this method). Others (ajuga is

Epimedium rubrum *(ten inches) has showy foliage; it needs protection from sun.*

one; succulent hen-and-chickens, another) have offsets from the mother plant that can be cut off with a sharp knife. Make sure you get some roots along with leaves of the offset. Then set them into the ground as you did when setting out the original plantings.

To keep ground covers vigorous, give them fertilizer in early spring.

The only other regular care they will need is a thorough soaking during a prolonged spell of hot, dry weather. It's also a good idea to water them heavily during a dry fall to ensure a winter supply of moisture.

Some of the dwarf evergreens—prostrate juniper, for instance—make handsome ground covers. Space the young plants two feet apart throughout the deeply dug area. Cover the exposed ground between plants with a mulch of fir or redwood bark chunks. Bark lasts for a number of years, so the initial expense is a bit deceiving. After a year or two, simply add a small amount each year to keep the mulch at a level of two inches. Within a few years, the evergreens will form a solid cover.

By blocking sun and drying winds, this kind of mulch can reduce water losses by as much as 50 percent. It helps soil moisture and nutrients go to the roots and stems of the plants, rather than to weeds or to the air through evaporation.

Among other less commonly used ground covers are certain wildflowers. Wild ginger looks great all summer in a shady area; bloodroot foliage is an unusual and attractive plant in shade. After delicate white flowers fade, the foliage continues to grow throughout the summer, keeping its green color until the first frost.

Herbs, too, can sometimes act as ground covers. Thyme is one of the most desirable ground covers because it does well in the winter from zone 5 southward. In its several varieties, thyme grows from two to 12 inches high. Planted between stepping-stones of a sunny path, a few strands will spread onto the stones. When you step on them, you release their aromatic scent. If you want to grow thyme this way, look in seed catalogs for a prostrate variety, such as *Thymus serpyllum*.

Hall's honeysuckle quickly spreads across any sunny area to form a ground cover up to two feet deep. It withstands drought well.

Ornamental Grasses

Seldom-used ornamental grasses deserve your attention as dramatic landscape accents. For greatest effect, clump two or more plants of one species near a similar group of another. Repeat these clumps at intervals for a balanced display. The dramatic grouping at the edge of a patio, below, is just one of the shows ornamental grasses can make. Three varieties are effectively teamed: at the back, tall *Spartina pectinata* or cordgrass; in the center is tasseled annual fountain grass or *Pennisetum setaceum;* and around the edges of the patio are tufts of *Festuca ovina* or blue fescue.

Another tall perennial ornamental worthy of consideration is *Erianthus ravennae* or plume grass; it sends up 12-foot plumes from 3-foot plants. Bamboo-like *Arundo donax,* 6 to 8 feet tall, is hardy in the South and makes a good potted plant in the North if you've a suitable spot to overwinter it indoors.

A popular edging plant with glossy foliage, liriope, above, blooms in summer, its flowers resembling grape hyacinth. Zone 5.

260

Blue fescue forms 10-inch clumps in sun or shade. Zone 3.

Another ornamental grass which is highly decorative is *Miscanthus sinensis,* a winter-hardy perennial that will grow as tall as 6 feet high. A variegated form of this species which is related to zebra grass is also available.

Carex morrowi variegata has white stripes on green leaves and is just 1 foot tall. In the entry planting, pictured at right, ornamental grass, *Helictotrichon sempervirens,* has been set into a bed of spring heath. Its distinctive, arching foliage and unusual color make it an excellent accent plant for the use illustrated, or for front-of-the-border placement in other garden locations.

Helictotrichon sempervirens, a member of the oats family, lends distinction to an entry planting in a bed of heath.

261

Enjoy Garden Flowers Indoors

Cut some of your garden flowers for enjoyment indoors. Roses, annuals, perennials, and bulbs are all good candidates for indoor arrangements. You may even elect to plant a cutting garden—a bed of flowers *intended* for plucking. Grow extras to share their beauty with friends and family.

Be creative. Don't hesitate to clip and carry flowers indoors simply because you've never studied traditional flower arranging. Professional styling has its place, but a handful of flowers placed casually and naturally in one of your favorite pitchers or vases can be equally charming. You can turn any receptacle into a flower container by lining it with one or more glass jars or even a plastic ice cream or whipped topping tub— anything that safely holds water and that can be concealed within a more decorative outer receptacle.

Place your gifts from the garden all over the house: a nosegay at the kitchen sink or breakfast table, a single bloom in a bud vase on the bathroom sink or bedside table, a cluster of flowers atop a table beside a favorite armchair.

You can create a big, lush bouquet with just a dozen blooms, as proven by these cottage tulips.

How to Handle Cut Flowers

One of the joys of growing a flower garden is the luxury of being able to cut a bouquet to bring indoors. Many that you can grow easily are simply not available as cut flowers at the florist's shop. And what fun to choose flowers for the table to carry out a color scheme.

But there are tricks to all trades—including how to cut and keep fresh the flowers from your garden. Here are some tips regularly used by florists and experienced arrangers of homegrown blooms.

Like any art or craft, flower arranging requires good tools. But, in this case, the essentials are relatively few and inexpensive. All you really need, other than flowers, are three or four containers in basic shapes, needlepoint holders, a sharp scissors or knife, and the other simple items shown here.

Before going out into the garden to gather flowers, read these tips. They can make the difference between a professional, long-lasting bouquet and one that quickly wilts.

If you plan to cut only a few stems to bring right indoors, always carry them head-down. This keeps stems straight and prevents heavy flower heads from being snapped off.

It's important to get cut flowers into water as soon as possible after cutting. Cut stems at an angle and plunge into a pail of tepid water deep enough to come just short of flower heads. If putting several kinds into one pail, wrap each kind in sheets of newspaper first.

If you didn't carry a pail of water into the garden with you as you were cutting, re-snip each flower stem at an angle underwater before plunging into a pail of lukewarm water. Place the pail in a cool spot out of the sun, and let stand until the water cools to room temperature— for several hours or, preferably, overnight—before arranging the cut flowers. This step is called "conditioning."

If stems are thick or woody, use your sharp scissors or knife to make 1- or 2-inch slits from the bases upwards. This assures that they'll soak in enough water to keep blooms supplied with moisture. If you fail to do this, flowers and foliage will shortly go limp and probably will not revive.

Another important factor in the good looks and long life of your bouquet is your choice of flowers. Avoid buds so tight that they'll never open, as well as full blooms that will soon pass their prime.

The roses sketched below are good examples of a too-tight bud, a flower at the perfect stage for cutting, and a fully open flower that will soon wilt or shatter and spoil the appearance of your arrangement. Some flowers at this advanced stage may, however, be floated on water inside a rounded glass bowl and remain attractive for several days if you freshen water daily.

If you grow many roses, you will certainly want the pleasure of cutting some to bring indoors. But first, you must realize that the fate of future bloom depends on how you go about your cutting. Always leave at least two healthy five-leaflet leaves on the remaining stem to help the plant maintain vigor. If you cut very long stems, you probably will not have further bloom from them for the remainder of the rose season.

Another plant tempting to cut and bring indoors is the lily. Never cut a long stem, as the bulb needs the stem and foliage to form the strength to produce next year's bloom.

To assure the long life of your arrangement, be sure to place it where it is out of direct sunlight and protected from drafts—never in reach of air circulated by an air conditioner or a fan or the flower will dehydrate.

To save pricked fingers when you're arranging roses, hold stems high and clip off thorns at the level you will touch in the process of arranging. For *all* cut flowers, clip off all foliage that would otherwise be below water level in the finished arrangement. Such leaves would quickly disintegrate, foul the water, and shorten the life of your arrangement. Always wash containers thoroughly after using them so they will be fresh and clean for the next arrangement.

Poppies, dahlias, and some other garden flowers with hollow stems or stems that exude a milky liquid on cutting need to be seared with a flame. The burner from your chafing pan or an old candle will do nicely. It's wise to take this step immediately after cutting. Carry the candle or other means of producing flame right into the garden with you and sear at once. If you cut stems shorter later, re-sear.

Flowers whose stems have been seared still need conditioning by being plunged into a pail of lukewarm water and left there for several hours or overnight.

Sometimes heavy-headed flowers such as large mums or dahlias bend over, nearly snapping off. You can perform surgery by taking a sturdy toothpick—the kind that's pointed at both ends—and, holding bent stem in an upright position, plunge the toothpick through the bloom center and down into the stem. Such blooms aren't long-lasting.

Roses and tulips open in a hurry once they're cut and brought indoors. To slow the opening, use florist's tape to gently hold the blooms shut until just before the arrangement is to be put on view. Also, slow the opening process by keeping the arrangement in a cool place until you're ready to display.

If you want to use garden lilies in a centerpiece for the dining table, it's good practice to snip off all pollen-bearing stamens of each bloom before you make the arrangement. Bits of stamen are apt to drop off and stain the flowers themselves, and—more important—the tablecloth below. These stains are persistent and hard to remove.

Many florists habitually cut off all such stamens on Easter lily plants before they are placed on sale. However, some lily-fanciers object to this practice on the grounds that it takes away from the natural beauty of the bloom.

If you want to use some very wide-open chrysanthemums in a flower arrangement, use this tip to keep petals from dropping off in the handling process. Hold stems upside down and gently drip candle wax around the calyx—the outer circle of green that served to protect the flower when it was still in the bud stage. And a few drops of wax dripped into the bloom centers of flowers such as daylilies that tend to close early will help keep them open a bit longer.

265

Arranging Roses

Arranging your roses will bring the beauty of the garden indoors and brighten up any room of the house. Whether it be a casual or a formal treatment, the bouquet is a living expression of your personality and love.

The easiest arrangement is not really an arrangement at all. One flower in a bud vase is simple yet elegant and can easily be changed to fit your mood.

Most arrangements you will show off in your home will combine several varieties of roses and several different types of garden flowers or both. Those same companions you combined with your roses in the planting beds look equally as beautiful sharing a vase. With roses, try iris, lilies, delphinium, gladiolus, veronica, snapdragons, astilbe, stock, asters, chrysanthemum, or daisies of any type. Don't be afraid to experiment with flower combinations that might seem a bit unorthodox.

Formal occasions demand subtle colors and close harmony; informal settings call for bolder and brighter contrasts, with more varied colors and flowers. Fit the roses, the design, and the container to the room or the mood of the occasion.

When choosing a container, keep two things in mind. First is size; the container must be in scale with the roses. Second is the material of the container. Roses generally are thought to be elegant flowers. So, they're perfect in silver, porcelain, crystal, or china vases or bowls. They will do equally well, though, in casual arrangements in pewter, metal, or ceramic containers, or straw baskets. Old teapots or sugar bowls are also possible choices.

You don't have to put your roses in a vase—a shallow container is also an attractive possibility. To anchor the flowers and keep them standing tall and straight, use a pinholder or florists' foam. If foam is your choice, soak completely in water before you place the roses in it. With either, keep the water supply steady and changed at least once a day. Nothing will shorten the life of an arrangement quicker than fouled water.

The popularity of miniature roses has led to a whole new sub-hobby—collecting miniature containers. To show them off in perfect scale, put your minis in thimbles, doll house furniture, seashells, shot glasses, or medicine bottles.

When choosing roses to arrange, pick fully double varieties for best results. Flowers with fewer petals open flat quickly and need to be replaced more frequently. In general, the more double the rose, the slower it will open and the longer it will last. Most shrub and old-fashioned roses wilt quickly and are therefore not good in arrangements, but don't overlook their foliage and hips as fillers and as backgrounds.

Foliage accompanying roses in arrangements is important, too, and needn't be rose leaves alone. For tall and spiking arrangements, try iris, gladiolus, or canna leaves. For variegated foliage, snip a few hosta leaves, or cut artemisia for a silver-gray effect. One of the broadleaved evergreens can be used for its shiny green foliage. For delicacy and grace, try ivy or asparagus ferns. At Christmastime, combine roses with holly berries and sprigs of pine or yew.

The art of arranging roses involves organizing flowers, container, and accessories according to principles of design. The result should be simple, beautiful, expressive, and harmonious in detail.

To achieve these results, your arrangement should appeal to the senses, be pleasing in space, line, form, pattern, texture and color. Even fragrance should be considered. A too strongly scented arrangement can easily become overpowering.

Space available will determine the size and shape of the arrangement. A design for a buffet table should be low and long; that for a pedestal should be upright. Fill the space as though you were filling a picture frame. With line, the eye moves from one part of the arrangement to the others. Line may be long or short, straight or curved, delicate or bold, horizontal or vertical, so long as it is there.

Think of form when arranging your roses. This means thinking in three dimensions and not just height and width. This is very critical if the design is viewed from all sides of the room.

Within the form, the roses need to be arranged in a creative pattern. This can be achieved by the repetition of certain varieties or colors in a mass arrangement or by careful placement of the flowers, leaving open spaces between them.

Texture of the container, foliage, other flowers, and accessory material must be in character with the form and color of the roses. A fine-textured porcelain vase demands a delicate, light arrangement, while a design in a cast-iron kettle takes stronger colors and a heavier touch.

Color is perhaps the most important element of design and is inseparable from it. Color causes a psychological reaction, a sensation of the soul.

Choose your colors carefully to express your emotions. Your arrangement can be of various shades and tints of the same color, of closely related colors, or of opposite colors. For example, if yellow is your color, the arrangement can be of lemon through gold, or yellow with yellow-orange and orange, or yellow with mauve.

Use the elements of design in the right way, and your arrangement will be balanced. This does not necessarily mean it will be symmetrical; it means it will be in equilibrium. To assist in achieving balance, place buds toward the top and fuller roses toward the bottom. Darker colors should also weight the bottom. If the container is stronger on one side, the arrangement should be balanced in the same direction.

The last feature your design should have is rhythm. The eye must be carried easily from one part of the arrangement to another. This can be achieved by repetition of color or form, by progressing from bud to full open flower, or by the line.

Flower arranging is an art, not a science, and can be a very fulfilling sideline for rose growers. After a little practice, you'll be making flower arrangements for the porch or patio, the bathroom, the guest room. Your design will brighten up dark corners, mantels, pianos, the table. Formal or natural, let it be creative!

Deep red roses in a crystal vase spell refinement, elegance, and dignity.

Arranging Roses

The only color on this table is that of the roses, making a dramatic contrast to the black and white of the china and accessories.

Dried blue-violet statice enhance the beauty of pink roses.

Just because it's winter doesn't mean you have to be without roses for the house or table. The same care you gave to roses from the garden should be given to those bought in a store. As soon as you get them home, re-cut them under water and store them in water in a cool place for several hours before making the arrangement.

Should your roses prematurely wilt, revive them by cutting the stems under water and placing the roses in a bucket of lukewarm water, up to the neck of the flower, for several hours.

If your arrangement is going to be viewed from all sides, be sure it is equally attractive all around. To make this task easy, put your arrangement together on something that revolves, a Lazy Susan, for instance.

And if your arrangement will be set close to the viewers, pick roses for their fragrance as well as their eye appeal. Also, don't overlook the effect that white or colored light will have on bringing out the tones and luster of the cut roses. Adjust it as needed, but be careful you don't overdo the effect.

Sing 'Auld Lang Syne' with a holiday arrangement of greens.

ROSE FAVORITES

The American Rose Society, a national association of amateur and professional rose growers, has categorized all old garden, shrub, hybrid tea, floribunda, grandiflora, polyantha, climbing, and miniature roses into sixteen separate color classifications. This list of classifications makes the job of picking the best roses a lot easier.

w—white or near white
my—medium yellow
dy—deep yellow
yb—yellow blend
ab—apricot blend
ob—orange and orange blend
o-r—orange-red

lp—light pink
mp—medium pink
pb—pink blend
mr—medium red
dr—dark red
rb—red blend
m—mauve
r—russet

Each year, members of the American Rose Society are surveyed to establish ratings for the varieties grown across the country. The rating system is based on a ten-point scale.

10.0 Perfect (never achieved)
9.0-9.9 Outstanding
8.0-8.9 Excellent
7.0-7.9 Good
6.0-6.9 Fair
5.9 and lower (of questionable value)

The results of this annual survey are published in the "Handbook for Selecting Roses," available from the American Rose Society for 25 cents. Write to Box 30,000, Shreveport, Louisiana 71130. It lists over 1,000 different rose varieties. The roses listed here have all attained a rating of 8.0 or higher.

HYBRID TEAS

White
Garden Party w
Pascali w

Yellow
Peace yb
Susan Massu yb

Orange
Fragrant Cloud o-r
Tropicana o-r

Pink
Century Two mp
Chicago Peace pb
Confidence pb
Dainty Bess lp
Duet mp
First Prize pb
Miss All-American Beauty mp
Royal Highness lp
Swarthmore pb
Tiffany pb

Red
Big Ben dr
Chrysler Imperial dr
Double Delight rb
Granada rb
Mister Lincoln dr
Wini Edmunds rb

Mauve
Lady X m

GRANDIFLORAS

Pink
Pink Parfait pb
Queen Elizabeth mp

FLORIBUNDAS

White
Evening Star w
Iceberg w
Ivory Fashion w

Yellow
Little Darling yb

Orange
Bahia ob
City of Belfast o-r
Ginger o-r
Matador ob
Orangeade o-r
Sarabande o-r

Pink
Betty Prior mp
Gene Boerner mp
Sea Pearl pb
Red Europeana dr

Mauve
Angel Face m

POLYANTHA

Pink
The Fairy lp

CLIMBERS

Apricot
Royal Sunset ab

Pink
Climbing First Prize pb

Red
Don Juan dr
Handel rb

MINIATURES

White
Cinderella w
Easter Morning w
Popcorn w
Simplex w
Starglo w

Yellow
Yellow Doll my

Apricot
Baby Darling ab
Mary Adair ab

Orange
Hula Girl ob
Mary Marshall ob
Scarlet Gen o-r
Sheri Anne o-r
Starina o-r

Pink
Baby Betsy McCall lp
Chipper lp
Hi Ho dp
Janna pb
Jeanne Lajoie mp
Judy Fischer mp
Kathy Robinson pb
Pink Cameo dp
Pixie Rose dp

Red
Beauty Secret mr
Dwarfking mr
Jeanie Williams rb
Kathy mr
Magic Carrousel rb
Over the Rainbow rb
Top Secret mr

ALL-AMERICA ROSE SELECTIONS

In 1938, rose producers and introducers banded together and formed the All-America Rose Selections (AARS). This organization was set up to test new roses and determine which, if any, were worthy of recommendation to the buying public.

Plants are grown in 26 test gardens across the United States and Canada so that each rose tested is exposed to a variety of soil and climatic conditions. They are rated on habit, vigor, hardiness, disease resistance, repeat bloom, foliage, form, substance, opening and finishing color, fragrance, and novelty. After a two-year test, those rose varieties with the highest scores are awarded the green and white AARS stamp. They are then released for sale to the public.

Year	Award Winner	Color	Class	Originator
1979	Friendship	Pink	Hybrid tea	Robert Lindquist Sr.
	Paradise	Lavender and pink	Hybrid tea	O. L. Weeks
	Sundowner	Orange	Grandiflora	Sam McGredy IV
1978	Charisma	Multicolor red/yellow	Floribunda	Robert Jelly
	Color Magic	Coral blend	Hybrid tea	Wm. Warriner
1977	Double Delight	Red and white bicolor	Hybrid tea	H. C. Swim
	First Edition	Coral	Floribunda	Georges Delbard
	Prominent	Hot orange	Grandiflora	Reimer Kordes
1976	America	Salmon	Climber	Wm. Warriner
	Cathedral	Golden apricot	Floribunda	Sam McGredy IV
	Seashell	Peach & salmon	Hybrid tea	Reimer Kordes
	Yankee Doodle	Sherbet orange	Hybrid tea	Reimer Kordes
1975	Arizona	Bronze-copper	Grandiflora	O. O. Weeks
	Oregold	Pure yellow	Hybrid tea	Matthias Tantau
	Rose Parade	Pink	Floribunda	J. Benjamin Williams
1974	Bahia	Orange-pink	Floribunda	Lammerts
	Bon Bon	Pink and white bicolor	Floribunda	Warriner
	Perfume Delight	Clear pink	Hybrid tea	Weeks
1973	Electron	Rose-pink	Hybrid tea	Sam McGredy IV
	Gypsy	Orange-red	Hybrid tea	O. L. Weeks
	Medallion	Apricot-pink	Hybrid tea	Wm. Warriner
1972	Apollo	Sunrise yellow	Hybrid tea	D. L. Armstrong
	Portrait	Pink	Hybrid tea	Carl Meyer
1971	Aquarius	Pink blend	Grandiflora	D. L. Armstrong
	Command Performance	Orange-red	Hybrid tea	Lindquist
	Redgold	Red edge on yellow	Floribunda	Dickson
1970	First Prize	Rose-red	Hybrid tea	Boerner
1969	Angel Face	Lavender	Floribunda	Swim & Weeks
	Comanche	Scarlet-orange	Grandiflora	Swim & Weeks
	Gene Boerner	Pink	Floribunda	Boerner
	Pascali	White	Hybrid tea	Louis Lens
1968	Europeana	Red	Floribunda	G. deRuiter
	Miss All-American Beauty	Pink	Hybrid tea	Meilland
	Scarlet Knight	Scarlet red	Grandiflora	Meilland
1967	Bewitched	Clear, phlox-pink	Hybrid tea	Lammerts
	Gay Princess	Shell pink	Floribunda	Boerner
	Lucky Lady	Creamy, shrimp-pink	Grandiflora	D. L. Armstrong & Swim
	Roman Holiday	Orange-red	Floribunda	Lindquist

Year	Award Winner	Color	Class	Originator
1966	American Heritage	Ivory tinged carmine	Hybrid tea	Lammerts
	Apricot Nectar	Apricot	Floribunda	Boerner
	Matterhorn	White	Hybrid tea	D. L. Armstrong & Swim
1965	Camelot	Shrimp pink	Grandiflora	Swim & Weeks
	Mister Lincoln	Deep red	Hybrid tea	Swim & Weeks
1964	Granada	Scarlet-yellow	Hybrid tea	Lindquist
	Saratoga	White	Floribunda	Boerner
1963	Royal Highness	Clear pink	Hybrid tea	Swim & Weeks
	Tropicana	Orange-red	Hybrid tea	Matthias Tantau
1962	Christian Dior	Crimson-scarlet	Hybrid tea	F. Meilland
	Golden Slippers	Orange-gold	Floribunda	Von Abrams
	John S. Armstrong	Deep red	Grandiflora	Swim
	King's Ransom	Chrime yellow	Hybrid tea	Morey
1961	Duet	Salmon-pink, orange-red	Hybrid tea	Swim
	Pink Parfait	Dawn pink	Grandiflora	Swim
1960	Fire King	Vermillion	Floribunda	F. Meilland
	Garden Party	White	Hybrid tea	Swim
	Sarabande	Scarlet orange	Floribunda	F. Meilland
1959	Ivory Fashion	Ivory	Floribunda	Boerner
	Starfire	Cherry red	Grandiflora	Lammerts
1958	Fusilier	Orange-red	Floribunda	Morey
	Gold Cup	Golden yellow	Floribunda	Boerner
	White Knight	White	Hybrid tea	F. Meilland
1957	Golden Showers	Daffodil yellow	Climber	Lammerts
	White Bouquet	White	Floribunda	Boerner
1956	Circus	Multicolor	Floribunda	Swim
1955	Jiminy Cricket	Coral orange	Floribunda	Boerner
	Queen Elizabeth	Clear pink	Grandiflora	Lammerts
	Tiffany	Orchid pink	Hybrid tea	Lindquist
1954	*Lilibet	Dawn pink	Floribunda	Lindquist
	Mojave	Apricot orange	Hybrid tea	Swim
1953	Chrysler Imperial	Crimson red	Hybrid tea	Lammerts
	Ma Perkins	Coral-shell pink	Floribunda	Boerner
1952	*Fred Howard	Yellow, penciled pink	Hybrid tea	F. H. Howard
	Helen Traubel	Apricot pink	Hybrid tea	Swim
	Vogue	Cherry coral	Floribunda	Boerner
1951	None of the 1951 introductions was equal to the rigid AARS standards.			
1950	Capistrano	Pink	Hybrid tea	Morris
	Fashion	Coral pink	Floribunda	Boerner
	Sutter's Gold	Golden yellow	Hybrid tea	Swim
1949	Forty-niner	Red and yellow	Hybrid tea	Swim
	*Tallyho	Two-tone pink	Hybrid tea	Swim
1948	Diamond Jubilee	Buff	Hybrid tea	Boerner
	Nocturne	Dark red	Hybrid tea	Swim
	Pinkie	Light rose pink	Floribunda	Swim
	Taffeta	Carmine	Hybrid tea	Lammerts
1947	Rubaiyat	Cerise red	Hybrid tea	McGredy
1946	Peace	Pale gold	Hybrid tea	F. Meilland

No longer generally available.

How to Dry Flowers

Enjoy your garden flowers indoors all winter by preserving them. Here are the various techniques, along with recommended flowers for each.

AIR DRYING

Cut flowers when dry and at their best (midday); strip leaves and secure in small bunches with elastic ties. Then, hang them upside down in a dark ventilated attic or room for a period of two to three weeks. Avoid picking flowers after heavy rains or when covered with dew.

Some excellent garden varieties for this method include cockscomb (celosia), larkspur, annual statice, acacia, bells-of-Ireland, blue salvia, Chinese-lanterns, globe amaranth, hydrangea (Pee Gee), delphinium, yarrow, artemisia, heather, honesty (silver dollars), and strawflowers (strawflowers should be picked and wired when buds are just opening).

Likewise, many of the field flowers such as dock, goldenrod, pampas grass, pearly everlasting, teasel, and tansy dry well using this method.

SILICA GEL

Your favorite garden flowers—including zinnias, marigolds, roses, shasta daisies, dahlias, delphiniums, snapdragons, feverfew, ranunculus, and peonies—are great candidates for desiccant drying. Remember, however, that the finished product is only as good as the original flower specimen you picked to preserve! Try to avoid broken or damaged flowers.

Place a base of 1 or 2 inches of silica gel granules in the bottom of a cookie tin or coffee can and insert the short-cut stem of the flower *face up* in the drying medium. Be careful not to overlap any of the petals between flower specimens. Gently sprinkle more of the granules over the flowers until they are completely covered with silica gel to a depth of about 1 inch. *Cover tightly* and tape name of flower and date on top of container. Place tin in a dark, dry place for the required drying time (from two to six days, see chart). If in doubt, lift lid and check to see if the petals feel brittle and papery to the touch; if not, replace cover.

When ready to remove, slowly pour off the silica gel and cup your hand under the flower head. Gently shake off drying compound, and if necessary, remove stubborn granules with a soft artist's brush. Store flowers in airtight boxes until ready to use (stem ends may be inserted erect in blocks of dry floral foam). To keep dried material in top condition, especially over prolonged periods or when excessive humidity may be a problem, add 3 to 4 tablespoons of silica gel to the storage container. If a petal should fall off, dab on a small amount of white glue with a toothpick and join it to the flower center.

Though delphiniums and larkspur may be air-dried, they retain form and color perfection in silica gel. Delphiniums, larkspur, rose buds, lilacs, and snapdragons should be dried in a horizontal position. Avoid drying dark red flowers, as they turn black. But don't forget to dry flower buds and leaves for more effect.

Silica gel, available at craft shops, can be reused indefinitely, but must be heated in the oven at 250° F. for one hour when restoration of the blue crystals is necessary.

BORAX

Ordinary household borax also may be used as drying medium. Follow the silica gel directions with two exceptions—place the flower *face down* in the container and leave the *lid off* while drying. Though less expensive than silica gel, it takes twice as long to act as a desiccant, and the color retention is less effective.

PRESSED

For the avid pressed-flower enthusiast, a flower press, complete with blotting paper, is available in craft shops. But for the average pressed-flower lover, a telephone book will suffice. At 1-inch intervals

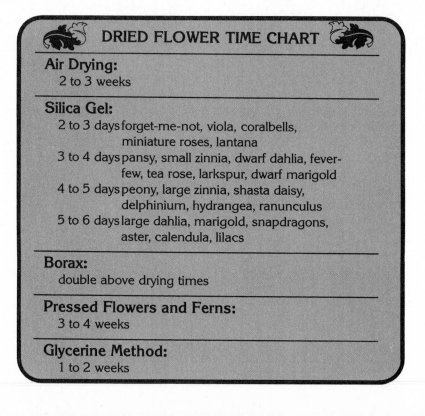

DRIED FLOWER TIME CHART

Air Drying:
2 to 3 weeks

Silica Gel:
2 to 3 days forget-me-not, viola, coralbells, miniature roses, lantana
3 to 4 days pansy, small zinnia, dwarf dahlia, feverfew, tea rose, larkspur, dwarf marigold
4 to 5 days peony, large zinnia, shasta daisy, delphinium, hydrangea, ranunculus
5 to 6 days large dahlia, marigold, snapdragons, aster, calendula, lilacs

Borax:
double above drying times

Pressed Flowers and Ferns:
3 to 4 weeks

Glycerine Method:
1 to 2 weeks

in the book, spread facial tissue in newspaper. Place flowers flat and avoid overlapping. Cover flowers with tissue, then newspaper, so that newspaper print will not be picked up by the flowers while pressing.

If possible, use an even thickness of materials on each page for even drying. Remember to include buds and curve some stems and leaves for graceful positioning when dried. Weight with books and store for 3 to 4 weeks away from sunlight.

Some garden favorites for pressing include buttercup, daisies, verbena, dusty miller, hydrangea florets, lobelia, delphinium spikes and florets, sweet alyssum, pansies, violas, and almost all types of fern.

When ready to create pressed flower pictures, use eyebrow tweezers and a tiny dot of white glue to anchor the flowers to the background material. Let the finished design dry overnight before inserting the glass and making the back airtight with tape.

FOLIAGE (GLYCERINIZED)

Leaves such as peony, oak, and beech may be pressed or dried in silica gel, but they will never be as supple and useful as when treated with glycerine. In a jar, mix a solution of one part glycerine to two parts hot water and shake well. After scraping or pounding the cut young branch ends, place them in 2 to 3 inches of the solution. Let stand for one to two weeks, or until leaves have finished absorbing the mixture and feel pliable. Usually they change to dark green or soft shades of brown and rust, depending upon their foliage. The glycerinized material may be used with fresh flowers, too, as water causes no injury.

Additional foliage to treat includes eucalyptus, holly, laurel, aspidistra, pyracantha, sycamore, yew, and crab apple. Foliage to be treated should be gathered before mid-August while still tender. And the glycerine solution may be used over again if stored in a tightly covered jar.

DRIED ARRANGEMENTS

Combine glycerinized foliage with dried flowers in a foam-filled container, after using floral wire and tape to extend the flower stems. Insert the foliage first, using it as a guide for height and outline (about 1½ times the height of the container). After the filler material, place large and darker flowers in the lower center section of the arrangement for visual interest. Fill in with the rest of the flowers. Place the completed arrangement away from direct sun.

Air drying of tansy, pearly, everlasting, yarrow, lady's-mantle, and three kinds of statice.

273

How to Preserve Roses

Enjoy the beauty and pleasure of your rose garden long after autumn leaves have fallen and plants have faded from bloom.

For potpourris and rose recipes, use only fragrant petals and hips cut from plants that have not been sprayed with pesticides. Gather the petals in the morning after the dew is gone, and remove the green or white base from the petals; known as the heel, it has a bitter taste. Rinse the petals lightly and pat dry.

Potpourri

Take the cover off a potpourri jar, and fill the room with the pleasant fragrance of roses and spices.

There are two types of potpourri: dried and moist. The same recipe can be used for either; only the method varies. Moist potpourri has a heavier scent.

For dried potpourri, pick roses in the morning after the dew has lifted, when they are one-third to one-half open. Place the petals on screens or trays in a dry, airy room away from the sun, turning every day until they are crisp.

Dry petals all summer, storing them in dark, airtight containers. When you've collected enough, mix one tablespoon of fixative (orris or storax, for example) and one tablespoon of spices like cinnamon, mace, cloves, or allspice, with every quart of rose petals. Add other dry ingredients to the mixture—dried and crushed citrus peel, rose leaves, lavender, lemon balm, heliotrope, and rosemary. Add a few drops of fragrant oil, mix, age for six weeks.

For moist potpourri, dry rose petals until they are limp. In a jar, alternate ½-inch layers of petals with one tablespoon of non-iodized salt. After two weeks, add spices, fragrant oil, and partially dried flowers. Age for a month or more.

Dried Roses

Color your home with dried roses long after the garden has faded from bloom.

For drying, pick dry flowers (not wet with rain or dew) in the stage of bloom you want to preserve.

Place a base of one to two inches of silica gel granules in the bottom of a cookie tin or coffee can, and insert the short cut stem of the flower, face up in the drying medium. Be careful not to overlap any of the petals between flower specimens. Gently sprinkle more of the granules over the flowers until they are completely covered with silica gel to a depth of about one inch. Cover tightly, and tape the name of the flower and the date on top of the container. Leave the tin in a dark, dry place for the required drying time (from two to six days). If in doubt, lift the lid and check. The petals should feel brittle and papery; if they don't, replace cover and let the flowers dry longer. When they are ready to remove, slowly pour off the silica gel, and cup your hand under the flower head. Shake off the drying compound gently, and, if necessary, remove stubborn granules with a soft artist's brush. Store the flowers in airtight boxes until ready to use. For neat storage, insert the erect stem ends in blocks of dry floral foam. To keep dried material in top condition, especially over prolonged periods or when excessive humidity may be a problem, add three to four tablespoons of silica gel to the storage container. If a petal falls off, use a toothpick to dab a small amount of white glue on the end of the petal, and, with tweezers, join it to the flower center. Don't forget to dry flower buds and leaves to enhance your arrangements. Dark red flowers aren't suitable for drying because they turn black.

Silica gel, available at craft shops, can be reused indefinitely but must be heated in the oven at 250 degrees Fahrenheit for one hour to restore the blue crystals to full potency.

Pressed

The avid pressed-flower enthusiast can buy a flower press, complete with blotting paper, at a craft shop. For the average pressed-flower lover, however, a thick telephone book will suffice. At one-inch intervals in the book, spread facial tissue on newspaper. Place the flowers flat. Avoid overlapping. Cover the flowers with tissue, then newspaper. In this way, the newsprint will not be picked up by the flowers while they're being pressed. Repeat the process until the book is filled. If possible, use materials of even thickness on each page for even drying. Remember to include buds, and curve some stems and leaves for graceful positioning when dried. Put a weight on the book, and store for three to four weeks away from sunlight in a dark, dry place.

Attar of Roses

Fill an earthen jar with rose petals, cover with water, and set in the sun. After one week, the oil will form on the surface. Soak up with a cotton swab and squeeze into a vial. For best results, use Damask rose petals.

Rose Beads

Years ago, young brides had their wedding bouquets made into rosary beads to remind them of their special day and to freshen newly stored linens.

Mix 1¾ cups of flour with four tablespoons of salt and enough water to make a smooth dough. Press into this mixture three cups of finely chopped, fragrant rose petals. Flour a bread board, and roll out the dough ¼ inch thick. Cut out circles with a thimble, and roll them into beads. String with wire, and hang in the dark until the beads are dry. Then re-string them to get the finished product. Beads will dry to brown unless they're colored with three drops of oil paint. Add ten drops of rose oil to increase the fragrance.

Rose Frosting

Mix three ounces of cream cheese with one tablespoon of milk. Sift 2½ cups of confectioners' sugar, and add it gradually, blending well. Add one teaspoon of rose water and food coloring, if desired. Spread the frosting on the cake, and sprinkle with chopped nuts. For best flavor, serve the cake chilled.

To make a potpourri mix pleasing to the eye as well as the nose, add some dried whole flowers for color.

Special Uses for Herbs

For Delightful Scents

The aromatic herbs have a charm and mystique all their own. Through the ages, they have been used in bath and breath fresheners, hair rinses, soap powders, room deodorizers, and even insect repellents. They are also some of the main ingredients in sweet-scented potpourris, sachets, and pillows.

To make a potpourri like the one at left, you'll need a collection of dried rose petals. Clip them during the summer and dry in a shady well-ventilated place. Store the dried petals in airtight containers until you're ready to make the potpourri, but be sure to stir them every few days. If you don't have a source of rose petals, rose geranium leaves can be substituted.

Next, crush a mixture such as lavender, orris root, tonka bean, sandalwood, lemon verbena, frankincense, and myrrh until you have a pleasing scent combination (orris root is a scent preservative that is available at most pharmacies). Thoroughly mix these ingredients with the dried rose petals, and cure in a covered container for five or six weeks, stirring the mixture every few days.

After curing, you can use the potpourri mix in sachets, or just store it in jars, opened occasionally to add fragrance to a room. Potpourris also can be placed in open bowls for a continuous fresh fragrance, but such a mix will not hold its scent for as long a time.

Perhaps the best way to make a potpourri mix pleasing to the eye as well as to the nose is to add some dried whole flowers for color. The bowl at left is filled with a potpourri mix attractively concealed beneath a layer of dried flowers. The flowers —camellia, pansy, alyssum, rue, apricot geranium, azalea, nastur-

tium, and forsythia—were dried with commercial drying powders.

Lavender sticks add a delightful fragrance to trunks, closets, and dresser drawers. To make a lavender stick, clip an odd number of lavender flower stalks just before they are completely open. Be sure to clip as much stem as possible. It's a good idea for beginners to start out with about eleven flower stalks.

Bunch the flower heads and tie the stems together just at the base of the flower heads. Use about a yard of narrow ribbon, leaving a long length on one side. Gently fold up the stems, one at a time, over the flower heads (stems will form a kind of "cage" with the flower heads in the center).

After the stems are folded, draw the long free end of the ribbon through the stems from inside, weaving in and out, and over and under the stem "cage," below. Be sure the ribbon stays flat, and that each weave is flush with the next. Continue weaving until the flower

heads are completely covered.

To keep the sticks from unraveling, tie the free end of the ribbon into a knot at the base of the woven head, and add a decorative bow over the tied knot. A rubber band placed around the free stem ends will keep them from spreading as the sticks dry. It also will make the stems less likely to break off.

To make a lavender pillow, above, simply remove the lavender flowers from their stalks and stuff and sew them into a dainty pillow, along with some powdered orris root as a scent preservative. Use pillows in closets, trunks, dresser drawers or in gift packages. Pillows retain their scent for several months.

Zones of Plant Hardiness

Throughout this book, we have referred to zone numbers that represent the northern limits of successful culture for certain plants.

Zone boundary lines are not absolute. You can expect temperatures to vary as much as 5° from those given on the opposite page. You must also consider localized conditions. Hills and valleys in certain areas do not always have the same high and low temperatures as those recorded at the official weather bureau stations.

Still other conditions to consider before selecting plants are rainfall, humidity, snow coverage, wind, and soil type. A specific perennial may survive in zone 3 in Maine, for example, but be completely unadapted to that same zone in North Dakota—simply because of differences in rainfall and humidity.

For assured success, start with local plant favorites. Your added care will help the natives prosper in domestic situations. And often they'll do better than plants brought in from distant places at surviving freakish weather, hail, flood, drought, or early and late frosts.

Be flexible. When certain plants prosper unexpectedly in your garden, consider adding more of them—perhaps in additional varieties or different colors. If others do poorly, don't hesitate to replace them with more hardy plants.

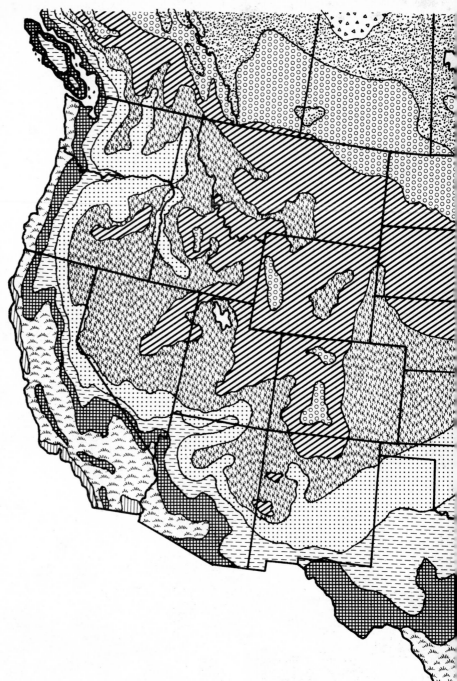

Source: United States Department of Agriculture

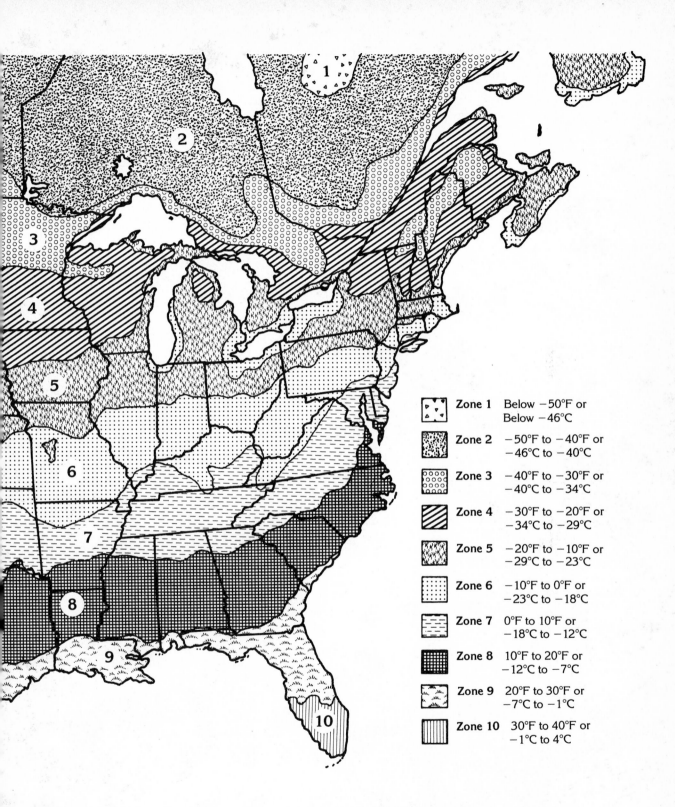

	Zone 1	Below −50°F or Below −46°C
	Zone 2	−50°F to −40°F or −46°C to −40°C
	Zone 3	−40°F to −30°F or −40°C to −34°C
	Zone 4	−30°F to −20°F or −34°C to −29°C
	Zone 5	−20°F to −10°F or −29°C to −23°C
	Zone 6	−10°F to 0°F or −23°C to −18°C
	Zone 7	0°F to 10°F or −18°C to −12°C
	Zone 8	10°F to 20°F or −12°C to −7°C
	Zone 9	20°F to 30°F or −7°C to −1°C
	Zone 10	30°F to 40°F or −1°C to 4°C

INDEX

A

AARS (All-America Rose
   Selections), 270–271
Abronia, 257
Accent rose, 205
Achillea, 8, 10, 64
Achimenes, 251
Acidanthera, 248
Aconite, winter, 230
Aconitum, or monkshood, 51–52
Acroclinium, or helipterum, 115
Actaea, 254
Adonis vernalis, 27
Agapanthus, 249
Ageratum, 27, 70, 72, 73, 74, 80,
   87, 102, 107, 115
Air drying, 272
Ajuga, 258
Alba rose, 147, 180, 187
Alcea rosea, 10, 67
Alfred de Dalmas rose, 189
Alkanet, 11, 27–28
All-America Rose Selections
   (AARS), 270–271
Allium, 232, 233, 235, 251
Aloha rose, 213
Alpine forget-me-not, 66
Alumroot, 35, 254
Alyssum, 9, 11, 12, 27, 73, 80, 85,
   86, 87, 91, 92, 94, 95, 98, 102,
   103, 112, 115–116, 168, 273
Amaranth, globe, 102, 128, 272
Amaranthus, 73, 84, 87, 103, 116
Amaryllis, 251
American Heritage rose, 170, 195
   AARS, 271
American Rose Society, 269
America rose, 213
   AARS, 270
Ammobium, 116
Anabell rose, 170, 205
Anchusa, 10, 11, 27–28, 31,
   116–117
Anemone, 10, 11, 231, 234, 251,
   254, 256
Anemonella, 254
Angel Face rose, 170, 172, 205,
   264
   AARS, 270

Anthemis tinctoria, 28
Antigua, 195
Antirrhinum. *See* Snapdragon
Apache Tears rose, 205
Aphids, 182
Apollo rose, 195
   AARS, 270
Apricot Nectar rose, 170, 205
   AARS, 271
Aquarius rose, 203
   AARS, 270
Aquilegia, 10, 11, 34–35, 254
Arbutus, trailing, 254
Arctotis, 80. *See also* African daisy
Arisaema triphyllum, 252, 255
Arizona rose, 203
   AARS, 270
Armeria maritima, 62
Armstrong, John S., rose, 203
   AARS, 271
Arranging roses, 266–268
Artemisia, 10, 11, 28
Arundo donax, 260
Asarum, 255
Asclepias tuberosa, 10, 11, 32, 254
Aster, 10, 11, 28–29, 71, 78, 80, 82,
   87, 96, 102, 117
   Stoke's, 10, 61
   wood, blue, 257
Astilbe, 10, 11, 29
Attar of rose, 274
Aurinia saxatilis, 27
Austrian Copper rose, 189
Avens, 41
Azalea, 8, 9, 224

B

Baby Betsy McCall rose, 217, 269
Baby-blue-eyes, 80, 102, 134
Baby Darling rose, 217, 269
Baby Masquerade rose, 217
Baby's-breath, 8, 10, 11, 29, 64,
   128–129
Bachelor's-buttons, 33, 61, 73, 80,
   102, 123
Bahia rose, 149, 170, 205, 269
   AARS, 270
Balloon flower, 10, 11, 29–30
Balsam, bush, 80, 117
Baneberry, 254

Baptisia, 10, 13, 30
Baroness Rothschild rose, 188
Basket-of-gold alyssum, 11, 12, 27
Beads, rose, 274
Bean
   castor, 73, 103, 107, 121
   scarlet runner, 88, 91, 100, 102
   tonka, 277
Beauty Secret rose, 217, 269
Beds, rose, 156, 158
Bee-balm, 8, 10, 11, 30, 53
Beetle, Fuller rose, 182
Begonia
   Rieger, 92
   tuberous, 109, 242–243, 251
   wax, or fibrous, 80, 88, 90, 92,
      94, 95, 96, 102, 103, 113, 118
Belinda rose, 192, 193
Bellflower, 10, 11, 32
Bellis perennis, 10, 31–31, 66
Bells-of-Ireland, 80, 118
Bellwort, 254
Bergamot, 30
Bermudiana rose, 167
Betony, stachys, or lamb's-ears,
   60–61
Betty Prior rose, 205, 269
Bewitched rose, 195
   AARS, 270
Big Ben rose, 170, 195, 269
Bishop's-cap, 254
Black-eyed susan, 57, 88, 100,
   103, 254
Black spot disease, 177, 182, 187
Blanc Double de Coubert rose, 191
Blanket flower. *See* Gaillardia
Blaze rose, 213
Bleeding-heart, 10, 11, 13, 31
Bloodroot, 254
Bluebell, 47, 254
   Virginia, 10, 11, 38, 50, 64
Bluebonnet, Texas, 131
Blue fescue, 255
Blue flag, 255
Blue gentian, 255
Blue lace flower, 102, 118
Blue Moon rose, 170, 195
Blue phlox, 256
Blue violet, 257
Blue wood aster, 257
Bon Bon rose, 205
   AARS, 270
Bo-Peep rose, 217
Bourbon rose, 147, 187
Brachycome. *See* Daisy, Swan River

Breeding roses, 220–221
Browallia, 80, 88, 94, 102, 119
Brunnera macrophylla, 31
Budding, rose, 221
Bud union, 174, 176, 179, 180, 181, 182
Buff Beauty rose, 192
Bugloss, Siberian, 31
Burning bush. *See* Kochia
Buttercup, 31–32
  crowfoot, 255
Butterfly flower, 102, 119
Butterfly weed, 10, 11, 32, 254

C

Cabbage rose, 147, 187
Caladium, 84, 96, 99, 244, 251
Calendula, 8, 73, 74, 75, 78, 80, 81, 82, 86, 102–103, 272
California poppy, 256
Calliopsis. *See* Coreopsis
Callistephus. *See* Aster
Caltha, or marsh marigold, 252, 256
Camaieux rose, 188
Camassia, 233, 235
Camelot rose, 203
  AARS, 271
Campanula, 10, 11, 32, 66
Candy Stripe rose, 195
Candytuft, 10, 11, 32–33, 80, 120.
  See also Iberis
Cane borer, 182
Canker, 182
Capistrano rose, AARS, 271
Cardinal climber, 100
Cardinal de Richelieu rose, 188
Cardinal flower, 49
Carex morrowi variegata, 261
Carla rose, 195
Carnation, 85, 103, 121
Carrousel rose, 203
Catananche caerulea, 36
Catchfly, 51
Cathedral bells vine, 101
Cathedral rose, 205
  AARS, 270
Catherine Mermet rose, 189
Cecile Brunner rose, 208
Celosia, 73, 76, 80, 85, 87, 102, 121, 272
Celsiana rose, 188
Centaurea, 33, 80, 102, 123–124, 125–126
Centifolia, 147, 180, 187, 189

Centranthus, 10, 47
Century Two rose, 170, 195, 269
Cerastium, 9, 33
Ceratostigma, 48
Charisma rose, 205
  AARS, 270
Charles de Mills rose, 188
Charlotte Armstrong rose, 195, 214, 220
Chelone, 257
Chestnut rose, 189
Chevy Chase rose, 213, 215
Chicago Peace rose, 170, 195, 269
China Doll Rose, 208
China rose, 147, 148, 188
Chinese-lantern, 33–34, 103, 272
Chionodoxa, 230, 233, 234
Chipper rose, 217, 269
Christmas rose, 11, 43–44
Chrysanthemum, 10, 11, 24–25, 34, 38–39, 43, 52–53, 59–60, 85, 90, 110, 122
Chrysler Imperial rose, 170, 195, 214, 269
  AARS, 271
Cigar plant. *See* Cuphea
Cimicifuga, 257
Cinderella rose, 217, 269
Cineraria, 107
Cinquefoil, 10, 57, 254
Circus rose, 206
  AARS, 271
City of Belfast rose, 206, 269
Clarkia, 80, 122, 128
Claytonia, 257
Cleome, 73, 76, 80, 87, 102, 103, 122–123
Climbers, rose, 148, 150, 154, 156, 166, 175, 180, 189, 192, 211, 213–214
  AARS, 270–271
  pruning, 177
Cobaea, 76, 100, 101, 102, 103
Cockscomb, *See* Celosia
Colchicum, 233
Coleus, 73, 80, 84, 88, 113, 123
Color combinations, rose, 170–173
Color Magic rose, 195
  AARS, 270

Columbine, 10, 11, 34–35, 61, 254
Columbus Queen rose, 196, 197
Comanche rose, 203
  AARS, 270
Command Performance rose, 196
  AARS, 270
Common Moss rose, 189
Coneflower, 10, 57–58
  prairie, 254
  purple 254
Confidence rose, 196, 269
Container roses, 160–163
Convolvulus, 123
Coralbells, 10, 11, 35
Coral Dawn rose, 213
Coraldrops, 251
Cordgrass, 260
Coreopsis, 10, 11, 35, 73, 78, 80, 86, 102, 103, 123,
Cornelia rose, 192
Cornflower, 33, 73, 87, 102, 103, 123–124
Cosmos, 70, 73, 78, 80, 82, 84, 87, 86, 102, 103, 124
Cottage tulips, 262
Cowslip, blue, 50
Crested Moss rose, 189
Crimson Glory rose, 196, 214
Crimson Rambler rose, 148
Crocus, 10, 11, 12, 234
Crowfoot, buttercup, 255
Crown gall, 182
Cuddles rose, 217
Cup-and-saucer vine, 100, 101, 102, 103
Cupflower, 94, 124
Cuphea, 124
Cupid's-dart, 36
Cyclamen, hardy, 13, 233
Cynoglossum, 124–125
Cypress, summer, 119
Cypripedium, 255

D

Daffodil, 9, 225, 228–229, 231, 262, 263. *See also* Narcissus
Dahlia, 70, 71, 76, 78, 80, 103, 109, 125, 239–240, 250, 251, 272
  dwarf, 250
Dainty Bess rose, 196, 269
Daisy
  African, 103, 114, 115
  blue, 38
  cape, 120
  dahlberg, 125

Daisy *(continued)*
English, 10, 30–31, 66, 67, 110
gloriosa, 8, 76, 80, 84, 103
michaelmas. *See* Aster
mountain, or fleabane, 39
painted, 10, 34, 52–53, 103
shasta, 10, 11, 34, 55, 59–60, 78, 272
Swan River, 80, 103, 140
tahoka, 103, 141
transvaal. *See* Gerbera
Damask rose, 147, 188, 274
Daylily. *See* Hemerocallis
De la Grifferaie rose, 211
Delicata rose, 192
Delphinium, 10, 11, 12, 36–37, 80, 164, 166, 167, 266. *See also* Larkspur
Dentaria, 257
Desert-candle. *See* Eremurus
Devil-in-a-bush. *See* Nigella
Diamond Jubilee rose, 196
AARS, 271
Dianthus, 11, 37, 67, 71, 73, 82, 84, 85, 102, 107, 121, 136, 141
Dicentra. *See* Dutchman's-breeches
Dicentra spectabilis, 31
Dictamnus, 10, 11, 40
Digitalis, 10, 55, 66–67
Dimorphothea, 120
Dior, Christian, rose, 170, 195
AARS, 271
Diseases, rose, 162, 176–178, 182, 187
Dr. Huey rose, 180, 221
Dodecatheon, 257
Dog-tooth violet, 253
Don Juan rose, 213, 269
Doronicum, or leopard's-bane, 37–38
Dortmund rose, 192
Double Delight rose, 170, 196, 201, 269
AARS, 270
Downy phlox, 256
Dragonhead, false, 55
Dried flowers, 272–273
Dropmore lythrum, 49
Dropwort, or meadowsweet, 51
Duet rose, 170, 196, 269
AARS, 271
Dusty miller, 28, 84, 102, 103, 125–126, 273
Dutchman's-breeches, 252, 255
Dwarfking rose, 217, 269
Dyssodia, 125

E

Easter Morning rose, 217, 269
Echinacea, 254
Echinops, or globe thistle, 10, 11, 42
Echium, 80
Eclipse rose, 196
Eglanteria rose, 146, 191
Eglantine, 146
Eiffel Tower rose, 196
El Dorado rose, 158
Electron rose, 158, 170, 196
AARS, 270
Else Poulsen rose, 148, 206
Entryways, roses for, 154
Epigaea, 254
Eranthis, 223, 230, 234
Eremurus, 233
Erianthus ravennae, 260
Erigeron sp., 39
Erythronium, 233
Eschscholzia, 120, 256
Eucomis, 247
Eupatorium coelestinum, 27
Euphorbia, 60, 80, 126
Evening primrose. *See* Oenothera
Evening Star rose, 206
Evergreens, 259
dwarf, 259
Everlasting, 102, 139

F

Faberge rose, 206
Fairy, The, 208, 211
Fairy rose, 148, 218, 269
False dragonhead, 55
False miterwort, 255
Farewell-to-spring. *See* Godetia
Fashion rose, 206
AARS, 271
Father Hugo's rose, 189
Felicia amelloides, 38
Fern, 258
Fertilizer, 160, 162, 175, 179, 181
Fescue, blue, 260
Festuca ovina, 260
Feverfew, 10, 34, 38–39, 102, 103, 126, 272

Filipendula vulgaris, 51
Fire bush. *See* Kochia
Firecracker plant. *See* Cuphea
Fire King rose, 206
AARS, 271
Fire-on-the-mountain, 126
First Edition rose, 206
AARS, 271
First Love rose, 196
First Prize rose, 156, 196, 214
AARS, 270
F. J. Grootendorst rose, 152
Flag, blue, 255
Flax, or linum, 10, 39, 73, 126–127
Fleabane, 39
Floribunda rose, 152, 160, 175, 176, 177, 180, 181, 205–208, 211
AARS, 270–271
color, 269
Flossflower. *See* Ageratum
Foamflower, 255
Foetida, hybrid, 188
Forget-me-not, 28, 31, 72, 73, 86, 102, 110, 116–117, 124, 255
Alpine, 66
Siberian, 31
Forty-niner rose, AARS, 271
Fountain grass, 260
Four-o'clock, 73, 76, 80, 82, 85, 102, 103, 127
Foxglove, 7, 10, 53, 55, 66–67, 91, 110
Fragrant Cloud rose, 166, 170, 196, 269
Frau Karl Druschki rose, 188
Freesia, 251
Fred Howard rose, AARS, 271
Friendship rose, 196
AARS, 270
Fritillaria, 235
Frühlingsgold rose, 189
Fuchsia, 83
Fuller rose beetle, 182
Funkia. *See* Hosta
Fusilier rose, AARS, 271

G

Gaillardia, 10–11, 39–40, 53, 73, 80, 102, 103, 127
Galanthus, 233, 231, 234

Gallica roses, 188
Galtonia, 251
Garden Party rose, 170, 196, 269
    AARS, 270
Gas plant, 10, 11, 40, 65
Gay Princess rose, 169, 230
Gazania, 69, 73, 82, 103, 127
Gene Boerner rose, 170, 206, 269
    AARS, 270
General Jacqueminot rose, 189
Gentian, 40, 255
Geranium, 78, 80, 84, 85, 87, 88,
    89, 91, 94, 103, 107, 113, 127–
    128, 157, 255
Geranium, cranesbill, 10, 41
Gerbera jamesoni, 41
Geum, 41–42
Ghost weed. See Euphorbia
Ginger, 206, 269
    ground cover, 259
    wild, 259
Gladiolus, 239, 251
Globeflower, or trollius, 13, 42
Globe thistle, or echinops, 10, 11, 42
Gloire des Mousseux rose, 189
Gloriglo rose, 218
Glory-of-the-snow. See Chionodoxa
Glycerinized foliage, 273
Godetia, 73, 103, 122, 128
Gold Coin rose, 218
Gold Cup rose, AARS, 271
Goldenrod, hybrid, 10, 60
Golden Showers rose, 154, 213
    AARS, 271
Golden Slippers rose, AARS, 271
Golden Wings rose, 192
Gomphrena. See Amaranth, globe
Gourds, ornamental, 100
Grafting, 208, 221
Granada rose, 170, 196, 269
    AARS, 271
Grandiflora rose, 160, 175, 176, 181,
    203, 211, 269
    AARS, 270–271
Grand Slam rose, 196
Grass, ornamental, 260–261
Green Ice rose, 160, 218
Green rose, 188
Grootendorst, F.J., rose, 152
Ground covers, 258–259
Gypsophila, 10, 11, 29, 73, 80, 102,
    103, 128–129, 168
Gypsy rose, 160, 161, 196
    AARS, 270

H

Hall's honeysuckle, 258
Handel rose, 213, 269
Harison's Yellow rose, 188
Harlequin bug, 182
Heat Wave rose, 170
Hedges, rose, 152
Heidelberg rose, 192
Heirloom rose, 170, 196
Helenium, 10, 11, 42
Helen Traubel rose, AARS, 271
Helianthus, 10, 43, 257. See
    also Sunflower
Helichrysum. See Strawflower
Helictotrichon sempervirens, 261
Heliopsis, or oxeye, 8, 10, 11, 43
Heliotrope, 10, 80, 85, 103, 129
Helipterum, or acroclinium, 115
Helleborus, 43–44
Hemerocallis, or daylily, 10, 11, 12,
    15, 20–21, 36
Hen-and-chickens, 259
Hepatica, 255
Herbs
    ground covers, 259
    scents, 277
Hermosa rose, 188
Heuchera, 10, 11, 35, 254
Hibiscus, 10, 256
High Noon rose, 213
Hi Ho rose, 269
Hollyhock, 7, 10, 66, 67, 73, 80,
    96, 129
Honesty, 67
Honeysuckle, Hall's, 258
Hops, 100
Hosta, 9, 13, 44, 258
Hula Girl rose, 218, 269
Humulus japonicus, or hops, 100
Hyacinth, 10, 11, 12, 223, 230–231,
    235
Hybrids, rose
    creating, 147, 220–221

Hybrids (continued)
    Foetida, 188
    Moschatas, 192
    Moyesi, 191
    Perpetual, 145, 188–189
    Rugosa, 191–192
    Spinosissima, 189
    See also Tea, Hybrid
Hymenocallis, 251
Hypericum, 44–45

I

Iberis, 10, 11, 12, 32–33, 120
Iceberg rose, 170, 206, 269
Ice plant, 129–130
Impatiens, 76, 80, 83, 84, 88, 90,
    92, 96, 97, 103, 113, 130
Indigo, blue false, 10, 13, 30
Iris, 10, 11, 12, 16, 17, 42, 45–47,
    234, 255
    Dutch, 46
    dwarf bearded, 10, 11, 16, 46
    flag, blue, 255
    Japanese, 10, 16, 46
    Siberian, 13, 16, 46
    spuria, 10, 16, 46–47
    tall bearded, 16, 46
Irish Gold rose, 170, 196
Isabel de Ortiz rose, 196
Ismene, 251
Ivory Fashion rose, 170, 206, 269
    AARS, 271

J

Jack-in-the-pulpit, 255
Jacob's-ladder, 47, 255
Jacques Cartier rose, 189
Jadis rose, 196
Janna rose, 218, 269
Japanese beetle, 182
Jeanie Williams rose, 218, 269
Jeanne Lajoie rose, 218, 269
Jiminy Cricket rose, AARS, 271
John F. Kennedy rose, 196
Josephine, Empress, rose, 147
Joseph's Coat rose, 214
Judy Fischer rose, 218, 269
Juniper, 98
    prostrate, 259
Jupiter's-beard. See Centranthus

K

Kale, flowering, 84
Kathy Robinson rose, 218, 269
Kathy rose, 218, 269
Kennedy, John F., rose, 196
King's Ransom rose, 170, 198
  AARS, 271
Kniphofia, or poker plant, 56
Kochia, or burning bush, 80, 119
Königin von Dänemark rose, 187
Kordesi roses, 192
Kordes' Perfecta rose, 198

L

Lady Penzance rose, 191
Lady slipper
  balsam, 117
  cypripedium, 255
Lady X rose, 170, 198, 269
Laing, Mrs. John, rose, 189
Lambelin, Roger, rose, 189
Lamb's-ears, stachys, or betony,
  60–61
Lantana, 103, 130
La Reine Victoria rose, 187
Larkspur, 73, 80, 82, 102, 103, 130–
  131, 272
Lathyrus. See Sweet pea
Laura rose, 156
Lavender, 10, 47–48, 277
  cotton, 58
Lavender Lace rose, 218, 219
Leadwort, or plumbago, 48
Leaf cutting bee, 182
Leaf rollers, 182
Lemon Spice rose, 166, 170, 198
Lemon verbena, 276–277
Lenten rose, 43–44
Leopard's-bane, or doronicum,
  37–38
Leucojum aestivum, or snowflake,
  233
Liatris, 10, 11, 48, 80, 82
Lice, plant, 182
Lily, 10, 11, 12, 22–23
  Aztec, 251
  calla, 246, 251
  canna, 109, 245, 251
  foxtail, 233, 251
  gloriosa, 247, 251
  hardy, 48–49, 91
  Madonna, 15, 48

Lily (continued)
  martagon, 48
  pineapple, 247
  plantain. See Hosta
  spider, 205
  torch. See Kniphofia
  trout. See Erythronium
Lily-of-the-valley, 223
Limonium, 139
Linaria, 131
Linum, or flax, 10, 39, 126–127
Liriope, 260
Little Darling rose, 206, 269
Littlest Angel rose, 218
Lobelia, 10, 11, 49, 73, 78, 80, 85,
  87, 88, 91, 92, 93, 94, 102, 103,
  131, 256, 273
Loosestrife. See Lythrum
Lord Penzance rose, 191
Love-in-a-mist. See Nigella
Love-lies-bleeding, 116
Lucky Lady rose, AARS, 270
Lupine, 10, 50, 61–62, 73, 91, 103,
  131–132
  Carolina, 10, 11, 61–62
Lychnis, 51
Lycoris, 233
Lythrum, 8, 10, 11, 13, 49–50

M

Madam Hardy rose, 188
Magic Carpet polygonum, 80
Magic Carrousel rose, 218, 269
Maiden's Blush rose, 187
Mallow rose, 256
Maltese-cross, 51
Maman Cochet rose, 189
Mandrake, or mayapple, 256
Ma Perkins rose, AARS, 271
Marechal Niel rose, 189
Margo Koster rose, 208
Marguerite
  blue, or felicia, 38
  golden, or anthemis, 28

Marigold, 69, 70, 71, 73, 76, 78, 80,
  81, 82, 84, 85, 87, 98, 99, 102,
  103, 107, 132, 166, 260, 272
Marsh marigold, or caltha, 252, 256
Mary Adair rose, 218, 269
Matador rose, 170, 206, 269
Matricaria, or feverfew,
  annual, 126
  perennial, 38–39
Matterhorn rose, 170, 198
  AARS, 271
Matthiola. See Stocks
Max Graf rose, 154, 192
Mayapple, or mandrake, 256
Meadow rue, 61
  early, 256
  tall, 256
Meadowsweet, or dropwort, 51
Medallion rose, 155, 170, 198
  AARS, 270
Mertensia virginica, or Virginia
  bluebells, 10, 11, 38, 64, 253
Mesembryanthemum. See Ice plant
Mexican fire plant, 126
Michelle Meilland rose, 170, 198
Midge, rose, 182
Mignonette, 80, 85, 132
Mildew, rose, 182
Milkwort, or spurge, 60
Miniature roses, 148, 150, 152, 154,
  156, 160, 162, 166, 174, 175, 177,
  211, 216–217
Mirabilis. See Four-o'clock
Mirandy rose, 198
Miscanthus sinensis, 261
Miss All-American Beauty rose,
  198
  AARS, 270
Mister Lincoln rose, 162, 170,
  198, 269
  AARS, 271
Mist flower. See Ageratum
Mitchella, or partridgeberry, 256
Mitella, 254
Mojave rose, 170, 198
  AARS, 271
Moluccella. See Bells-of-Ireland
Monarda. See Bee-balm
Monkshood, or aconitum, 51-52
Montbretia, 248
Montezuma rose, 203

Moonflower, 100, 102, 103
Morning-glory, 76, 82, 88, 91, 100, 101, 102, 103, 123
Moschatas, hybrid, 192
Moss rose, or centifolia, 147, 180, 189
Moss rose, or portulaca, 102, 137, 143, 258
Mountain bluet, 33
Mount Shasta rose, 170, 203
Mousseline, or Alfred de Dalmas, rose, 189
Moyesi, hybrid, rose, 191
Mullein, or verbascum, 10, 62
Muscari, 11, 230, 234, 235
Musk rose, 148, 192
Myosotis. See Forget-me-not

N

Narcissus, 10, 12, 223, 225, 228–229, 232, 234–235, 237, 263
Nasturtium, 73, 80, 85, 86, 88, 94, 96, 100, 102, 103, 133
Nematodes, 182
Nemesia, 73, 80, 102, 133
Nemophila, 80, 102, 134
Neue Revue rose, 170, 198
Nevada rose, 191
New Dawn rose, 214
Neyron, Paul, rose, 189
Nicolas, Dr. J.H., rose, 213
Nicotiana, 73, 76, 80, 85, 102, 103, 134
Nierembergia, 94, 124, 134
Nigella, 73, 80, 134–135
Nocturne rose, AARS, 271
Noisette rose, 147, 148, 189

O

Obedience plant, 55
Oenothera, 52, 255
Oklahoma rose, 198
Old Blush rose, 188
Old garden roses, 180, 181, 187–189, 269
Oldtimer rose, 198
Olé rose, 203
Orangeade rose, 170, 206, 269

Oregold rose, 170, 198
AARS, 270
Ornamental grasses, 260
Ornithogalum umbellatum, 235
Orris root, 277
Over the Rainbow rose, 218, 269
Oxalis, 251
Oxeye. See Heliopsis
Oxypetalum, 80

P

Paeonia sp. See Peony
Painted tongue. See Salpiglossis
Pansy, 8, 67, 70, 72, 73, 77, 80, 86, 91, 92, 94, 95, 102, 103, 107, 112, 135, 272, 273
Papa Meilland rose, 198
Papaver. See Poppy
Paquerette rose, 148
Paradise rose, 170, 198
AARS, 270
Parsley, curly, 87
Partridgeberry, or mitchella, 256
Pascali rose, 170, 171, 198, 269
AARS, 270
Pasqueflower, 256
Patient lucy. See Impatiens
Paul's Scarlet Climber rose, 214
Peace rose, 170, 198, 214, 269
AARS, 271
Chicago, 170, 195, 269
Pink, 170, 198
Peer Gynt rose, 170, 198
Pelargonium, 41. See also Geranium
Pennisetum setaceum, 260
Penstemon, 53
Peony, 10, 11, 15, 18–19, 53–54
Perfume Delight rose, 198, 199
AARS, 270
Periwinkle. See Vinca

Perpetual, hybrid rose, 147, 177, 188–189
Stanwell, 189
Persian yellow rose, 147
Pests, rose, 182–183
Petite de Hollande rose, 187
Petunia, 69, 70, 72, 73, 74, 76, 78, 80, 84, 85, 86, 87, 88, 90, 92, 94, 98, 99, 102, 103, 107, 135, 157
Pharaoh rose, 156, 198
Phlox, 8, 9, 10, 11, 54–55, 72, 73, 78, 102, 103, 136, 256
Physalis alkekengi. See Chinese-lantern
Picnic rose, 206
Pinata rose, 214
Pincushion flower. See Scabiosa
Pink Cameo rose, 269
Pinkie rose, AARS, 271
Pink Parfait rose, 203
AARS, 271
Pink Peace rose, 170, 198
Pinks, 8, 10, 37, 51, 80, 102, 136
Pixie Rose, 218, 269
Plant companions for roses, 164–169
Plant lice, 182
Platycodon grandiflorus, 10, 11, 29–30
Plumbago, or leadwort, 10, 48
Plume grass, 260
Plumosa. See Celosia
Podophyllum, or mayapple, 256
Poinsettia, annual, 80
Poker plant, or kniphofia, 56
Polemonium caeruleum, 47, 255
Polyantha rose, 148, 150, 152, 160, 177, 181, 208, 211, 269
Polygonatum, or solomon's-seal, 257
Polygonum, 80, 258
Poppy, 10, 11, 81
Alpine, 136
California, 72, 73, 102, 103, 120, 136, 256
Iceland, 8, 45, 72, 73, 86, 103, 114, 136
Oriental, 15, 26, 45, 56
shirley, 88, 136
Portland rose, 147, 189
Portrait rose, 170, 198
AARS, 270
Portulaca, or moss rose, 102, 137, 143, 258

Potentilla, 10, 57, 254
Potpourri, 274, 276, 277
Prairie coneflower, 254
Preserving
  cut flowers, 272–273
  roses, 274
Pressed flowers, 272, 274
Primrose, 9, 10, 13, 80, 86, 90, 92
  evening, 52, 255
Pristine rose, 170, 198
Prominent rose, 170, 203
  AARS, 270
Promise rose, 170, 200
Proud Land rose, 173, 200
Pruning roses, 162, 175, 176–177,
  180, 181
Puerto Rico rose, 163
Pulmonaria, 50
Purple coneflower, 254
Puschkinia, 231, 234
Pyrethrum. *See* Daisy, painted

Q

Queen-anne's-lace, 103
Queen Elizabeth rose, 148, 170,
  203, 214, 269
  AARS, 271

R

Ramblers, rose, 148, 150, 214. *See
  also* Climbers
Ranunculus, 31–32, 249, 251,
  255, 272
Ratibida, 254
Red Cascade rose, 150, 154, 160,
  218
Red Devil rose, 200
Red Fountain rose, 214
Redgold rose, 170, 206, 207
  AARS, 270
Red Lion Rose, 170, 200
Red Masterpiece rose, 170, 200
Reseda. *See* Mignonette
Rhonda rose, 214
Ricinus. *See* Castor bean
Rock cress, 9
Rocky Mountain garland, 122
Roman Holiday rose, AARS, 270

Rosa sp., 256
  alba, 147
  borboniana, 147
  centifolia, 147
  chinensis, 147, 148
  damascena, 147
  foetida, 147
  gallica, 147
  kordesi, 148
  moschata, 147
  multiflora, 147, 148, 152, 180,
    211, 214, 221
  noisettiana, 147
  odorata, 147
  rouletti, 148
  rugosa, 154, 211
  wichuraiana, 148, 150, 154, 211
Rose,
  Christmas, 43–44
  lenten, 43–44
  mallow, 256
  prairie, 256
Rose
  arranging, 266–268
  beds, 156, 158
  beetle, Fuller, 182
  breeding, 220–221
  budding, 221
  chafer, 182
  color combinations, 170, 173
  container, 160–163
  cut, 264–265
  dried, 274
  entryway, 154
  frosting, 274
  hedge, 152
  plant companions for, 164–169
  scale, 182
  slug, 182
Rose de Meaux, 187
Rose de Rescht, 188
Rose Gaujard, 200
Rose Mundi, 188
Rose Parade, 170, 208
  AARS, 270
Rosmarin rose, 218

Royal Gold rose, 214
Royal Highness rose, 170, 200, 269
  AARS, 271
Royal Sunset rose, 214, 269
Rubaiyat rose, 200
  AARS, 271
Rudbeckia, 9, 10, 11, 13, 57–58,
  102, 137, 254
Rugosa, hybrid, rose, 195
Rust, roses, 182

S

Sage, 10, 11, 58
Sage, scarlet, 102, 138
St. John's wort, 44–45
Salet rose, 189
Salpiglossis, 69, 80, 137–138
Salvia, 10, 11, 58, 69, 76, 80,
  138, 272
Sand verbena, 257
Sanguinaria, 254
Santolina chamaecyparissus, 58
Sarabande rose, 153, 170, 208
  AARS, 271
Satinflower. *See* Godetia
Sawtooth sunflower, 257
Scabiosa, 58–59, 69, 138
Scarlet Gem rose, 218, 269
Scarlet Knight rose, 203
  AARS, 270
Scarlet star glory, 100
Schizanthus. *See* Butterfly flower
Scilla, 11, 234
Scotch rose, 189
Seabreeze rose, 218
Sea Foam rose, 150, 192, 211
Sea lavender. *See* Statice
Sea Pearl rose, 208, 269
Sea pink, or thrift, 62
Seashell rose, 170, 200
  AARS, 270
Secret Love rose, 159
Sedum, 11, 59, 87, 99
Seventh Heaven rose, 166
Sheri Anne rose, 218, 269
Shooting-star, 257
Shrub roses, 150, 152, 154, 168,
  175, 177, 180, 181, 191–192, 266,
  269
Siberian bugloss, 31

Siberian forget-me-not, 31
Silver King artemisia, 28
Silver Lining rose, 200
Silver Mound artemisia, 10, 11, 28
Simplex rose, 218, 269
Slopes, 258
Smoky rose, 156
Snakeroot, 257
Snapdragon, 70, 73, 76, 78, 80, 81, 82, 84, 102, 138–139, 272
Sneeze-weed, 42–43
Snowdrop, 223, 231
Snowfire, 160, 200
Snowflake, or *Leucojum aestivum*, 233
Snow-in-summer, 9, 33
Snow-on-the-mountain, 80, 126
Soer Therese rose, 220
Soil, 162, 175, 180
Solidago, 60, 78, 80
Solomon's-seal, 257
Sonia rose, 203
Sonoma rose, 155
Southern star, 80
Southernwood, or artemisia, 28
South Seas rose, 200
Souvenir de la Malmaison rose, 187
Spanish Sun rose, 170, 208
Sparrieshoop rose, 192
Spartan rose, 208, 209
Spartina pectinata, 260
Species, roses, 189
Speedwell. *See* Veronica
Spellbinder rose, 200
Spiderflower. *See* Cleome
Spider mite, 182
Spiderplant. *See* Cleome
Spiderwort, 10, 11, 257
Spinosissima, hybrid, rose, 189
Spiraea latifolia, 51
Spirea, false, 29
Spotted cucumber beetle, 182
Sprekelia, 251
Spring-beauty, 257
Spurge, 60
Stachys, betony, or lamb's-ears, 60–61
Stanwell Perpetual rose, 189

Starfire rose, AARS, 271
Starglo rose, 269
Starina rose, 218, 269
Statice, 73, 76, 86, 102, 103, 139, 272
Sterling Silver rose, 200
Stocks, 80, 85, 103, 139
Stokesia, 10, 61
Stonecrop, 59
Strawflower, 139, 272
Sugar Elf rose, 160
Summer cypress. *See* kochia
Summer Sunshine rose, 170, 200
Sundowner rose, 170
    AARS, 270
Sundrops. *See* Oenothera
Sunflower
    annual, 102, 140
    false, 42–43
    Mexican, 96, 107, 141
    perennial, 10, 43
    sawtooth, 257
Sunset Jubilee rose, 170, 200
Sunsprite rose, 154, 168, 170, 208
Susan Massu rose, 170, 200, 269
Sutter's Gold rose, 200, 214
    AARS, 271
Swarthmore rose, 200, 269
Sweetbrier rose, 146, 191
Sweet pea, 82, 85, 100, 102, 103, 140
Sweet-sultan, 85, 103, 140–141
Sweet william, 8, 37, 67, 70, 80, 88, 103, 141

T

Taffeta rose, AARS, 271
Tagetes. *See* Marigold
Talisman rose, 214
Tall meadow rue, 256
Tallyho rose, AARS, 271
Tamango rose, 208
Tarnished plant bug, 182

Tea rose, 147, 160, 189
    hybrid, 159, 162, 175, 176, 177, 181, 195–200, 211, 214, 269
    AARS, 270-271
Temperature, 279
    and protection, 180–181
Tempo rose, 214
Texas bluebonnet, 131
Thalictrum, 61, 256
Thermopsis, 10, 11, 61–62
Thrift, 62
Thyme, 259
Thymus serpyllum, 259
Tiarella, or foamflower, 255
Tickseed, perennial, 35
Tiffany rose, 170, 200, 269
    AARS, 271
Tigridia, 251
Tithonia, 96, 102, 107, 141
Toadflax, 131
Tobacco, flowering or ornamental. *See* Nicotiana
Toothwort, 257
Top Secret rose, 218, 269
Torenia, 102, 141–142
Toro rose, 200
Touch-me-not, 117–118
Toy Clown rose, 218
Trachymene. *See* Blue lace flower
Tradescantia, 10, 11, 257
Trailing arbutus, 254
Traubel, Helen, rose, 196
Tree roses, 150, 154, 156, 160, 177, 179, 211
Trillium, 253
Trillium grandiflorum, 253
Triteleia laxa, 235
Tritonia, 251
Trollius, or globeflower, 13, 42
Tropaeolum. *See* Nasturtium
Tropicana rose, 166, 200, 214, 269
    AARS, 271
Tuberose, 251
Tulip, 9, 10, 11, 12, 91, 222, 223, 224, 225, 226–227, 232, 234, 262, 263
    botanical, 235, 237
    season of bloom, 235
    species, 235, 237
Turtlehead, 257

U

Uncle Joe rose, 200
Uvularia, or bellwort, 254

V

Valerian
  Greek, 47
  red, 47
Variegata di Bologna rose, 187
Velvet flower. *See* Salpiglossis
Verbascum, 10, 62
Verbena, 73, 80, 85, 94, 102, 103,
  113, 142, 257, 273, 276–277
Veronica, 10, 11, 63
Vinca, 80, 82, 142
Vinca minor, 258
Vin Rose, 173

Viola, 8, 10, 11, 63, 70, 157. *See
  also* Pansy
Violet
  blue, 257
  dog-tooth, 233, 253
Virginia bluebells, 253
Vogue rose, 208
  AARS, 271

W–X

Wax begonia. *See* Begonia, wax
White Bouquet rose, AARS, 271
White Dawn rose, 214
White Knight rose, 172, 200
  AARS, 271
White Masterpiece rose, 170, 200
Wild columbine, 254
Wildflower, 7, 31, 34–35, 40, 51, 55,
  61, 252–257
Wild ginger, 257
Will Scarlet rose, 192
Winged everlasting, 116
Wini Edmunds rose, 200
  AARS, 271
Winter
  container roses, 160
  protection for roses, 180

Wishbone flower, 141–142
Woburn Abbey rose, 170, 208
Wood aster, blue, 257
Wormwood. *See* Artemisia

Y

Yankee Doodle rose, 200
  AARS, 270
Yarrow, 10, 11, 64
Yellow Doll rose, 269
Yellow lady's-slipper, 255
Yucca, 10, 64

Z

Zinnia, 69, 70, 73, 76, 78, 80, 82,
  84, 85, 86, 94, 96, 102, 103, 107,
  142, 272
Zone map, 279–280